Information Visualization

Springer

London
Berlin
Heidelberg
New York
Hong Kong
Milan
Paris
Tokyo

Chaomei Chen

Information Visualization
Beyond the Horizon

Second Edition

Springer

Chaomei Chen, PhD, MSc, BSc
College of Information Science and Technology, Drexel University,
3141 Chestnut Street, Philadelphia, PA 19104-2875, USA

British Library Cataloguing in Publication Data
Chen, Chaomei, 1960–
   Information visualization: beyond the horizon. – 2nd ed.
   1. Information visualization   2. Virtual reality
   1. Title   II. Chen, Chaomei, 1960–. Information visualization
   and virtual environments
   006

ISBN 1852337893

Library of Congress Cataloging-in-Publication Data
Chen, Chaomei, 1960–
   Information visualization: beyond the horizon/Chaomei Chen.
      p. cm.
   Rev. ed. of: Information visualisation and virtual environments, c1999.
   Includes bibliographical references and index.
   ISBN 1-85233-789-3 (hc.: alk. paper)
   1. Information visualization.   2. Virtual reality.   I. Chen, Chaomei, 1960– Information
   visualisation and virtual environments.   II. Title.

   TK7882.I6C477 2004
   006.6–dc22   2004045618

ISBN 1-85233-789-3 Springer-Verlag London Berlin Heidelberg
Springer-Verlag is part of Springer Science+Business Media
springeronline.com

Typesetting by Gray Publishing, Tunbridge Wells, Kent, UK
Printed and bound at Kyodo Printing Co (S'pore) Pte Ltd
34/3830-543210 Printed on acid-free paper SPIN 10945360

To Baohuan, Calvin, and Steven

Foreword

It is with enthusiasm and excitement that I join the community of information visualization researchers and designers in celebrating our still fresh accomplishments of the past decade. However, even as we take pride in how far we have come, we should acknowledge that these are just the first steps of a much longer journey.

This book and the rich literature from conferences, journals, and a few pioneering books reveals a flourishing, but still emerging academic field, that fights for recognition every day. Similarly, the product announcements from new and mature companies, demonstrate the passionate commitment of venturesome entrepreneurs who struggle to cross the chasm to commercial success.

Readers of the academic literature and corporate press releases probably believe that the allure of information visualization is in finding appropriate representations of relationships, patterns, trends, clusters, and outliers. This belief is reinforced by browsing through conference titles that weave together technical topics such as trees, networks, time series, and parallel coordinates, with exotic verbs such as zoom, pan, filter, and brush. However, I believe that the essence of information visualization is more ambitious and more compelling; it is to accelerate human thinking with tools that amplify human intelligence.

Chaomei Chen captures the spirit of this emerging academic discipline in this second edition and cleverly uses knowledge domain visualization to trace the growth and spread of topics. His survey highlights the dramatic progress during the past five years in a way that celebrates and challenges researchers and developers. His numerous screenshots of research and commercial systems give a glimpse of what is possible, but readers will have to see the demos for themselves and view working products to get the full impact of the interaction dynamics.

Chen's book shows us how the rapidly maturing information visualization tools are becoming as potent as the telescope and microscope. A telescope enabled Galileo to see the moons of Jupiter, and a microscope made it possible for Pasteur to see bacteria that enabled him to understand disease processes. Similarly, remarkable technologies such as radar, sonar, and medical scanners extend human vision in powerful ways that facilitate understanding. The insights gained provide support for air traffic controllers, naval officers, physicians, and others in making timely and effective decisions.

The payoffs to users of information visualization tools will be in the significant insights that enable them to solve vital problems at the frontiers of their fields. By extending their vision to higher dimensional spaces, users of information visualization tools are making meaningful and sometimes surprising breakthroughs. These users, such as genomic researchers, financial analysts, or patent lawyers, are often struggling to understand the important relationships, clusters, or outliers hidden in their data sets. Their quest may last days or years as they seek to identify surprising groupings hidden among naturally occurring combinations or distinguish novel trends from well-understood seasonal variations. The outcome may be to discover secondary functions of known genes, or stocks that will outperform others in their industry group.

The users' goals are often noble, valuable, and influential. Which sets of genes limit cancer growth? Which stock movements are often precursors of a major market rise? Which companies are distinctively active in developing new patents in wireless applications for e-commerce? In other circumstances, the users of information visualization deal with difficult topics such as tracking epidemics, uncovering fraud, or detecting terrorists.

The process of information visualization is to take data available to many people and to enable users to gain insights that lead to significant discoveries. Chen appropriately focuses attention on how information visualization techniques "make the insights stand out from otherwise chaotic and noisy data". The often noisy data must be cleaned of anomalies, marked for missing values, and transformed in ways that are more conducive to insight and discovery. Then users can choose the representations that suit their tasks best. Next, users can adjust their view by zooming in on relevant items and filtering out unnecessary items. Settings of control panels may have to be changed to present the items in appropriate colors, positions, shapes, orientation, etc.

Some parts of this process can be automated, and some data mining or statistical algorithms can be helpful, but often the insight comes to those who have a hypothesis to test or who suspect a novel relationship. Visualizations are especially potent in promoting the intuitions and insights that lead to breakthroughs in understanding the relevant connections and salient features.

Typically, the quest for understanding requires looking at the details of an outlier or a surprising correlation. At that point, the benefit of domain knowledge and the need for more data becomes strong. Chen's practical examples illustrate this process and the role of domain knowledge, especially in the case of detecting abrupt changes and emerging trends. Only the experienced geneticist can make the leap to recognize how a raised level of gene expression signals its participation in a meaningful biological pathway. Only the knowledgeable stock market analyst recognizes that the reason for a sudden rise in value is due to a successful marketing trial of a new product.

There are three implications of the situated nature of information visualization that will influence future research and the success of products: (1) input data usually needs to be cleansed and transformed to support appropriate exploration, (2) related information is often needed to make meaningful judgments, and (3) effective presentation of results is critical to influence decision-making.

Sources of input data need to be trusted and possibly consulted to understand its meaning and resolve inconsistencies. Then these data can be cleansed of anomalies, transformed to appropriate units, and tagged for missing values. Sometimes data needs to be aggregated to an appropriate level of analysis, such as web log data that is grouped by session, by hour, or by domain name.

The source data may need to be supplemented by related information to provide context for decisions. For example, sales data that records customer zip codes, may only become meaningful when the zip code demographics, geographic location, or income distribution is accessible. It will be no surprise that ski equipment is sold heavily in mountain states, but the surprising insight may be the high level of sales in wealthy southern cities. Similarly, genomic researchers need to know how a tight cluster of highly expressed genes relates to the categories of molecular function in the gene ontology. Stock market analysts will want to understand why a group of stocks rose and then fell rapidly by studying recent trading patterns and industry news reports.

Since effective presentation of results is critical to influence decision-making, designers must understand how users collaborate. The first step is simply recording the state of a visualization by allowing the saving of settings. Other important services are to support extraction of subsets, posting results to a web page, and producing high quality printed versions. Chen reports on the collaborative environments that allow simultaneous viewing of a shared display, accompanied by a synchronous chat window, voice conversation, or instant messaging, are increasingly common. Asynchronous environments with web-based discussion boards, are also important as they better support larger communities, where co-ordination for a synchronous discussion is difficult. Chen deals with this topic, as well as the visualization of group processes in online communities.

These three aspects of effective information visualization are in harmony with Geoffrey Moore's analysis in his insight-filled book *Crossing the Chasm* (1991). His formula for successful software products is that they are "whole product solutions" which solve a known problem with an end-to-end solution (no additional components needed). He cautions that training has to be integrated, benefits have to be measurable, and users have to be seen as heroes. Many early products failed to adhere to this formula, but newer offerings are in closer alignment.

Researchers can also learn from this formula, because it encourages a practical approach. Professor Fred Brooks long ago encouraged researchers to focus on a "driving problem". His advice remains potent, especially for those who are entranced with colorful animated displays and elaborate statistical manipulations. Explorers of the vast multidimensional spaces are more likely to make important discoveries if they keep their mind's eye focused on solving their driving problem. They are also more likely to experience those wonderful Aha! moments of insight that are the thrill of discovery.

Then researchers and developers will need to get down to rigorous evaluations. Chaomei Chen places a strong emphasis on empirical studies to help researchers and developers get past their understandable infatuation with their innovations. Rapid progress will be made as more evaluations are done using benchmark tasks and standard data sets, coupled with carefully reported in-depth case studies of collaborations with problem solvers in many disciplines.

There's work to be done. Let's get on with it!

Ben Shneiderman
University of Maryland

Preface for the Second Edition

When the original version of *Information Visualisation and Virtual Environments* (IVVE) was published in the summer of 1999, the only book available to readers anywhere on the globe was the now widely cited volume of 52 pioneering articles ingeniously interwoven together by the three masterminds – the "Readings". As it turned out, a few more people were simultaneously working on their own books to introduce and redefine the subject. Five years on, the field of information visualization has grown in leaps and bounds. Practitioners and researchers now enjoy a wealth of books on the subject of information visualization from a rich spectrum of perspectives: Colin Ware's thorough coverage of the foundation of perception and cognition, Bob Spence's well-articulated text on the fine details of the work of many creative minds, Martin Dodge and his colleagues' hand-picked exemplars from a geologist's mindset, and Ben Bederson and Ben Shneiderman's more recent touch with the years of work from their lab at the University of Maryland. Since 2002, the field has its own journal – *Information Visualization* (IVS) – and numerous conferences where information visualization has its place.

What are the most significant changes over the past five years? Do we have more successful stories to tell about information visualization? What are the remaining challenges? And what are the new ones lurking from the most unexpected directions? My original intention in 1999 was two-fold: (1) providing an integrative introduction to information visualization and (2) establishing a connection between information visualization and virtual environments. With hindsight, the first goal echoes the first of the two generations of information visualization, which I will explain shortly, whereas the second goal may correspond to the second generation. There is increasingly prolific evidence that we are experiencing a profound but underlying transition from the first to the second.

The history of information visualization can be characterized by two distinct but often overlooked focuses: structure and change. The majority of the showcase information visualization work is about structure. The holy grail of information visualization is to make the insights stand out from otherwise chaotic and noisy data. Naturally, the mission of the first generation in the 1990s and the beginning of 2000s has been revealing structures that would be otherwise invisible. The unique position of structure is also evident from various navigation strategies, from the focus + context design rationale to the so-called drill-down tactics. Although the content is always a part of the equation, it has never been the real rival of structure.

The first part of the book closely reflects the *structure-centric* tradition – everything is a structure. The process of abstracting structures from seemingly unstructured data is not something unique to information visualization. Cartographers, for example, have established a complete line of business that can represent the geographic features of the real world on various maps. The tradition of structuralism is most apparent in one of the earliest columns of information visualization – graph drawing. Until recently the level of clarity and aesthetics of how the structure of a given graph can be drawn algorithmically has been the predominant driving force behind the development of various increasingly sophisticated graph drawing algorithms.

The second part of the book, consisting of individual differences studies and spatially organized multi-user virtual environments, was an attempt to establish the potentially fruitful connection between the two communities. Information visualization models embedded in shared virtual environments call for explicit and direct attention to an extensible framework that can accommodate the growth of such information visualization models, especially when the virtual environment itself drives the subsequent evolution. However, back in 1998 I was preoccupied with our own research findings and wanted to use the book as a vehicle to convey as much as our research. Furthermore, many things we take for granted today were unheard of, or more precisely, unseen five years ago. And this is the time to address the second generation.

The second generation is about change. It is *dynamics-centric*. It is about growth, evolution, and development. It is about sudden changes as well as gradual changes. A good starting point for explaining the second generation would be a well-known example in scientific visualization – the storm, how it started, evolved, and eventually came to an end. One of the often quoted definitions of information visualization is that information visualization deals with data that do not have inherited geometry. In other words, one has the freedom of mapping the underlying data to any geometric forms so long as one asserts meanings, no matter how arbitrarily, to the end product of such mapping. As a result, it does not come easy to put my visualization and your visualization side by side and compare even if they are about the same underlying phenomena. The key question is: what distinguishes scientific visualization and information visualization? Are they really that different?

On the surface, scientific visualization appears to have the blessing of scientific theories that can quantify the meaning of each pixel and leave no room for ambiguity or misconception. If scientific visualization is a mapping from a physical phenomenon to its visual representation, this is like saying that the mapping is unique and it is complete because the geometry is more likely than not to be inherited in the underlying scientific model. In most geographic visualizations, the geographic framework is retained and the mapping preserves the geometry. On the other hand, Harry Beck's classic schematic design of the London underground map in 1933 constantly reminds us that a good design is not necessarily built on geometric details even if it comes with the data. Charles Minard's classic map depicting Napoleon's disastrous retreat from Moscow has set a good example of what information visualization should achieve. If a picture is worth thousands of words, then Mindard's map unfolds a vivid story.

Behind scientific visualization, we are likely to find the provision of not only quantitative and geometric models, but also models that govern the dynamics of an underlying phenomenon. Just as in the storm example, scientific visualization typically works with data that are either readily presentable in visual forms or readily computable to a presentable level. In contrast, information visualization is often characterized by the absence of such readiness. Typical information data are not readily presentable due to the lack of built-in visual–spatial attributes. They are not readily computable due to the lack of an underlying computational model. Information visualization, therefore, faces a much tougher challenge because one has to fill up the two gaps before reaching starting points of scientific visualization. Meanwhile, the tight coupling between visualizations and underlying theoretical models in scientific visualization has left something to be desired in information visualization, such as the descriptive and predictive power and reasoning capabilities.

The need to fill up the two gaps is echoed by the emergence of the second generation of information visualization. Information visualization has to re-examine the nature of a semantic mapping and the meaning of visual–spatial configurations in the context of intended cultural and social settings.

The recent citation analysis of information visualization clearly identifies the role of earlier pioneers such as Edward Tufte and Jacques Bertin. Tufte's three books have been the source of inspiration for generations of researchers and practitioners in information visualization and design. In August 2003, I searched for "information visualization" on Google's three billion-strong indexed web pages and it returned 44,500 hits. Adding a more specific term to the query rapidly reduced the number. The following numbers may give us a glimpse of what information visualization is about, at least on the web: focus + context (6980), evolution (4370), graph drawing (3200), empirical study (2750), fisheye (1960), hyperbolic (1910), treemap (934), Spotfire (808), SOM (659), semiotics (563), detect trend (356), Pathfinder (300), and detect abrupt change (48).

The focus + context issue is the most widely known, followed by evolution, graph drawing and empirical studies. Specific visualization techniques and systems are topped by fisheye and hyperbolic views, which are in line with the popular awareness of the focus + context issue. Although it commanded 563 hits, semiotics as a relatively broad term is apparently underrepresented in information visualization. The least popular topic in this group is "detect abrupt change," which is a precious 48 out of three billion web pages. This second edition of the book pays particular attention to empirical studies accumulated over the past five years, the role of semiotics in information visualization, and the need for detecting emerging trends and abrupt changes.

This edition continues the unique and ambitious quest for setting information visualization in an interdisciplinary context, especially in relation to virtual environments because they provide a particularly stimulating context for us to understand theoretical and practical implications of various fundamental issues and specific information visualization features. This new edition is particularly tailored to the need of practitioners, including a number of newly added in-depth analyses of successful stories and entirely new chapters on semiotics and empirical studies. A number of chapters are thoroughly updated. The new edition is also suitable for an introductory course to information visualization.

The new edition is entitled *Information Visualization: Beyond the Horizon*. In part, this refers to the transition that is quietly taking place, which will ultimately transcend the first, structure-centric, generation of information visualization to the emerging second, dynamics-centric, generation. Furthermore, there are a number of promising trends on the horizon of information visualization, notably the vibrating area of Knowledge Domain Visualizations (KDViz), new perspectives on the role of information visualization in detecting abrupt changes and emerging trends, and a whole new front of empirical studies of information visualization.

Among the eight chapters in the new edition, the degree of update and revision varies a great deal, from new chapters, substantially updated chapters, to moderately updated chapters. I have particularly concentrated on two new chapters: Chapter 6 on empirical studies of information visualization and Chapter 8 on detecting abrupt changes and emerging trends. I regard these two topics as having the most profound implications on information visualization in the next five years. There are simply so many grounds to cover in each of the topics. Chapter 5 contains some of the materials in the original Chapter 4 in the first edition, plus a new study on visualizing scientific paradigms. Several sections in Chapter 4 have been substantially rewritten. Chapter 7 includes a new study of group tightness. The remaining chapters have been updated to a much less degree, although all chapters are reorganized accordingly.

Acknowledgements

I'd like to take this opportunity to thank so many people for their valuable help, persistent encouragements and selfless support, especially Ben Shneiderman (University of Maryland, USA), Mary Czerwinski (Microsoft Research, USA), Eugene Garfield (Institute for Scientific Information, USA), Ray J. Paul (Brunel University, UK), Roy Rada (University of Maryland, USA), Henry Small (Institute for Scientific Information, USA), Bob Spence (Imperial College, University of London, UK), and Howard D. White (Drexel University, USA). I am also grateful to my collaborators, including Jasna Kuljis (Brunel University, UK), Vladimir Geroimenko (University of Plymouth, UK), Diana Hicks (Georgia Tech, USA), Katy Börner and Shashikant Penumarthy (Indiana University, USA) for a study described in part in Section 7.4, Kevin Boyack (Sandia National Laboratories, USA). Thanks to John Schwarz (CalTech, USA) and Edward Witten (Princeton University, USA) for their help in interpreting the superstring visualizations described in Chapter 8.

The work is in part supported by the 2002 ISI/ASIS&T Citation Analysis Research award and the earlier grants from the British Engineering and Physical Science Research Council (grant number: GR/L61088) and the Council for Museums, Archives and Libraries. I'd also like to acknowledge the visiting professorship with Brunel University in 2003.

Special thanks to Rebecca Mowat and Jenny Wolkowicki at Springer-Verlag for their efficient and professional work.

Drexel University   Chaomei Chen
Philadelphia, PA   January 2004

Contents

Chapter 1
Introduction

Knowledge comes, but wisdom lingers.
Lord Alfred Tennyson

Information visualization as a distinctive field of research has less than ten years of history, but has rapidly become a far-reaching, interdisciplinary research field. Works on information visualization are now found in the literature of a large number of subject domains, notably information retrieval (IR), hypertext and the World Wide Web (WWW), digital libraries (DL), and human–computer interaction (HCI). The boundary between information visualization and related fields such as scientific visualization and simulation modeling is becoming increasingly blurred.

Information visualization represents one of the latest streams in a long-established trend in modern user interface design. The desire to manipulate objects on a computer screen has been the driving force behind many popular user interface design paradigms. Increasing layers of user interface are being added between the user and the computer, yet the interface between the two is becoming more transparent, more natural, and more intuitive, as, for example, the "what-you-see-is-what-you-get" (WYSIWYG) user interfaces, "point-and-click and drag-and-drop" direct manipulation user interfaces, and "fly-through" in virtual reality worlds.

The fast advancement of information visualization also highlights fundamental research issues. First, the *art* of information visualization perhaps appropriately describes the state of the field. It is currently a challenging task for designers to find out the strategies and tools available to visualize a particular type of information. Information visualization involves a large number of representational structures, some of them well understood, and many less so. Furthermore, new ways of representing information are being invented all the time. Until recently, systematic integration of information visualization techniques into the design of information-intensive systems has not occurred. An exceptional trend is the use of cone trees and fisheye views to visualize hierarchical structures. For example, cone trees are used in LyberWorld (Hemmje et al., 1994), Cat-a-Cone (Hearst and Karadi, 1997), and Hyperbolic 3D (Munzner, 1998b). The WWW has significantly pushed forward the visualization of network structures and general graphs. Nevertheless, a taxonomy of information visualization is needed so that designers can select appropriate techniques to meet given requirements. It is still difficult to compare information visualization across different designs.

The second issue is the lack of generic criteria to assess the value of information visualization, either independently, or in a wider context of user activities. This is a challenging issue, since most people develop their own criteria for what makes a good visual representation. The study of individual differences in the use of information visualization systems is a potentially fruitful research avenue. Much attention has been paid to a considerable number of cognitive factors, such as spatial ability, associative memory, and visual memory. These cognitive factors, and various cognitive styles and learning styles, form a large part of individual differences, especially when visual representations are involved.

The third issue is the communicative role of information visualization components in a shared, multi-user virtual environment. It is natural to combine information visualization with virtual reality, and the use of virtual reality naturally leads to the construction and use of virtual environments. The transition from information visualization to multi-user virtual environments marks a significant difference in user perspective. Individual perspectives are predominant in most information visualization design, while social perspectives are inevitable in a virtual environment.

Individuals may respond with different interpretations of the same information visualization. In a virtual environment, the behavior of users and how they interact with each other is likely to be influenced by the way in which the virtual environment is constructed. So far, few virtual environments are designed using abstract information visualization as an overall organizational principle. How do we ascertain the influence of information visualization techniques on the construction of a virtual environment, on user behavior, their understanding, interpretation, and experiences? Do people attach special meanings to these abstract information visualization objects? And in what way will visualized information structures affect social interaction and intellectual work in a virtual environment? To answer these questions may open a new frontier to research in information visualization. More fundamentally, appropriate theories and methodologies are needed to account for such cognitive and social activities in relation to information visualization.

In this book, we use some representative examples of information visualization to illustrate these issues and potential research areas in information visualization and virtual environments. We aim to take a step towards a taxonomy of information visualization, by highlighting and contrasting the commonality and uniqueness of existing information visualization designs in terms of overall design rationale, interaction metaphors, criteria and algorithms, and evaluation. Three empirical studies are included, which concern the relationships between individual differences, namely three cognitive factors, and the use of a user interface design based on a visualized semantic space for information foraging. The studies provide the reader with some results of our latest research.

Each chapter in the book addresses one main topic. Chapter 2 introduces methods for finding or extracting backbone structures from a complex set of information. Chapter 3 focuses on techniques for generating spatial layouts and graph drawing techniques. General criteria for visualizing hierarchical and network structures are also highlighted. Chapter 4 collects and arranges representative information visualization designs and systems into several broad categories, in order to highlight their similarities and distinctiveness of design. Chapter 5 looks at the emerging field of Knowledge Domain Visualization (KDViz). Chapter 6 covers empirical studies of information visualization. This is essentially a new chapter. Chapter 7 deals with virtual environments with a number of substantial updates, including a study of group tightness. The final chapter, Chapter 8, is a new chapter on detecting abrupt changes and emerging trends. This chapter looks beyond the current horizon of information visualization and identifies a number of areas that information visualization must deal with in its further advances, for example, a closer incorporation of knowledge discovery and data mining techniques.

We will start with examples of geographical visualization, in which information is organized on a geographical framework. Information visualized in this way tends to be intuitive and easy to understand, and will provide a starting point for us to proceed to visualizing more abstract information, where we may not be able to map information onto a geographic map, or a relief map of the earth. We must, therefore, find new ways to organize and accommodate such information, and create data structures capable of representing characteristics of an abstract information space. There will also be some discussion of optimal foraging theory and cognitive map theories, and their implications on information visualization.

1.1 A Roadmap of Information Visualization

We begin our journey with an intellectual roadmap of information visualization (see Figure 1.1). The roadmap will guide us to the most influential works in the field, a glimpse to the underlying knowledge structure, and the time when they entered the mainstream of the field. The construction of such maps is detailed in later chapters. Here is a brief description of what the map is telling us.

This is a co-citation map of articles in the literature of information visualization between 1993 and 2003. A co-citation is an instance when two articles are referenced by a third article. The co-citation relationship tells us how often scientists endorse the connection in terms of the corresponding co-citation frequency. In general, the more often two articles are cited side by side, the stronger the intellectual tie between the two articles is likely to be.

First of all, the roadmap shows various sized dots – nodes – and different colored lines – links. Each node denotes a published article about information visualization,

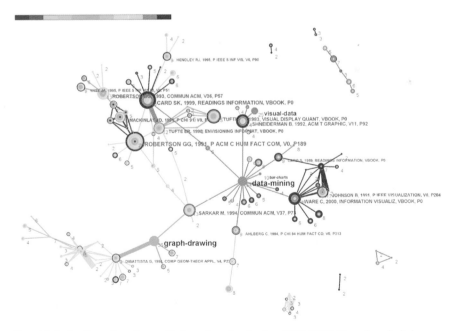

Figure 1.1 An intellectual roadmap of information visualization (1993–2003). The color of a link corresponds to the year in which the co-citation frequency for the first time exceeds a co-citation threshold.

and each link denotes a co-citation relationship. The size of a node is proportional to the number of times the underlying article is cited or referenced by other articles. So the larger a node, the more frequently it is cited. The length and thickness of a line are proportional to the strength of a co-citation measurement. In other words, a shorter and thicker link depicts a stronger co-citation relationship than a longer and thinner one. The color of a link indicates the time when the link becomes strong enough for the first time. See Chapters 5 and 8 for more in-depth descriptions of the method. The center of a star-shaped cluster is often a significant article. The change of link colors is an indicator of when scientists change their focuses. The size of a node label is also proportional to its citations – more frequently cited articles have larger labels. In this map and other maps in this chapter, we refer to an article by its first author, even if it may have multiple authors. So what is the map telling us? The map depicts highly cited articles as color-coded citation treerings. The larger the diameter of a treering, the more frequently the associated article was cited. Highly cited articles are also labeled by their references in blue. Title phrases and abstract phrases with a surge of popularity in citing articles are labeled in red. For example, the map shows a recent surge of phrase *data-mining* in 2002 and an earlier surge of phrase *graph-drawing* in 1998. Such phrases are good indicators of the nature of citations to articles adjacent to the phrases.

The most cited article in the map, with the largest treering to the middle left, is the original article on cone tree visualizations by Robertson et al. (1991). Located slightly above the cone tree article is *Readings in Information Visualization* by Card, Mackinlay, and Shneiderman (1999), which has rapidly become the bible of the field. The map also reveals other highly cited publications such as Tufte's 1983 book *The Visual Display of Quantitative Information*, located to the right next to the original treemap article by Shneiderman (1992). Treemap visualizations are one of the most popularized and successful techniques. We will return to the topic in later chapters.

The "data mining" cluster is connected to the book *Information Visualization* by Ware (2000) to the right of the map, which is in turn frequently co-cited with the first treemap article by Johnson and Shneiderman (1991). The cone tree article, the *data-mining* cluster, and the *graph-drawing* cluster are joined together at the center of the map by Sarkar and Brown (1994). The leading publication in the *graph-drawing* cluster is by Di Battista et al. (1994). We will take a closer look at graph drawing in Chapter 3.

Outside the mainframe of the map there is an island cluster, in the upper right corner of the map including White and McCain's 1998 author co-citation analysis of information science using multidimensional scaling (MDS), and Chen's 1999 author co-citation analysis of hypertext, in which Pathfinder network scaling was adapted for the first time for visualizing a network structure beyond the traditional scope of Pathfinder studies in cognitive science. The island cluster on this map is in fact the tip of a much bigger iceberg, involving scientometrics, bibliometrics, and other fields. Its relatively low-profile presence on this map is because we aim our camera at the center of the information visualization field. As a result of a growing interest in tracking the evolution of a knowledge domain's intellectual structure (Chen and Paul, 2001; Chen et al. 2001a; Chen 2003; Chen et al. 2002; Chen and Kuljis, 2003; Small 1999a,b, 2003), a relatively new field of Knowledge Domain Visualization (KDViz) is rapidly gaining popularity. Chapter 5 includes more detailed examples. *Mapping Scientific Frontiers* (Chen, 2003) is also recommended as further reading on the subject.

The overall map has shown us the most significant intellectual landmarks. In fact, the overview map is the result of superimposing co-citation maps of consecutive

Table 1.1 Groundbreaking articles of the field revealed by the 1993 co-citation map

Year	Author	Topic	Source
1986	Furnas	Fisheye View	CHI'86
1988	Fairchild et al.	SemNet	Book
1990	Feiner and Beshers	Worlds within Worlds	UIST'90
1991	Mackinlay et al.	Perspective Wall	CHI'91
1991	Card et al.	Information Visualiser	CHI'91
1991	Robertson et al.	Cone Trees	CHI'91

Figure 1.2 The 1993 co-citation map of information visualization.

years. If each year's co-citation map is like a patch, then the overall map stitches these patches into a single piece. Individual maps are more detailed, showing probably more articles that may not be prominent in the overall map.

No significant co-citation structures were detected by the co-citation data in 1990, 1991, and 1992. The earliest detectable co-citation map of information visualization starts from 1993, containing six articles – the articles that eventually sparked the field of information visualization (see Table 1.1 and Figure 1.2). The 1995 co-citation map only contains three articles and they are among the six: the *Perspective Wall* article, the *Fisheye View* article, and the *Cone Tree* article.

Next is the 1998 co-citation map of two clusters (Figure 1.3): the cluster on the left – Cluster L, and the cluster on the right – Cluster R. Cluster L includes Tufte's 1983 and 1990 books, Foley's book on computer graphics, Cleveland's 1993 book, and two books of Nielsen. Cluster R includes two fisheye view articles – one by Furnas (1986) and one by Sarkar and Brown (1994) – the spring embedder article by Eades (1984), the annotated bibliography of graph drawing algorithms by Di Battista et al. (1994) and several others, a graph drawing article by Misue et al. (1995), a tree map article, and a TileBars article from Marti Hearst (1995).

The 2000 co-citation map is dominated by a graph drawing cluster to the left, an upper right cluster, and a lower right cluster (Figure 1.4). The graph drawing cluster is centered on Di Battista et al. (1994). Seminal graph layout algorithm articles such as Eades (1984) and Fruchterman and Reingold (1981) also appear in this cluster. The upper right cluster contains Robertson et al. (1993), Hendley et al. (1995), and Sarkar and Brown (1994). *Readings in Information Visualization* (Card et al., 1999) appears for the first time in a co-citation map. The lower right cluster contains Tufte's 1983 and 1990 books and Shneiderman's 1992 treemap article.

The 2001 co-citation map reveals a number of new entries, such as Herman et al.'s 2000 survey of graph drawing techniques (Figure 1.5). The mainstream cluster is dominated by Robertson et al. (1991) and Card et al. (1999).

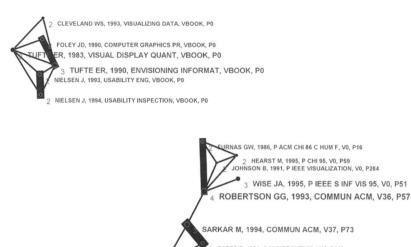

Figure 1.3 The 1998 co-citation map of information visualizaton.

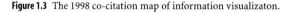

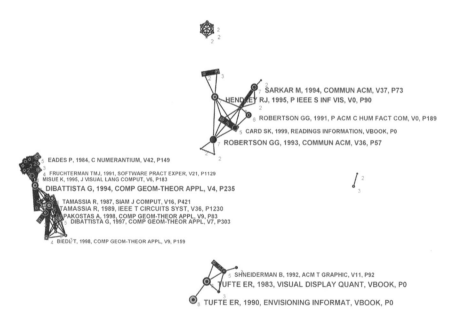

Figure 1.4 The 2000 co-citation map of information visualization.

The 2002 co-citation map shows two major clusters (Figure 1.6). The major cluster contains the *Readings*, Ware's 2000 *Information Visualization*, and Spence's 2001 *Information Visualization 1995 book*. The small cluster is scientific literature visualization, including Small's (1999b) *citation mapping* article, White and McCain's

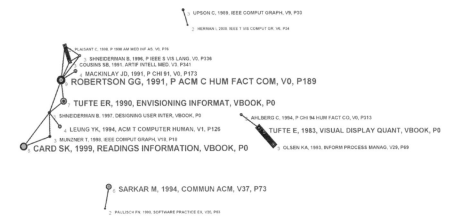

Figure 1.5 The 2001 co-citation map of information visualization.

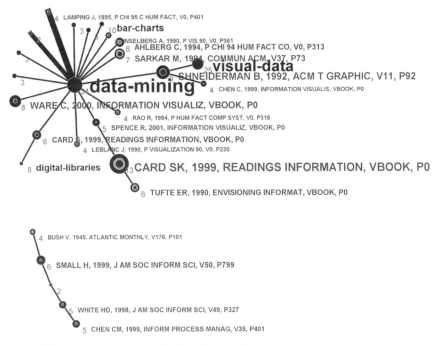

Figure 1.6 The 2002 co-citation map of information visualization.

1998 MDS-mapping of author co-citation networks of information science, and Chen's (1999b) Pathfinder network visualization of author co-citation of the hypertext literature.

Finally, the 2003 co-citation map, based on data retrieved in October 2003, reflects the latest snapshot of the field (Figure 1.7). The *Readings* continues to dominate the map. The second most significant position is taken by Ware (2000).

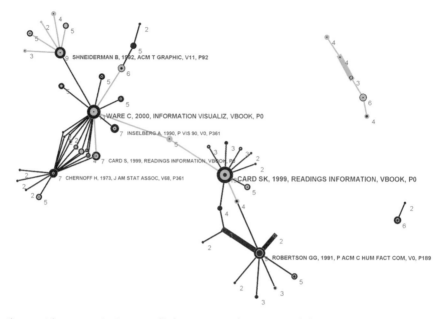

Figure 1.7 The 2003 co-citation map of information visualization (partial, data retrieved in October 2003).

1.2 Geographic Visualization

Information visualization is rooted in a number of closely related areas, particularly in geographical information. When geographical mapping is possible, information can be organized in association with geographical positions in a very natural and intuitive way. The influence of geographical and spatial metaphors is so strong that they can be found in most information visualization systems.

Spatial metaphors not only play a predominant role in information visualization, but also become one of the most fundamental design models of virtual environments. The central theme of this book is to reveal the underlying connection between information visualization and virtual environments, which are effectively brought together by spatial metaphors. Such integration sets information visualization in the wider, richer context of social and ecological dynamics, provided by a virtual environment. At the same time, virtual environments are better able to fulfill their ambitions with the power of information visualization.

1.2.1 The Loss of Napoleon's Army

One picture is worth a thousand words. A classic example is the compelling storytelling map by Charles Joseph Minard (1781–1870), which vividly reveals the losses of Napoleon's army in 1812 (Figure 1.8).

The size of Napoleon's army is shown as the width of the band in the map, starting on the Russian–Polish border with 422,000 men. By the time they reached Moscow in September, the size of the army dropped to 100,000. Eventually, only a small fraction of Napoleon's original army survived.

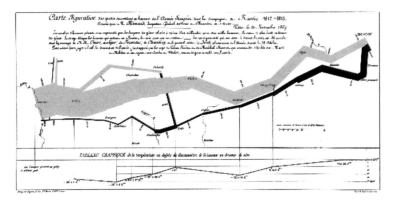

Figure 1.8 The paths of Napoleon's army.

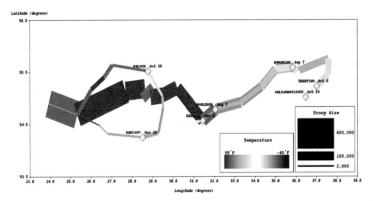

Figure 1.9 Napoleon's retreat, visualized by the SAGE system. Reprinted with permission of Mark Derthick.

Recently, the map was redrawn by a group of researchers at Carnegie Mellon University using an information visualization system called SAGE (Roth et al., 1997).[1] The new version of the map, shown in Figure 1.9, and drawn using almost the same techniques as Minard's original ones, aims to reveal various details and their relationships more accurately. The steadily dropping temperature was a major factor during the retreat. The SAGE version is able to represent such change of temperature in different colors along with the shrinking size of Napoleon's army. This color coding clearly shows the heat wave in the first few months, and the steady decline in temperature throughout the retreat. There was a spell of milder temperatures when the retreating army was between the cities of Krasnyj and Bobrsov.

Figure 1.10 is another map generated by SAGE, based on Minard's data. Here, time, place, and temperature are incorporated in the visual representation. The horizontal axis is the time line. Lengthy stays at particular places are shown as gaps between colored blocks, and battlefields are shown as diamonds. These improvements show something that was not so obvious in Minard's map, i.e. what happened

---

[1]See Chapter 4 for more details about SAGE.

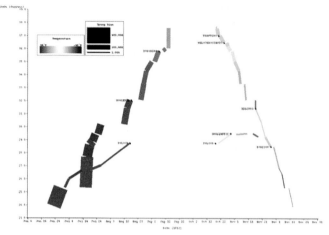

Figure 1.10 Time, place, and temperature are attributes of the movement. Reprinted with permission of Mark Derthick.

to the northern flank of Napoleon's army – it branched off from the main force, captured Polock in August, and remained there until after a second battle in October. Later in November, it rejoined the main retreat, as the temperature dropped dramatically.

Information visualization is often a powerful and effective tool for conveying a complex idea. However, as shown in the above example, one may often need to use a number of complimentary visualization methods in order to reveal various relationships.

1.2.2 Playfair

In a comprehensive review of graphical data analysis techniques, Howard Wainer (1981) introduced graphical statistical data analysis techniques, mainly developed by statisticians, to social scientists, especially psychologists. He identified two major approaches: rigorous, formal statistical models, and descriptive methods for exploratory rather than confirmatory analysis.

Wainer's historical account begins with the 1786 publication of Playfair's *Commercial and Political Atlas* – a major conceptual breakthrough in graphical presentation, which pioneers the use of spatial dimensions to represent non-spatial, quantitative, idiographic, empirical data (Figure 1.11). Wainer also identifies Tukey's 1962 visionary *Future of data analysis* as *prophetic* and Tukey's 1977 *Exploratory Data Analysis* (EDA) as a landmark event in graphical data analysis.

1.2.3 Cartography of the Internet

As we will see in later chapters, many information visualization systems are based on organizational principles rooted in the geographical paradigm, which is closely related to the more generic use of spatial metaphors in information visualization and virtual environments. Spatial metaphors are traditionally, and increasingly, popular in information visualization and virtual environments. A fruitful way to

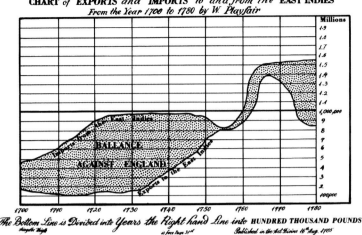

Figure 1.11 Playfair's exports and imports chart (1785).

explore their role is to examine the boundary conditions of when and where they would be an appropriate and adequate option.

The following examples represent some of the major developments in visualizing the Internet and its predecessors. Special attention is drawn to the role of the geographical paradigm in information organization and visualization.

Where Wizards Stay up Late: the Origins of the Internet, written by Hafner and Lyon (1996), provides a wonderful starting point to explore the early days of computer networks across universities, countries, and continents. It is a thought-provoking book to read, and to reflect upon today's widespread use of the WWW. There is a companion website, wizards,[2] aiming to establish a central repository for information concerning the origins of the Internet. Wizards website invites people to contribute and recommend new links to the site (e-mail: wizards@construct.net). Wizards contains dozens of diagrams, hand-drawn sketches and maps, photographs and technical papers, in particular, maps and drawings of the earliest networks.

In 1966, the US Defense Department's Advanced Research Projects Agency (ARPA) funded a project to create computer communication among its university-based researchers. This multimillion dollar network, known as the ARPANET, was launched in 1969 by ARPA, with the aim of linking dozens of major computer science labs throughout the country. An informative timeline of this part of its history is now available on the web.[3]

The first four sites chosen to form the ARPANET were University of California Los Angles (UCLA), SRI, University of California Santa Barbara (UCSB), and the University of Utah. Figure 1.12 is the initial configuration of this ARPANET. IMP is the packet switch scheme used on it.

---

[2]http://www.fixe.com/wizards/
[3]http://www.bbn.com/timeline/

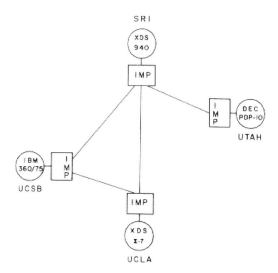

Figure 1.12 The initial four-node ARPANET.

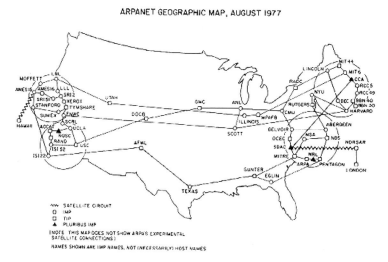

Figure 1.13 Geographic map of ARPANET in 1977.

The network had grown to 34 IMP nodes by September 1972. The first ARPANET geographic map (Figure 1.13) appeared in August 1977. Hubs at both the west and east coasts are clearly shown in the map, and links to Hawaii and London were based on satellite circuits.

Figure 1.14 is the geographic map of the ARPANET in October 1987, ten years later. NSFNET, commissioned by the National Science Foundation (USA), marks another historical stage in the development of global computer networks. The following section contains visualizations of NSFNET traffic in the 1990s. They are also based on geographical maps.

ARPANET Geographic Map, 31 October 1987

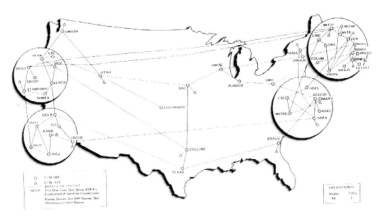

Figure 1.14 Geographic map of ARPANET in 1987.

1.2.3.1 Visualization of the NSFNET

NSFNET was commissioned by the National Science Foundation until April 1995. A number of commercial carriers have maintained the NSFNET backbone service. Donna Cox and Robert Patterson at the National Center for Supercomputing Applications (NCSA) visualized various traffics on the NSFNET, from 1991 until the NSFNET was decommissioned in 1995.[4]

Visualizations of the NSFNET include byte and billion-byte traffic into the NSFNET backbones at two levels: T1 backbone (up to 100 billion bytes) and T3 backbone (up to one trillion bytes from its client networks). The volume of the traffic is color-coded, ranging from zero bytes (purple) to 100 billion bytes (white).

Figures 1.15 and 1.16 are visualizations of inbound traffic measured in billions of bytes on the NSFNET T1 backbone in 1991. The volume of traffic is color-coded, ranging from zero bytes (purple) to 100 billion bytes (white). Traffic on the NSFNET has been vividly characterized by these powerful geographic visualizations. Figure 1.17 represents byte traffic into the ANS/NSFNET T3 backbone in November, 1993. The colored lines represent virtual connections from the network sites to the backbone.

1.2.3.2 Geographical Visualization of WWW Traffic

The WWW is by far the most predominant traffic on the Internet. There is a growing interest in understanding the geographical dispersion of access patterns to the WWW, especially from electronic commerce and commercial Internet service providers. A geographic visualization of the WWW traffic is presented by a group of researchers at the National Center for Supercomputing Applications (NCSA) (Lamm et al., 1995). Patterns of access requests received by the WWW server complex at the NCSA are mapped to geographic locations on the globe of the earth. Because the Mosaic WWW

---

[4]http://www.ncsa.uiuc.edu/SCMS/DigLib/text/technology/Visualization-Study-NSFNET-Cox.html

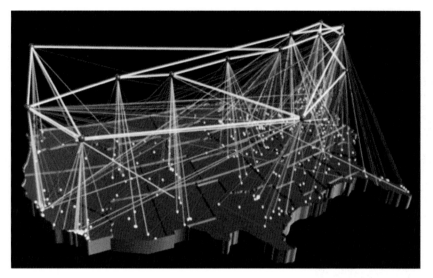

Figure 1.15 Billion-byte traffic into the NSFNET T1 backbone in 1991.

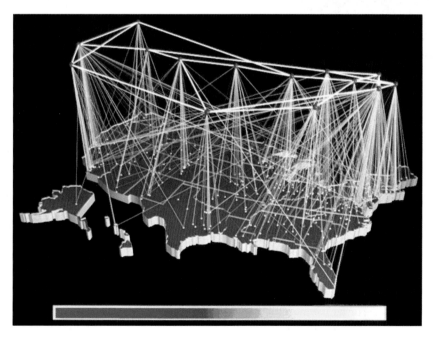

Figure 1.16 Billion-byte inbound traffic on the NSFNET T1 backbone in 1991.

browser was developed at NCSA, the access load on the NCSA WWW server is always high, which makes the NCSA WWW server an ideal high-load test bed.

All the WWW servers run NCSA's Hypertext Transfer Protocol Daemon (httpd), which deals with access requests. It maintains four logs on the local disk: document

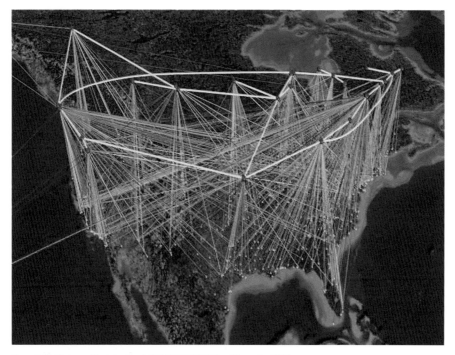

Figure 1.17 Byte traffic into the ANS/NSFNET T3 backbone in 1993.

accesses, agents, errors, and referers. NCSA's geographical map of the WWW traffic focuses on the document access logs, because they record interesting information about each access request. Nevertheless, other logs also provide potentially useful data. For instance, statistics of the use of Netscape or Internet Explorer can be obtained from the agent logs. More interestingly, one may identify how the user gets to the current link from the referer's logs.

Each entry of the access log includes seven fields, namely the IP address of the requesting client, the time of the request, the name of the requested document, and the number of bytes sent in response to the request. In particular, the file name usually contains further information about the nature of the request; the extension of a filename may reveal whether the requested file is text, an image, audio, video or special types of files.

Geographic mapping particularly relies on the information encoded in the IP address field of server access logs. Each IP address can be converted to a domain name. It is this domain name that can be used to match each access request to a geographical location, although this matching scheme may break down in certain circumstances.

NCSA's geographical visualization is based on IP addresses and domain names. The geographic mapping also relies on the InterNIC *whois* database containing information on domains, hosts, networks, and other Internet administrators, and, more usefully for geographical mapping, a postal address. Each access request is mapped to a city or the capital of a country if it is outside the US. The latitude and longitude of the city is then retrieved from a local database.

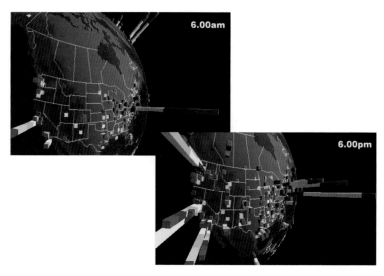

Figure 1.18 Access requests to NCSA's WWW server complex (Eastern Standard Time August 22, 1995, 6.00 am and 6.00 pm). Reprinted with permission of Daniel Reed.

Initially, the geographical mapping must rely on the results of queries sent to the remote *whois* database, but a local database is gradually replacing the need for accessing to a remote database, as a greater number of matched IP addresses are accumulated in the local database.

Figure 1.18 shows two snapshots of the NCSA geographic visualization. The surface of the earth is rendered according to altitude relief from the USGS ETOP05 database,[5] and political boundaries are drawn from the CIA World Map database.

Arcs and stacked bars are two popular methods of visualizing data on a sphere. Arcs are commonly used to display point-to-point communication traffic, for example, the visualization of the topology of MBone (Munzner et al., 1996).

Stacked bars are particularly useful for associating data to a geographical point, representing various data by position, height, and color bands. In NCSA's geographic visualization, each bar is placed on the geographic location of a WWW request to the NCSA's web server. The height of a bar indicates the number of bytes, or the number of requests relative to other sites. The color bands represent the distribution of document types, domain classes, or time intervals, between successive requests.

Figure 1.18 contains two snapshots of a single day, separated by 12 hours, on August 22, 1995. The first was in the morning Eastern Standard Time (6.00 am), and the second was in the evening (6.00 pm). Europe is a major source of activity at the NCSA WWW server. The first snapshot shows some high stacked bars in Europe, while most of the US sites were quiet. In the evening, access requests from the US were in full swing. Even now, one could still see a similar pattern as on the geographical map of the ARPANET 20 years ago – the west and east coasts generated by far the most access requests to NCSA's server. High population areas, such as New York and Los Angeles, are major sources of WWW traffic.

According to Lamm et al. (1995), large corporations and commercial Internet service providers tend to appear as the originating point for the largest number of

---

[5]http://www.usgs.gov/data/cartographic/

accesses. Smaller sites, such as universities, government laboratories, and small companies, constitute a large portion of all accesses, but they are geographically distributed more uniformly. Based on NCSA's data in 1994 and 1995, government and commercial access is growing much more rapidly than that of educational institutions. Lamm et al. also found that requests for audio and video files are much more common during the normal business day than during the evening hours. They conjecture that this reflects both lower band-width links to Europe and Asia, and low speed modem-based access via commercial service providers. Such findings have profound implications for the design of WWW servers and browsers, as well as Internet service providers.

The NCSA group is working on a geographical visualization that would allow users to zoom closer to selected regions, and gain a more detailed perspective than is presently possible with fixed region clustering. They are currently adding more detailed information to geographical databases for Canada and the UK.

1.2.3.3 Geographical Visualization of the MBone

The MBone is the Internet's multicast backbone. Multicast distributes data from one source to multiple receivers, with minimal packet duplication. A visualization of the global topology of the Internet MBone is presented by Munzner et al. (1996), again illustrating the flexibility and extensibility of the geographical visualization paradigm.

The MBone provides an efficient means of transmitting real-time video and audio streams across the Internet. It has been used for conferences, meetings, congressional sessions, and NASA shuttle launches. The MBone network is growing exponentially, without a central authority; visualizing the topology of the MBone has profound implications for network providers and the multicast research community.

Munzner et al. maps the latitude and longitude of MBone routers on 3D geographical information. The connections between MBone routers are represented as arcs. The geographical visualization of the MBone is made as an interactive 3D map using VRML – Virtual Reality Modeling Language (Figure 1.19). In Figure 1.20, the globe is wrapped with a satellite photograph of the earth surface.

1.2.3.4 Visualization of Routing Dynamics

How long will it take for packets to travel from one point to another on the Internet? CAIDA's Skitter[6] is designed to measure and visualize routing dynamics (CAIDA, 1998; Huffaker et al., 1998). The round-trip time taken from the source to the destination and back to the source is measured and visualized. Skitter measures the round-trip time by sending packets to a destination and recording the replies from routers along the way. Figure 1.21 shows a visualization of paths from one source host to 23,000 destinations.

Analysis of real-world trends in routing behavior across the Internet has direct implications for the next generation of networking applications. The primary design goal of Skitter was to visualize the network connectivity from a source host

---

[6]http://www.caida.org/Tools/Skitter

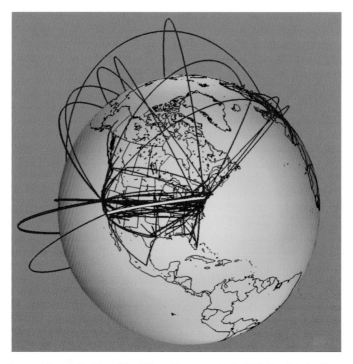

Figure 1.19 Geographic visualization of the MBone (Munzner et al., 1996). Reprinted with permission of Tamara Munzner.

Figure 1.20 Geographic visualization of the MBone on a satellite photograph of the earth surface (Munzner et al., 1996). Reprinted with permission of Tamara Munzner.

Figure 1.21 Skitter visualization of top autonomous systems (AS): a component of the network that controls its own routing within its infrastructure and uses an external routing protocol to communicate with other ASs. Reprinted with permission from CAIDA.

as a directed graph. Skitter probes destinations on the network. The results are represented as a spanning tree with its root node at the probing host, also known as the polling host. The data is then aggregated and shown as a top–down, macroscopic view of a cross-section of the Internet. Visualization of macro-level traffic patterns can give insights into several areas; for example, mapping dynamic changes in Internet topology, tracking abnormal delays, and identifying bottleneck routers and critical paths in the Internet infrastructure.

Interestingly, CAIDA is planning to tap the Skitter output data with a geographical database of various crucial backbone networks on the Internet, the MBone and caching hierarchy topology. These data together can help engineers to pinpoint routing anomalies, and track round-trip times and packet loss.

CAIDA's short-term plans include developing 3D visualizations of Skitter measurements, using additional active and passive measurement hosts throughout the Internet, and analyzing trends in these traffic data.

Similar work has been done at Matrix Information Directory Services (MIDS) in mapping the Internet. MIDS produces an animated map known as the Internet Weather Report[7] (IWR), which updates network latencies on the Internet six times a day, probed from MIDS's headquarters in Texas to over 4000 domains around the world.

Martin Dodge, at University College London, maintains a wonderful collection, called the Atlas of Cyberspace, of fascinating geographical visualization images on the web.[8] The original sources of some examples in this book were found via

---

[7]http://www.mids.org/weather/
[8]http://www.atlascyberspace.org/geographic.html

Figure 1.22 Another visualization of Skitter. Reprinted with permission from CAIDA.

hyperlinks from the atlas. The site also distributes a monthly newsletter on new updates on the gallery to subscribers. Subscription is free.

1.3 Abstract Information Visualization

We have seen some fascinating visualization works based on geographical maps. These visualizations appear to be simple, intuitive, and natural. They seem to break the barrier between a complex system and the knowledge of a specific subject domain.

This intuitiveness is largely due to the use of a geographical visualization paradigm – information is essentially organized and matched to a geographical structure. The visualizations are based on the world map that we are all familiar with, and yet a large amount of information is made available for people to understand. Having seen the power of geographical visualization paradigms, we will focus on some questions concerning information visualization and virtual environments more generally.

- Are these geographic visualization paradigms extensible to information that may not be geographical or astronomical in nature?
- How do we visualize abstract information spaces in general?
- What are the criteria for an informative and insightful visualization of an abstract information space?
- What are the human factor issues that must be taken into account?

The following sections will introduce optimal information foraging and cognitive maps, in order to understand the context in which information visualization might be useful.

1.4 Optimal Information Foraging

Information visualization often plays an integral part in more complex intellectual work. The value of specific information visualization techniques can only be fully appreciated in such contexts. The design of information visualization has produced numerous analogues and metaphors, the most influential ones being navigating in information landscape and treasure hunting in digital information spaces.

Information foraging theory is built on an ecological perspective to the study of information-seeking behavior (Pirolli and Card, 1995). Optimal foraging theory was originally developed in biology and anthropology, being used to analyze various food-foraging strategies and how they are adapted to a specific situation. Information foraging theory is an adaptation of the optimal foraging theory, to provide an analytic methodology to assess information search strategies in a similar approach. Like the original optimal foraging theory, it focuses on the trade-off between information gains and the cost of retrieval for the user.

Information foraging is a broad term. A wide variety of activities associated with assessing, seeking, and handling information sources can be categorized as information foraging. Furthermore, the term "foraging" refers both to the metaphor of browsing and searching for something valuable, and to the connection with the optimal foraging theory in biology and anthropology. In information foraging, one must make optimal use of knowledge about expected information value and expected costs of accessing and extracting the relevant information. Pirolli (1998) applies information foraging theory to the analysis of the use of the Scatter/Gather browser (Pirolli et al., 1996b), and particularly explains the gains and losses from the user's point of view in accessing the relevance of document clusters. The Scatter/Gather interface presents users with a navigable, automatically computed overview of the contents of a document collection, represented as a hierarchy of document clusters.

In hypertext, or on the web, we may experience common navigational behavior, known as branching, when we have to decide which thread of discussion we want to follow. Such decision-making has been identified as one of the major sources of cognitive overload for hypertext readers. Users cannot simply read *on*. They must choose, or gamble in many situations, the path that is most likely to be informative and fruitful to them. The cost of such decision-making is associated with how easy a user interface or the network connection allows users to *undo* their selected actions. Global overview maps are often used to help users make up their mind easily. Information visualization in an abstract information space is largely playing a similar role: to guide users to find valuable information with the minimum cost.

1.5 Exploring Cyberspaces

The concept of a cognitive map plays an influential role in the study of navigation strategies, such as browsing in hyperspace and wayfinding in virtual environments (Darken and Sibert, 1996). A cognitive map could be seen as the internalized analogy in the human mind to the physical layout of the environment (Tversky, 1993;

Thorndyke and Hayes-Roth, 1982; Tolman, 1948). The acquisition of navigational knowledge proceeds through several developmental stages, from the initial identification of landmarks in the environment to a fully formed mental map (Thorndyke and Hayes-Roth, 1982).

Landmark knowledge is often the basis for building our cognitive maps (Thorndyke and Hayes-Roth, 1982). The development of visual navigation knowledge may start with highly salient visual *landmarks* in the environment, such as unique and magnificent buildings, or natural landscapes. People associate their location in the environment with reference to these landmarks.

The acquisition of *route* knowledge is usually the next stage in developing a cognitive map. Those who have acquired route knowledge will be able to travel along a designated route comfortably without the need to rely on landmarks. Route knowledge does not provide the navigator with enough information about the environment to enable the person to optimize their route for navigation. If someone with route knowledge wanders off the route, it would be very difficult for that person to backtrack to the right route.

The cognitive map is not considered fully developed until *survey* knowledge has been acquired (Thorndyke and Hayes-Roth, 1982). The physical layout of the environment has to be mentally transformed by the user to form a cognitive map.

Dillon et al. (1990) point out that when users navigate through an abstract structure such as a deep menu tree, if they select wrong options at a deep level they tend to return to the top of the tree altogether, rather than just take one step back. This strategy suggests the absence of survey knowledge about the structure of the environment, and a strong reliance on landmarks to guide navigation. Existing studies have suggested that there are ways to increase the likelihood that users will develop survey knowledge of an electronic space. For instance, intensive use of maps tends to increase survey knowledge in a relatively short time (Lokuge et al., 1996). Other studies have shown that strong visual cues indicating paths and regions can help users to understand the structure of a virtual space (Darken and Sibert, 1996).

By and large, visual information navigation relies on the construction of a cognitive map, and the extent to which users can easily connect the structure of their cognitive maps with the visual representations of an underlying information space. The concept of a cognitive map suggests that users need information about the structure of a complex, richly interconnected information space. However, if all the connectivity information were to be displayed, users would be unlikely to navigate effectively in spaghetti-like visual representations. Give this conundrum, how do designers of complex hypertext visualizations optimize their user interfaces for navigation and retrieval?

One problem faced by designers is that detail concerning an explicit, logical structure may not be readily available in visualization form. An explicit organizing structure may not always naturally exist for a given data set, or the existing structure may simply be inappropriate for the specific tasks at hand. What methods are available for designers to derive and expose an appropriate structure in the user interface? How can we connect such designs with the user's cognitive map for improved learning and navigation?

1.6 Social Interaction in Online Communities

An example of a move from individualistic views of knowledge to socially constructed views has been found in the work of Barrett (1989), concerning the hypertext community. Most virtual environments on the Internet have a common goal of supporting social interaction in an electronic information space. Much attention has been devoted to the role of spatial metaphors in fostering social interaction in such environments. A powerful framework of navigation distinguishes three major paradigms: spatial, semantic, and social navigation (Dourish and Chalmers, 1994).

Spatial navigation mimics our experiences in the physical world. A virtual environment may be a geometric model of a part of the real world, such as a town hall, a bank, or a theatre. Users may navigate in the virtual world entirely based on their experiences in navigating through a city or a building in the real world.

Instead of following the geometric properties of a virtual world, in semantic navigation, navigation is driven by semantic relationships, or underlying logic. A good example of semantic navigation is navigation in hypertext. We follow a hypertext link from one part of the hyperspace to another because they are semantically related, rather than based on geometric properties. Finally, social navigation is an information browsing strategy that takes advantage of the behavior of like-minded people.

The use of spatial models in attempts to support collaborative virtual environments has been criticized as oversimplifying the issue of structuring, or framing, interactive behavior. Harrison and Dourish (1996) examine the notions of space and spatial organization of virtual environments. They call for a re-examination of the role of spatial models in facilitating and structuring social interaction. They highlight the critical distinction between space and place by arguing that it is the notion of place, rather than that of space, which actually frames interactive behavior.

According to Harrison and Dourish (1996), designers are looking for a critical property that can facilitate and shape interactive behavior in a distributed working environment. This critical property, called appropriate behavioral framing, will provide users with a reference framework in which they can judge the appropriateness of their behavior. Harrison and Dourish argue that spatial models are simply not enough for people to adapt their behavior accordingly. Rather, it is a sense of place and shared understanding about behavior and action in a specific culture that shapes the way we interact and communicate (Harrison and Dourish, 1996).

Context is a recurring concept in the design of a virtual environment that can support social interaction. Several methodologies from sociology, anthropology, and linguistics are potentially useful for exploring the structure of social interaction and how it reflects the influence of a meaningful context. Two concepts are particularly concerned with structures of social contexts: the concept of *contextualization cues* from linguistics (Gumperz, 1982), and the concept of *frames* from sociology (Goffman, 1974). The following review is partially based on Drew and Heritage (1992).

Sociolinguistics had initially treated context in terms of the social attributes that speakers bring to talk – for example, age, class, ethnicity, gender, geographical region, and other relationships. Studies of data from natural settings have shown that the relevance of these attributes depended upon the particular setting in which the talk occurred, and also upon the particular speech activities or tasks that speakers were engaged in within those settings.

The dynamic nature of social contexts and the importance of linguistic details in evoking them have been studied in Gumperz (1982). It is shown that any aspect of linguistic behavior may function as a contextualization cue, including lexical, phonological, and syntactic choices, together with the use of particular codes, dialects, or styles. These contextualization cues indicate which aspects of the social context are relevant in interpreting what a speaker means. By indicating significant aspects of the social context, contextualization cues enable people to make inferences about one another's communicative intentions and goals.

The notion of contextualization cues offered an important analytical way to grasp the relationship between language use and speakers' orientations to context and inference making. There is a significant similarity between the linguistic concept of contextualization cues as outlined by Gumperz (1982), and the sociological concept of *frames* developed by Goffman (1974). The notion of *frames* focuses on the definition which participants give to their current social activity, to what is going on, what the situation is, and the roles adopted by the participants within it. These two concepts both relate specific linguistic options to the social activity in which language is being engaged.

Activity theory is rooted in the work of the Russian psychologist L. Vygotsky. Traditionally, this theory has a strong influence in Scandinavian countries. Since the late 1980s however, there is an increasingly growing interest in activity theory in Human–Computer Interaction (HCI) (Nardi, 1996), Computer-Supported Cooperative Work (CSCW) (Kuutti and Arvonen, 1992), and Information Science (Hjorland, 1997).

According to activity theory, cognition is an adaptation of one's knowledge to ecological and social environments. The individual's information needs, knowledge, and subjective relevance criteria should be seen in a larger context (Hjorland, 1997).

This book aims to explore and develop virtual environments that take into account the dynamics of social structures, such as rules and resources, and to provide an environment for the social construction of knowledge. We are interested in building virtual environments in which spatial, semantic, and social navigation can be organically combined together. People will be able to chat and have light conversations, but also engage in social interaction as a part of collaborative intellectual work, in particular subject domains.

1.7 Information Visualization Resources

There has been a steady growth of interest in information visualization and in virtual worlds. Since 1999, several books have been available on the subject of information visualization, notably: Card et al. (1999), Ware (2000), Spence (2001), and the first edition of this book you are reading (Chen, 1999a). The number of conferences relevant to information visualization has been steadily increasing, including the IEEE symposium on Information Visualization (InfoVis) series, and the International Conference on Information Visualization (IV) series in London. A peer-reviewed international journal, *Information Visualization* (IVS), was launched in March 2002. The provision of a dedicated journal enables researchers and practitioners in the field to exchange ideas and thereby stimulate a healthy development of the field.

The growth of the information visualization literature over the last five years is tremendous. It is increasingly difficult to provide a comprehensive coverage of even only the important ones. This book does not attempt to present a comprehensive sweeping coverage of the field; instead, it focuses on a few areas in the

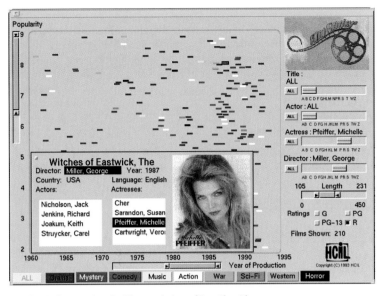

Figure 1.23 FilmFinder. Reprinted with permission of Ben Shneiderman.

rapidly growing field. For those who look for a broader picture, *The Craft of Information Visualization*, written and edited by Bederson and Shneiderman (2003) is a significant and ambitious addition to the information visualization literature. It provides a collection of 38 publications from their lab over the past two decades in information visualization, and reflections on key topics in the field. *The Craft of Information Visualization* is recommended for further reading on a much broader range of topics.

Paul Kahn at Dynamic Diagrams[9] presents a series of tutorials on information visualization, especially on site maps on the Web. MAPA, Dynamic Diagrams' own visualization tool, is introduced in Chapter 4.

During 1997, University of Maryland students built a comprehensive resource called Online Library of Information Visualization Environments (Olive) on the web.[10] Information is organized according to the underlying data structures, e.g. tree and network structures, and includes a bibliography reflecting work up to that time (Shneiderman, 1996). An earlier student project developed a website on virtual environments and telepresence,[11] providing a useful historical snapshot of work up to 1993. Figure 1.23 shows a screenshot of FilmFinder developed by the University of Maryland.

Iowa State University maintains a clearing house website of projects, research, products, and services concerning information visualization. The website is called the Big Picture,[12] covering issues from visual browsing on the web to navigating in databases, notably in MARC and bibliographical databases. A general bibliography of applicable works is also included.

---

[9]http://www.dynamicdiagrams.com
[10]http://otal.umd.edu/Olive/
[11]http://www.cs.umd.edu/projects/hcil/vrtp.html
[12]http://www.public.iastate.edu/~CYBERSTACKS/BigPic.htm

Finally, a wonderful collection of images and reference links on information visualization, called the *Atlas of Cyberspaces*,[13] is maintained on the web by Martin Dodge at University College London. It contains screenshots of various information visualization applications, with particular focus on geography, spatial analysis, and urban design.

1.8 Summary

In this chapter, we introduced geographical visualization as the starting point of our journey, emphasizing that the goal of information visualization is to represent abstract information spaces intuitively and naturally. We also pointed out that the power of information visualization will only be fully understood when information visualization becomes an integral part of users' activity. Optimal foraging theory and cognitive maps were introduced, to provide a wider context in which to shape the requirements for information visualization.

In Chapter 2, we focus on techniques to extract salient structures from a complex information system, for the purpose of information visualization. In subsequent chapters, we will demonstrate the visualization techniques available to deal with these structures.

---

[13]http://www.cybergeography.org/

Chapter 2
Extracting Salient Structures

---

*Art is the imposing of a pattern on experience, and our aesthetic
enjoyment is recognition of the pattern.*
Alfred North Whitehead

Information overload becomes a common problem in the exponential growth of widely accessible information in modern society, and efficient information filtering and sharing facilities are needed to resolve it. Information visualization has the potential to help people find the information they need more effectively and intuitively.

Information visualization has two fundamentally related aspects: (1) structural modeling, and (2) graphical representation. The purpose of structural modeling is to detect, extract, and simplify underlying relationships. These relationships form a structure that characterizes a collection of documents or other data sets. The following questions are typically answered by structural modeling: What is the basic structure of a complex network or a collection of documents? What are the mental models of a city or a zoo in different people's minds? What is the structure of the literature of a subject domain?

In contrast, the aim of the graphical representation is to transform an initial representation of a structure into a graphical one, so that the structure can be visually examined and interacted with. For example, a hierarchical structure can be displayed as a cone tree, or a hyperbolic graph.

Although the second aspect normally concentrates on the representation of a given structure, the boundary between the two aspects is blurred, as many information visualization systems are capable of displaying the same structure in a number of ways. In fact, the phrase *information visualization* sometimes refers to the second aspect specifically.

In this chapter, we focus on the first aspect of information visualization – structural modeling. Generalized similarity analysis (GSA), is introduced as a unifying framework, and as a starting point for us to interpret and evaluate visualization systems, and to understand the strengths of a particular technical solution. GSA provides a generic and extensible framework capable of accommodating the development of new approaches to visualization. This chapter and subsequent chapters include some examples of how we incrementally introduce Latent Semantic Indexing and Author Co-Citation Analysis into the framework.

This chapter first examines the automatic construction of hypertext, a rich source of inspiration for information visualization, then looks at the growing interest in the WordNet® database and its role in visualization applications, and finally, at GSA, introduced to provide a synthesized view of the literature, and to highlight some potentially fruitful areas for research.

2.1 Proximity and Connectivity

2.1.1 Semantic Distance

WordNet® provides a rich source of structures to describe the relationships between words. Research has shown that the perception of such relationships in a hierarchy may be affected by some interesting factors, which are likely to have significant effects on information retrieval, especially in assessing the query–document relevance. The following example explains two major effects based on a concept of semantic distance.

There is an increasing interest in the nature of online searching. According to a constructivist analysis, during online searching, the searcher continuously constructs meaning from the perceptual phenomena appearing on the computer screen as the result of a complex interplay of the work of indexers, database designers, and everyone else who has contributed to the development of the searching environment.

Online database searching and, more recently, web-based searching using various search engines, all resemble a black-box experience. One enters a search query and receives bibliographical records, or URLs, without a clear picture of why these results are presented, or whether they are indeed relevant. Relevance ranking algorithms cannot do the real work of information retrieval – searchers themselves must reach the ultimate judgment regarding the relevance of a listed document.

A key factor that distinguishes subject experts from non-experts is specialized vocabulary. Experts are individuals with special vocabulary and background knowledge, and they share presumptions and language.

The semantic distance model (SDM) of relevance assessment is proposed by Brooks (1995). The central concept of the SDM is semantic distance. Concepts are placed in a multidimensional space, according to their values on some dimension of meaning. To create a dimension of meaning, Brooks used the generic trees of descriptors found in an existing thesaurus or a hierarchical structure, in which the semantic distance between two items is defined as the number of steps from one to another along existing links in the structure.

Brooks has shown that relevance assessments declined systematically with an increase in semantic distance. Subjects gave the highest relevance assessments to the topical subject descriptor semantically closest to the bibliographical record, and then incrementally smaller relevance assessments to descriptors more distant. This was explained as a result of the so-called semantic distance effect.

In addition, the rate of decline of the assessed relevance appeared to be different for top and bottom record in the same generic tree. This was described as the influence of the semantic direction effect. Comparing a bibliographical record from the top of a generic tree to descriptors located below it produced a rapid decline in relevance assessment. In contrast, comparing a bibliographical record at the bottom of a tree to descriptors located above it produced a slower rate of decline in relevant assessment. In other words, the perceived distance downwards to non-relevance appeared to be shorter than the distance upwards to non-relevance.

Brooks found out that topical subject expertise enhances the effects of the SDM, and the strength of the SDM is contingent on phenomenological factors of the computer–human experience. This provides empirical support for the belief that relevance is a contingent, psychological construct. The effects of the SDM may be limited on term hierarchies in which terms are spaced so far apart that they lack internal coherence and do not converge into a cohesive semantic domain.

SDM can provide important input into information visualization, especially when dealing with a heterogeneous network of documents, topical descriptors, subject headings, and search queries.

2.1.2 Multidimensional Scaling

Scaling is an important concept in psychology, and can provide a rich source of visualization techniques. It derives a quantitative scale to represent an internal, psychological response or reaction to stimuli, such as preference and satisfaction. A number of techniques have been developed for a variety of scaling. Multidimensional scaling (MDS) includes a family of popular scaling methods that can map high-dimensional data into a two- or three-dimensional space. It is possible to capture the nature of a data set from groupings emerging from the spatial layout in MDS.

To use MDS, the data set must provide enough information to derive and represent the distance between a pair of data points. This type of data is known as proximity data. There are several ways of obtaining it, for example, judging the similarity between two documents directly, using sorting and clustering techniques.

A special type of MDS, known as *individual differences MDS* (INDSCAL), is designed for the study of the nature of individual differences. The input is a series of matrices. For example, White and McCain (1998) used author co-citation analysis to map the field of information science. Twelve key journals in information science between 1972 and 1995 were analyzed, and INDSCAL was used to identify trends in terms of top-cited authors in the field. The input was three periodical author co-citation matrices.

The results of MDS may not always be straightforward to interpret. Using the example of Boston tourist sites, according to Lokuge et al. (1996), trajectory mapping for high-dimensional feature spaces often captures the features of the data better than MDS. Instead of relying on similarity judgments as in MDS, trajectory mapping requires subjects to imagine a conceptual feature or property that links each pair of sites. The subject then extrapolates that feature in both directions, to pick two stimuli that would be appropriate from the remaining set.

A trajectory map for tourist sites in Boston is shown in Figure 2.1. The positions of the nodes are not important; instead, the mental model is captured by the connections between the nodes. It is the choice between using spatial proximity or using explicit links that distinguishes MDS and trajectory mapping. Similarly, Pathfinder networks, a key component in GSA, also highlight the role of explicit links in structuring and visualizing salient semantic structures.

In a series of studies, Chalmers and his group increasingly improved the running time of multidimensional scaling (Table 2.1). Recently, by using a hybrid strategy *Sampling → Spring → Interpolating → Refining*, they reported their new algorithm that can lay out 108,000 items in 360 seconds (Morrison et al., 2003).

2.1.3 Link-reduction in Graphs

The most widely known graph drawing techniques include force-directed graph drawing algorithms and spring-embedder algorithms (Eades, 1984). The primary

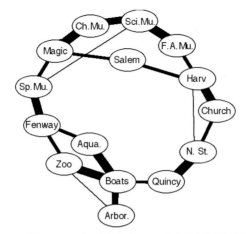

Figure 2.1 A trajectory map of Boston tourist sites (Lokuge et al., 1996). © 1996 ACM, Inc. Reprinted with permission.

Table 2.1 Fast Multidimensional Scaling (Fast MDS)

	Big O Notation	
MDS	N^3	$N^{12/4}$
Chalmers, 1996	N^2	$N^{8/4}$
Morrison et al., 2002	$N^{3/2}$	$N^{6/4}$
Morrison et al., 2003	$N^{5/4}$	$N^{5/4}$

goal of these algorithms is to optimize the arrangement of nodes of a network algorithmically, such that nodes connected by strong links in a graph-theoretical model appear close to each other in the final geometric representation, and weakly connected nodes appear far apart. Force-directed algorithms often lead to node placements that are aesthetically appealing. These algorithms, however, face some challenges in terms of efficiency, especially in terms of scalability, which is closely related to the clarity of a visualized network.

Cluttered network visualizations should be avoided whenever possible. An excessive number of links in a display may severely obscure the discovery of essential patterns. A commonly used strategy to reduce clutter is to reduce the number of links. There are several ways to achieve this goal. Three popular ones are analyzed below.

The first option is imposing a link weight threshold so that only links with weights above the threshold are included (Zizi and Beaudouin-Lafon, 1994). This approach is straightforward and easy to implement. However, it does not take the intrinsic structure of the underlying network into account, so the transformed network may not preserve the essence of the original network.

Minimum Spanning Tree (MST)

The second option is extracting a minimum spanning tree (MST) from a network of N vertices and reducing the number of links to $N - 1$. This approach guarantees the number of links in the transformed network is always $N - 1$, whereas option 3 may not have such upper bounds. For instance, we know that a Pathfinder network is the set union of all possible MSTs of the original network, but the number of distinct MSTs depends on the weight distribution of individual links. Therefore, the number of extra links varies not only from network to network, but also from measurement to measurement. For instance, Noel et al. (2002) showed that using document co-citation counts normalized as cosine coefficients or Pearson correlation coefficients can lead to MSTs of different topological properties, and that the former resulted in more favorable structures, i.e. the presence of highly connected nodes with a fixed number of links, although the size of their MST is relatively small, less than 200 nodes.

Pathfinder Network Scaling (PFNET)

The topology of a PFNET is determined by two parameters q and r and the corresponding network is denoted as $PFNET(r, q)$. The q-parameter specifies the maximum length of a path subject to the triangular inequality test. The r-parameter is the Minkowski metric used to compute the distance of a path. The most concise PFNET for visualization is PFNET ($q = N - 1$, $r = \infty$) (Chen, 2003; Chen and Paul, 2001; Schvaneveldt, 1990). In an author co-citation analysis (ACA), White (2003b) demonstrated that a 120-node PFNET derived from author co-citation counts was predominated by a number of high-degree nodes. In contrast, if author co-citation links were weighted by Pearson correlation coefficients, the resultant PFNET did not have this pattern. He concluded that using raw counts in ACA would be a preferred method. As a side note, the use of Pearson correlation coefficients is studied in Ahlgren et al. (2003), where an example is constructed to show that Pearson correlation coefficients could lead to counter-intuitive results in author co-citation analysis.

2.2 Clustering and Classification

The goal of cluster analysis is to divide a large data set into a number of sub-sets, called clusters, according to some given similarity measures. Not only has clustering analysis established many areas of application, for instance, constructing taxonomies in biology, but it can also play a significant role in information visualization. For example, the *Scatter/Gather* system developed at Xerox helps users to deal with a large information space by repeatedly clustering and aggregating documents at various levels in its user interface, so that the required information can be found more easily.

2.2.1 Clustering algorithms

Clustering algorithms rely on a definition of distance or similarity between two items in a data set. The Minkowski model provides a generic definition of distance:

$$d_{ij} = \left[\sum_{a=1}^{r} | x_{ia} - x_{ja} |^p \right]^{1/p} \quad (p \geqslant 1), \ x_i \neq x_j$$

where two data points are represented by vectors x_i and x_j. Several definitions of distances can be derived from this model; in particular, Euclidean ($p = 2$) and Dominance ($p = \infty$) can be derived from the Minkowski distance, as special cases.

A metric space is defined with the following two axioms:

1   Non-degeneracy: $d_{ij} = 0$ if and only if $i = j$.
2   Triangle inequality: $d_{ij} \leq d_{ik} + d_{kj}$.

The Minkowski distance defines a metric space. Pathfinder network scaling introduced in Chapter 3 relies on an extended triangle inequality condition. If the triangle inequality can be defined in a semantic space, based on some *semantic distance*, it is then a metric space. Clustering algorithms use distance as a yardstick to either group a pair of data points into the same cluster, or separate them into different clusters.

There are three basic categories of clustering methodologies: (1) *graph-theoretical*, (2) *single-pass*, and (3) *iterative* algorithms. A graph-theoretical algorithm relies on a similarity matrix representing the similarity between individual documents. Clusters are formed by closely related documents, according to a similarity threshold. Each cluster can be represented as a connected graph. Depending on how these documents are separated, the process is known as "single link", "group average", or "complete link" clustering (van Rijsbergen, 1979).

Seed-oriented clustering is an example of single-pass clustering algorithms. In the seed-oriented clustering, clusters grow from individual data points, called *cluster seeds*. For example, document clusters can be generated by adding the documents most similar to the seeds into existing clusters. The number of clusters must be known for seed-oriented clustering to occur.

Iterative algorithms attempt to optimize a clustering structure, according to some heuristic function. An iterative algorithm can use clusters generated by other clustering algorithms, such as seed-oriented clustering, as a starting point.

Some clustering analysis routines are provided in popular statistical packages such as SPSS.[1] SPSS provides the following clustering procedures in the Professional Statistics option:

- K-means cluster
- hierarchical cluster

K-means clustering algorithms can handle a large data set, but the number of clusters must be specified in advance. Hierarchical clustering algorithms merge smaller clusters into larger ones, without knowing the number of clusters in advance.

The example data set for the K-mean clustering method includes various personal profiles from 474 people, such as age, education, starting salary, and present salary. The goal of the example analysis is to divide these people into two groups based on their profiles. Two clusters are specified in advance, and the resulting clusters are shown in Table 2.2.

The data set is divided into two clusters by the K-mean procedure: cluster 1 contains 401 people and cluster 2 contains 73 people. People in cluster 2 seem to be younger, better educated, and earning higher salaries.

Clustering is a useful way of dealing with very large sets of documents. However, there are few *incremental*, or *maintenance*, clustering algorithms in the literature.

---

[1]www.spss.com

Table 2.2 Centroids of two clusters

Cluster	People	Age	Education	Salary (begin)	Salary (now)
1	401	37.55	12.77	5748.27	11290.35
2	73	35.20	17.47	12619.07	27376.99

It is common for the clustering procedure to be repeated entirely in response to the change of the original data set. For a dynamic and evolving data set, reclustering must be done from time to time on the updated data set, in order to keep the clusters up to date. Each time the data are updated, the whole set of clusters must be built all over again.

2.2.2 Incremental Clustering

To maintain clusters generated by graph-theoretical methods such as single-link, group-average, or complete-link clustering algorithms, similarity values are needed. Although the update cost of the single-link method is reasonable, the time and space requirements of the group-average and the complete-link approaches are prohibitive, because the complete knowledge of similarities among old documents is required. Therefore, an efficient maintenance algorithm would be preferable to reclustering the whole data set.

Fazli Can (1993) has developed an incremental clustering algorithm that can continuously update existing clusters. It was tested in an experiment based on the INSPEC database of 12,684 documents and 77 queries. Empirical testing suggests that the incremental clustering algorithm is cost-effective; more importantly, the clusters generated are statistically valid and compatible with those generated by reclustering procedures.

Can's algorithm is called *cover-coefficient-based incremental clustering methodology* (C^2ICM), and is a seed-oriented method. The cover-coefficient (CC) concept provides a measure of similarities among documents. It is first used to determine the number of clusters and cluster seeds. Non-seed documents are subsequently assigned to seeded clusters.

The CC concept is used to derive document similarities based on a multidimensional term space. An $m \times n$ (document by term) matrix D is mapped into an $m \times m$ matrix C (*cover coefficient*). Each c_{ij} ($l < i, j < m$) in the matrix C denotes the probability of selecting any term appearing in document d_i from document d_j. The probability is defined as follows:

$$C_{ij} = \alpha_i x \sum_{k=1}^{n} (d_{ik} \times \beta_k \times d_{jk})$$

where α_i, and β_k are the reciprocals of the ith row sum and kth column sum, respectively. Each document must contain at least one term and each term must appear at least in one document.

This probability indicates the similarity between documents d_i and d_j. The probability is demonstrated as follows. First, randomly choose a term t_k from document d_i. In c_{ij}, the probability of this random selection is denoted by $\alpha_i \times d_{ik}$. The next step is to select the term t_k from document d_j (the ball of that particular color); this probability is represented in c_{ij} by $\beta_k \times d_{jk}$. Finally, the contribution of each bag (terms of d_i) to the selection probability of a ball of that particular color (d_j) must be taken into account by adding these probabilities together for all.

This c_{ij} probability is a measure of similarity. It indicates the extent to which document d_i is "covered" by document d_j. If two documents have no terms in common, then they will not cover each other at all, and the corresponding c_{ij} and c_{ji} will be zero. In addition, Can (1993) introduces $\delta_i = c_{ii}$ as the *de-coupling coefficient* because it is a measure of how different document d_i is from all other documents. The de-coupling coefficient is defined as $\psi_i = 1 - \delta_i$

Based on the coupling and de-coupling coefficients, the number of clusters can be estimated as a function of the matrix D instead of a predefined parameter. This is the key to the incremental clustering method.

Can (1993) generated initial clusters using a method called C^3M (cover-coefficient-based clustering methodology). The incremental clustering algorithm C^2ICM is an extension of the C^3M method; both are seed-oriented clustering algorithms.

In a seed-oriented approach, a cluster seed must be able to attract some non-seed documents around itself, and, at the same time, must be separated from other seeds as much as possible. To satisfy these constraints, Can introduced another concept, the *cluster seed power*, such that documents with the highest seed powers are selected as the cluster seeds. Once seed documents are found, the remaining non-seed documents are allocated to a cluster if its seed can provide the best cover for them, or if it has the greatest seed power.

C^2ICM is a complex incremental clustering algorithm, but it is useful for updating clusters of very large and dynamic data sets. As many computational algorithms and software must be able to scale up to meet continuous challenges from increasingly large data sets, notably the web, methods such as the incremental clustering will be an increasingly useful and generic tool.

2.3 Virtual Structures

The outcome of structural modeling is a virtual structure. It is this virtual structure that information visualization aims to reveal to users in a graphical and visually understandable form. Virtual structures include structures derived from a wide range of data, using computational, statistical, or other modeling mechanisms. The term "virtual" is used here to emphasize that the structure does not exist in the original data in a readily accessible form.

A topical map of a collection of scientific papers published in a conference series is a good example to explain the difference between a virtual structure and an existing structure. The papers are independently written about related topical subjects, but they may or may not relate to each other in more specific aspects. The original data set does not usually have readily accessible information to specify whether or not two papers are related, and if so in what sense. Thus the topical map provides a means of describing the underlying connections within the collection, which is not readily available in any other form.

In order to demonstrate the process of structural modeling, we include some theoretical and practical examples, in areas such as automatic construction of hypertext, manually constructed thesaurus, and the GSA framework.

2.3.1 Automatic Construction of Hypertext

Many systems have been designed on the basis of classic information retrieval models. The most common requirement for generating hypertext automatically is to identify passages in the text that are good candidates for a hypertext link. Automatic construction of hypertext is closely related to the creation of an automatic overview map, an information visualization area in its own right.

Automated link generation presents some of the most challenging tasks for extracting and visualizing abstract information spaces. A variety of techniques have been developed; among them the classic vector space model has a profound impact on the development of visualization systems for information retrieval. In fact, a wide range of information visualization systems use the basic idea of a vector space model in one way or another.

The process of constructing a hypertext consists of two broad phases. In the first, known as information chunking, a document is segmented into nodes to be interconnected in the final hypertext. The second phase is linking: nodes are connected by hypertext links according to a story line, some underlying logic, or other heuristics, into a hypertext. Research in information retrieval has used clustering methods to link documents by their containing cluster.

Most approaches inspired by information retrieval models have paid little attention to the nature of the relationship underlying automatically generated links. Allan (1997), however, particularly focused on how link types can be found automatically, and how these links can be appropriately described. He classified links into three categories – manual, pattern matching, and automatic – based on whether or not their identification can be achieved automatically. For example, pattern-matching links typically rely on existing mark-ups in the text, whereas automatic link types can be derived with or without existing mark-ups. Automatic links are further divided into sub-categories, such as revision, summary and expansion, equivalence, comparison and contrast, tangent, and aggregate links. Equivalence links represent strongly related discussions of the same topic.

2.3.2 The Vector Space Model

Much of the work on automatic hypertext generation in large document collections has been formulated as a special case of the more general information retrieval (IR) problem. The basic premise underlying most current IR systems is that documents that are related in some way will use the same words. If two documents have enough terms in common, then we can assume that they are related, and should therefore have a link placed between them.

The vector space model (VSM) has a great impact, not only on information retrieval, but also on the design of many information visualization systems. The SMART information retrieval system introduces the vector space model, in which both queries and documents are represented as vectors in a high-dimensional space. The dimensionality is determined by the number of unique terms in the given document collection. The magnitude of a vector in a particular dimension represents the importance of the specific term in the corresponding document (Salton et al., 1994).

Since the vector space model maps both queries and documents into vectors, one can compute document–document relevance, as well as query–document relevance. The well-known $tf \times idf$ weighting scheme is typically used to compute the vector coefficients. The weight of term T_k in document D_i is defined by w_{ik} as follows:

$$w_{ik} = \frac{v_{ik}}{\sqrt{\sum_{j=1}^{t} v_{ij}^2}}$$

$$v_{ik} = tf_{ik} \cdot \log\left(\frac{N}{n_k}\right)$$

where N is the number of documents in the collection, tf_{ik} is the number of times term T_k occurs in document D_i, and n_k is the number of documents in which term T_k occurs at least once. The denominator plays a role known as *length normalization*, which reduces the bias in favor of long documents, because they tend to have larger tf values.

The vector space model has several appealing features for information retrieval and information visualization. Both queries and documents are represented as vectors. The focus of traditional information retrieval is on query–document relevance ranking, in order to find the document which best matches a given query. In contrast, information visualization has special interests in inter-document similarities, as measured by the distance between corresponding document vectors.

Many visualization systems are designed to visualize a sub-set of a particular collection of documents, in response to a search query. The original collection is therefore narrowed down by the search query. For example, Allan (1997) describes automated construction of hypertext with such a scenario. A hypertext, based on the results of an initial search query, is automatically generated. Users can find documents related to a chosen document in the vector space by selecting documents immediately surrounding the vector of the document.

Allan presents an example in which the user's goal was to find documents related to an encyclopedia article on "March music". Many of the documents retrieved according to the vector proximity turned out to be relevant to the topic. However, a number of documents retrieved in this way were not relevant, because the meaning of the word "March" is ambiguous: it could refer to a type of music, a month of the year, or other meanings. This is a well-known problem, known in the information retrieval community as the vocabulary mismatch problem, and has drawn much attention from researchers.

The way to distinguish the meanings of words like "March" or "Bank" is to examine the contexts in which they occur. Latent semantic indexing (LSI) demonstrates how this problem can be tackled (Deerwester et al., 1990) (see section 2.3.3). Lexical chaining (see section 2.3.5) represents an alternative approach, in which the accurate information about connections between different words is derived from a thesaurus, and the information used to reduce the ambiguity of words as their contexts is taken into account (Green, 1998).

Allan (1997) describes yet another approach, where the vector space model is applied to finer-grained analysis within documents. In addition to document vectors, paragraphs and sentences in each document are also represented in the vector space model. First, two documents are divided into smaller pieces so that they can be compared at a finer-grained inspection, for example, sentence by sentence, or paragraph by paragraph. Second, sentences are transformed into vectors. These sentence vectors are compared, to determine whether or not the documents share a similar context. In Allan's example, the following criteria are used to select relevant documents:

- there must be at least one pair of sentences in the two documents with a similarity of 70%;
- there must be at least one pair of sentences with at least two terms in common; and
- the most heavily weighted term must contribute more than 95% of the similarity.

There exist other alternatives to take the role of a context into account. Latent semantic indexing (LSI), also known as singular value-decomposition (SVD), is such a candidate.

2.3.3 Latent Semantic Indexing

Latent semantic indexing (LSI) is designed to overcome the so-called vocabulary mismatch problem faced by information retrieval systems (Deerwester et al., 1990; Dumais, 1995). Individual words in natural language provide unreliable evidence about the conceptual topic or meaning of a document. LSI assumes the existence of some underlying semantic structure in the data, which is partially obscured by the randomness of word choice in a retrieval process, and that the latent semantic structure can be more accurately estimated with statistical techniques.

In LSI, a semantic space, based on a large term $\times$ document matrix, is constructed. Each element of the matrix is the number of occurrences of a term in a document. The document plays a contextual role, specifying the meaning of the term. LSI uses a mathematical technique called singular value decomposition (SVD). The original term $\times$ document matrix can be approximated with a truncated SVD matrix. A proper truncation can remove noise data from the original data, as well as improve the recall and precision of information retrieval. The diagram in Figure 2.2 illustrates how a large matrix is truncated into a smaller one.

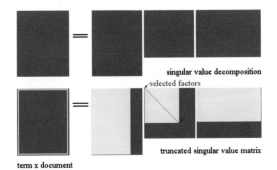

Figure 2.2 Singular value decomposition (SVD) and a truncated SVD matrix.

Perhaps the most compelling claim from the LSI is that it allows an information retrieval system to retrieve documents that share no words with the query (Deerwester et al., 1990; Dumais, 1995). Another potentially appealing feature is that the underlying semantic space can be subject to geometric representations. For example, one can project the semantic space into a Euclidean space for a 2D or 3D visualization. On the other hand, in practice, large complex semantic spaces may not always fit into low-dimension spaces comfortably.

LSI reduces the dimensionality of a data set in a similar way to standard factor analysis. Each data point can be represented by a smaller number of underlying factors identified by LSI. In Figure 2.3, (a) is a 2D scatter plot of the ACM SIGCHI conference data set, containing 169 documents published between 1995 and 1997. This data set appears to be relatively well captured by the first two dimensions. In contrast, Figure 2.3 (b) shows a scatter plot of the CACM collection, containing more than 3200 documents. A large number of documents are plotted close to the original, suggesting that their positions in the semantic space cannot be adequately represented within its sub-spaces.

The two diagrams in Figure 2.4 represent the singular values of the CHI and CACM data sets based on the output of LSI. They were plotted in a similar way to eigenvalue curves in standard factor analysis. The value of each point indicates the uniqueness or significance of a given factor. A higher singular value indicates that the underlying factor explains more variance than a factor with a lower singular value. The first few dimensions typically explain a large amount of variance. Both data sets have a long, flat tail, suggesting that they are high-dimensional spaces in nature.

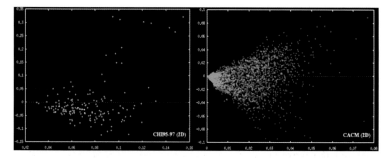

Figure 2.3 Scatter plot of CHI 95–97 (left) and the CACM collection (right).

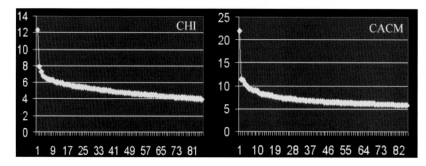

Figure 2.4 The singular value curves of the CHI and CACM data sets.

2.3.4 The Use of WordNet®

WordNet® is an on-line lexical database developed by the Cognitive Science Laboratory at Princeton University,[2] on the basis of contemporary psycholinguistic theories of human lexical memory. It was first created in 1985 as a dictionary based on psycholinguistic theories, and now contains over 50,000 words and 40,000 phrases, collected into more than 70,000 sense meanings.

The basic concepts and construction of WordNet® are explained in the so-called "Five Papers on WordNet", available on the web.[3] A comprehensive bibliography, maintained by Joseph Rosenzweig at the University of Pennsylvania, is also available on the web.[4]

WordNet® divides words up into synonym sets, also known as synsets. Each synonym set includes words that are synonyms of one another. These synsets are then connected by a number of different relations such as "is-a", "has-a", or "includes". A particular word may appear in several synonym sets, depending on how many senses it has. Each sense of a word is identifiable by the word and a sense number.

A number of browsers have been designed to facilitate the access to the WordNet®. WordNet Navigator[5] is a graphical user interface, developed at the Universidad Complutense de Madrid, Spain. It can be used to display how words are related in the WordNet®. While its user interface was mainly written in Java, the communication with the WordNet® is handled in C. These two components are integrated on the web using Common Gateway Interface (CGI).

The information is displayed on the screen in four categories: (1) Navigation Tree, a diagram of relations between words; (2) Node Info, information about a particular word; (3) Control and (4) Navigation Mode, for inputting control parameters and link types for navigation.

The local structure surrounding a given word is displayed in the navigation tree, in which nodes represent words, and edges indicate relations such as "is-a", "has-a", or "include". Each node contains a word and a *sense number*, which identifies its synonym set. The node info displays information about synonyms and definitions. The control specifies the word with which to start. The navigation mode specifies whether the current navigation is based on the structure determined by "is-a" or by "has-a" links.

For example, suppose we are interested in the word "place" and its synonyms. To start the navigation, type the word "place" into the control section. The sense number is optional. If a sense number is given, only one node will appear on the screen; otherwise, the navigation tree will include all the meanings of the word "place". If nothing matches the query word "place", then we may try a different word or sense number. Once the navigation tree returns, it is time to specify the navigation mode: whether the navigation should rely on "is-a" or "has-a" relationships. If the user selects a node in the navigation tree, the selected node, its parent, siblings, and children will be displayed, according to the chosen navigation mode. This graphical browser provides simple but useful access to the internal structure of the WordNet®.

---

[2]http://www.cogsci.princeton.edu/~wn/
[3]ftp://ftp.cogsci.princeton.edu/pub/wordnet/5papers.pdf
[4]http://www.cis.upenn.edu/~josephr/wn-biblio.html
[5]http://bogart.sip.ucm.es/demos/navword/

2.3.5 Lexical Chaining

The classic vector space model and its variants are by far the most popular options in visualizing abstract information spaces for retrieval and exploration. The following example illustrates how the WordNet® can provide semantic knowledge of relationships between words, in the estimation of inter-document similarities.

An interesting alternative, lexical chaining, is described by Green (1998)[6] in an attempt to deal with two major linguistic factors that may undermine the effectiveness of traditional information retrieval models, namely, synonymy and polysemy. Synonymy refers to the use of different words to describe the same concept, for example, "dog" and "puppy". Polysemy, on the other hand, refers to the use of the same word to describe different concepts, for example, "bank". Consequently, term occurrences may underrepresent the connection between synonym words, or overrepresent the connection between documents using the same word in different senses.

A lexical chain is a sequence of semantically related words occurring in a document. For example, if text contains the words "apple" and "fruit", then they should both appear in a chain, since an apple is a kind of fruit. It is believed that the organization of the lexical chains in a document reflects the discourse structure, or the main theme of the document.

Lexical chains in text can be recovered using any lexical resource that relates words to their meanings. For example, *Roget's International Thesaurus* (Chapman, 1992) and the WordNet® database (Beckwith et al., 1991) have been used to provide such semantics. Estimating the similarity between two documents is therefore equivalent to finding the similarity between lexical chains associated with these documents. Lexical chaining appears to be a promising alternative to the existing information visualization paradigms.

2.4 Complex Network Theory

Statistical mechanics of complex networks have recently become the center of attention in several scientific communities, including statistical physics, computer science, and information science (Albert and Barabási, 2002; Barabási et al., 2000; Barabási et al., 2002; Dorogovtsev and Mendes, 2002; Girvan and Newman, 2001). These studies focused on the topological properties of large networks (the Internet, the web, scientific networks) and found some surprising similarities. The latest advances are primarily rooted in two types of networks known as small-world networks (Watts and Strogatz, 1998) and scale-free networks (Barabási et al., 2000). This line of research particularly focuses on mechanisms that can explain, in statistical terms, topological properties demonstrated by a class of networks. Even so, the findings from these studies are not readily adaptable to information technology research and development, and large-scale, detailed experimental studies are necessary to establish links between statistical physics and other fields of study where understanding the dynamics of large-scale network evolution is also of central concern.

---

[6]http://www7.conf.au/programme/fullpapers/1834/com1834.htm

2.4.1 Topological Properties of Networks

Small-world networks are large networks characterized by the existence of short-cut links and tighter clustering of nodes than one would find in a random network. The existence of short chains of acquaintances has been documented by social-network scientists for over four decades (Huberman, 2001). The web is one of the first identified small-world networks (Barabási et al., 2000). Scientific collaboration networks based on co-authorship also demonstrate small-world network properties (Newman, 2001a, b).

The degree of a node is the number of links to the node. Scale-free networks are characterized by an extremely skewed distribution with a long tail (Albert and Barabási, 2002). Mathematically, such distributions can be described by a power law, which means that the probability of finding a node with k links to other nodes is proportional to $k^{-\gamma}$. The size of the exponent γ has been the focus of a large number of studies. For instance, it was found to be 1.5 for networks of words, 2.2 for metabolic networks, 2.5 for protein–protein interactions, 2.5 for collaboration networks, and between 2.5 and 3.0 for citation networks (Dorogovtsev and Mendes, 2002).

The power law distribution implies that the majority of nodes have only one or a few links, while a small but significant amount of nodes have a large number of links (Barabási, 2002). Exceedingly well-connected nodes are also known as hubs. The web is a scale-free, as well as a small-world, network. Scale-free networks have a noticeable resilience to random connection failures without losing their global connectivity (Pastor-Satorras and Vespignani, 2001)

Topological properties of networks may have far-reaching implications – for example, on the understanding of the spread of disease and rumors, or on the most effective way to search through the web (Barabási, 2001). Recently, research has focused on modeling the growth mechanisms of small-world or scale-free networks. The main interest is whether it is possible to duplicate the evolution of a network so that topological properties of a simulated network match to the real one. However, it should be noted that the analysis of structural and dynamic properties of networks in this context usually did not take into account the nature of individual nodes and links.

2.4.2 Preferential Attachment

The simplest network growth model adds one new node at a time and links the new node with a randomly chosen node from the current network. Attachment mechanisms like this have no preference in selecting where the new link should grow. The resultant networks tend to have an exponential degree-distribution. They are called exponentially growing networks (Dorogovtsev and Mendes, 2002).

The growth of scale-free networks has been intensively studied. Most network formation mechanisms in this category are motivated by the rich-get-richer effect, also known as the Matthew Effect and cumulative advantage. Instead of randomly selecting a node and linking it to a new node, a new link is most likely given to a node that already has the most links (Barabási, 2002). This mechanism is called preferential attachment. If the preferential attachment probability p is a linear function of the degree k, this method produces a scale-free network with an exponent γ of 3. Barabási and his colleagues (Barabási et al., 2002) found that preferential attachment mechanisms could produce the topological properties of the co-authorship networks of mathematicians and neuroscientists over an eight-year period (1991–1998). Steyvers and Tenenbaum (2001) experimented with a growth model for three semantic networks – associative networks, the WordNet®, and *Roget's Thesaurus* – by preferentially choosing well-connected concepts and preferentially connecting to nodes with high utility. Their model produced small-world properties and the power-law degree distributions. However, it has been shown that preferential attachment in general does not guarantee a scale-free network (Krapivsky et al., 2000).

Mechanisms for generating scale-free networks without preferential attachment have also been proposed (Caldarelli et al., 2002). It has been shown that, without making rich-get-richer attachments, it is possible to obtain a scale-free network. Rather than relying on the popularity of nodes, the alternative mechanism relies on the fitness of each node and implies that the fitness is a major source of attraction; such nodes are more likely to become hubs. Such mechanisms are called the good-get-richer mechanisms. Similarly, Melian and Bascompte (2002) analyzed the relation between the connectivity of a species and the average connectivity of its nearest neighbors in three of the most resolved community food webs. They found that two highly connected nodes are unlikely to be connected between each other in protein networks, but the reverse happens in food webs.

Decay is an equally important part of network evolution: a network may lose its nodes and links over time as well as gain new ones. Prior to the recent interest in statistical mechanics, van Raan and his colleagues in the scientometrics community (van Raan, 2000) identified that the growth of scientific publications and citations is characterized by growing and aging processes.

2.4.3 Challenges

It should be noted that the lack of detailed, comprehensive empirical investigations of these statistical mechanisms in the context of an underlying phenomenon is a significant gap between the theories in statistical physics and the potential practice of analyzing large-scale network evolution in specific application domains. Few empirical studies have examined changes in the topological properties of a network over time. The lack of good time-resolved data on how networks grow has been the principal reason (Newman, 2001a). Some of the fundamental challenges are as follows.

- Perspectives of statistical mechanics at the global, system level do not necessarily lead to detailed, context-dependent decisions at the local, operational level. Knowing that the topology of a large network has small-world properties is one thing; knowing how to algorithmically find a short-cut path is quite another. Kleinberg's local search algorithm for finding short-cuts in a small-world network is an excellent example of the fundamental connections one needs to build between statistical models and IT-enabled instrumental tools. Related questions include how to actually find hubs if statistical properties suggest their existence.
- Preferential attachment relies on an assumption that the degree function is readily accessible throughout the entire network in question. In reality, this may not be the case. For instance, in citation networks, which we will discuss in subsequent sections, it is unrealistic to assume that scientists have a global knowledge of the popularity of articles within the entire scientific literature. Detailed empirical examinations are necessary to identify the underlying

context-dependent variables so that one can be aware of the validity of such assumptions. For instance, by examining the growth of a citation network, one can reveal the nature of discrepancies between a preferentially growing simulated network and the growth of a real network.

- In order to maximize the potential of information technology, one needs to know not only the overall statistical properties of the topology of a network, but also the meaning and implications of local and moment-by-moment fluctuations associated with individual nodes and links on our understanding of the underlying phenomenon. Information technology – particularly, animated visualizations of time series of the states of a network – can significantly facilitate information processing and analysis at this level.

- Statistical mechanics of large-scale networks provide generic mathematical foundations for network analysis. Adapting and incorporating theories of statistic mechanics has a great potential to strengthen and improve the practice of network analysis outside the statistical physics community. For instance, few traditional network visualization studies have statistical mechanics as an integral part of the network, and even fewer have connected visual–spatial properties of the visualization model to statistical properties that may identify the growth pattern of the underlying network. This is a fundamental but potentially rewarding challenge.

These challenges become apparent if one considers complex network theory in the context of information technology. Some challenges identify the potential contributions from information technology to complex network theory, and others the reverse. In one way or another, most challenges have a root in inter-disciplinary differences in terms of perspectives and the level of granularity.

2.5 Structural Analysis and Modeling

Botafogo et al. (1992) analyze the structure of a hypertext using graph decomposition methods. A graph can be decomposed into sub-graphs, so that each sub-graph is connected. Using similar methods, several different types of nodes, based on their positions in the graph, are identified. For example, two structural metrics – the relative out centrality (ROC) and relative in centrality (RIC) – are introduced to identify various structural characteristics of a node.

The ROC of a node measures whether the node is a good starting point to reach out for other nodes, whereas the RIC of a node indicates how easily the node can be found. Using a high-ROC node as a starting point, the structure of the hypertext can be transformed to one or more hierarchies, and large hierarchies can be displayed with fisheye views, which balance local details and global context (Furnas, 1986). Several examples of how hierarchical structures can be visualized are considered in Chapter 4, including fisheye and hyperbolic views in particular.

2.5.1 Discovering Landmarks in a Web Locality

A web locality often refers to a collection of web documents. Documents on a particular HTTP server, a collection of documents gathered from the web using a "spider", or perhaps even the search results returned by a web search engine, all constitute a web locality. Landmarks in a web locality are simply those nodes important to the locality. However, identifying good landmarks automatically is, in general, a complex and challenging task.

Mukherjea and Hara (1997) adopt three heuristic metrics in order to identify landmark nodes within a web locality, including connectivity, frequency of access, and depth in a hierarchy.

A landmark node should be highly connected to other nodes. If all roads lead to Rome, then Rome must be a landmark place on this planet. First of all, the "out degree" of a node is the number of outgoing links provided by the node, whereas the "in degree" is the number of incoming links received by the node. A node with high out and/or in degrees should be marked as a landmark.

In addition to the first-order connectivity, the second-order connectivity has also been used to identify landmark nodes. This is defined as the number of nodes that can be reached from a particular node by no more than two links. Botafogo et al. (1992) suggest that nodes with high back second-order connectivity also make good landmarks. The back second-order connectivity is defined as the number of nodes that can reach the given node by no more than two links. For example, an index page including many anchors on the web tends to have high connectivity, while the home page of a large corporation is likely to have high back connectivity.

Purely connectivity-based heuristics may miss nodes that are significantly important, but are unlikely to be singled out in terms of connectivity alone. Mukherjea's formula thus takes the frequency of access into account in attempts to identify landmark nodes with reference to the perception of users. The more frequently a node is visited, the more likely that the node should be made a landmark.

The majority of web sites put general information higher up in the hierarchy of the web locality. Detailed information, on the other hand, is likely to be placed lower down in the hierarchy. Mukherjea suggests that the depth of a node indicates its importance. The depth of a document on the web can be detected by decomposing its URL. For example, http://www.acm.org/ is a node with a depth of one, whereas http://www.acm.org/sigchi/chi97/ has a depth of three.

The following formula is adopted from Mukherjea and Hara (1997) for dis covering landmark nodes (with simplified notations and symbols):

$$landmark(\lambda) = \frac{connectivity}{max(connectivity)} \cdot \omega_{connectivity}$$
$$+ \frac{access}{max(access)} \cdot \omega_{access} + \frac{1}{depth} \cdot \omega_{depth}$$

$$connectivity = (in + out) \cdot \omega_{first} + (in\,2 + out\,2) \cdot \omega_{second}$$
$$\omega_{first} + \omega_{second} = 1$$
$$\omega_{connectivity} + \omega_{access} + \omega_{depth} = 1$$

where ω_x is a weight that can be configured by users. To be a landmark, the landmark value must exceed the threshold value λ to ensure that only real landmark nodes are selected. The default threshold value is 0.1. By default, the first-order connectivity (in and out) is weighted slightly more than the second-order connectivity (in 2 and out 2).

A landmark view generated by this formula is shown in Figure 2.5, which visualizes the Georgia Technical College of Computing web server. The aesthetic layout

Figure 2.5 Landmark nodes in a web locality. The taller a node, the greater its importance. Brighter colored nodes are more popular. Reprinted with permission of Sougata Mukherjea.

of the landscape is generated using a force-directed graph layout algorithm (Szirmay-Kalos, 1994). In this map, landmarks are displayed proportional to their importance values. The height of a node represents the importance of the node. Popular nodes are in bright colors, while less popular nodes are displayed in darker colors. The landscape view enables the user to locate important nodes in the web locality quickly, by navigating through the 3D space using mechanisms provided by the VRML browser.

2.5.2 Trajectory Maps

So far we have discussed structural models based on feature vectors of documents, images, or other types of objects. In addition to these vector-based models, a structure may represent the dynamics between documents and generic objects. An important family of such structures is known as procedural models, including user-centered information structures. Here, the interrelationship between two objects is determined on the basis of actions or events that directly involve the two objects.

When a user navigates the web, a link-following event relates the source document with the destination document. Such events collectively indicate the perceived connection between the two documents. In other words, such interrelationships can be derived from behavioral models of browsing patterns. Similarly, as two publications in the literature are repeatedly cited together, the bond between them is reinforced and strengthened dynamically. Sometimes such structures are referred to as mental maps (Lokuge et al., 1996). The following example is based on Lokuge et al. (1996) and Lokuge and Ishizaki (1995), in which mental maps of various facilities in Boston are derived as user-centered information structures.

There are many tourist attractions in Boston. How are these attractions interrelated from the point of view of an individual? Are mental models different from one individual to another? Lokuge et al. (1996) describe a method to structure such information using multidimensional scaling and trajectory mapping techniques.

Fifteen different tourist sites are chosen from a tourist guide to form the mental map. The interrelationships between these sites are high dimensional in nature, because they may be uniquely related in a number of ways according to different features, and they tend to vary from individual to individual.

At least two mental models of these tourist sites can be derived: one based on their geographic locations, and one based on their functions. To generate these mental models using multidimensional scaling, two subjects gave pairwise similarity judgments according to geographic locations and functions. The judgments based on geographic similarity (Figure 2.6) are completely different from judgments based on content (Figure 2.7). The distance-based MDS plot is similar to the

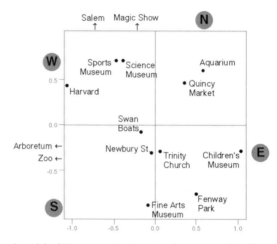

Figure 2.6 The mental model of Boston tourist sites, based on geographical locations (Lokuge et al., 1996). © 1996 ACM, Inc. Reprinted with permission.

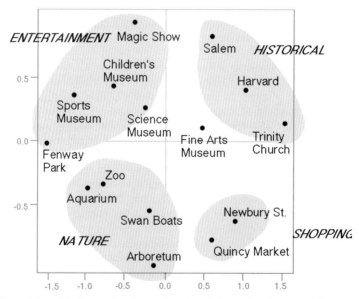

Figure 2.7 The mental model of Boston tourist sites, based on their functions (Lokuge et al., 1996). © 1996 ACM, Inc. Reprinted with permission.

actual map of Boston. In the function-based MDS plot, similar tourist sites, such as the Aquarium and the Zoo appear near each other.

2.5.3 Pathfinder Network Scaling

Pathfinder network scaling is a structural modeling technique originally developed by Schvaneveldt et al. (1989) for the analysis of proximity data in psychology. It simplifies a complex representation of data to a much more concise and meaningful network – only the most important links are preserved, to create a Pathfinder network (PFNET).

If we consider the following three examples, the major problems with an excessive number of links in a graphical representation of a network should become clear. Figure 2.8 shows a network structure visualized by the NavigationView Builder (Mukherjea et al., 1995), one of the most widely cited works in information visualization. It is clear from this example that a large, connected graph would have even more edges crossing each other. One of the common criteria for general undirected graph drawing is to avoid such crossings if possible.

This illustrates the fact that underlying patterns in a complex network can be lost in a large number of links. There are several options to avoid displaying redundant links. For example, multidimensional scaling (MDS) does not usually display any links at all. The relationships between objects are purely represented by their positions in the spatial configuration. In fact, a special class of hypertext, called spatial hypertext, also known as linkless hypertext because of its reliance on spatial proximity (Marshall and Shipman, 1995), is taking a similar approach. Alternatively, redundant links from the original data may be removed in advance, including algorithms such as Pathfinder network scaling and minimal spanning trees. The spanning tree approach is used in LyberWorld (Hemmje et al., 1994) and Hyperbolic 3D (Munzner, 1998b).

Visualizing complex information structures is much more difficult than representing regular hierarchical structures. Zizi and Beaudouin-Lafon designed

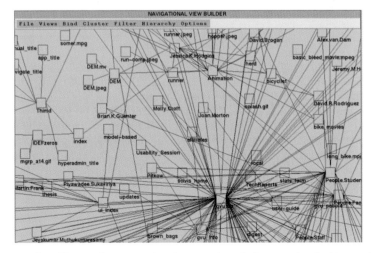

Figure 2.8 A real-world network may contain a large number of edges. Reprinted with permission of Sougata Mukherjea.

SHADOCS, a document retrieval system, to incorporate interactive dynamic maps into the user interface (Zizi and Beaudouin-Lafon, 1994). SHADOCS uses a dynamic clustering technique to divide a large set of document descriptors into smaller clusters. Graphical overview maps are subsequently generated on the screen using a space-filling algorithm. Each region in a map corresponds to a cluster of descriptors, and the size of a region is proportional to the relative importance of those descriptors in the underlying documents. This is very similar to the representation of self-organized maps.

There are two types of approach towards the issue of scalability, focusing on either the size (in terms of the number of nodes), or the density of the network (in terms of the number of links). The scalability issue, in terms of the size of new networks, has been largely resolved (Zizi and Beaudouin-Lafon, 1994) by systems such as SHADOCS, which separate large networks into a number of smaller networks by dynamic clustering algorithms. However, a density-related scalability issue turns out to be more difficult.

The total number of links in a network consisting of n nodes could be as many as n^2. A commonly used strategy is to set a threshold value, and only consider links with values above the threshold. SHADOCS uses a straightforward threshold to control the number of links to be displayed on the screen map. Since the spatial relations have not been taken into account, the linkage in a pruned network may look rather arbitrary, and incompatible with the spatial layout. After all, scalability implies the ability to maintain the original integrity, consistency, and semantics associated with the network representation of an implicit structure. Pathfinder network scaling algorithms provide a useful means of dealing with this challenging problem in a more harmonious way.

Pathfinder network scaling can be seen as a link reduction mechanism that preserves the most salient semantic relations. A key assumption is the triangle inequality condition; only those links that satisfy this condition will appear in the final network. In essence, the rationale is that, if the meaning of a semantic relation can be more accurately or reliably derived from other relations, then this particular relation becomes redundant and can therefore be safely omitted. GSA extends this method to a variety of proximity data estimated by statistical and mathematical models (Chen, 1997a, 1998b). A distinct advantage is that the same spatial metaphor can be consistently used across a range of proximity data, a significant advantage for maintaining the integrity of the semantic structures generated by different theories and techniques.

Pathfinder relies on Pathfinder network scaling, the so-called triangle inequality to eliminate redundant or counter-intuitive links. The principal assumption is that if a link in the network violates this condition, then the link is likely to be redundant or counter-intuitive and should be pruned from the network.

The topology of a PFNET is determined by parameters r and q: the resultant Pathfinder network is denoted as PFNET(r, q). The weight of a path is defined, based on Minkowski metric with the r-parameter. The q-parameter specifies that the triangle inequality must be maintained against all the alternative paths with up to q links connecting nodes n_1 and n_k:

$$w_{n_1 n_k} \leq \left(\sum_{i=1}^{k-1} w_{n_i n_{i+1}}^r \right)^{1/r} \qquad \forall\, k = 2, 3, \ldots, q$$

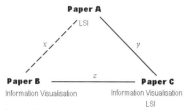

Figure 2.9 Triangle inequality: the path y–z presents more salient information than link x.

For a network with N nodes, the maximum value of the q-parameter is $N - 1$. PFNET ($r = 1, q = N - 1$) consists of the least number of links, where each path is a minimum-cost path. If there is more than one path connecting the same pair of nodes, they must have the same weight. The tightest triangle inequality ($q = N - 1$) is normally imposed, in order to achieve a concise Pathfinder network for visualization purposes, and must be maintained throughout the entire network.

A Pathfinder network can be generated from an existing minimal spanning tree (MST) of the original network by including additional links, provided new links do not violate the triangle inequality. In fact, the minimum-cost Pathfinder network (MCN) is the set union of all the possible MSTs so that the structure of an MCN is unique for each original proximity network. The software allows us to choose an MST instead of a PFNET to represent a large network.

Figure 2.9 illustrates how the triangle inequality filter works and how its outcome should be interpreted. Suppose there are three papers: A, B, and C. Paper A describes LSI. Paper B is about information visualization. Paper C applies LSI to an information visualization design. The relationship between papers A and B is established by the content of Paper C. Therefore the path along links y and z reflects the nature of this relationship more profoundly than link x does. Link x becomes redundant and should be removed.

Graphical representations of Pathfinder networks are generated using force-directed graph drawing algorithms (Fruchterman and Reingold, 1991; Kamada and Kawai, 1989), which are increasingly popular in information visualization because they tend to lay out similar nodes near to one another, and put dissimilar ones farther away. Similar algorithms are used by Bead (Chalmers, 1992) and SPIRE (Hetzler et al., 1998).

The value of Pathfinder network scaling in visualization is its ability to reduce the number of links in a *meaningful* way, which results in a concise representation of clarified proximity patterns, a desirable feature for visualizing a complex structure. Pathfinder networks provide not only a fuller representation of the salient semantic structures than minimal spanning trees, but also a more accurate representation of local structures than multidimensional scaling techniques.

Let us compare two Pathfinder networks, based on the same set of papers from the CHI 96 proceedings, but with different q parameters. The link structure in Figure 2.10, PFNET($r = 2, q = 1$), keeps all the links derived from the proximity data. The meaning of $q = 1$ is that the triangle inequality is not imposed on alternative paths consisting of two or more links. In contrast, the link structure in Figure 2.11, PFNET ($r = 2, q = N - 1$), preserves only paths that have the minimal weights, in order to highlight salient relationships with an improved clarity. Such simplified graphs provide a natural basis for an overview map of the information space.

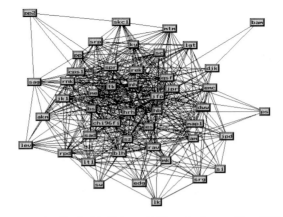

Figure 2.10 CHI 96 papers visualized with all the available paths. Source: Chen (1997a).

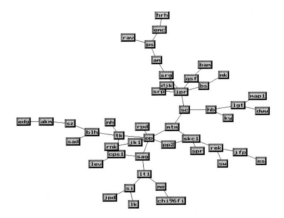

Figure 2.11 CHI 96 papers visualized with PFNET links only. Source: Chen (1997a).

Pathfinder networks have demonstrated various useful features in co-citation studies (Chen, 2003; White, 2003b). However, the Pathfinder network-scaling algorithm has its limitations. In order to achieve a network of high clarity and legibility, it is necessary to impose the so-called triangular inequality throughout the network. While this requirement leads to the simplest representation of the essence of an underlying proximity network, this is at a considerable computational cost. Additionally, as the size of the original network increases, the algorithm requires a considerable amount of memory to run. Therefore, it would be desirable if either an equivalent but more efficient algorithm can be developed, or a hybrid approach can be used to achieve cost-effectiveness. In contrast, MST algorithms such as Kruskal's algorithm and Prim's algorithm can be efficiently implemented, but may not capture local structures as accurately as Pathfinder. Now the question is how these properties influence the visualized network evolution. To our knowledge, this issue has not been specifically addressed.

One of the problems in visualizing complex networks is caused by their structural complexity. A number of algorithms are available to reduce the complexity of a network by reducing the number of links but maintaining the most salient structure untouched; commonly used algorithms include minimum spanning trees (MSTs) and the relatively less known Pathfinder networks (PFNETs). Pathfinder networks are a generalization of MSTs in that an MST is a special subset of a Pathfinder network. The algorithm is originally developed by cognitive scientists to build procedural models based on subjective ratings (Chen, 1998a,b; Chen & Paul, 2001; Schvaneveldt, 1990). The unique advantage of the Pathfinder algorithm is that it can remove a large number of links and retain the most important ones by using a more sophisticated elimination mechanism as compared to, for example, MST. It has increasingly become a strong candidate in a series of KDViz studies (Chen et al., 2001; Chen et al., 2002; Chen and Kuljis, 2003; White, 2003b).

The goal of applying the Pathfinder algorithm is, in essence, to prune a dense network to its backbone structure. The topology of a Pathfinder network is determined by two parameters r and q. The r parameter is used to define a metric space over a given network based on the Minkowski distance so that one can measure the length of a path connecting two nodes in the network. The Minkowski distance becomes the familiar Euclidean distance when $r = 2$. A particularly interesting case is when $r = \infty$, in which the weight of a path is defined as the maximum weight of its component links, which is why it is also called the maximum value distance.

Given a metric space, a triangle inequality can be defined as:

$$w_{ij} \leqslant (\Sigma_k\, w_{n_k n_{k+1}}^r)^{1/r}$$

where w_{ij} is the weight of a direct path between i and j, $w_{n_k n_{k+1}}$ is the weight of a path between n_k and n_{k+1}, for $k = 1, 2, ..., m$. In particular, $i = n_1$ and $j = n_k$. In other words, the alternative path between i and j may go all the way round through nodes $n_1, n_2, ..., n_k$ as long as each intermediate link belongs to the network.

If w_{ij} is greater than the weight of alternative path, then the direct path between i and j violates the inequality condition. Consequently, the link $i - j$ will be removed because it is assumed that such links do not represent the most salient aspects of the association between the nodes i and j.

The q parameter specifies the maximum number of links that alternative paths can have for the triangle inequality test. The value of q can be set to any integer between 2 and $N - 1$, where N is the number of nodes in the network. If an alternative path has a lower cost than the direct path, the direct path will be removed. In this way, Pathfinder reduces the number of links from the original network, while all the nodes remain untouched. The resultant network is also known as a minimum-cost network.

However, this is a computationally expensive algorithm; the published algorithm is in the class of $O(N^4)$ (Figure 2.12). KDViz approaches built on the Pathfinder network scaling algorithm have a potential bottleneck if one needs to deal with larger and larger networks. The strength of Pathfinder network scaling is its ability to derive more accurate local structures than other comparable algorithms such as multidimensional scaling (MDS) and minimum spanning tree (MST). The best results are achieved when $q = N - 1$ and $r = \infty$; not surprisingly, this is also the most expensive because all the possible paths must be examined for each link. In addition, the algorithm requires a large amount of memory to store

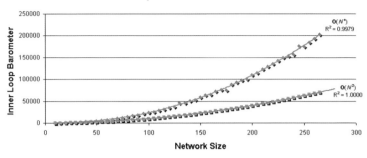

Figure 2.12 Pathfinder's inner loop is in the order of $O(N^4)$.

the intermediate distance matrices. These scalability problems are the major motivations for us to consider a divide-and-conquer strategy.

2.6 Generalized Similarity Analysis

Generalized similarity analysis (GSA) is a unifying framework developed through a series of studies in structuring and visualizing complex information spaces (Chen, 1997a, b, 1998a, b; Chen and Czerwinski, 1997, 1998). GSA aims to provide a consistent framework, with associated modeling and visualization tools, to extract and transform a wide variety of structures inherited in a collection of documents into spatial models. For example, a number of inter-document similarity matrices have been derived: content-based similarity, cross reference-based similarity, and usage pattern-based similarity. A key element is the use of Pathfinder network scaling techniques (Schvaneveldt et al., 1989).

Visualizing a complex graph often needs to address a challenging problem, caused by an excessive number of links. In a spatial layout of a network representation with a large number of links, fundamental patterns may be lost in a cluttered display, and users may experience a cognitive overload.

Pathfinder network scaling simplifies the structure of a network by extracting and displaying only the most salient relationships, and eliminating redundant or counter-intuitive ones from the original network. Pathfinder has some desirable features over techniques, including multidimensional scaling (MDS).

In our earlier work (Chen, 1997a), we used the classic vector space model with $tf \times idf$ weighting (Salton et al., 1994) to compute interdocument similarities. However, the vector space model is subject to an assumption that terms used in document vectors are independent, and it was realized that this assumption may oversimplify the interrelationships between the use of particular terms and their context, consequently leading to counter-intuitive results. Latent semantic indexing (LSI) (Deerwester et al., 1990) was subsequently incorporated into the framework, in order to reveal underlying semantic structures as reflected through a collection of publications in a specific subject domain. (See Sections 2.5.3 and 2.3.3, respectively, for more detailed descriptions of Pathfinder network scaling and LSI.)

The development of GSA was initially based on three distinct interconnectivity models associated with documents on the web: hypertext linkage, term distributions, and navigation patterns. These three examples are included in order to illustrate the extensibility of the framework.

2.6.1 Scalability of Networks

Visualizing complex information structures must address two different types of scalability issue: the size of the network (in terms of the number of nodes), and the density of the network (in terms of the number of links).

SHADOCS is a document retrieval system that incorporates interactive dynamic maps into the user interface (Zizi and Beaudouin-Lafon, 1994). A large set of document descriptors is divided into smaller clusters using a dynamic clustering technique. Graphic overview maps are generated on the screen using a space-filling algorithm; each region in a map corresponds to a cluster of descriptors. The size of a region is proportional to the relative importance of those descriptors in the underlying documents.

On the one hand, a large network can be separated into a number of smaller networks by dynamic clustering algorithms, for example in SHADOCS. On the other hand, a density-related scalability issue remains a relatively challenging one. The maximum number of links in a network consisting of N nodes is N^2. When we deal with a network with a large number of nodes, we must also deal with an even larger number of links.

A commonly used strategy is to set a threshold, and consider only links whose weights are above the threshold. For instance, SHADOCS uses a straightforward threshold to control the number of links to be displayed on the screen map. However, threshold values may not adequately reflect the intrinsic structure of a network. As a result, a pruned network may look rather arbitrary, and incompatible with the layout nodes. Scalability is the ability to maintain the original integrity, consistency, and semantics associated with the network representation of an implicit structure. In the next section, this challenging problem is addressed in a more harmonious way, by a useful approach based on Pathfinder network scaling algorithms.

2.6.2 Hypertext Linkage

The structure of a network can be represented as a matrix. A network of a hypertext with N document nodes can be represented as a distance matrix, an $N \times N$ matrix. Each element d_{ij} in the matrix denotes the distance between node i and j. Botafogo et al. (1992) introduced two structural metrics, the relative out centrality (ROC) and relative in centrality (RIC) metrics, to identify various structural characteristics of a node.

A node with a high ROC would be a good starting point to reach out for other nodes, while a node with a high RIC should be readily accessible. Using a high-ROC node as a starting point, the structure of the hypertext can be transformed into one or more hierarchies. Botafogo et al. suggest that large hierarchies may be displayed with fisheye views, which balance local details and global context (Furnas, 1986). Chapter 4 includes several examples of how hierarchical structures can be visualized, using fisheye and hyperbolic views.

HyPursuit is a hierarchical network search engine based on semantic information embedded in hyperlink structures and document contents (Weiss et al., 1996). HyPursuit considers not only links between two documents, but also how their ancestor and descendant documents are related. For example, if two documents have a common ancestor, they are regarded as more similar to each other. In HyPursuit, document similarity by linkage is defined as a linear combination of three components: direct linkage, ancestor, and descendant inheritance. More recently, the design of a very large web search engine, known as Google, also relies on hypertext links to enhance the precision of search results. The Google search engine is described in Chapter 4.

Pirolli et al. (1996a) at Xerox also use hypertext links to characterize web documents. Documents in a web locality, a closed subset of WWW documents, can be represented by feature vectors based on attributes such as the number of incoming and outgoing hyperlinks of a document, how frequently the document has been visited, and content similarities between the document and its children. These feature vectors can be used to describe the nature of a page and predict the interests of visitors to that page.

In generalized similarity analysis (GSA), document proximity is defined based on similarities between documents. The document similarity by hypertext linkage in GSA is defined as follows:

$$sim_{ij}^{link} = \frac{link_{ij}}{\sum_{k=1}^{N} link_{ik}}$$

where $link_{ij}$ is the number of hyperlinks from document D_i to D_j in a collection of N documents from the WWW, for example, from a particular server or on a specific topic. Higher-order interrelationships with ancestors and descendants are not considered, because they can be resolved by Pathfinder network scaling algorithms. This definition allows asymmetrical as well as symmetrical relationships between documents. The Pathfinder network scaling algorithms can handle both symmetric and asymmetric data. Without losing generality, we assume that these measures are symmetric unless otherwise stated. According to this definition, a similarity of 0 between two documents implies $link_{ij} = 0$, which means that one document is not linked to the other at all. On the other hand, a similarity of 1 implies $link_{ik} = 0$ for all the $k \times j$, which means that the two documents are connected by hyperlinks to each other, but not to any other documents.

Figure 2.13 shows the structure of a WWW site (SITE$_A$) according to hypertext linkage. Pathfinder extracted 189 salient relationships from 1503 initial similarity measures. The spring energy in this PFNET is less than 0.005 (four isolated nodes are not shown).

Structural analysis based on hypertext links can be used to detect general interests from one website to others. Chen et al. (1988a) present a connectivity analysis of the web sites of computer science departments in 13 universities in Scotland. Figure 2.14 shows the number of outgoing hypertext links from each of the 13 departmental websites in Scottish universities.

Table 2.3 shows the top ten American and British commercial websites most frequently cited by the 13 Scottish computer science sites. A commercial site was

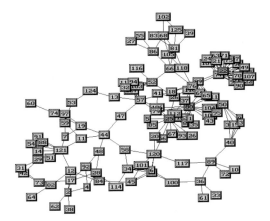

Figure 2.13 The structure of SITE$_A$ with 198 salient hyperlinks, shown as a PFNET($q = N - 1 = 126$, $r = \infty$).

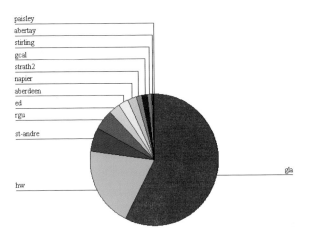

Figure 2.14 Outgoing hyperlinks from each of the 13 Scottish university sites. Source: Chen et al. (1998a).

Table 2.3 Top ten most popular American and British commercial sites cited by Scottish universities (Data: Aug/Sept, 1996)

Rank	US Site	Count	Type	UK Site	Count	Type
1	Java	188	Software	Demon	63	ISP
2	Yahoo	124	Search Engine	Telegraph	27	Media
3	AltaVista	34	Search Engine	Bookshop	35	Publisher
4	Lycos	29	Search Engine	Web13/Future	28/28	ISP/Media
5	Microsoft	30	Software	Cityscape	26	Media
6	AT&T research	51	Research	Nexor	34	ISP
7	Netscape	32	Software	OUP	16	Publisher
8	NBA	36	Sport/Music	Almac	16	ISP
9	Digital research	44	Research	Musicbase	18	Sport/Music
10	Lights	36	Others	Virgin Records	17	Sport/Music

identified by its domain name, i.e. .com for an American site, and .co.uk for a British site. They were ranked by the number of unique Scottish sites that linked to them. For example, 10 out of 13 Scottish sites had links to Java Development Toolkit at *java.sun.com*, at the time of the analysis.

An interesting pattern emerged. Links to American sites were dominated by companies providing leading Internet-related technologies and services, such as Java programming tools, Yahoo and AltaVista. On the other hand, links to British sites were predominated by mass media and entertainment such as the *Daily Telegraph* and Channel 4 (at www.cityscape.co.uk).

The profile of top-ranked popular commercial sites is mapped into a two-dimensional configuration using multidimensional scaling (MDS). Each site is represented as a vector, based on how frequently it was referenced across the 13 Scottish sites. The frequencies are standardized over all the Scottish sites, to minimize the bias towards large sites in Scotland. Figure 2.15 shows the MDS map generated by SPSS, a popular statistical package. It explains 85% of the variance. Annotations in the map are added by hand with lines, to highlight sites that are similar to each other.

Along Dimension 1, research laboratories in large American companies are located on the one hand, namely, AT&T and Digital, while two sites at the other end are particularly devoted to music, e.g., Virgin Music Group (VMG).

In contrast, Dimension 2 may reflect some aspects of particular cultures. For example, National Basketball Association (NBA) (American) is on the top map, whereas the *Daily Telegraph* (British) is at the bottom. The positions of Yahoo and AltaVista suggested some connections to the generic nature of their indexing and search facilities. On the other hand, popular British commercial sites clearly reflected the British culture, for example, *Daily Telegraph*, Channel 4, and Oxford University Press (OUP).

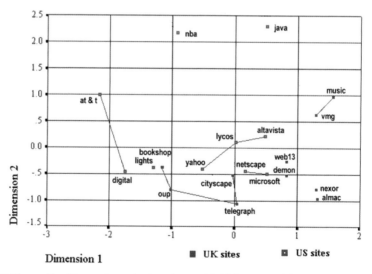

Figure 2.15 The profile of the most popular American and British commercial sites to Scottish universities. Source: Chen et al. (1998a).

2.6.3 Content Similarity

The vector-space model was originally developed for information retrieval (Salton et al., 1994, 1996). It is an influential and powerful framework for analyzing and structuring documents. Each document is represented by a vector of terms, and terms are weighted to indicate how important they are in representing the document. The distance between two documents can be determined according to corresponding vector coefficients.

A large collection of documents can be split into a number of smaller clusters such that documents within a cluster are more similar than documents in different clusters. By creating links between documents that are sufficiently similar, Salton et al. automatically generated semantically-based hypertext networks using the vector-space model (Salton et al., 1994).

In GSA, we have several options to derive interdocument similarities according to term distributions. These may include, among others, the classic vector space model, the latent semantic indexing model, and dice coefficients. The following example is based on the well-known $tf \times idf$ model, term frequency $\times$ inverse document frequency, to build term vectors. Each document is represented by a vector of T terms with corresponding term weights. The weight of term T_k to document D_i, is determined by:

$$w_{ik} = \frac{tf_{ik} \times \log\left(\dfrac{N}{n_k}\right)}{\sqrt{\displaystyle\sum_{j=1}^{T} \left(tf_{ij}\right)^2 \times \log\left(\dfrac{N}{n_j}\right)^2}}$$

where tf_{ik} is the occurrences of term T_k in D_i, N is the number of documents in the collection (such as the size of a WWW site), and n_k represents the number of documents containing term T_k. The document similarity is computed as follows, based on corresponding vectors: $D_i = (w_{i1}, w_{i2}, ..., w_{iT})$ and $D_j = (w_{j1}, w_{j2}, ..., w_{jT})$:

$$sim_{ij}^{content} = \sum_{k=1}^{T} w_{ik} \times w_{jk}$$

Figure 2.16 shows a PFNET for another departmental WWW site, SITE$_B$, with 172 HTML documents. The network has 172 nodes and 242 links. The screen display becomes crowded even if numerical IDs are used in the graphical representation. This is an example of the famous "focus *versus* context" problem: users need to access local details, while maintaining a meaningful context. In order to resolve this problem, virtual reality modeling language (VRML) comes into play. VRML provides not only new ways of interacting with graphic representations in a two- or three-dimensional space, but also a new metaphor of interaction, ranging from individual use to collaborative work.

A graph representation takes shape as the overall spring energy reduces below a threshold given in advance. Figure 2.17 shows the node placement process for CHI

96 papers at six discrete points. The value of spring energy at each point is given at the right-hand corner. For example, at an early stage, the energy of the spring system is 0.999, the energy is systematically reduced to 0.900, 0.500, 0.200, 0.100, and eventually the process is terminated at the threshold, 0.005.

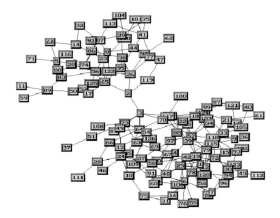

Figure 2.16 The structure of SITE$_B$ by content similarity, preserving 242 links (PFNET, $q = N - 1 = 171$, $r = \infty$). Source: Chen (1997a).

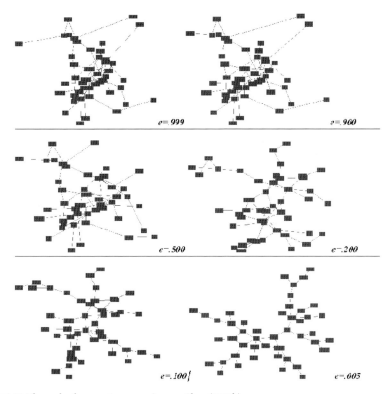

Figure 2.17 The node placement process. Source: Chen (1998b).

2.6.4 State-transition Patterns

There is a growing interest in incorporating usage patterns into the design of large, distributed hypermedia systems, notably on the WWW. Access logs maintained by many WWW servers provide a valuable source of empirical information on how users actually access the information on a server, and which documents appear to attract the attention of users. Sequential patterns of browsing indicate, to some extent, document relatedness perceived by users. For example, Pirolli et al. (1996) use the number of users who followed a hyperlink connecting two documents in the past to estimate the degree of relatedness between the two documents.

The dynamics of a browsing process can be captured by state-transition probabilities. Transition probabilities can be used to indicate document similarity with respect to browsing, to some advantage. For example, the construction of the state-transition model is consistent with linkage- and content-based similarity models. In our example, one-step transition probability p_{ij} from document D_i to D_j is estimated as follows:

$$p_{ij} = \frac{f(D_i, D_j)}{\sum\limits_{k=1}^{N} f(D_i, D_k)}$$

where $f(D_i, D_j)$ is the observed occurrences of a transition from D_i to D_j, and $f_k(D_i, D_k)$ is the total number of transitions starting from D_i. Transition probability p_{ij} is used to derive the similarity between document D_i and D_j in the view of users:

$$sim_{ij}^{usage} = p_{ij}$$

The following example is based on state-transition patterns derived from server access logs maintained at $SITE_A$.

Figure 2.18 shows three Pathfinder networks, corresponding to three bi-monthly access log data between September 1996 and January 1997, associated with external users' access to the author's homepage. A number of predominant cycles emerged

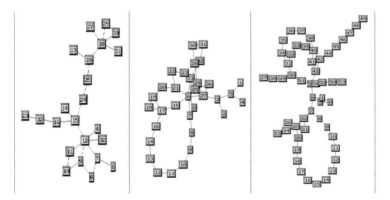

Figure 2.18 The structure of $SITE_A$, containing personal web pages, by usage patterns. Source: Chen (1997a).

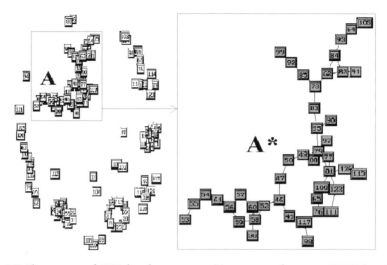

Figure 2.19 The structure of SITE$_A$ based on state-transition patterns, shown as a PFNET ($q = N - 1$, $r = \infty$). Source: Chen (1997a).

from the graph. In fact, there seemed to be some correspondence between a cycle and a set of documents of a particular type. For example, the largest cycle corresponds to top-level documents regarding general information about the homepage (Node 7), the page counters and plans. The cycle (17-19-20-21-6-15) corresponds to some research papers. The cycle (21-22-23-33-6) corresponds to documents used in teaching. It also seemed that larger cycles corresponded to deeper browsing sequences, whereas smaller cycles tended to relate to more specific topics and shorter browsing sequences. Node 0 is an artificial node, to indicate the end of a browsing sequence.

A total of 22,209 access requests were made between July 30 and September 31, 1996, from 1125 sources. The behavior of the top 30 most active users is used to establish representative behavioral patterns in terms of first-order state transitions. These 30 users account for 10.7% of all the users who visited the site during this period. The number of pages visited by each of these users varied from 13 pages to 115 pages. Figure 2.19 shows a PFNET derived from similarities based on first-order state-transition probabilities. Cluster A is enlarged to Cluster A*.

The spike at the lower left half and the ring in Cluster A* essentially associate with master's student's project on web-based interface design. The spike at the upper right half corresponds to some research papers on hypertext.

It is possible to integrate several virtual structures derived from the same data using different structural modeling mechanisms. In the following generic formula, an existing hyperlink structure is adjusted, by incorporating the underlying semantic structure derived from content similarities:

$$sim_{ij}^{combined}(\omega_{ij}) = \frac{\omega_{ij} \cdot hyperlinks_{ij}}{\sum_{k=1}^{N} \omega_{ik} \cdot hyperlinks_{ik}}$$

$$sim_{ij}^{link+content} = sim_{ij}^{combined}\left(\omega_{ij} = sim_{ij}^{content}\right)$$

Table 2.4 Pearson's and cosine correlation coefficients among similarities based on linkage, content and usage patterns associated with the $SITE_A$

$SITE_A$ ($N = 127$)	Linkage	Content	Usage
Mean	0.0735	0.1671	0.0020
Std Dev	0.1413	0.3121	0.0357

$SITE_A$ ($N = 127$)	Pearson	Sig.	Cosine
Linkage–Content	0.3201	0.000	0.4682
Linkage–Usage	0.0184	0.017	0.0423
Content–Usage	0.0429	0.000	0.0644

where the resultant similarity, $sim_{ij}^{link+content}$, represents a virtual structure, based on both hypertext linkage and term distributions.

2.6.5 Meta-similarities

A meta-similarity is an overall estimate of the strength that two similarity variables are related. To illustrate this concept, we computed Pearson's and cosine correlation coefficients among three sets of similarities associated with the website $SITE_A$, according to hyperlinks, content terms, and usage patterns. A total of 127 valid documents from the $SITE_A$ were included in our study. The linkage-content meta-similarity has the highest score on both Pearson's and cosine correlation coefficients ($r = 0.3201$ and $r_c = 0.4682$, $N = 127$) (Table 2.4). The linkage-usage meta-similarity has the lowest score on both Pearson's and cosine correlation coefficients ($r = 0.0184$ and $r_c = 0.0644$, $N = 127$).

We analyzed the changes in usage patterns associated with a collection of documents maintained by the author on the WWW over six consecutive months between August 1996 and January 1997. By comparing usage pattern-based similarity measures between adjacent months, it was found that the meta-similarity increased from 0.1967 to 0.4586 over the six months. It appears to be a trend that the meta-similarity is increasing with time. A possible explanation is that usage patterns become increasingly similar as the underlying structure settles down, at least for frequently visited documents. Experimental studies, and a thorough examination of specific documents and associated usage patterns, may lead to further insights into the pattern.

2.6.6 Structuring Heterogeneous Information

This example briefly illustrates the design of a novel user interface for exploiting documents accumulated in an information filtering and sharing environment. In addition to visualizing interdocument relationships, the visual user interface reveals the interconnectivity between user profiles and documents. The role of user profiles, based on the notion of reference points, is explored.

The exponential growth of widely accessible information in modern society highlights the need for efficient information filtering and sharing. Information filtering techniques are usually based on the notion of user profiles, in order to estimate the relevance of information to a particular person.

Jasper is an information filtering and sharing system (Davies et al., 1995), maintaining a growing collection of annotated reference links to documents on the WWW. Currently, the interconnectivity among these accumulated documents and user profiles is not readily available in Jasper. In this chapter, we describe the design of a novel visual user interface in order to uncover the interconnectivity.

The concept of reference points was originated in psychological studies of similarity data and spatial density (Kruskal, 1977). The underlying principle is that geometric properties such as symmetry, perpendicularity, and parallelism are particularly useful in communicating graphical patterns. For example, people often focus on structural patterns such as stars, rings and spikes, in a network representation. Reference points, conceptually or visually, play the role of a reference framework in which other points can be placed.

In this example, it is hypothesized that a number of star-shaped, profile-centered document clusters would emerge if the role of reference points was activated by user profiles. Users would be able to share information more effectively, based on the additional information provided by user profiles through the visual user interface.

Based on a random sample of 127 documents and 11 user profiles from Jasper, the heterogeneous information structure is visualized within the generalized similarity analysis (GSA) framework. First, we extract and preserve only the most salient semantic relationships, in order to reduce the complexity of the visualization network. Second, we incorporate user profile-based reference points in order to improve the clarity of the visual user interface.

Unique behavioral heuristics are applied to distinguish user profiles and documents, in order to speed up the convergence of our self-organized clustering process. These emergent structures are derived without any prior knowledge of structural relationships. Additional structural cues are likely to result in more efficient results.

The impact of user profile-based reference points can be seen in Figure 2.20. The left sub-figure shows the self-organized spatial layout without using the mechanism of reference points. The sub-figure in the middle shows the layout if the mechanism of reference points was utilized.

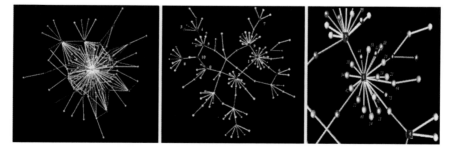

Figure 2.20 The role of reference points: disabled (left), enabled (middle), and a close-up look at a cluster (right) (cube = profile; sphere = document).

In fact, the 11 user profiles, which make up merely 8% of the 138 nodes, were associated with 69% of the links in the network, whereas the remaining 127 documents, which make up 92% of the nodes, only shared 31% of the links. Reference points have clearly improved the clarity of the overall structure. Users may now track relevant documents based on their knowledge of their colleagues' expertise.

The quality of information visualization can be improved by incorporating user profile-based reference points, which is potentially useful for visual user interface design. The focus of empirical analyses on this type of visual user interface is usually the human factors. There are many usability evaluation methodologies available to assess whether a particular design feature, or the entire ecological system, is appropriate for users.

2.7 Summary

In this chapter, we have introduced several major aspects of information visualization: structural modeling, in particular, the use of the vector space model and its variants, multidimensional scaling and trajectory mapping.

There was also an introduction to the generalized similarity analysis (GSA) framework, giving several examples to illustrate its extensibility and flexibility. More examples are cited in subsequent chapters.

The next chapter focuses on graphic representation, another fundamental aspect of information visualization, introducing some of the most popular and advanced spatial layout algorithms.

Chapter 3
Graph Drawing Algorithms

Beauty in things exists in the mind which contemplates them.
David Hume

This chapter focuses on the second aspect of information visualization – graphic representation, or more generally, visual representation. Spatial layout and graph drawing algorithms play a fundamental role in information visualization. A good layout effectively conveys the key features of a complex structure or system to a wide range of users and audience, whereas a poor layout may obscure the nature of an underlying structure.

Graph drawing techniques have been used in information visualization, as well as in VLSI design and software visualization. Most graph drawing algorithms agree on some common criteria for what makes a drawing good, and what should be avoided, and these criteria strongly shape the final appearance of visualization.

Clustering algorithms often go hand in hand with graph drawing algorithms, and also provide an important means of dealing with increasingly large data sets. For example, several popular graph drawing algorithms have been developed to deal with relatively small data sets, from dozens of nodes to several hundreds. An ultimate test for such algorithms is to scale up, in order to deal with several hundreds of thousands of nodes, notably for visualization applications on the web. In this chapter, the terms *graph drawing* and *network visualization* are equivalent.

3.1 An Overview

Figure 3.1 is generated by CiteSpace, a system we explain in more detail in Chapter 8. CiteSpace visualizes the most salient co-citation network of articles published in a subject domain. In this figure, it is the graph drawing domain. It patches individual snapshots of co-citation networks taken from different time slices into a panoramic view. The important visual and structural attributes include hubs and pivot points. A hub is simply a node with the highest node degrees. A pivot point is a joint between individual snapshots. Since links in each snapshot network have the same color, a pivot point is the only gateway between two snapshot networks. Pivot points in the graph drawing map include the widely cited force-directed placement paper by Fruchterman and Reingold (1991), which joins a pink branch (1993–1995) and a light red branch (1999–2001), and the article by Tamassia et al. (1988), entitled *Automatic graph drawing and readability of diagrams*. Two articles are both hubs and pivot points: *Methods for visual understanding of hierarchical system structures* by Sugiyama et al. (1981) and *Algorithms for drawing graphs: An annotated bibliography* by Di Battista et al. (1994). The 1999 book by Di Battista et al. is a hub but not a pivot. The latest connection added to the map is the 1993 article by Gansner et al. (1993) on AT&T's graph drawing software *dot*. Like

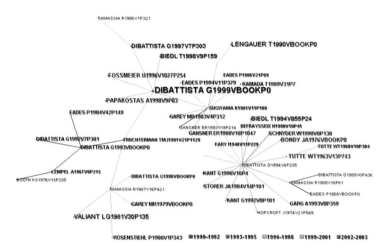

Figure 3.1 A co-citation map of graph drawing articles (1990–2003). See section 8.5.2 for technical details of the mapping.

a roadmap, we can use such maps to find not only articles that we are familiar with, but also apparently highly cited articles that we are not aware of.

The most traditional way of visualizing a network is to use node-and-link graphical representations. Graph drawing is an established field that is concerned with how to draw a network algorithmically in compliance with a set of aesthetic criteria. In the field of graph drawing, much of the attention has been given to the efficiency of algorithms and the clarity of end results.

Network visualization is a major line of research in information visualization, which is concerned with representing the meaning of abstract information intuitively. Just as the Hubble Space Telescope helps astrophysicists to study galaxies in deep space, network visualization techniques enable analysts to explore the topology of a network. Network visualization is necessary for examining the dynamic process of network evolution chronologically and for examining the behavior of individual nodes and links in context. Researchers have developed numerous network visualization systems (Di Battista et al., 1999), including maps of the Internet connectivity, large networks of telephone calls, the structure of science shown as citation networks, and the progressive visualization of how a knowledge domain evolves. On the other hand, the scalability of the current generation of network visualization algorithms remains one of the toughest challenges. There is still a huge gap, conceptually as well as algorithmically, between structural and dynamic patterns that one would like to access at various levels of granularity. Advances in statistical mechanics of large-scale network evolution have the potential for widening the scope of available methods and techniques with a much increased scalability.

3.1.1 Challenges

Algorithmically visualizing large-scale networks poses a number of theoretical and technical difficulties. Until very recently, network visualization had not paid much attention to statistical properties in helping users understand real-world networks and designing more effective visualization techniques. Network analysis traditionally focuses on strong ties rather than weak ties in networks. Link reduction algorithms typically remove weak links and preserve strong ones. The practical significance of weak ties in social networks was established by sociologist Granovetter (1973). Burt (1992) further indicated that the role played by weak ties depends on the existence of a structural hole in one's social network – when a person's social network has strong between-cluster ties but weak within-cluster ties. Sparrow (1991) identifies three additional problems of criminal network analysis: (1) hidden nodes and links, (2) blurred boundaries between a network and its environment, and (3) structural changes and changes in nodes and links. Krebs (2002) studied a social network of the 19 hijackers involved in the World Trade Center attack of September 11, 2001, based on school chums, shared accommodations, and kinship ties, and found that the essential links were rooted in ties of deep trust, which are hard to detect from the outside. In contrast to the rapidly increasing number of strong-tie studies of statistical mechanics, few studies have focused on the role of weak ties (White and Houseman, 2002). Citation network analysis has not paid enough attention to weak ties either.

- The scalability of layout algorithms for visualizing large-scale networks is both a technical and a methodological issue. Algorithms tend to break down if applied to large-scale complex networks.
- Current layout algorithms are inefficient in incrementally updating the layout when nodes and links are added or removed.
- Clustering algorithms do not scale well across networks of varying density.
- Graph-theoretical network decomposition methods are unable to distinguish links of different strengths.
- Networks with heterogeneous link types or node types cannot be efficiently handled. A smooth transformation between topologies on different types is a challenge perceptually, cognitively, and algorithmically.
- The majority of network analysis algorithms exclusively focus on strong ties, or heavyweight links. Social network studies have proven the special role of weak ties and structural holes. It is important for IT research to clearly identify the implications of weak ties and structural holes on large-scale network visualization.
- The nature and practical implications of information lost in link-reduction and network scaling processes are not well understood. Statistical properties of a network before and after being processed by routinely used network transformation algorithms can provide valuable and far-reaching insights. If a particular algorithm does not preserve probabilistic distributions, what are the implications on interpretation and evaluation?

3.1.2 Scalability

The most widely known graph drawing techniques include force-directed graph drawing algorithms and spring-embedder algorithms (Eades, 1984). The primary goal of these types of techniques is to optimize the arrangement of nodes of a network algorithmically, such that in the ultimate geometric model, strongly connected nodes appear close to each other, and weakly connected nodes appear far apart. This optimization is known as the layout process, which is a key topic in the graph drawing community. The strength of the connection between a pair of nodes is typically measured by conceptual similarity, computational relatedness, or conditional probabilities. Examples in this category include Galaxies and SPIRE developed at Pacific Northwest National Laboratories (Wise et al., 1995). Several public-domain software packages, such as Pajek (Batagelj and Mrvar, 1998), provide implementations of force-directed graph drawing and spring-embedder algorithms. The strengths of force-directed algorithms include the aesthetic appearance of layout and intuitive good fits between visualization models and underlying network data. The scalability issue is one of the serious drawbacks of these algorithms. Most of these algorithms do not scale well as the size and density of a network increases. Visualizing the evolution of large-scale networks over time poses additional scalability challenges.

To reduce the complexity of a network visualization task, it is common to prune the original network by link reduction algorithms, or to divide a large network into its smaller components. There are several ways to reduce the number of links in a network: using minimum spanning trees to proximate the original network (MSTs) (Munzner, 1997; Robertson, Mackinlay, and Card, 1991), removing links if their weights are below a threshold (Zizi and Beaudouin-Lafon, 1994), or applying network scaling algorithms such as Pathfinder network scaling (Schvaneveldt, 1990). Using MSTs can considerably reduce the complexity of network visualization, especially for large-scale networks. Studies using Pathfinder network scaling in the visualization of citation networks will be discussed in more detail later. In general, there is a limit for what link reduction can accomplish in resolving the scalability issue. In the divide-and-conquer category, clustering and classification algorithms are the major approaches. Although clustering algorithms can often identify component sub-graphs in a network, there is little that clustering algorithms can do if the network contains giant components and the giant components themselves must be divided. Traditional graph-theoretical algorithms based on connectivity also belong to this category.

In addition to the most widely used node-and-link representations, there are other types of visualization models, for instance, space-filling algorithms such as Tree Maps (Johnson and Shneiderman, 1991), self-organized Kohonen maps (Lin et al., 1991), Botanic Trees, and information landscapes (Chalmers, 1992). The advantages of these alternatives remain to be empirically examined.

Visualizing large-scale networks also faces another challenge: limited screen real estate. Sometimes there are simply not enough pixels on the computer display to accommodate a large-scale complex network, even if we really want to depict one node as one pixel. This challenge is related in part to the divide-and-conquer strategy but also to the focus + context problem, a long-standing challenge in the information visualization community. Solutions proposed so far include distortion-based displays, notably fisheye views (Furnas, 1986), multi-scale, or zoomable, interfaces (Furnas and Bederson, 1995). Techniques of this type are particularly useful for examining local details in a meaningful context.

Few studies have specifically addressed the challenge of large-scale network visualization. NicheWorks (Wills, 1999) is a notable exception. NicheWorks was designed to visualize networks of tens or hundreds of thousands of nodes. It was tested for analyzing websites and detecting international telephone fraud. The strategy taken by NicheWorks is to relax optimization criteria often applied to layout algorithms for smaller networks with the number of nodes ranging from

100 to 1000. Other examples include Cichild (Brown et al., 2000), Caida (CAIDA, 1998), Network Simulator (NS[1]) and Network Animator (Nam[2]), and MAGE.[3] Although a number of statistical mechanics studies used Pajek (Batagelj and Mrvar, 1998) to illustrate network topologies, the scale-up challenge is evident, which echoes our earlier discussion on force-directed approaches.

3.1.3 Visualizing Evolving Networks

Few examples of visualizing the evolution of networks over time are available in the literature. In one, Branigan and Cheswick (1999) used the Internet Mapping techniques to show how the accessibility of the Yugoslavian network was affected by the war. They used a sequence of daily maps of the Yugoslavian network to identify the disappearing and reappearing components of that part of the Internet.

Research in information visualization has addressed issues of evolving information structure, including Disk Trees and Time Tubes (Chi et al., 1998), which display the changes of a website over time. However, empirical studies suggested that a casual user may not easily find useful patterns (Robertson et al., 2002). Kleiberg et al. (2001) visualized large hierarchical data structures as botanical trees, using strands to mimic the internal vascular structure of a botanical tree. Chen and Carr (1999b) visualized the evolution of the field of hypertext using author co-citation networks over a period of nine years. More recently, we developed animated visualization techniques to track competing paradigms in scientific disciplines over much longer periods, ranging from 18 years to more than 50 years (Chen et al., 2002). However, studies in this category have not taken statistical mechanics into account. Although the detection of communities and the movement of dynamic processes over a network's topology have been studied, the methodologies used have little connection to the concepts of small-world networks and scale-free networks.

Visualizing a variety of dynamic processes on a complex network is technically challenging as well as conceptually complex. Pickover (1988) noted that there has been little research in the rich fractal patterns produced by complicated networks as a result of the propagation of signals through such networks. Nodes in such networks denote signal-processing variables. Convergence maps distinguish regions of stable behavior from divergent, exploding behavior.

The significance of understanding the evolution of a complex network is widely recognized. For example, recent research in complex network theory has focused on statistical mechanisms that govern the growth of small-world networks (Watts and Strogatz, 1998) and scale-free networks (Barabási et al., 2000). Scale-free networks are characterized by a power law degree distribution. A major concern is how to simulate the evolution of a network that demonstrates such special topological properties so that one can improve the understanding of real-world networks. Few empirical studies have examined changes in the topological properties of a network over time.

Visualizing fundamental changes in scientific networks is one of the toughest challenges for research in information technology. The shortage of comprehensive

---

[1]http://www-mash.cs.berkeley.edu/ns/
[2]http://www.isi.edu/nsnam/nam/index.html
[3]http://kinemage.biochem.duke.edu

examinations of the evolution of citation networks is due to various reasons, including the lack of an overarching framework that accommodates underlying theories and system functionalities across relevant disciplines, the lack of integrated network analysis and visualization tools, the lack of widely accessible longitudinal citation network data, and the lack of tools that specifically facilitate the analysis of network evolution.

A common problem with visualizing a complex network is that a large number of links may prevent users from recognizing salient structural patterns. A practical strategy is to reduce the number of links shown. There are several link reduction algorithms. The question is which one preserves the underlying topological properties best. Furthermore, as far as an evolving network is concerned, the resultant network should also preserve dynamical properties that characterize the evolution.

In the following example, we compare the role of two link reduction algorithms in visualizing the evolution of networks. A minimum spanning tree (MST) is widely known and commonly used in information visualization. On the other hand, Pathfinder network scaling is a procedural modeling algorithm originally developed by cognitive psychologists to capture salient relationships between concepts (Schvaneveldt, 1990). The strengths of such relationships are typically measured by human experts' subjective ratings of how similar those concepts are. Prior studies exclusively used Pathfinder networks to represent interrelations between concepts or keywords. Our earlier work has extended the use of Pathfinder networks to a much richer range of applications, especially co-citation networks (Chen, 1998a,b; Chen and Paul, 2001). In fact, an MST is a special case of a Pathfinder network because a Pathfinder network is the set union of all the possible MSTs derived from a network (Schvaneveldt, 1990).

There are a number of issues concerning visualizing the evolution of a network with special reference to the use of MST and PFNET. (1) What should be a preferable topological structure of a visualized network? (2) What are the additional criteria for visualizing the evolution of a network? (3) To what extent can MST and PFNET be expected to meet such criteria? (4) What are the implications of our finding on visualizing the evolution of a network in general?

3.2 Drawing General Undirected Graphs

General undirected graphs are one of the most useful data structures. We can all think of many examples of using graphs. However, the large variety of graphs and the general problems of information visualization have caused researchers to focus on various special cases or special appearances of the layout, such as trees and directed acyclic graphs (Davidson and Harel, 1996). A comprehensive discussion and annotated bibliography of a wide range of graph drawing algorithms can be found in the literature (Di Battista, 1998; Di Battista et al., 1994).

Drawing general undirected graphs presents a challenging area to a variety of graph drawing algorithms. They need to meet one or both of the two important requirements: (1) to draw a graph well, and (2) to draw it quickly. To meet the first requirement, algorithms may follow several commonly used heuristics. To meet the second, algorithms may need to scale up to be able to handle a large graph.

Drawing undirected graphs can be traced back to a VLSI design technique called *force-directed placement*, whose aim is to optimize the layout of a circuit with the least number of line crossings. Eades (1984) introduced the spring-embedder model, in which vertices in a graph are replaced by steel rings, and each edge is replaced by a spring. The spring system starts with a random initial state, and the vertices move accordingly under the spring forces. An optimal layout is achieved as the energy of the system is reduced to a minimal.

This intuitive idea has inspired many subsequent works in drawing undirected graphs, notably Kamada and Kawai (1989), Fruchterman and Reingold (1991), and Davidson and Harel (1996). Here their works are summarized and compared, to illustrate the influence of the spring-embedder model in graph drawing and information visualization. The insights inspired by these works are invaluable for information visualization in general.

3.2.1 Aesthetic Criteria

Different graph drawing algorithms may have their own aesthetic criteria to follow. Important aesthetics for general graph drawing are given by Di Battista et al. (1994). Coleman (1996) also gives a list of properties towards which good graph layout algorithms should strive, covering notions of clarity, generality and ability to produce satisfying layouts for a fairly general class of graphs. Speed is also a criterion. Table 3.1 shows various criteria for drawing undirected, straight-line edge graphs. Most emphasize evenly distributed vertices and uniform edge lengths. Some algorithms make explicit efforts to minimize edge crossings, while others do not.

Some of these criteria can be mutually exclusive. For example, a symmetrical graph may require a certain number of edge crossings, even if they may be avoided. And uniform edge lengths may not always produce the most appropriate results. A pragmatic approach is to allow sufficient flexibility to allow algorithms to be tailored to particular applications.

3.2.2 The Spring Model

The spring-embedder model was originally proposed by Eades (1984), and is now one of the most popular algorithms for drawing undirected graphs with straight-line edges, widely favored in information visualization systems for its simplicity and intuitive appeal.

Table 3.1 Criteria for graph drawing algorithms

Criteria	Di Battista et al. (1994)	Eades (1984)	Kamada and Kawai (1989)	Fruchterman and Reingold (1991)	Davidson and Harel (1996)	NicheWorks (1997)
Symmetric	✓	✓	✓			
Evenly distributed nodes	✓		✓	✓	✓	Clustered
Uniform edge lengths	✓	✓	✓	✓	✓	Weights
Minimized edge crossings	✓		✓	✓	✓	

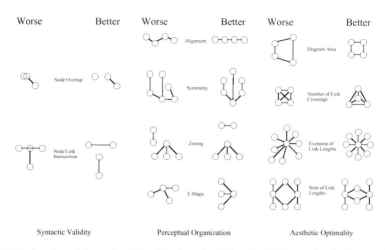

Figure 3.2 Preferred graph layout heuristics (Kosak et al., 1994). © 1994 IEEE. Reprinted with permission.

Eades' algorithm follows two aesthetic criteria: uniform edge lengths and symmetry as far as possible. In the spring-embedder model, vertices of a graph are denoted by a set of rings, and each pair of rings is connected by a spring. The spring is associated with two types of forces: *attraction* forces and *repulsive* forces, according to the distance and the properties of the connecting space.

The drawing of a graph approaches optimal as the energy of the spring system is reduced. An attraction force (f_a) is applied to nodes connected by a spring, while a repulsive force (f_r) is applied to disconnected nodes. These forces are defined as follows:

$$f_a(d) = k_a \log(d)$$
$$f_r(d) = k_r / d^2$$

The k_a and k_r are constants and d is the current distance between nodes. For connected nodes, this distance d is the length of the spring. The initial layout of the graph is configured randomly. Within each iteration the forces are calculated for each node, and nodes are moved accordingly, in order to reduce the tension. According to Eades (1984), the spring-embedder model ran very fast on a VAX 11/780 on graphs with up to 30 nodes. However, the spring-embedder model may break down on very large graphs.

3.2.3 Local Minimum

The spring-embedder model has inspired a number of modified and extended algorithms for drawing undirected graphs. For example, repulsive forces are usually computed between all the pairs of vertices, but attractive forces can be calculated only between neighboring vertices. The simplified model reduces the time complexity: calculating the attractive forces between neighbors is $\Theta(|E|)$, although the repulsive force calculation is until $\Theta(|V|^2)$, which is a great bottleneck of *n*-body algorithms in general. Kamada and Kawai (1989) introduced an algorithm based

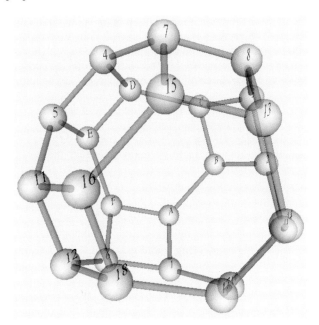

Figure 3.3 A graph drawn by vrmlgraph, a 3D VRML graph drawing package in Java. The source code and JAR are available: http://sourceforge.net/projects/vrmlgraph.

on Eades' spring-embedder model, which attempts to achieve the following two criteria, or heuristics, of graph drawing:

- The number of edge crossings should be minimal.
- The vertices and edges are distributed uniformly.

The key is to find local minimum energy according to the gradient vector $\sigma = 0$, which is a necessary, but not a sufficient, condition for a global minimum. In nature's terms, this search is asking much, so additional controls are often included in the implementation to ensure that the spring system is not trapped in a local minimum valley.

Unlike Eades' algorithm, which does not explicitly incorporate Hooke's law, Kamada and Kawai's algorithm moves vertices into new positions one at a time, so that the total energy of the spring system is reduced with the new configuration. It also introduces the concept of a desirable distance between vertices in the drawing: the distance between two vertices is proportional to the length of the shortest path between them.

Following Kamada and Kawai's notation (1989), given a dynamic system of n particles mutually connected by springs, let $p_1, p_2, \ldots, p_n$ be the particles in the drawing area corresponding to the vertices $v_1, v_2, \ldots, v_n \in V$, respectively. The balanced layout of vertices can be achieved through the dynamically balanced spring system. Kamada and Kawai formulated the degree of imbalance as the total energy of springs:

$$E = \sum_{i=1}^{n-1} \sum_{j=i+1}^{n} \frac{1}{2} k_{ij} \left(\left| p_i - p_j \right| - l_{ij} \right)^2$$

Their model implies that the best graph layout is the state with minimum E. The distance d_{ij} between two vertices v_i and v_j in a graph is defined as the length of the shortest paths between v_i and v_j. The algorithm aims to match the spring length l_{ij} between particles p_i and p_j, with the shortest-path distance, to achieve the optimal length between them in the drawing. The length l_{ij} is defined as follows:

$$l_{ij} = L \times d_{ij}$$

where L is the desirable length of a single edge in the drawing area. L can be determined based on the largest vertex-to-vertex distance in the graph. If L_0 is the length of a side of the square of drawing area, L can be derived as follows:

$$L = \frac{L_0}{\max_{i<j}(d_{ij})}$$

The strength of the spring connecting p_i and p_j is denoted by parameter k_{ij}:

$$k_{ij} = \frac{K}{d_{ij}^2}$$

where K is a constant. Both l_{ij} and k_{ij} are symmetrical; therefore this design yields symmetrical layouts whenever possible.

Finding a global minimum is difficult in a large search space. The strategy used in Kamada and Kawai's algorithm is to find a local minimum first. Nodes are moved into new positions if the movement leads to the fastest reduction of the total energy. The procedure is repeated until it converges – when the maximum improvement is less than a small fixed threshold ε. The algorithms may continuously search for a new local minimum by swapping over pairs of nodes and repeating the above procedure, provided this swapping over yields a further decrease in the energy. In genetic programming, such swapping operations are known as cross-over operations.

Kamada and Kawai's algorithm has been extended from a two-dimensional space to a three-dimensional version (Kumar and Fowler, 1995).[4] The necessary condition of local minimum energy E is specified by the following equation:

$$\frac{\partial E}{\partial x_m} = \frac{\partial E}{\partial y_m} = \frac{\partial E}{\partial z_m} = 0, \quad 1 \leqslant m \leqslant n$$

A distinct feature of Kamada and Kawai's algorithm is that only one vertex is moved at a time, while other vertices are frozen. Typically the algorithm chooses to move the vertex v_m that is in the "worst place", i.e. which has the largest Δ_m as defined below:

$$\Delta_m = \sqrt{\left\{\frac{\partial E}{\partial x_m}\right\}^2 + \left\{\frac{\partial E}{\partial y_m}\right\}^2 + \left\{\frac{\partial E}{\partial z_m}\right\}^2}$$

[4] http://bahia.cs.panam.edu/info_vis/spr_tr.html

The following pseudo-code of the algorithm is adapted from Kamada and Kawai (1989) and Kumar and Fowler (1995). Let $p_1, p_2, ..., p_n$ denote the vertices in a graph of N nodes, and $d_{ij}, l_{ij}, k_{ij}, \varepsilon$ as defined above. δx, δy, and δz denote the corresponding movement in along x, y, and z dimensions.

```
compute d_ij for 1 ≤ i ≠ j ≤ N
compute l_ij for 1 ≤ i ≠ j ≤ N
compute k_ij for 1 ≤ i ≠ j ≤ N
initialize p_1, p_2, ... , p_n
while (max_iΔ_i > ε) {
    let p_m be the vertex satisfying Δ_m = max_iΔ_i
    while (Δ_m > ε) {
        compute δx, δy, and δz
        x_m = x_m + δx
        y_m = y_m + δy
        z_m = z_m + δz
    }
}
```

The time complexity of the algorithm in Kamada and Kawai (1989) cannot be represented as a function of $|V|$ and $|E|$. Kamada and Kawai (1989) suggested a method to deal with weighted graphs. For example, l_{ij} can be defined as the sum of weights on the shortest path between i and j. In Pathfinder network scaling, the generic Minkowski metric can be used to compute the length of a path.

Some of the common criteria are not explicitly controlled in the spring-embedder model. For example, it does not provide an explicit mechanism to detect and minimize the number of edge crossings. Several implementations based on the spring-embedder model have introduced optimization mechanisms. The greatest advantage of formulating such graph drawing problems as an optimization problem is that algorithms can be made more flexible by incorporating the required criteria into the optimization process.

3.2.4 Force-directed Placement

A significant enhancement and adaptation of the spring-embedder model (Eades, 1984) has been made by Fruchterman and Reingold (1991). Their algorithm follows generally accepted aesthetic criteria for graph drawing, including evenly distributed vertices, minimized edge crossings, and uniform edge lengths. As in Eades (1984), attraction forces are calculated only for neighboring nodes, and repulsive forces are calculated for all pairs of nodes. According to Fruchterman and Reingold, nodes at distance d are attracted to each other by the following attraction force f_a:

$$f_a(d) = \frac{d^2}{k}$$

and they are pushed apart by the repulsive force f_r:

$$f_r(d) = -\frac{k^2}{d}$$

where k is the optimal distance between nodes in the graph, calculated from the number of nodes and the size of the drawing area. In Fruchterman and Reingold (1991), the process is carried out iteratively. Within each iteration, the forces are calculated for each node, and at its end all nodes are moved simultaneously. The process is also controlled by a temperature parameter, in a similar way to simulated annealing (see Section 3.3.5). The algorithm uses 50 iterations, and all the examples shown in their article were drawn in 10 seconds or less on a SparcStation. The force-directed placement algorithm in Figure 3.4 is adapted from Fruchterman and Reingold (1991).

```
{ a drawing frame: W × L }
G := (V, E);
k := √(W * L/ | V |);
function fₐ(x) := begin return x²/k end;
function fᵣ(x) := begin return −k²/x end;

for i := 1 to iterations do begin
   {calculate repulsive forces}
   for v in V do begin
      {each vertex has two vectors: .pos and .disp}
      v.disp := 0;
      for u in V do
         if (u≠v) then begin
            Δ := v.pos − u.pos;
            v.disp := v.disp + (Δ/|Δ|)*fᵣ(|Δ|);
         end
   end

   {calculate attractive forces}
   for e in E do begin
      Δ := e.v.pos − e.u.pos;
      e.v.disp := e.v.disp − (Δ/|Δ|)*fₐ(|Δ|);
      e.u.disp := e.u.disp + (Δ/|Δ|)*fₐ(|Δ|);
   end

   {limit the maximum displacement to the temparature t}
   {and prevent from being displaced outside frame}
   for v in V do begin
      v.pos := v.pos + (v.disp/|v.disp|)*min(v.disp, t);
      v.pos.x := min(W/2, max(−W/2, v.pos.x));
      v.pos.y := min(L/2, max(−L/2, v.pos.y));
   end
   {reduce the temperature as the layout approaches a better configuration}
   t := cool(t);
end
```

Figure 3.4 Force-directed placement (Fruchterman and Reingold, 1991) © John Wiley & Sons Limited. Reproduced with permission.

3.2.5 Simulated Annealing

Davidson and Harel (1996) describe how *simulated annealing* is applied to graph drawing. Their algorithm is also based on the spring-embedder model for drawing general undirected graphs with straight-line edges, and particularly emphasizes the aesthetic quality of graph drawing. For example, nodes and edges should be placed so that the picture is clear and pleasing. Several simple criteria are used to improve the aesthetic quality of the graph.

Simulated annealing is a flexible optimization method originating in statistical mechanics (Kirkpartrick et al., 1983; van Laarhoven and Aarts, 1987). It has been applied successfully to classical combinatorial optimization problems, such as the *traveling salesman* problem, and the design of VLSI. Simulated annealing differs from standard *greedy* optimization methods by allowing *uphill* moves, which may temporarily lead to a higher energy, but which are necessary to make a configuration out of the trap of a local minimum, and eventually reach a global minimum.

The major weakness of simulated annealing is its efficiency – simulated annealing algorithms in general are relatively slow. More fundamentally, simulated annealing may break down if the size of the graph to be drawn is very large. Davidson and Harel note that their algorithm can handle graphs of up to around 30 nodes and 50 edges, but the quality of the output deteriorates rapidly on larger graphs. In fact, their procedure is so time-consuming that they only use it to fine-tune a rough solution found using other techniques.

The major strength of simulated annealing is its ability to deal with optimization problems in a discrete configuration space which is too large for an exhaustive search. The aim is to minimize or maximize a cost function. Simulated annealing typically starts with a randomly chosen initial configuration and repeatedly searches for configurations that can reduce the value of the cost function.

The key function of simulated annealing is to ensure that the search does not stop at a local minimum, rather than the global minimum. It is based on an analogy to the physical *annealing* process, in which liquids are cooled to a crystalline form.

When a liquid is cooled slowly, it reaches a totally ordered *crystal* form, which represents the system with the least amount of energy. In contrast, if it is cooled rapidly, the energy of the system is higher than a crystallized state. When a liquid is cooled slowly, the atoms have time to reach a thermal equilibrium at every temperature. In this state, the system obeys the Boltzmann distribution:

$$p(E) \approx e^{-E/kT}$$

where $p(E)$ specifies the probability distribution of the energy values of the states E, as a function of the temperature T and the Boltzmann constant k. The energy is decreasing as the temperature approaches zero.

Metropolis et al. (1953) simulated this annealing procedure by a series of sequential moves based on a basic rule. The probability of the system changing from one state (with energy $E1$) to another state (with energy $E2$) is:

$$e^{-(E2-E1)/kT}$$

According to this rule, whenever the energy $E2$ of the new candidate state is lower than the current energy $E1$, the system will take the move. But if $E2 > E1$, the state change is probabilistic. Kirkpatrick et al. (1983) generalized this procedure for general optimization problems. A general simulated annealing algorithm is structured as follows:

{set initial configuration σ}
$\sigma := \sigma_{random}$;
{set initial temperature}
$T := T_0$;
while (*control condition*):
    {choose a new configuration σ' from the neighborhood of σ}
    $\sigma' := \sigma + \Delta$;
    {let E and E' be the values of the cost function at σ and σ'}
    if ($E' < E$) {
        {accept new configuration}
        $\sigma := \sigma'$;
    } else {
           if ($r < e^{(E-E')/T}$) {
           {accept new configuration}
           $\sigma := \sigma'$;
           }
    }
    {reduce temperature T}
    $T := cooling(T)$;
}
return final configuration σ.

Many variations on this general scheme are available in the literature; for example, van Laarhoven and Aarts (1987) describe simulated annealing in detail, and also provide an abundance of references. Simulated annealing is very good at finding minimum values that are *close* to the global minimum, but seldom does it detect the global minimum itself.

The neighborhood of a configuration σ is defined by the set of configurations that differ from σ by the location of a single node. Each new configuration is achieved by moving a particular node to a new location. In particular, Davidson and Harel chose to limit such moves within a circle of decreasing radius around the original location of the node. The radius of the circle is relatively large at the beginning of the process so that each node has sufficient freedom to move around, but it becomes smaller and smaller as the algorithm proceeds. In fact, in their algorithm, the distance between the new location and the original location had to equal the radius of the circle, to ensure that nodes were moved around within the shrinking circle as far away as possible, throughout the process.

A key element in simulated annealing is the cost function. It is this cost function that is to be optimized. This cost function must incorporate criteria to be met by the final drawing. Great care should be taken when defining the cost function because it is the most heavy-duty computation component of the algorithm. Davidson and Harel have considered a number of criteria in their cost function.

Even node distribution in the drawing space is handled by two components in Davidson and Harel's cost function, also known as the *energy function* in this case. The first component prevents the nodes from being placed too close to each other, equivalent to the repulsive force in the spring-embedder model, while the second component deals with the placement near to the borders of the drawing space. The repulsive effect is based on the electrical potential energy. For each pair of nodes i and j, the repulsive effect is inversely proportional to the distance between them, and the energy function includes the first component as follows:

$$\sum_{i,j} \frac{\lambda_1}{d_{ij}^2}$$

where d_{ij} is the Euclidean distance between i and j. Here, λ_1 is a normalizing factor defining the relative importance of this criterion compared to the others. Increasing λ_1 relative to the other normalizing factors increases the cost of the repulsive effect. Therefore, more compact configurations are preferable.

In order to prevent nodes from being placed too close to the borders of the drawing space, the following term is included in the energy function:

$$m_i = \lambda_2 \left(\frac{1}{r_i^2} + \frac{1}{l_i^2} + \frac{1}{t_i^2} + \frac{1}{b_i^2} \right)$$

where r_i, l_i, t_i and b_i are the distances between node i and the right, left, top and bottom sides, respectively. Increasing λ_2 relative to λ_1 rewards configurations with more nodes towards the center, while decreasing it results in using more of the drawing space near to the borders.

Davidson and Harel included a component in their energy function to shorten the edges to the necessary minimum, without packing the entire graph too tightly. As a result, long edges are penalized in the energy function. For each edge k of length d_k, the edge length component is defined as follows:

$$C_k = \lambda_3 d_k^2$$

where λ_3 is a normalizing factor. As a by-product, the short-edge criterion can effectively eliminate most unnecessary edge crossings. However, some graphs may need a more specific treatment for these.

In general, minimizing the number of crossings is important, but difficult to achieve. If the graph is planar, it is possible to eliminate all the edge crossings. Algorithms do exist for producing a crossing-free picture of a planar graph, but many algorithms rely on more essential criteria to eliminate them. Although the number of crossings might not be minimal (and some crossings might remain even in planar graphs), the resultant graph drawing could still be pleasant and satisfactory.

Davidson and Harel deal with edge crossings by adding a simple constant penalty, λ_4, to the cost function for every pair of crossing edges. Increasing λ_4 imposes a heavier penalty to edge crossings, and results in drawings with fewer crossings on average, probably at the expense of other aesthetics.

The cooling schedule is one of the most delicate parts of the annealing algorithm. Since the initial configuration of the system is chosen at random, the initial temperature can be set high enough to accept almost any move at the beginning. The goal is to "shake" the graph thoroughly. The exact value of the temperature parameter needs to be determined empirically. Davidson and Harel used a geometric cooling rule. If T_p is the temperature at stage p, then the temperature at the next stage is given by

$$T_{p+1} = \gamma T_p$$

which falls between 0.6 and 0.95. Davidson and Harel (1996) use $$ 0.75 in most of the examples, to achieve a relatively rapid cooling. Cooling too rapidly results in sub-optimal drawing. Davidson and Harel (1996) use a linear number – 30 times the number of nodes – to determine the number of trials at each temperature. For particularly difficult examples, running the algorithm with a larger number of trials per temperature may yield only marginal improvement. Davidson and Harel's algorithm runs in time at most $O(|V|^2|E|)$.

Figure 3.5 includes nine snapshots of a simulated annealing process, using an energy function based on Kamada and Kawai's algorithm. The energy function is based on Kamada and Kawai's partial differential equation's solution, in an attempt to identify a local minimum, as part of our GSA environment.

The graph is a 25-node grid. The initial configuration of the node positions is randomly assigned. The energy function also includes a component that prevents nodes being placed too near to each other. Edge crossings are neither to be specifically detected, nor particularly penalized. A number of iterations are made at each temperature, and each not only attempts to move a node closer to a local minimum, but also randomly accepts a move such that a node may escape the valley of local minimum and lead to a global minimum. The magnitude of a move reduces as the temperature gradually decreases.

The first snapshot was made at the early stage of the simulated annealing, when the temperature was 1000. The layout revealed little about the structure of the grid.

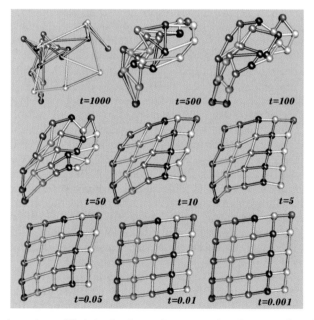

Figure 3.5 Snapshots of a modified simulated annealing process, based on Kamada and Kawai's local minimum partial differential equations.

In the second and the third, the structure started to emerge, and became clearly visible by the time the temperature was decreased to 10. Finer tuning is shown in the last three snapshots, in which the basic shapes of these drawings are essentially the same, while some local adjustments took place.

The temperature was gradually decreased through the simulated annealing process, although actually decreasing very quickly, although a slower decreasing rate may be appropriate for a more complex graph. The curve of the energy function was rapidly reduced at the early stage of simulated annealing. As the temperature approached zero, the reduction of the energy was slowed down, and the process converged when the reduction of the energy was less than a small threshold.

3.3 Examples of Graph Drawing

The following examples represent applications of graph drawing techniques. Chapter 4 also includes visualization systems that use graph drawing techniques in a number of ways.

3.3.1 Representing Structures Using Graphs

Much attention has been given to the study of social networks as a potential application area; graph drawing techniques have been used to reveal their structures. Figure 3.6 is a social network in which an industrial organization has access to various parts of a network of research laboratories sponsored by the German government.

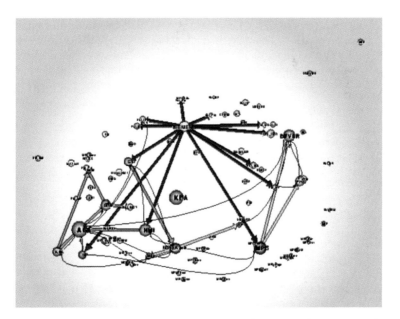

Figure 3.6 Access of an industrial organization to various parts of a network of state sponsored research laboratories. Reprinted with permission of Lothar Krempel.

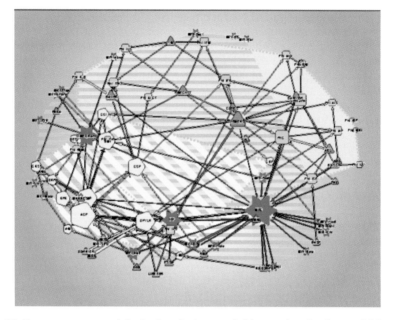

Figure 3.7 Heterogeneous research institutions: basic research (blue stars), national research laboratories (yellow pentangles), applied research (green squares), and industrial organizations (red triangles).
Reprinted with permission of Lothar Krempel.

Many networks are homogenous, containing a single type of node, whereas heterogeneous networks contain several types of nodes. As in LyberWorld for example,
a network of an information space may contain documents, terms, and queries as
nodes. It is important to find out how these nodes are distributed and connected in
a graphic representation. This task is equivalent to finding the two-dimensional
convex hull for each of these data types. A convex hull[5] marks an area populated by
all members of a given type of node. Analyzing the distribution of various types of
data can lead to valuable insights into profound connections between different
types of data.

Figure 3.7 shows an interesting example. Several different types of research
institutions in Germany are included in a heterogeneous network. For example,
blue stars represent basic research institutions; yellow pentangles represent
national research laboratories; green squares represent research institutions that
focus on applied research; and red triangles represent industrial organizations.
The visualized network provides a valuable resource for industrial partners and
others who want to find out about the invisible network of research organizations.

A rapidly growing application of graph drawing techniques is in visualizing
information spaces, to visualize a network of documents. Figure 3.8 displays a
visualization of the ACM SIGCHI's conference proceedings (1995–1998) as a
semantic graph, rendered in VRML. The edges in the graph represent the strongest
semantic relationships derived from the contents of documents within the GSA
framework. The use of GSA in information visualization and virtual environments
is further discussed in subsequent chapters.

---

[5]http://www.geom.umn.edu/

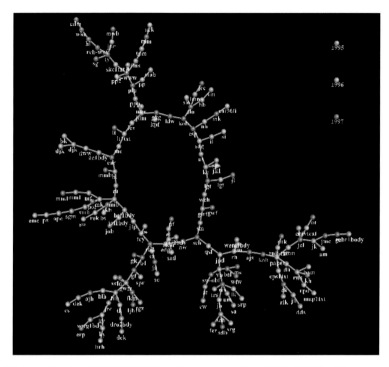

Figure 3.8 A visualization of ACM SIGCHI's conference proceedings (1995–1997) in GSA.

The graph in Figure 3.9, also rendered in VRML, represents the structure of a network of Gopher servers in Europe. Connections are denoted by links between different nodes. This example is included in the Atlas of Cyberspace, maintained at the University College London.

3.3.2 Drawing Large Graphs

Harel and Koren (2000) reported a multiscale layout algorithm for the aesthetic drawing of undirected graphs with straight-line edges. The algorithm is extremely fast, and is capable of drawing very large graphs. They showed a drawing of a graph with over 15,000 vertices (Figure 3.10). With their new algorithm, drawing graphs of 1000 vertices can be done in about 1 second. This is certainly exciting news.

Nguyen and Huang (2003) described a new approach, called *space-optimized tree*, to the visualization of very large hierarchies in a two-dimensional space. The idea is to recursively place children of a sub-tree into polygon areas and still use a node-link diagram to present the entire hierarchical structure. Space-optimized tree combines two viewing methods, the *modified semantic zooming* and a *focus + context* technique. Examples are shown in Figure 3.11.

A number of graph drawing packages have been made available beyond the graph drawing community, notably Pajek and TouchGraph. Pajek supports a still increasing set of functions for network analysis. It also integrates graph drawing functions based on Kamada and Kawai's algorithm and Fruchterman and

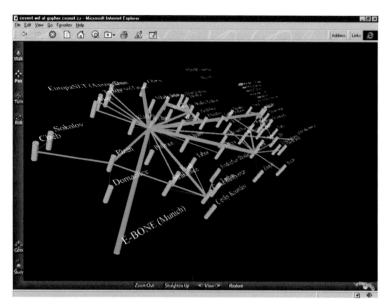

Figure 3.9 A Cesnet Map visualizing a network of Gopher servers in Europe. http://gopher. cesnet.cz/ cesnet.wrl

Figure 3.10 A large graph drawn by the multiscale layout algorithm (Harel and Koren, 2000), containing 15,606 vertices and 45,878 edges. Reprinted with permission of David Harel.

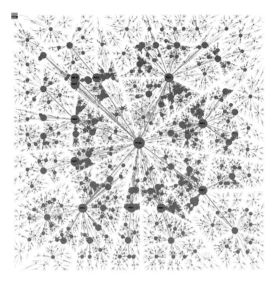

Figure 3.11 Space-optimized tree recursively places subtrees into polygon areas (Nguyen and Huang, 2003). © 2003 Palgrave-Macmillan. Reprinted with permission.

Reingold's force-directed placement algorithm. Batagelj and Mrvar (1998) des-cribed the Pajek system and its role in large network analysis.

TouchGraph is a promising open source project with an emphasis on incorp-orating graph drawing techniques with search engines such as Google and the online bookstore Amazon. TouchGraph provides some user-friendly controls of a graph drawing. Figure 3.12 shows a snapshot of TouchGraph's AmazonBrowser, which visualizes the search results of books on *mass extinction*. Users can check a brief description and even go and buy books with Amazon; and I bought two books as a result of this search!

3.3.3 Summary

Davidson and Harel's simulated annealing approach is more similar to Kamada and Kawai (1989) than to those of Eades (1984) or Fruchterman and Reingold (1991). In Kamada and Kawai (1989), the energy of the spring system is reduced in stages, node after node, as in simulated annealing, but in a deterministic way. An attractive feature of Kamada and Kawai's algorithm is that only one expression is needed for the energy function. In order to escape from a local minimum, the loca-tions of two nodes can be swapped in simulated annealing.

Fruchterman and Reingold's algorithm (1991) has a unique feature: all the nodes are moved together, making it possible to reach configurations that are not necessarily in the vicinity of the current local minimum.

There is flexibility in the construction of the cost function: other criteria for aes-thetics could probably be added without much trouble, and the relative weights of the criteria can be varied, thus making it possible to have some control over the final appearance of the graph.

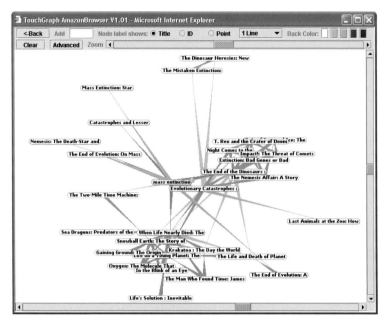

Figure 3.12 TouchGraph's AmazonBrowser on mass extinction books.

The simulated annealing approach is competitive in terms of the quality of the resulting layouts, although, as mentioned earlier, it inherits its unattractive running time from the general framework of simulated annealing.

Simulated annealing does not scale up well. An alternative is to use simulated annealing only after a rather complex series of preprocessing stages.

Simulated annealing can indeed be used in graph drawing, but is probably better employed in a tandem system whose front-end contains more specific heavy-duty tools for finding a reasonable first-cut solution.

The following chapters include a wider variety of works in both information visualization and virtual environments. The major graph drawing criteria and heuristics described in this chapter may provide a useful standing point for the reader to assess the design rationale of particular information visualization. Further usability criteria will be introduced in Chapter 5, taken from the perspective of individual differences in cognition.

3.4 Graph Drawing Resources

There are a number of graph drawing packages available in the public domain. Many of them implement the spring-embedder model or its variants.

GraphViz[6] is a set of graph drawing software developed at AT&T Research Laboratories. It includes software for drawing undirected and straight-line edges. GraphViz 1.3 can be downloaded from AT&T's website.[7]

---

[6]http://www.research.att.com/sw/tools/graphviz
[7]http://www.research.att.com/sw/tools/graphviz/download.html

Table 3.2 Drawing undirected graphs: the spring-embedder and its variants

Models	Attraction force	Repulsive force	Energy function
Eades (1984) Spring-embedder	$f_a(d) = k_a log(d)$	$f_r(d) = k_r/d^2$	
Kamada and Kawai (1989) Local minimum			$$E = \sum_{i=1}^{n-1} \sum_{j=i+1}^{n} \frac{1}{2} k_{ij} \left(|p_i - p_j| - l_{ij} \right)^2$$
Fruchterman and Reingold (1991) Spring-embedder	$f_a(d) = d^2/k$	$f_r(d) = -k^2/d$	
Davidson and Harel (1996) Simulated annealing			uneven-node-distribution-penalty + edge-crossing-penalty + long-edge-length-penalty

Table 3.3 Personal pages on the web, leading to resources of graph drawing

Name	URL on the web
David Eppstein	http://www.ics.uci.edu/~eppstein/gina/gdraw.html
Arne Frick	http://i44s11.info.uni-karlsruhe.de:80/~frick/former.html
Lothar Krempel	http://www.mpi-fg-koeln.mpg.de:80/~lk/netvis/
Tamara Munzner	http://graphics.stanford.edu/courses/cs348c-96-fall/resources.html
Georg Sander	http://www.cs.uni-sb.de/RW/users/sander/
Roberto Tamassia	http://www.cs.brown.edu/people/rt/gd.html

GEM3D[8] is software for drawing undirected graphs in three dimensions, based on the spring-embedder model. Edges are drawn as straight lines, and the length of edges is as uniform as possible. It is designed for fast interactive 3D graph visualization. Arne Fricks has been maintaining information about *GEM3D* on the web (see Table 3.2).

Another interesting graph layout tool in the public domain is *VGJ*, written in Java. *VGJ* includes routines for drawing hierarchies, undirected graphs (using the spring-embedder model), and hierarchical directed graphs (using clan-based decomposition). The tool supports 3D and file input/output in GML, an upcoming graph specification standard.

Not surprisingly, the web has been the major source of graph drawing literature. An annotated bibliography of graph drawing can be found on the web.[9] The following personal pages are from people who are active in graph drawing, and have maintained informative resource links on the Web.

"Graph Drawing" is an annual conference devoted to graph drawing algorithms, theories, and applications. Links to previous Graph Drawing conferences can be found on Tamassia's web page listed in Table 3.3.

---

[8]ftp://i44ftp.info.uni-karlsruhe.de/pub/papers/frick/gem3Ddraw.tar.gz
[9]http://www.graphdrawing.org/literature/gdbiblio.pdf

Chapter 4
Systems and Applications

Vision is the art of seeing things invisible.

Jonathan Swift

In Chapters 2 and 3, essential methods and quality criteria for analyzing and modeling implicit and explicit structures were introduced. A graph drawing algorithm, for example, usually aims to achieve a layout with the least number of edge crossings, an even distribution of nodes, and/or uniform edge lengths. This chapter illustrates some of the most interesting applications of information visualization.

Pragmatic implications of choosing a particular visualization technique should be analyzed by taking into account the original design principles. Chapter 5 will further investigate the impact of information visualization on navigation and information retrieval.

4.1 Trees

Trees, or hierarchies, are commonly used abstractions of information structures. The organizational structure of a file system can be represented as a hierarchy; the structure of a classification system is a hierarchy; and a biological classification of all animals is also hierarchical. Visualizing hierarchies is one of the most mature and active branches in information visualization. The tree data structure not only plays a significant role in its own right in information visualization, but also provides a crucial means of representing more complex structures.

There are many efficient visualization algorithms for hierarchical structures than there are for general networks. As a result, a commonly used strategy is to simplify a network by extracting a tree structure and then apply an efficient tree visualization algorithm. Furthermore, a number of approaches to visualizing hierarchical information structures have focused on the so-called *focus versus context* problem.

A representative approach to displaying and visualizing a large hierarchical structure is to use cone trees. These were originally developed by George Robertson and his colleagues at Xerox PARC (Robertson et al., 1991). The idea of cone trees has had a profound impact on information visualization, and has been adopted in the design of a number of systems that visualize hierarchical structures. In fact, several systems derive hierarchical structures from more general network structures, and use cone trees to visualize the resultant hierarchies.

Tree maps are described by Johnson and Shneiderman (1991) and Shneiderman (1992) as a space-filling approach to the visualization of hierarchical information. Space-filling approaches have also been used in representing self-organizing maps; for example, the computer display area can be partitioned into a number of regional areas, each corresponding to an underlying topic (Lin et al., 1991; Lin, 1997).

A related concept, also developed at the University of Maryland, is elastic windows, in which the screen is tiled by all the available windows in various sizes, so that the user can easily bring a window into focus. Further details about elastic windows can be found in Kandogan and Shneiderman (1997).

4.1.1 Cone Tree

Three-dimensional cone trees were introduced by Robertson et al. (1991). Cone trees are interactive, rendered with shadows, transparency, and animated movements (Figure 4.1). In general, cone trees are not regarded as distorted displays. On the other hand, it is straightforward to incorporate cone trees in a multiscale display, i.e. a zoomable display. The 1991 cone tree article has become an archetype of information visualization ever since. The co-citation maps of information visualization underline its significance to the information visualization community.

One of the well-known visualization systems for information retrieval, LyberWorld, uses NavigationCones to visualize the context of searching. A good example is provided by Tamara Munzner (1998b) in the design of H3 – a 3D hyperbolic layout system. Her algorithm draws 3D cone trees in a hyperbolic space in order to overcome common problems encountered by tree drawing algorithms. She also uses a spanning tree as the backbone of her cone trees in a hyperbolic space, which effectively simplifies the visualization of a general graph into the visualization of a hierarchical structure.

4.1.2 LyberWorld

LyberWorld (Hemmje et al., 1994) is a well-known example of applying metaphors of spatial navigation to abstract information spaces. The design of LyberWorld focuses on a network representation of an information space. It consists of two types of nodes: document nodes and term nodes, and three types of links: document–term links, term–term links, and document–document links.

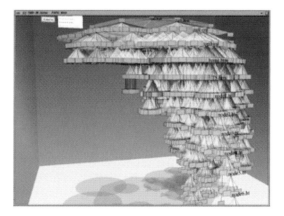

Figure 4.1 A cone tree visualization. Reprinted with permission of George Robertson.

Navigation in LyberWorld relies on the concepts of content and context spaces. The content space is the entire search space, whereas the context space is the sub-space the user has visited. Instead of using computationally expensive graph layout algorithms to map the content network into a three-dimensional space, LyberWorld derives hierarchies from the network representation of the content space and maps them onto a visualization tool, called NavigationCones. NavigationCones visualize the navigation history of a user in the content space, along content-oriented search paths, which connect different documents in the content space.

In LyberWorld, document–term relevance is visualized by the RelevanceSphere. Here, terms are placed on the surface of a sphere, while documents are positioned within the sphere, based on their relevance to each of the terms. Documents closer to the surface are of a greater overall relevance. This visualization aims to improve the user's understanding of the query results, and the structure of the document space. However, no empirical studies have been found in the literature, based on the use of LyberWorld.

4.1.3 Cat-a-Cone

Many information visualization systems map each document to a single point of a semantic space, in which documents are clustered according to overall interdocument similarities. A cluster-based visualization can be useful for many purposes, such as getting an overview of a collection's contents. On the other hand, an alternative way to visualize document similarities is to display documents according to orthogonal semantic attributes or category labels, such as the Dewy Decimal Classification Scheme. The design of Cat-a-Cone reflects some interesting insights into this issue (Hearst and Karadi, 1997).

Marti Hearst explains that when documents are clustered or grouped according to their overall similarities, it becomes harder for users to find out the unique distinctions between documents. Cat-a-Cone is designed to match the results of a search, in the context of a cone tree. It uses animation and a 3D graphical information workspace to accommodate the category hierarchy, and to store intermediate search results in a book.

Cat-a-Cone was built on the basis of 3D cone-tree visualization and animation from the Xerox PARC Information Visualizer (Robertson et al., 1993). Cone trees are used in order to fit the entire display of a very large category hierarchy into one window. Category labels displayed in the cone tree can be easily rotated from the background to the foreground with a simple click on the label of their parent category. The user may control the details displayed in the hierarchy by pruning or growing a particular part of the hierarchy.

Another important component used in Cat-a-Cone is based on the WebBook, also developed at Xerox PARC (Card et al., 1996). The WebBook and the WebForager are designed to provide a more intuitive way for users to access interconnected information.

Figure 4.2 is a screenshot of the Cat-a-Cone user interface, with the cone tree in the background. Category labels are only displayed if they match the current document displayed in the focal book in the foreground. This information workspace also includes a bookcase. The user can search the collection of documents and save the results of a search as a book. If a book is not currently in use, it can be put into the bookcase. The example shown in the figure is a sub-structure of the Yahoo hierarchy.

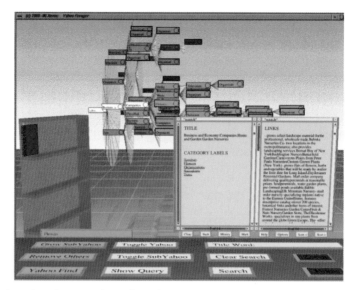

Figure 4.2 Cat-a-Cone (Hearst and Karadi, 1997). © 1997 ACM, Inc. Reprinted with permission.

A unique and significant design feature of Cat-a-Cone is the separation of the categorical hierarchy and the content of a document. It is also an example of how local details and a global context can be balanced using information visualization techniques. The cone tree provides a global context, while the WebBook provides details of the focal point. The focal point is mirrored in the cone tree, because only category labels relevant to the current document are displayed.

4.1.4 Botanical Tree

Kleiberg et al. (2001) develop a botanical visualization of huge hierarchies (Figures 4.3 and 4.4). The botanical trees are visually intriguing, although it remains to be seen whether empirical evidence can reveal further insights into the practical value of a creative design like this. Botanical tree is a particularly valuable contribution to the information community by exploring such an innovative design metaphor of a hierarchical structure.

4.1.5 Tree maps

The *TreeMap* visualization technique is another classic technique that supports browsing hierarchically organized files on computer (Johnson and Shneiderman, 1991; Shneiderman, 1992). TreeMap utilizes a space-filling algorithm that fills recursively divided rectangle areas with components of a hierarchy.

Tree maps have been adopted in several visualization projects, including SmartMoney (Figure 4.5), which gives an overview of the rises and falls of stock prices. Figure 4.6 shows an interesting extension of the traditional 2D tree map

Figure 4.3 A botanical visualization of a hierarchy (Kleiberg et al., 2001). © 2001 IEEE. Reprinted with permission.

Figure 4.4 A closer view of a botanical tree visualization (Kleiberg et al., 2001). © 2001 IEEE. Reprinted with permission.

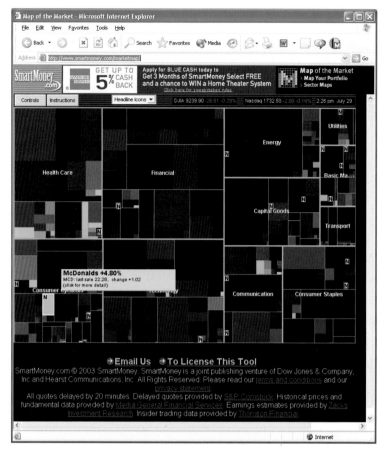

Figure 4.5 SmartMoney. http://www.smartmoney.com/marketmap/

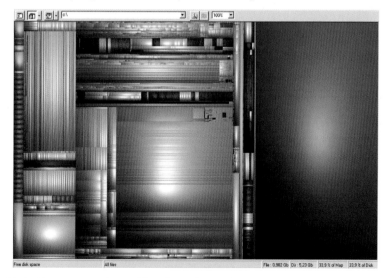

Figure 4.6 Cushion tree map (van Wijk and van de Wetering, 1999). © 1999 IEEE. Reprinted with permission.

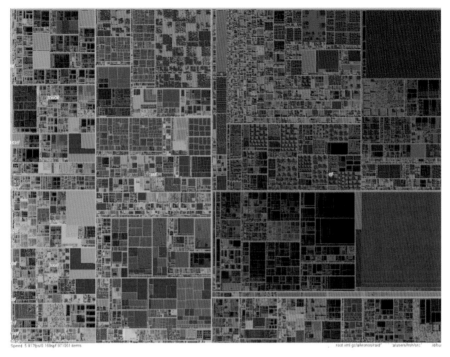

Figure 4.7 Million pixel treemap (Fekete and Plaisant, 2002). © 2002 IEEE. Reprinted with permission.

displays – a cushion tree map, which makes the tree map rectangles easy to recognize. Figure 4.7 shows a more recent experiment with the tree map design; the picture depicts a million pixels.

4.2 Networks

Network visualization is a cornerstone of today's information visualization. The complexity and diversity of network visualization and issues such as scalability and incremental updatability have made network visualizations one of the most interesting and challenging areas of information visualization.

4.2.1 SemNet

SemNet (Fairchild et al., 1988) is a classic study of 3D visualization. It is designed to help people understand the complex relationships within large knowledge bases. SemNet visualizes relationships that already exist within a knowledge base (Figure 4.8).

Fairchild et al. discuss a number of design issues in association with mapping a high dimensional data set into a 3D space. They analyze the complexity issue for

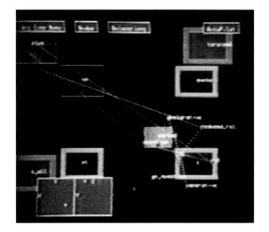

Figure 4.8 SemNet. Reprinted with permission of Kim Fairchild.

displaying the semantic network derived from very large knowledge bases and rightly point out that simply using a graphical representation does not solve the problems inherent in exploring, manipulating, understanding and modifying large knowledge bases. This highlights an important need to reduce the visual complexity of graphical representations.

The layout of SemNet is designed to reflect the relatedness between nodes, measured by the number of interconnections. Highly interconnected nodes are placed much closer together than unconnected nodes. SemNet has had a profound influence on subsequent works in information visualization.

4.2.2 NicheWorks

NicheWorks (Wills, 1999) is a visualization tool developed at Bell Laboratories, which aims to help an analyst work on very large networks of telephone-calling data. A crucial requirement for NicheWorks is the ability to lay out a group of 10,000–100,000 nodes. Another important requirement is that it should be able to display both graph structure and attributes associated with node and edge, to reveal hidden patterns and information for investigating and exploring such large, complex data sets.

One strategy used by NicheWorks is to relax some of the optimization criteria in order to speed up the process. For example, the aesthetics of evenly distributed nodes is not required for investigating traffic on a telephone network, so that this criterion was considerably relaxed by including only a final polishing algorithm to separate overlapping nodes.

NicheWorks presents a graph with straight-line edges. Instead of keeping edge lengths uniform, it is more important if the length of an edge can reflect the weight on the edge. In NicheWorks, the length of an edge is inversely proportional to the weight on the edge, so that the strongest linked nodes are closest together in the ideal layout. Figure 4.9 shows a graph in NicheWorks.

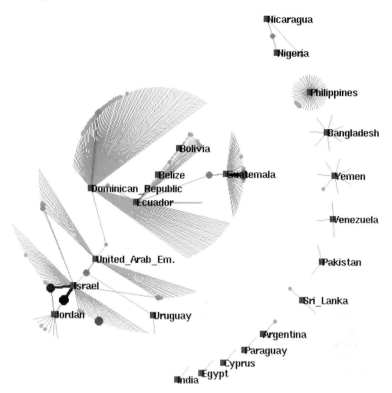

Figure 4.9 A telephone calling network visualized in NicheWorks. Reprinted with permission of Graham Wills.

4.2.3 3D Spring-Embedder Model and Narcissus

Kamada and Kawai's influential algorithm was originally presented for graph drawing in a 2D drawing space, but the extension of a drawing space from 2D to 3D is relatively straightforward. A 3D version[1] of Kamada and Kawai's algorithm is described in Kumar and Fowler (1994).

Narcissus is an information visualization system developed at the University of Birmingham (Hendley et al., 1995). It aims to visualize highly interconnected structures in a 3D space, for software visualization, and is based on self-organized graph-drawing techniques and virtual reality, to reveal a complex structure. It is proposed to use Narcissus to display the dependencies between various components of a software system.

Figure 4.10 is a screenshot of the Narcissus system. The graph layout is generated by following the same principle as the spring-embedder model, and was drawn in a 3D space. Ray-tracing techniques are used to render the final display. It is clear from the layout that Narcissus clusters nodes as much as possible, instead of producing an even distribution. Layout of the graph is performed using a self-organized graph-drawing technique. New nodes are introduced into the structure by being assigned a random location.

---

[1]http://bahia.cs.panam.edu/info_vis/spr_tr.html

Figure 4.10 Visualization in Narcissus rendered by ray-tracing. Reprinted with permission of Bob Hendley.

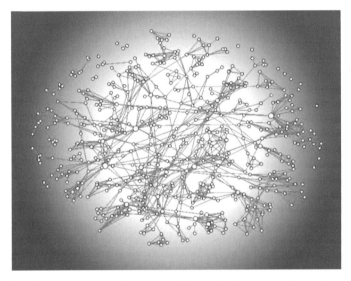

Figure 4.11 Visualization of co-authorships among 555 scientists. Reprinted with permission of Lothar Krempel.

Simulated annealing algorithms in general can be degenerated quickly as the size of a graph increases. The spring-embedder model and its variants are likely to break down on very large graphs. For example, Figure 4.11 is a visualization of co-authorships among 555 scientists, generated with a method similar to the spring-embedder model. Its aim is to reveal patterns in a social network of co-authorships.

The spatial layout here appears to be cluttered with links crossing each other over long distance. It highlights two issues: first, a highly interconnected graph like this is unlikely to be planar. It is difficult to project such graphs onto a two-dimensional space without losing clarity. The second observation is that the size of the graph becomes too large for self-organized graph-drawing heuristics to handle.

To address the first issue, the interconnectivity of the graph can be simplified by deriving representative sub-structures from it, such as a minimal span-ning tree, or a Pathfinder network. Chapter 5 includes an example in which a fundamental structure is derived from a substantial part of the literature of hypertext. This structure is then simplified into a Pathfinder network for visualization.

To address the second issue, a hybrid strategy may work well. A very large data set may be divided into smaller, more homogenous sub-sets using various clustering algorithms. Self-organized graph drawing algorithms are used only if the clustering process results in clusters that can be comfortably handled. Alternatively, as with NicheWorks, one can always relax certain less important criteria to improve the overall quality of a graph drawing.

A serious problem with self-organized graph drawing techniques, including the spring-embedder model, is that the configuration in the drawing space is not a continuous function of the underlying structure of the graph; a small change in the graph structure can lead to a much altered configuration in its layout. Instead of placing new nodes randomly in the drawing space, a more sensible approach would be to use methods equivalent to incremental clustering techniques (see section 3.1.2), so that the essential structure can be carried out into new configurations in a meaningful way. An incremental update of spatial layout would help users to reduce their cognitive load in dealing with these graphic representations.

An alternative to incremental updates is to animate the transformation from a previous drawing to the current one so that the user can see the changes in the structure as they are taking place. For example, in VRML 2.0 two consecutive frames can be interpolated to form an animation. More examples of information visualization are included in Chapter 5, with emphasis on the connection between a visualized structure and the mental model of the user.

4.2.4 Network Evolution

There is an increasing interest in the literature in visualizing the growth of an evolving network. The evolution of discourse is visualized in a recent example (Brandes and Willhalm, 2002). An et al. (2001) suggested that the evolution of citation networks could be useful in predicting research trends and in studying a scientific community's life span. Chen and Carr (1999a) represent the evolution of the field of hypertext by visualizing its author co-citation networks over consecutive periods of time. An interesting study by Powell et al. (2002) analyzed the evolution of the biotechnology industry through a study of a network of contractual collaborations in the field between 1988 and 1999. The nodes in the networks are organizations and the links are collaborative ties. Various stages of the network were visualized. No link reduction or pruning was made. It appears to be particularly problematic to identify significant topological and dynamical patterns in such visualization models because of the high density of the underlying network.

Two criteria are derived based on the above analysis for qualitatively evaluating network visualization.

Criterion I: Topological Properties

The most recognizable patterns in a network are stars, rings, and spikes (Rosch et al., 1976). The first criterion for selecting a preferable topological structure of a visualized network is the presence of hubs, or stars, in derived networks. The notion of reference points is proposed in Krumhansl (1978), referring to conceptually or visually salient or distinctive points in a geometric model. Such reference points play the role of a reference context to which other points are seen "in relation". For instance, a star in a network is a node which is the only node many nodes connect to. The "starness" of a pattern is also studied by Rosch et al. (1976). A star pattern indicates that the star node carries the most information, processes the highest cue validity and is the most differentiated from one another. It has been demonstrated in Chen and Davies (1999) that star patterns emerged in a hybrid PFNET of documents and users' profiles and profiles are in the center, connecting to documents. The preference of star-like patterns is also implicit in Salton's model of an effective indexing space for information retrieval (Salton, 1989). In such indexing spaces, similar documents should be easily separable from the rest of documents so that as one is retrieving a relevant document, it is possible to scoop many other relevant ones in its vicinity and to reject documents located remotely.

Existing studies appear to suggest that co-citation counts are likely to form such star patterns in both MST and PFNET. In terms of small-world networks, star-rich networks have relatively high clustering coefficients; we will return to this subject later. The first part of our study is to identify the boundary conditions of this claim so that one can select the most appropriate method for a given network.

Criterion II: Dynamical Properties

Our second criterion focuses on the need for visualizing the evolution of a network. What makes a good visualization of an evolving network? The second criterion imposes additional constraints on the visualization of network evolution. Criterion I emphasizes the topological properties of preferable network visualization. Criterion II requires that the changes of topological properties over time must preserve the integrity of emergent trends or patterns. Visualizing network evolution should not merely inform users of changes of individual nodes and links; rather, it is essential to inform users how an intrinsically cohesive structure changes locally and globally inorganically. A fragmented growth picture cannot be considered as an adequate visual representation. For instance, Branigan and Cheswick (1999) use their Internet Mapping techniques to show how the Internet in Yugoslavia was affected by the war. The focus is no longer on an individual connection; instead, it is now on the connectivity of a subset of nodes. It also follows that Criterion II implies a level of predictability; a good visualization should give the user various clues of where a new node is likely to appear and where a new path is likely to emerge.

Pearson's, r: PFNET versus MST

Both MST and PFNET appear to be capable of meeting the first criterion when conditions on the proximity measurements are satisfied. For instance, MSTs of similarity measures normalized by cosine coefficients tend to have several hubs or star nodes, whereas PFNETs of author co-citation counts with no normalization at all were found to have similar clustering patterns. MST is a common choice in information visualization. Clusters in MST appear to reflect the concepts of hubs and authorities. We also know that MST algorithms are more efficient than PFNET algorithms. Therefore, a number of theoretically and practically important questions now need to be addressed. Will MSTs be a generally better choice? As far as co-citation networks are concerned, will MSTs in general meet the second criterion? To what extent will the topological properties of highly clustered PFNETs be preserved by the use of raw author co-citation counts? Will PFNETs stand up the second criterion for visualizing the evolution of document co-citation networks?

Botulinum Toxin Research (1945–2002)

Chen and Morris (2003) studied animated visualization models of the evolution of botulinum toxin research from 1945 through 2002 based on both MST and PFNET and compared the resultant models against the two criteria derived earlier. The evolution of the underlying research field is represented by the evolution of its co-citation network over its 58-year span. The nature of components of the co-citation network is identified in both MST and PFNET models using an independent method – accumulative co-citation clustering.

Botulinum toxin is a poison produced by the anaerobic bacteria *Clostridium botulinum* (Jankovic and Brin, 1997). The toxin is one of the most potent poisons known, as little as 0.1 to 1 µg of toxin can be fatal to humans. Botulism, the medical condition caused by botulinum toxin, was first systematically studied by J. Kerner, a German medical officer, in the 1820s. The bacteria *C. botulinum* itself was first isolated and its toxin identified by Ermengem in 1897. Most of the different toxin types were identified in the first half of the twentieth century. Modern toxin research started with a seminal paper by Burgen et al. (1949), which revealed that the toxin attacked the neuromuscular junction.

Co-citation networks of botulinum toxin research were derived from a citation dataset, containing citation records from 1945 to 2002. The following discussion primarily focuses on a 516-node co-citation network. The weight of a link in the network was calculated in two ways: first, weight links by direct co-citation counts; secondly, weight links by normalized co-citation coefficients. The following normalization (I) is used in this study:

$$sim(d_i,d_j) = \frac{cc(d_i,d_j)}{\sqrt{c(d_i) \cdot c(d_j)}} \tag{I}$$

where $cc(d_i, d_j)$ is the number of times document i and document j are cited together, and $c(d_i)$ and $c(d_j)$ are the number of times document i and document j are cited respectively. Alternatively, one may choose to use the following normalization (II):

$$sim(d_i,d_j) = \frac{cc(d_i,d_j)}{c(d_i) + c(d_j) - cc(d_i,d_j)} \tag{II}$$

MSTs were extracted using Prim's algorithm. PFNETs were extracted using the algorithm described in Schvaneveldt (1990). Both types of network models were examined against the first criterion given earlier. In order to examine the compliance to the second criterion, animated visualizations were generated as a sequence of annual snapshots of the evolving network throughout the 58-year period. The animated visualization revealed two types of state transitions as originally specified in Chen and Kuljis (2003). The connectivity of the underlying co-citation network was represented by three node states and three link states. The three node states (NS) of an article are:

- NS1 – pre-publication state.
- NS2 – published but not yet cited.
- NS3 – first citation detected.

Similarly, a co-citation link connecting two articles has three states (LS) as well. Suppose article A_i was published earlier than article A_j.

- LS1 – both A_j and A_j in NS1.
- LS2 – both A_j and A_j in NS2 or NS3.
- LS3 – first co-citation detected.

Research fronts are considered as collections of papers on specific research problems in a field (Morris et al., 2003). Base reference clusters are groups of references that represent the foundational knowledge used by workers when investigating research problems. Research fronts can be found by clustering documents that tend to cite the same references, using bibliographic coupling (Kessler, 1963) as the basis for measuring similarity between pairs of papers. Base reference clusters can be formed by clustering references that tend to be cited together, using co-citation (Small, 1997) as the basis for measuring similarity between pairs of references.

In this study, research fronts were identified by agglomerative clustering using only papers that had at least five bibliographic coupling counts with some other paper in the dataset. Similarity calculation was based on Salton's cosine coefficient (Salton, 1989) applied to bibliographic coupling counts. The titles for each research front were derived manually by exploring titles of papers within each research front for common themes. Base reference clusters were formed by agglomerative clustering using only references that had been cited 10 or more times. Similarity calculation was based on Salton's cosine coefficient applied to co-citation counts. For each base reference cluster, labels were found by using the label of the research front that contained the most citations to references in the cluster. A map of the references in the Pathfinder network was produced identifying each reference by its base reference cluster membership, which allowed labeling of sections of the Pathfinder network based on base cluster labels.

Figure 4.12 shows the 516-node MST based on the normalized co-citation counts. The MST model indeed contained many clusters. A three-dimensional visualization with the citation counts depicted in the third dimension also confirms that the cluster centers tend to have higher citation counts than non-center members of clusters. The MST model in this particular case evidently met the first criterion and it would be reasonable to hypothesize that MSTs can meet the criterion in a broader range of networks.

However, an examination of the animated visualization over the 58-year span indicates that the MST model did not meet the second criterion, which requires the visualized network to convey the evolution of globally and locally cohesive structures. A key question is how the relationship between the center of a cluster and other non-center members in the cluster was depicted over the course of evolution. In

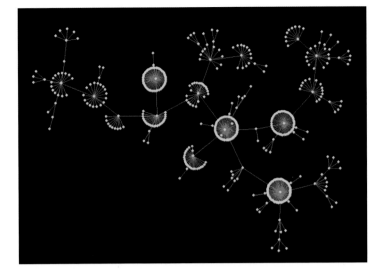

Figure 4.12 The MST visualization of the 516-node co-citation network on botulinum toxin (1945–2002) is predominated by star nodes. Co-citation counts are normalized (I) (Chen and Morris, 2003). © 2003 IEEE. Reprinted with permission.

general, due to the arbitrary choice inherited from the MST algorithms, one cannot guarantee the uniqueness of an MST. As a result, an MST may not preserve all the necessary links for representing the growth of a co-citation network. If this is the case, then important diffusion patterns may be distorted or inadequately represented by the extracted MST model. Users will probably find it hard to understand the way new nodes and new links emerge. The nature of the problem will become clear shortly when we contrast the growth animation of the PFNET and MST models.

The 516-node PFNET ($q = N - 1$, $r = \infty$) is shown in Figure 4.13. The two parameters q and r were chosen to ensure that the extracted PFNET has the least number of links. The network in this case contains 525 links, which gives the node–link ratio of 0.98. A number of visualization methods can be used to identify local structures of a PFNET, including node color mapping based on principle component analysis (PCA) on co-citations normalized as cosine coefficients, chronologically synchronized animated visualizations of state transitions for both nodes and links, and base reference cluster memberships based on the clustering algorithm, where clusters are formed independently from algorithms used in modeling the network. In Figure 4.13, each node is depicted as its cluster number. The PFNET and the clustering methods appear to have a nearly perfect match between each other. Figure 4.14 is the same network partitioned by PCA factor loadings.

Several distinct research fronts emerged in the 1980s. Gene sequencing research on *C. botulinum* started in the early 1990s. Toxin research base references are located in the areas slightly above the center of the map. Furthermore, research fronts have opened up on C2 cytotoxin and C3 exoenzyme recently. Additional research in botulinum toxin is using the C3 exoenzyme to study Rho proteins. C3 exoenzyme is also being studied as a possible neurotrophic drug, used for encouraging nerve growth. Base references related to C-2 and C-3 toxins are located in the south-western region of the map in Figure 4.13.

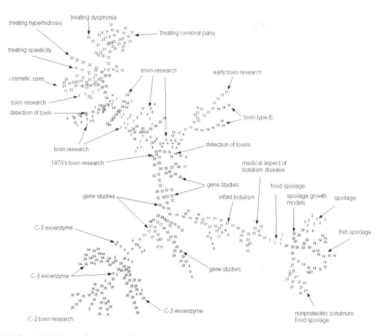

Figure 4.13 The PFNET visualization of the 516-node co-citation network ($q = N - 1, r = \infty$), containing 525 links (Chen and Morris, 2003). © 2003 IEEE. Reprinted with permission.

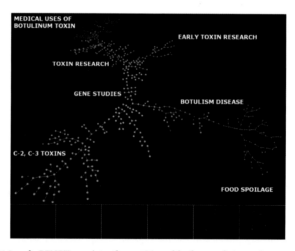

Figure 4.14 The 516-node PFNET consistently partitioned by base reference clusters and PCA factors. The PFNET is predominated by strongest paths (Chen and Morris, 2003). © 2003 IEEE. Reprinted with permission.

Other research fronts in botulinum toxin research have focused on the mechanisms of food spoilage (located in the south-eastern region of the PFNET), the medical aspects of botulism (along the branch stretching towards the east), and infant botulism (also in the same branch), which is often attributed to cases of sudden infant death syndrome. Research is also being carried out to develop methods of detecting and assaying the botulinum toxin in the environment. Botulinum toxin can be used as a chemical/biological warfare agent and possible bioterror weapon, making the search for a cheap and efficient detection method an important area for research. There does not appear to be a consistent set of base references for botulinum toxin bioterrorism and biological warfare as there is for the case of anthrax (Morris et al., 2003).

The medical uses of botulinum toxin have received a great deal of public attention. Scott et al. (1973) described experiments on monkeys to treat eye alignment disorders. In the 1980s it was noticed that many patients being treated for blepharospasm (a disorder of clamping of eyelids) using botulinum toxin exhibited reduced facial wrinkles and improved cosmetic appearance. Based on this effect, Carruthers (1992) reported the use of botulinum toxin for cosmetic purposes. The toxin has gained wide use for this purpose and as a result, the toxin is the current focus of much public attention.

In the 1990s botulinum toxin was studied for the treatment of spasticity, dysphonia (clamping muscles), achalasia (a disorder of clamping throat muscles that interferes with swallowing and food ingestion), cerebral palsy, hyperhidrosis (excessive sweating), anal fissures, and more. Jankovic (1991) presented an important review on medical uses of botulinum toxin. Most medical uses of botulinum toxin are based on toxin type A, which is manufactured under the commercial name of Botox.

The PFNET in Figure 4.14 was colored by factor loading from PCA based on cosine coefficients of co-citation frequencies. It is clear from Figures 4.13 and 4.14 that base reference clusters and PCA factors are consistent with each other. For instance, C-2 and C-3 toxins base references identified by timeline visualization correspond to the area in light blue, which is consistently identified by PFNET and PCA.

Unlike the MST model, the PFNET model was not predominated by high-degree nodes. If we use the first criterion alone, MSTs would be a more preferable choice than PFNETs. In addition, PFNETs derived from raw co-citation counts appear to form more interpretable structures than normalized versions (White, 2003a). However, our further study of the second criterion indicates that this may not be the case if we take the temporal factor into account.

The examination of the second criterion was based on animated visualizations of the 58-year growth history of the field. Figure 4.15 shows some of the frames in the animation sequence. The enlarged frame shows the diffusion process of how several base reference clusters emerge and spread. State transitions were shown by changing the transparency level of nodes and links in question. The four smaller frames in the figure were selected from the animation sequence to show the emergence of early toxin research in the late 1940s and the research front of gene studies formed at the center more recently.

The animated PFNET visualization model demonstrated that nodes with similar colors often emerged simultaneously and formed local structures. And these local structures were reinforced by the timely emergence of salient co-citation links. The growth process can be represented by the dynamics shown in such local structures. Features such as continuity, predictability, and local cohesiveness in the PFNET indicated that the second criterion was met. More significantly, it was found that these properties were missing from the MST model (see Figures 4.16 and 4.17). In PFNET, five pioneering toxin research articles formed a distinct thread, or a pathway. One can follow the development of the thread visually as new nodes and new links extend the pathway. In contrast, in the MST model, four

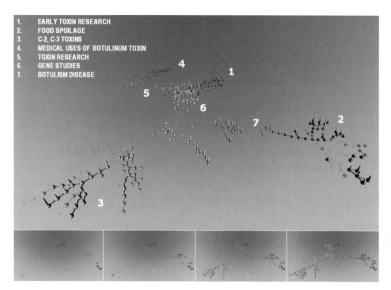

1. EARLY TOXIN RESEARCH
2. FOOD SPOILAGE
3. C-2, C-3 TOXINS
4. MEDICAL USES OF BOTULINUM TOXIN
5. TOXIN RESEARCH
6. GENE STUDIES
7. BOTULISM DISEASE

Figure 4.15 The animated PFNET sequence shows the evolution of the field as the PFNET network becomes populated (Chen and Morris, 2003). © 2003 IEEE. Reprinted with permission.

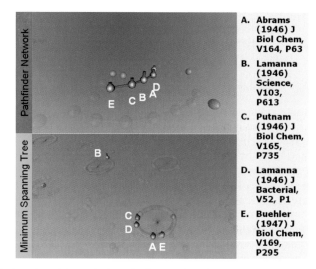

A. Abrams (1946) J Biol Chem, V164, P63

B. Lamanna (1946) Science, V103, P613

C. Putnam (1946) J Biol Chem, V165, P735

D. Lamanna (1946) J Bacterial, V52, P1

E. Buehler (1947) J Biol Chem, V169, P295

Figure 4.16 The integrity of the evolution of a five-article pathway is well preserved in PFNET (top), whereas the same pathway is fragmented in MST (bottom) (Chen and Morris, 2003). © 2003 IEEE. Reprinted with permission.

of the five articles were in the same cluster and one article was found in a different cluster.

The animation showed that the pathway clearly captured by PFNET was simply not in the MST model. None of the four articles was the center of the cluster. Each article in the cluster connected to the center through a single co-citation link. However, such links in MST were not necessarily the earliest or the most salient

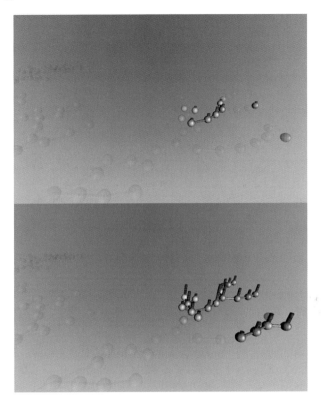

Figure 4.17 Two snapshots of PFNET taken subsequently clearly show the organic growth of the co-citation pathways. Such pathways were destroyed in MST (Chen and Morris, 2003). © 2003 IEEE. Reprinted with permission.

co-citation links. MST may have excluded some vital links in the crucial pathways in the course of evolution.

The advantage of the PFNET is evident; it clearly shows the evolution of the co-citation network, starting with the short pathway at first, and then continuing the growth by the emergence of the second pathway alongside. The two frames were separated by a few years. Users can easily recognize the nature of the newly added nodes.

Given the findings of this study, several lines of research are worth considering: (1) visualizing the evolution of co-citation networks in other subject domains, (2) visualizing scientific networks other than co-citation networks, such as citation networks, bibliographic coupling networks, co-authorship networks, and social networks, (3) visualizing a wider range of networks, for example, small-world networks and scale-free networks, and (4) visualizing the evolution of complex systems that are not necessarily represented as networks.

4.3 Spatial Information Exploration

Spatial metaphors are among the most popular design options in information visualization, for instance, SemNet (Fairchild et al., 1988), Bead (Chalmers, 1992),

Figure 4.18 Geographical layout is the most natural organizational principle (Lokuge et al., 1996). © 1996 ACM, Inc. Reprinted with permission.

LyberWorld (Hemmje et al., 1994), Starfield (Ahlberg and Shneiderman, 1994), VR-VIBE (Benford et al., 1995), SPIRE (Hetzler et al., 1998), VxInsight (Davidson, Hendrickson et al., 1998).

Earlier geographical information systems (GIS) have been a major source of inspiration for the design of more recent information visualization systems, using the universe, the solar system, galaxies, or other spatial metaphors. In a GIS system, tourist attractions, electricity consumption, water supply, crime, spending power and many other types of information can be intuitively superimposed over the natural layout framework provided by geography. Figure 4.18 shows the appealing features of a geographical information system of the Boston area, and Chapter 2 discussed how multidimensional scaling and trajectory mapping techniques were used to derive structural connections among various tourist sites in Boston.

4.3.1 Bead

Bead (Chalmers, 1992) is well known for its design rationale, which is based on the metaphor of information landscape, and generated using multidimensional scaling. The interrelationships among a set of documents are mapped to a geographical-like model within the DIVE virtual reality environment. Bead makes use of a variant of simulated annealing to lay out documents within a 3D space. The layout algorithm aims to map a semantic space into a 3D space, so that semantic proximity is preserved in the 3D representation. The similarity between two documents is based on co-occurrences of terms, and measures the number of words occurring in both documents. This is very similar to the Dice coefficients, normalized word co-occurrences between two documents.

Experiences with Bead highlight some challenging issues concerning the visual complexity of 3D models and navigating within them. As a result, Bead restricts the layout of documents to a flatter landscape model – a small range of fluctuation is allowed in the third dimension. This is why a space is sometimes called a 2.1D or 2.5D space. The document nodes are meshed together by polygonal shapes, and

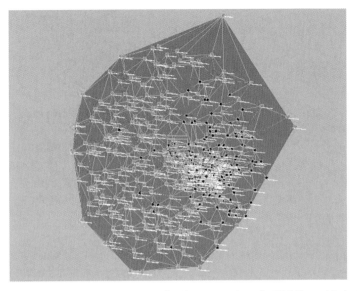

Figure 4.19 A bibliographic landscape in BEAD, showing an overview of 500 bibliographical references. Reprinted with permission of Matthew Chalmers.

distribution of the nodes in the landscape model tends to resemble the population on the land and on the coast to the sea. The colors in Figure 4.19 clearly reinforce this land-and-sea metaphor, the central area being the land, and the surrounding area the sea. Bead is in fact a multi-user virtual environment; the information landscape can be populated by multiple users.

It also supports search facilities. The results of a search are highlighted in the visualized document landscape. If a document is relevant in a search, then its neighbors are likely to be worth pursuing as well, even if they are not shown as relevant to the initial search. The layout algorithm tends to place documents that are marginally related to the main theme towards the coastlines. This geographical metaphor, the coastline and the mainland, is powerful and intuitive. Users can build their own mental model of how the data are organized, and their implications in terms of their locations in the visualization.

4.3.2 VR-VIBE

VR-VIBE is a virtual reality-based information system developed at the University of Nottingham. It is an extension of the *Visual Information Browsing Environment* (VIBE) originally developed at the University of Pittsburgh (Olsen et al., 1993).

VR-VIBE represents the interrelationships among documents in response to queries based on user-specified keywords, in a three-dimensional space rendered in virtual reality (Figure 4.20). VR-VIBE is designed to visualize the results of a search query in such a space. A virtual reality scene in VR-VIBE is based on a number of keywords initially specified by users, and the documents that are relevant to these keywords. Both keywords and resultant documents are placed in the three-dimensional space. The document–keyword relevance is based on the number of matches of the keyword in the given document and the position of a document

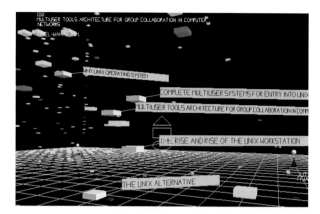

Figure 4.20 VR-VIBE. Reprinted with permission of Steve Benford.

is constrained according to the significance of each keyword given by the user. A document placed an equal distance from two keywords would be equally relevant to both keywords, while a document next to a particular keyword should be strongly relevant to that keyword. Only documents that are closely relevant to query keywords are displayed according to a threshold. Less relevant documents are omitted from the scene. VR-VIBE also enables multiple users to browse the same scene.

4.3.3 SAGE

SAGE[2] is an integrated visualization environment developed by a group of researchers at Carnegie Mellon University, incorporating a variety of graphic design tools, interactive exploration techniques, and information visualization facilities. SageBook is an application from the SAGE environment (Chuah et al., 1995).

SAGE supports *spatial shift* tasks. One can select objects or substructures of the original model and move a copy of them to a new place (see Figures 4.21 and 4.22). In Figure 4.21, the spatial shift operation moves a group of objects upwards from the original visualization model, so that the structure of this group is clear and easy to understand. In Figure 4.22, the spatial shift operation moves the selected sub-structure horizontally.

4.3.4 SPIRE

SPIRE[3] – Spatial Paradigm for Information Retrieval and Exploration – is a suite of information visualization tools developed at Pacific Northwest National Laboratory (PNL) in the USA. It aims to help users explore a large number of textual documents with an intuitive spatial metaphor (Wise et al., 1995; Hetzler et al., 1998). One of the design requirements of SPIRE is that users without special domain knowledge should be able to use these visualization tools to explore and

---

[2]http://www-2.cs.cmu.edu/Groups/sage/sage.html
[3]http://www.pnl.gov/infoviz/

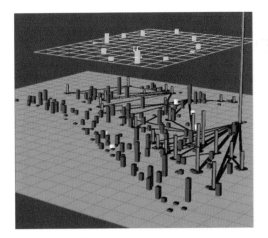

Figure 4.21 A spatial shift operation allows the user to manipulate selected components in a spatial model (vertical movement). Reprinted with permission of Mark Derthick.

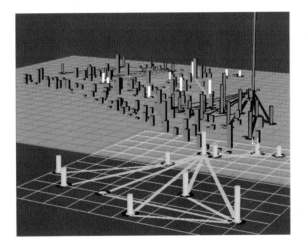

Figure 4.22 A horizontal spatial shift operation. Reprinted with permission of Mark Derthick.

discover topical themes and other underlying relationships among documents. The design of SPIRE is based on word similarities and themes within text. SPIRE supports two types of visualization: "galaxies" and "themescapes".

Visualization in galaxies is based on the popular document-clustering concept. It provides an overview of the entire set of documents; documents are represented as a galaxy of star clusters in the night sky (see Figure 4.23). These stars are called *docustars* in the galaxy visualization. Like many other visualization systems using spatial metaphors, similar documents are represented by stars near to each other in the galaxy, whereas documents about different topics are separated by greater distance. This metaphor intuitively suggests that documents within each cluster are closely related, and documents between different clusters are less closely related. Analytical tools provided by SPIRE may be used to investigate the document groupings, query the document contents, and investigate time-based trends.

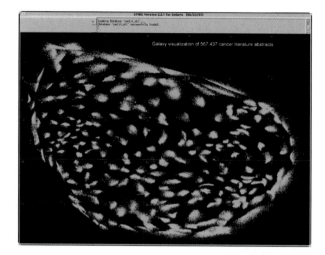

Figure 4.23 Galaxy visualization of 567,437 abstracts from the cancer literature. Reprinted with permission of Beth Hetzler.

Themescape visualizes the presence of specific themes across different documents as mountains in a relief map of natural terrain. The height of a peak indicates the relative strength of a given topic in the document set. Similar themes are grouped into a neighborhood, whereas unrelated themes are separated by greater distance. These visualization tools can be used to identify unanticipated relationships and examine changes in topics over time. One may also examine these thematic spaces over time, in order to understand vast interrelated dynamic changes simply not possible to detect using traditional approaches. Structuring abstract digital documents in general presents a challenging issue.

In the themescape visualization, the mountains in the visualization indicate dominant themes. The height of the peaks indicates the relative strengths of the topics in the document set (Figure 4.24). Again, similar themes are grouped into neighborhood, while themes separated by larger distances are unlikely to be related. Analysts can use this tool to identify unanticipated relationships, and examine changes in topics over time. Users can identify themes and concepts found among thousands of pages of text, and then further explore areas of interest.

SPIRE was originally developed for the US intelligence community, and has a wide variety of potential applications. Corporations researching competitive products, health care providers searching patient records, or attorneys reading through previous cases could all benefit from the SPIRE technology. For example, a researcher could use SPIRE to find out the direction in which the United States was heading in breast cancer research. Drawing from a large, unstructured document base of information, the researcher uses SPIRE's visualization tools to automatically organize the documents into clusters according to their content similarities, and into thematic terrain according to the themes in the text. Observation of these thematic spaces over time will help the user to understand vast interrelated dynamic changes simply not possible to detect using traditional approaches.

This technology has been used on many topical and current issues of national security, and results have yielded insight into complex issues, with enormous time

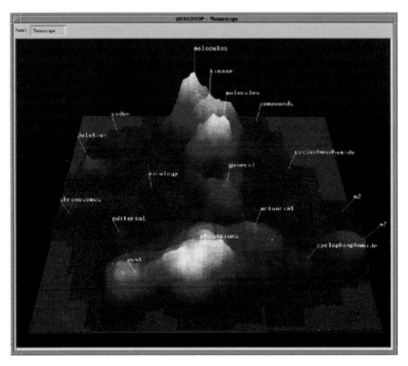

Figure 4.24 Thematic peaks and valleys in ThemeView™. Reprinted with permission of Beth Hetzler.

savings. Discovering trends, finding interrelationships among topics, and rapidly identifying key issues are all benefits of using SPIRE.

4.3.5 Starlight

The Startlight Information Visualization System was developed by the Pacific Northwest National Laboratory (PNNL). Starlight integrates information modeling and management functionality with a visualization-oriented user interface (Figure 4.25).

The designers of Starlight presented various scenarios of how Starlight can lead to a new style of data analysis based on multisource and heterogeneous data input. Starlight allows the analyst to assemble various elements of information into a coherent picture.

Figure 4.26 shows a Starlight visualization of a collection of approximately 1500 pages found by Google on *information visualization*. Nodes represent web pages, and edges represent hyperlink references among the pages. The majority of pages are from organizations who are actively engaged in information visualization research, chiefly universities. A collection of pages associated with the 2000 and 2001 IEEE Information Visualization conferences can be found in the upper left corner of the image. A group of pages from the site of publishers Morgan Kaufmann are also visible. The large collection of pages from the Union of International

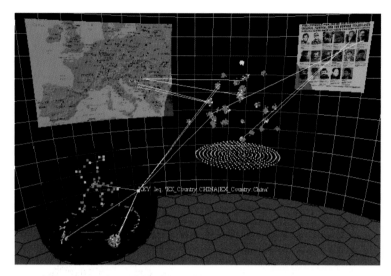

Figure 4.25 Starlight overview. http://starlight.pnl.gov. Reprinted with permission of John S. Risch.

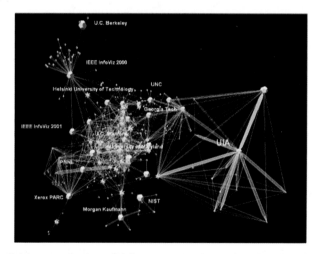

Figure 4.26 Starlight's network view of information visualization. Reprinted with permission of John S. Risch.

Associations (UIA) website suggests that UIA was apparently experimenting with techniques for visualizing its contents.

4.3.6 Self-organizing Maps

Self-organizing Maps, commonly known as SOMs, were developed by Teuvo Kohonen from 1982. The term *self-organizing* refers to the unsupervised learning approach in SOM. Today, SOMs have been used in a wide range of disciplines for data mining and data visualization. The strength of SOM is its ability to handle

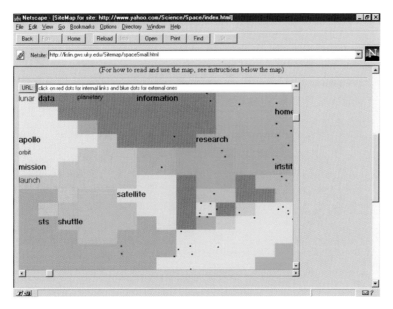

Figure 4.27 A SOM sitemap. Reprinted with permission of Xia Lin.

high-dimensional and non-linear problems such as feature extraction, image classification, and error-tolerant signal transmission in telecommunications.

There has been a growing interest in the role of SOM in visualizing documents. Lin et al. (1991) used SOM to cluster documents into various regions of a two-dimensional map. Each region is likely to contain documents that are similar to each other within the same region. Figure 4.27 is an example of Lin's work. The map shows documents drawn from the Science category at Yahoo! Words in the map. Labels such as lunar, Apollo, and mission indicate the general topics of the documents grouped in these regions.

ET-Map is another example of site maps on the web. It is a prototype Internet homepage categorization system developed at the University of Arizona (Chen, Houston, Sewell, and Schawtz et al., 1998), and aims to demonstrate a scalable, automatic, and concept-based approach to Internet homepage categorization and search. ET-map represents more than 100,000 entertainment-related documents on the web.

Figure 4.28 shows the top layer of a multilayered map, based on the contents of more than 110,000 entertainment-related homepages. These maps are generated automatically using artificial neuro-network techniques, and each layer has different subject regions. Larger subject regions occupy a larger space on the map, and conceptually related subjects are often grouped in close proximity. Regions which contain 100 URLs or more produce another map; regions which contain fewer than 100 URLs produce a ranked list of URL summaries. Figure 4.29 artistically illustrates how the user can use the ET-map in a search.

WebSOM is an application of the SOM techniques. It organizes textual documents for exploration and search. WebSOM has been used to map discussion groups and several other applications (Kohonen, 1998). Figure 4.30 shows the top level of a WebSOM map of a newsgroup on neural networks. Clicking in any area on the map will lead to a zoomed view (Figure 4.31). Color denotes the density or

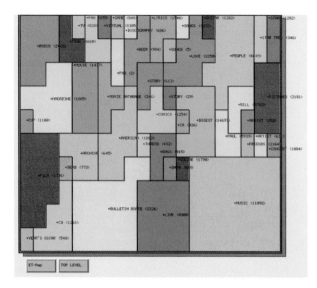

Figure 4.28 ET-map, a SOM map of over 100,000 entertainment-related web pages (Figure 4.39 in 1st edition). Reprinted with permission of Hsinchun Chen.

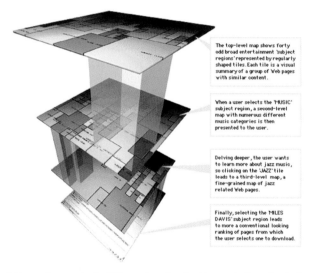

The top-level map shows forty odd broad entertainment 'subject regions' represented by regularly shaped tiles. Each tile is a visual summary of a group of Web pages with similar content.

When a user selects the 'MUSIC' subject region, a second-level map with numerous different music categories is then presented to the user.

Delving deeper, the user wants to learn more about jazz music, so clicking on the 'JAZZ' tile leads to a third-level map, a fine-grained map of jazz related Web pages.

Finally, selecting the MILES DAVIS' subject region leads to more a conventional looking ranking of pages from which the user selects one to download.

Figure 4.29 A multi-layered access in the ET-map. Reprinted with permission of Hsinchun Chen.

the clustering tendency of the documents: lighter areas are clusters, and darker areas are empty space between the clusters.

The most specific discussions are mostly found in the clearest "clusters", i.e. light regions surrounded by darker color. Near the edges of the map are typically the most "unusual" documents represented on the map. In the central areas, the discussions are more "typical", or may concern many different topics found on the map.

In a series of studies, Skupin (2002) developed a unique style of SOM maps. He integrated the SOM approach with traditional cartography and produced abstract

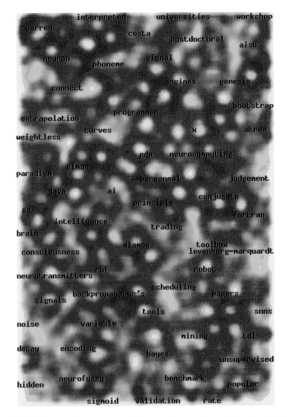

Figure 4.30 The top-level of a WebSOM map of comp.ai.neural-nets. Reprinted with permission of Samual Kaski. See Kohonen et al. (2000) for the most up-to-date descriptions.

SOM maps with the look and feel of an ordinary geographic map. For example, he visualized 2220 conference abstracts by simultaneously overlaying three levels of a hierarchical clustering tree of SOM neurons: 10-cluster solution (red); 25-cluster solution (green); and 100-cluster solution (black) (Figure 4.32). Cluster labels are scaled according to rank within the respective cluster.

Ontrup and Ritter (2001) introduced a new variation of SOM for visualizing high-dimensional text data. The new method is called the hyperbolic SOM. Figure 4.33 shows two screenshots of the hyperbolic SOM, in which ten different glyphs were used to represent the ten most frequent categories. The resulting hyperbolic SOMs are based on a tesselation of the hyperbolic plane and their lattice neighborhood reflects the hyperbolic distance metric that is responsible for the non-intuitive properties of hyperbolic spaces.

4.4 Focus + Context

When displaying a complex information structure in a limited viewing area, there is a tension between showing more low-level details and showing more

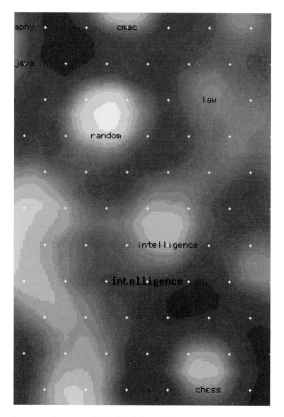

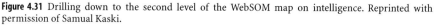

Figure 4.31 Drilling down to the second level of the WebSOM map on intelligence. Reprinted with permission of Samual Kaski.

high-level contextual information. The consensus is that users need to access both. The challenge arises when users need an easy access not only to local details of focal objects in a display, but also to global information that can help them stay oriented. The question is how to compromise the limited size of the drawing board. And the bottom line is that one has to prioritize what should be shown and what is not.

There are three general approaches to ease the tension: (1) overview + detail views – displaying overview and detailed information in multiple views, (2) zoomable views – displaying objects on multiple scales, also known as multiscale displays, and (3) focus + context views – displaying local detail and global context in integrated but geometrically distorted views. All these approaches have their strengths and weaknesses in terms of simplicity, ease of use, and overall effectiveness. The first approach becomes problematic when users have to move back and forth between the split displays of overview and detail. The second approach may temporarily lose the contextual information. The third approach may lose the sense of continuity if users switch their focal points drastically. It is necessary to consider remedies such as animating view-by-view transformations so as to smooth out potential cognitive pitfalls.

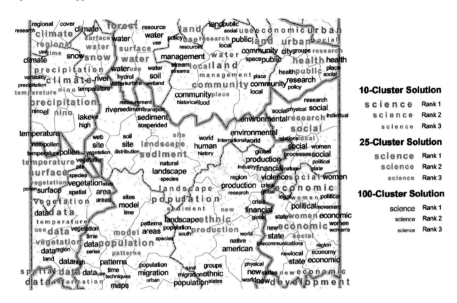

Figure 4.32 An abstract SOM map with the look and feel of an ordinary geographic map (Skupin, 2002). © 2002 IEEE. Reprinted with permission.

The most widely known examples of distorted displays include bifocal displays (Spence and Apperley, 1982), fisheye view displays (Furnas, 1986), the perspective wall display (Mackinlay, Robertson, and Card, 1991), and hyperbolic view displays (Lamping and Rao, 1996; Munzner, 1997, 1998a,b). The best example of multiscale displays is Pad++ (Bederson et al., 1996).

In general, a distorted display combines multiple scales in the same view; typically, the focal area is displayed on a finer scale, whereas peripheral areas are shown on coarser scales. In contrast, zoomable displays can change from one scale to another as the user zooms in or out, but it is often for the user to deal with one scale at a time. Studies of these approaches have been largely limited to hierarchical information structures. A recent evaluative study of hyperbolic view displays acknowledges some of the challenging issues if these techniques are applied to more complicated network structures (Pirolli et al., 2003).

Various strategies can be combined to achieve desired effects. An interesting addition is from a cartographic perspective: labels on a geographic map are often hierarchically organized and displayed such that country names are displayed in the largest font size, major cities' names in smaller font sizes, and smaller cities' names in even smaller font sizes. Some intriguing examples of cartographic-like visualizations are made by Skupin (2002).

4.4.1 Fisheye View

Furnas (1986) laid down the foundation of fisheye view displays. In particular, he formalized the definition of degree of interest (DOI) as a function to determine how fast the size of an object should be diminishing in a fisheye view. A fisheye

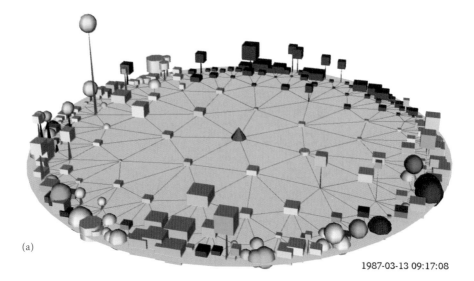

1987-03-13 09:17:08

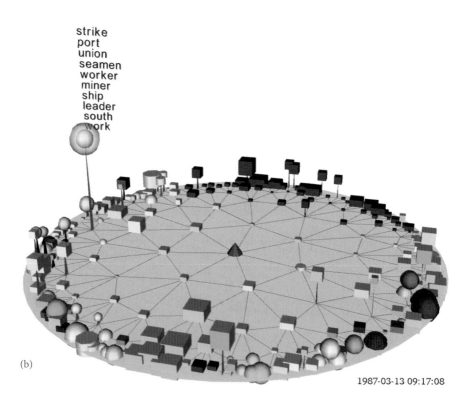

(b)

1987-03-13 09:17:08

Figure 4.33 Hyperbolic SOM for semantic browsing (Ontrup and Ritter, 2001). Reprinted with permission of Jörg Ontrup.

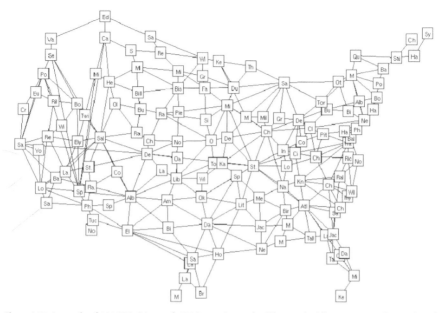

Figure 4.34 A graph of 134 US cities and 338 inter-city paths. The a priori importance value assigned to each vertex is proportional to the logarithm of population of the corresponding city (Sarkar and Brown, 1994). © 1994 ACM, Inc. Reprinted with permission.

view is indeed a combination of a perspective view and a semantic view. In general, remote objects look smaller than their counterparts near to the focal point; however, this rule can be overwritten by objects that have high DOI scores. A related concept is called semantic zooming. Sticky objects are another relevant concept; changing views or scales has no effect on the appearance of sticky objects.

Sarkar and Brown (1994) presented one of the highly cited works in fisheye view related visualizations. They used a graph of US cities to illustrate their fisheye view techniques. By comparing maps generated by various parameters, the power of a generalized fisheye view is easy to understand. Figure 4.34 shows a graph of 134 US cities and some inter-city paths. Figure 4.35 shows the same graph except that a fisheye view filter was applied.

Figure 4.36 shows an interesting 3D bi-focal fisheye view presented by Carpendale et al. (1997). The neighborhood of each focal point has a much lower density of nodes, which gives them higher readability.

4.4.2 Perspective Wall

The earliest version of the idea was demonstrated by Spence and Apperley (1982), showing messages as parallel strips on a computer screen. The width of each strip varies: the central strip is the widest, but surrounding strips are shrunk so that all strips can fit into the single display. Once the user selects a strip, it moves to the center and becomes a full-sized strip.

Mackinlay et al.'s Perspective Wall (1991) is a computerized, automated three-dimensional implementation of the bifocal display. A perspective wall has

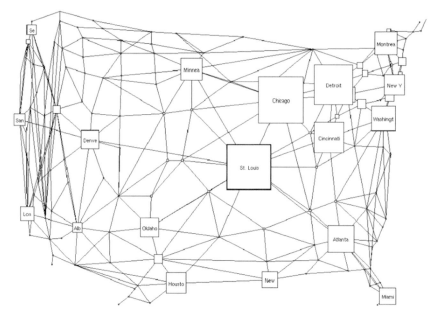

Figure 4.35 A fisheye view version of the graph in Figure 4.34. The important vertices are enlarged in this version, while the unimportant ones are shrunk (Sarkar and Brown, 1994). © 1994 ACM, Inc. Reprinted with permission.

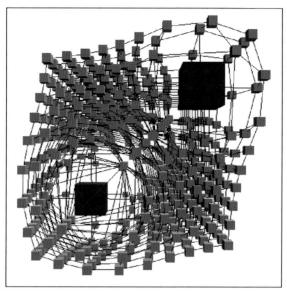

Figure 4.36 3D fisheye view (Carpendale et al., 1997). © 1997 IEEE. Reprinted with permission.

three panels. The central panel displays information that the user is currently focusing on. The two side panels, receding to the distance, form the context. The user can easily bring the information in the context into the focal panel.

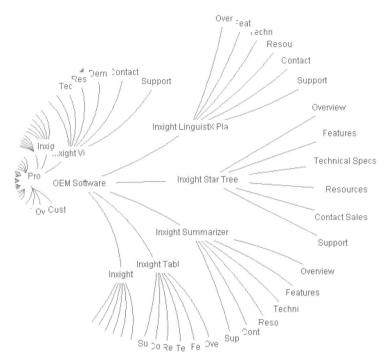

Figure 4.37 Inxight's hyperbolic display.

4.4.3 Hyperbolic View

Cone trees can display many more nodes on the screen than traditional two-dimensional tree diagrams, and can be rotated so that users can examine a node of a tree in the display more closely. However, in a Euclidean space, there is a limit to how large a cone tree can be squeezed into a display area without losing legibility.

Hyperbolic view displays are a relatively recent visualization technique for displaying a large hierarchical information structure developed at Xerox PARC (Lamping and Rao, 1995, 1996; Pirolli et al., 2003). The basis of a hyperbolic view is a mathematical model of a hyperbolic space. Hyperbolic models are suitable to display a large, unbalanced hierarchical structure. Hyperbolic views offer an elegant solution to the focus + context problem. Nodes at the center of the view are displayed in higher resolutions, whereas neighboring nodes are displayed in diminishing size. Users can select any nodes from the context into the center of the view and examine local details.

An increasing number of empirical studies appear in the literature with special focus on hyperbolic views' efficiency and accuracy. See Chapter 6 for more detailed discussions of empirical studies involving hyperbolic views as well as other information visualization features.

A significant extension of hyperbolic views is Tamara Munzner's Hyperbolic 3D viewer, or simply H3 (Munzner, 1997, 1998a,b). In Lamping and Rao's original design, a hyperbolic space is projected onto a two-dimensional disc. Munzner's H3 display projects a hyperbolic space onto a sphere. H3 trims a general network down

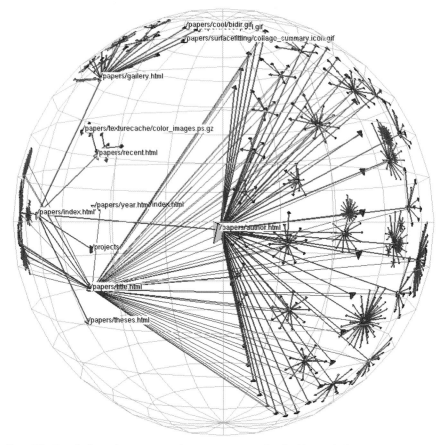

Figure 4.38 Hyperbolic 3D (Munzner, 1997). © 1997 IEEE. Reprinted with permission.

to a spanning tree as the backbone of the display, and subsequently embeds cone trees in a hyperbolic space. The hyperbolic space is eventually projected onto a sphere in a three-dimensional Euclidean space.

Spectacular spherical hyperbolic displays are produced by the Walrus tool developed by Young Hyun at CAIDA based on Munzner's work, although Walrus is independently implemented. Walrus' gallery is available on the Internet, containing still images as well as animations.[4] Walrus is implemented in Java3D.

4.4.4 Zooming User Interfaces

The term *zoomable user interface* (ZUI) is relatively new, although similar ideas and techniques have been used in computer systems for remote sensing image processing and geographical information systems for years. The most essential

---

[4]http://www.caida.org/tools/visualization/walrus/gallery1/

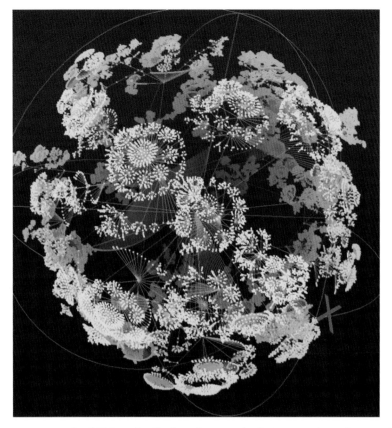

Figure 4.39 An example of Walrus visualization of a network of 535,102 nodes and 601,678 links. http://www.caida.org/tools/visualization/walrus/gallery1/lhr-old.png

requirement for a ZUI is that the user interface must allow the user to zoom in and out freely and easily, across various levels of detail.

One representative ZUI example is Pad++, a multiple scale display tool jointly developed by a number of universities, including New York University and the University of Maryland. A ZUI designed with PAD++ would enable users to zoom across a wide range of granularities. For example, one could design a ZUI of our universe and allow users to explore the universe at various levels. Users can infinitely zoom in and out: from an overview of our solar system, the earth, London, to a model of a human body, the human's heart, blood cells, and so on. A description of the design and evaluation of PAD++ in visualization is presented in Hightower et al. (1998). ZUI is closely related to the notion of multiscale interfaces, as introduced by Furnas (1997). The system resembles a fractal graphical user interface, in which one can explore structures infinitely.

The ability to move freely in a spatial user interface is a desirable feature of a modern information system. It is not uncommon to find information visualization systems incorporating virtual reality techniques to enable users to explore an information space in more intuitive ways. Many system designers and analysts choose to use open standard virtual reality techniques, namely virtual reality modeling language (VRML). Approaches based on open standards have the obvious advantages of easy exchange, and a wider community.

4.5 Visualizing Search Results

Many information visualization systems are designed to make information retrieval tasks easier, especially in terms of assessing the document–query relevance. The examples included in this section demonstrate how individual components can be usefully incorporated into a larger system.

4.5.1 Envision

Envision is one of the pioneering multimedia digital libraries of computer science literature (Fox et al., 1993; Heath et al., 1995). It includes publications of the ACM, and other literature to meet the needs of computer science researchers, teachers, and students at all levels of expertise. Envision was designed with full text searching and content retrieval capabilities. Search results from the Envision database can be visualized as a matrix of icons (Nowell et al., 1996), which enable users to assess the results of a search graphically, based on a variety of document attributes. For example, a year-by-relevance layout can reveal peaks and valleys of document– query relevance at a glance. The design of the Envision user interface uses colors and shapes to convey important characteristics of documents. The color of an icon indicates the degree of relevance: the most relevant documents in orange, documents marked by users as useful in red, and documents marked by users as not useful in white. A star icon indicates that the document is in the top 35% of relevance range; a diamond indicates its position in the next 35% of the range; and a triangle denotes a document in the bottom 30% of the range. The notion of peaks and valleys of relevance has also been used in more recent visualization systems, especially ones with various spatial metaphors.

4.5.2 TileBars

TileBars offers an intuitive and easily understandable display of query–document relevance in information retrieval (Hearst, 1997; Hearst and Karadi, 1997). The distribution of each term in a query is marked in corresponding positions in a document (Figure 4.40). Based on where a term occurs, the user can quickly decide the nature of specific query–document relevance. For example, if a term is evenly distributed throughout a document, then the document has some profound relations with the query. On the other hand, if the term only appears at the beginning of a document, then the document is probably only marginally related to the query. TileBars also enables the user to detect the context of term occurrences. For example, the tilebars of three sets of terms can be easily compared to determine the nature of their contexts.

Figure 4.41 shows the results of a search on "landmark" and "California", in an attempt to search for landmarks in California. The summary shows that there is

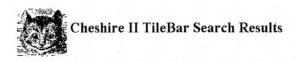

Figure 4.40 TileBars. Term distributions in documents are visualized (Hearst, 1995). © 1995 ACM, Inc. Reprinted with permission.

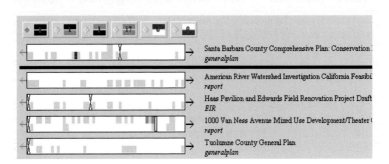

Figure 4.41 TileBar on the web.

Figure 4.42 NASA's neighborhood. Reprinted with permission of Tim Bray.

one strong co-occurrence of the two terms. For example, they may occur within the same sentence.

4.6 The Web and Online Communities

The World Wide Web (WWW) has sparked many challenging problems concerning information visualization, especially site maps or visualization of navigation trails. One of the earliest attempts to visualize the web was done by Tim Bray (1996). Here, websites are represented as ziggurats with globes on top: the diam-eter of the base indicates the number of pages, the height represents the visibility, the luminosity is denoted by the size of the globe on the top, and the domain of a site is color-coded.

Websites are placed in space, based on the strength of the linkages between them. Figure 4.42 shows the group of websites most closely linked to NASA (the red site in the middle). Government sites are colored in red, academic sites in green, and non-profit organizations in gold. CMU, where the Web Consortium site resides, provides a large number of outgoing links. NASA itself provides relatively few links to other sites.

Bharat and Broder (1998) estimated that by November 1997 the total size of the static web was 200 million pages, and search engines indexed only 160 million pages. It was estimated that Alta Vista indexed 100 million pages, Hot Bot 77 million, Excite 32 million and Infoseek 27 million.

The web is not only growing fast, but also changing rapidly. The average life span of documents on the web is around 50 days, broken links occur with 5–7% of access requests, and redirected links are between 13 and 19% of access requests.

4.6.1 Searching and Exploring the Web

Millions of users on the Internet are by now familiar with the fact that they have a variety of search engines at their disposal, but exactly how these search engines work behind the scenes still remains a mystery to them. Search engines tend to give little information to the user about why documents in the search results are indeed *relevant* to a search query; users must judge this for themselves.

Exploring the web, or information foraging on the web, for particular topical subjects across a number of web servers, is one area in which information

Figure 4.43 WebBook (Card et al., 1996). © 1996 ACM, Inc. Reprinted with permission.

visualization has been actively pursued. The following examples include search engines that use hypertext linkage to improve the precision of search results, as well as information visualization designed to help users to access information on the web in a more intuitive way.

One of the most in-depth public descriptions of a large-scale search engine to date is provided by Brin and Page (1998). They describe the now famous Google engine. Google now indexes 4.3 billion pages.[5] It aims to improve the precision of retrieval. A unique feature of the Google search engine is that information conveyed via hypertext links is heavily used to provide a better assessment of document–query relevance.

Google takes into account information reflected by hyperlinks on web resources, in order to improve the quality of search results. Such techniques can be used for searching resources that cannot be directly indexed, for example, Postscript files, images, computer software, and multimedia files.

An alternative to standard search engines' ranked lists of search results is to use information visualization techniques to represent a set of documents as a whole, so that users can explore an information space at their own pace. Such examples include IBM's WebCutter,[6] presented at the sixth WWW conference, Silicon Graphics' Site Manager (see also Hyperbolic 3D, discussed in Section 4.4.3), and WebQuery.[7]

The WebBook™ is a 3D interactive book of HTML pages. It allows rapid interaction with objects at a higher level of aggregation than pages. The WebForager™ is an application that embeds the WebBook™ and other objects in a hierarchical 3D workspace. Both designs are developed at Xerox PARC, intended as exercises to play off against analytical studies of information workspaces. Both WebBook™ and WebForager™ are explained in Card et al. (1996).

Figure 4.43 is a screenshot of WebBook™, which uses a book metaphor to organize web pages. A collection of web pages can be displayed as a collection using an augmented simulation of a physical book. 3D graphics and interactive animation are used to give the user a clear indication of the relationship between the pages of the book. Each page of the WebBook™ is a page from the web. The color of a link helps the user to distinguish a reference within the same book (red links) from a reference outside the book (blue links). Choosing a red link will animate the turning of pages to the desired page; choosing a blue link will close the current WebBook and look for the page elsewhere. If the page is in another

---

[5]http://www.google.com
[6]http://decweb.ethz.ch/WWW6/Technical/Paper040/Paper40.html
[7]http://www.cgl.uwaterloo.ca/Projects/Vanish/webquery-1.html

WebBook stored on a bookshelf, then that WebBook is opened and turned to the desired page. If the page is in none of the WebBooks, then the WebForager is used to display the individual page in the user's information workspace.

Figure 4.44 shows the WebForager workspace. This is arranged hierarchically (in terms of interaction rates) into three main levels:

1 a full-sized book or page is called a focus place, for direct interaction between the user and the content;
2 the desk and the surrounding space implies an immediate memory space, where pages or books can be placed when they are in use, but not the immediate focus, and
3 the bookcase represents a tertiary place where many pages and books can be stored.

4.6.2 Site Maps

Site maps are one of the most predominant applications of information visualization on the web. There is a wide variety, ranging from hand-made site maps, to automatically generated ones.

Figure 4.44 WebForager (Card et al., 1996). © 1996 ACM, Inc. Reprinted with permission.

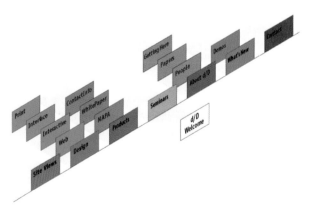

Figure 4.45 MAPA by Dynamic Diagrams. Reprinted with permission of Paul Kahn.

MAPA is a site map construction tool developed by Dynamic Diagrams. Figure 4.45 is a site map of their own homepage, generated by MAPA. The three-dimensional layout is based on existing hypertext links. MAPA relies on a web walker, or web spider to gather documents for pre-processing. Its design is a good example of a site map that is simple, clear, and easy to follow.

Figure 4.45 shows a screenshot of a site map created by MAPA for the java.sun.com website. To some extent the site map looks like several different types of cards placed on a table. Some cards represent pages containing higher level information, while some represent the pages themselves.

4.7 Commercial Systems

In this section, we present a swift tour of several commercially successful adventures of information visualization. The number of commercial information visualization systems is increasing. What is increasing even faster is the number of information visualization components embedded in a much wider range of commercial software products. We are particularly interested in successful knowledge transfer from the scientific community to the industry, including Spotfire and the bloom of treemaps-based commercial products.

In a special report entitled *Get the Picture* on January 12, 2004, The Wall Street Journal Online featured a few commercial visualization systems, including products from Spotfire and Antarctica Systems (Borzo, 2004). It is the time for information visualization techniques to play a more important role by saving time, identifying crucial connections, and maintaining a competitive edge. In this section, we first introduce some earlier commercial systems, then demonstrate the use of several more recent commercial systems, and finally summarize the commonality and uniqueness of these commercialization efforts.

4.7.1 Earlier Commercial Systems

AVS[8] – Advanced Visual Systems is a 12-year-old company specializing in data visualization products. It now has over 10,000 licensed users. One of its most known products is OpenViz, which is designed for corporate decision-makers and application developers. It supports visualizations through various interactive charts and highly integrated components.

Many software producers and venders have been increasingly integrating visualizing techniques into their commercial products. For example, DataDesk[9] has developed Viz!on ["vision"] as an Excel add-in for data exploration and visualization. SPSS/SigmaPlot[10] provides graphics components embedded in Microsoft Excel worksheets. Similarly, SAS/GRAPH®[11] software, the high-resolution graphics component of the SAS System, supports a wide range of color graphics capabilities,

---

[8]http://www.avs.com/
[9]http://www.datadesk.com/products/data_analysis/vizion/
[10]http://www.aspiresoftwareintl.com/html/sigmaplot.html
[11]http://www.sas.com/technologies/bi/query_reporting/graph/

including maps, charts, and plots. One can create choropleth maps, prism maps, and surface maps with SAS/GRAPH. The software also supports graphics editing, video editing and compositing, and batch processing of high-volume graphics.

The major difference between this group of commercial systems and research systems in the information visualization community is the number of ways available to the user to visualize, explore, and analyze data. Scalability, stability, responsiveness, and simplicity are evident in these systems and embedded visualization components. In addition, these systems are used in a wide range of application areas, although the majority of applications involve numeric analysis. In other words, semantic-based analysis and applications are still relatively rare.

4.7.2 Spotfire®

With 20,000 paying users at more than 500 sites, Spotfire[12] is surely a commercial success. Furthermore, Spotfire is one of the most successful examples of knowledge transfer and commercialization. One of the cornerstones of Spotfire's product line is the idea of dynamic queries (Ahlberg and Shneiderman, 1994). Christopher Ahlberg, Spotfire's CEO, co-founded Spotfire in 1996. Spotfire's customers are wide ranging, including companies in pharmaceuticals, biotechnology, chemicals, manufacturing, and semiconductors, and academic research institutions.

Spotfire® DecisionSite™ is Spotfire's flagship analytic application environment. DecisionSite enables users to access and merge data from a variety of sources and dynamically interact with this data through direct information interaction and analytical tools. Spotfire also has more specialized products, for example, DecisionSite for Lead Discovery for chemists, and DecisionSite for Functional Genomics for biologists.

Spotfire DecisionSite for Functional Genomics, for example, supports dynamic queries as pioneered in scatter plots, hierarchical clustering diagrams, three-dimensional plots of principal component analysis, and more specialized gene profile visualizations (see Figure 4.46). Spotfire's products support the fundamental need for data analysis and discovery; these products enable users to study data sets from a variety of sources in various perspectives and that leads to the discovery of insightful patterns. Spotfire enables its users to accomplish such tasks at ease. As Ben Shneiderman put it: "Spotfire is like a telescope for studying galaxies of data. It gives faculty and research staff unusual powers to explore and understand large data sets and, best of all, the chance to make discoveries of our own."

4.7.3 Inxight

Inxight[13] is one of the earliest commercialization adventurers capitalized on information visualization. It was founded in 1997 as a spin-off from Xerox PARC. Its business focus is on unstructured data management. Inxight has established an extensive network of 250 customers, especially in enterprise, government, publishing, and pharmaceuticals. Inxight's competitive edge is in part reflected by its

---

[12]http://www.Spotfire.com
[13]http://www.inxight.com/

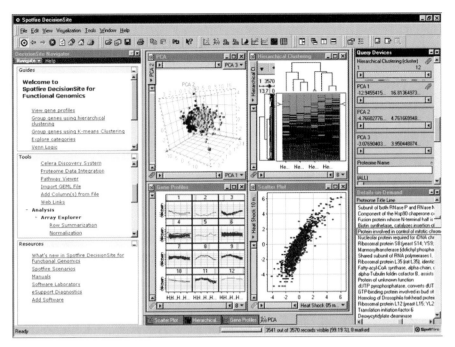

Figure 4.46 Spotfire DecisionSite for Functional Genomics. http://www.spotfire.com/academics/products-fg.htm

70 patents in information visualization, natural language processing, and information retrieval.

The hyperbolic tree visualization technique developed at Xerox PARC is one of the most notably techniques used in Inxight's products such as Inxight VizServer. VizServer is a scalable enterprise solution for visualizing and exploring large information collections. Inxight's website claims that with VizServer, users can locate information by as much as 62.5% faster than standard navigation methods. Chapter 6 covers empirical evaluations relevant to the hyperbolic view visualization.

Hyperbolic tree visualizations are tools for viewing hierarchical information. As we mentioned earlier, one of the most developed areas in information visualization is tree visualization. The following three examples are all about another tree visualization invented in early 1990s – tree maps. Tree map visualizations stand out on the horizon of the commercialization of information visualization research. The proliferation of tree maps in the commercial systems obviously benefits from the open source model associated with the tree map development at the University of Maryland. The first example, SequoiaView, is not a commercial product per se, but it is freely downloadable and provides an interesting reference point for other tree map implementations.

4.7.4 SequoiaView

SequoiaView is a disk browsing tool developed by the Department of Mathematics and Computer Science of the Technische Universiteit Eindhoven. SequoiaView 1.3

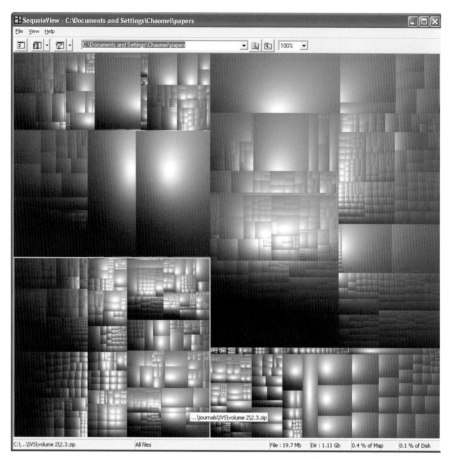

Figure 4.47 SequoiaView shows a cushion tree map of 5628 files and 667 folders in the papers directory on my desktop computer. The red rectangle frame highlights a zipped file containing manuscripts for volume 2 issue 3 of *Information Visualization*.

was launched in November 2002; I was the 267,185th visitor to download the software on January 23, 2004.[14]

SequoiaView implements the idea of cushion tree maps. Cushion tree maps were invented by Jack van Wijk to increase the readability of the original slice-and-dice space-filling tree maps. Each time a rectangle is subdivided, ridges are added. The result is a pattern of hierarchical cushions that show the structure in the directories and files (see Figure 4.47).

The user may control the height of the ridges as well as using lower ridges for deeper nested levels. Users can define different color schemes to facilitate identification of certain file types or apply a ready-made color scheme loaded from disk. For example, bitmaps could be colored in red, compressed files in purple, and so on.

The following two examples are both commercial products.

---

[14]http://www.win.tue.nl/sequoiaview/

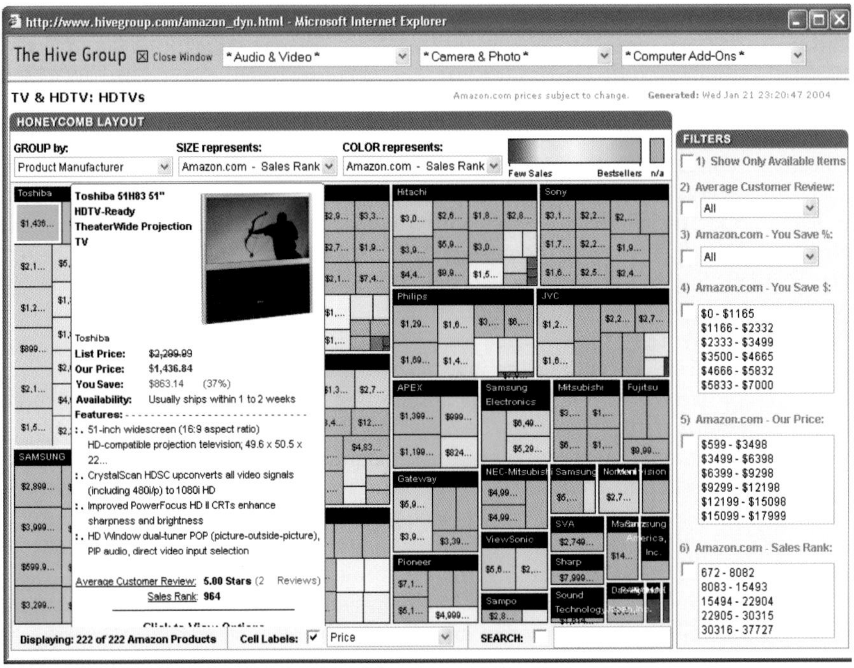

Figure 4.48 The Hivegroup tree map front-end to Amazon.com's TV section. Items are grouped by manufacture. Bestsellers are shown as larger-size and greener blocks.

4.7.5 Hivegroup

Hivegroup's Honeycomb is a tree map implementation for commercial use.[15] Honeycomb represents an interesting extension of the traditional use of tree map visualizations of file systems, although in a sense this is very similar to what SmartMoney has done, i.e. the size of a space-filling component can represent something other than the physical size of a computer file. Figure 4.48 shows the Honeycomb layout as part of a visual interface to the TV section on Amazon.com.[16] Items are grouped by product manufacture. The user controls what the size and the color mean. In this example, both the size and the color represent an item's sales rank, which is a popularity rank. If I am looking for a bestseller, I would be interested only in large and green areas. Such areas are quite easy to spot in the tree map-like layout. The upper left-hand corner and the lower right-hand corner appear to be the most interesting spots within each group. Honeycomb provides a very flexible set of controls over the visualization. The user may choose to use color to represent the amount of saving or the percentage of saving on each item.

4.7.6 ILOG

ILOG was founded in 1987. It has over $90 million revenues in 2003, 600 employees, and 2500 customers worldwide. ILOG's products provide comprehensive, flexible,

---

[15]http://www.hivegroup.com
[16]http://www.hivegroup.com/amazon_dyn.html

and extensible Java, .NET and C++ graphics libraries and visualization compon-
ents[17]. ILOG Visualization Suite includes ILOG JViews, ILOG JTGO, and ILOG
Views Component Suite for C++ GUIs. Furthermore, ILOG Server and ILOG DB
Link provide support for C++ and Java.

JViews[18] is ILOG's premium suite for delivering high-end interfaces. It includes
a number of extensible packages, including a Graph Layout package, a Maps package, and several other packages. The Graph Layout package[19] is 100% written
in Java, supporting rendering functions based on Java 2D. The package's open API
allows developers to extend and customize their own algorithms and applications.
For Java developers, JViews provides a strategic extension to Java Swing package
with extensible graphics visualization components. There is a 15-day free trial version available. At the starting price for $3000, this is a very attractive product for
network visualization. There is an even better deal for non-commercial research.
ILOG offers licenses for research. A single-user full-featured and full-powered
license of JViews costs $995.

ILOG Views Component Suite is another example that unifies interactivity, flexibility, and comprehensiveness of visualization in an integrated environment. For
example, it supports interactive 2D graphics, charts, map data reading and man-
aging, graph layout management, standard dialog controls, connections to databases
or XML, and interactive scheduling and planning.

ILOG[20] Discovery[21] includes a tree map visualization tool called File System
Analyzer. As we have seen earlier in this chapter, the original idea of tree map was
invented in early 1990s as a space-filling algorithm to visualize hierarchical information (Johnson and Shneiderman, 1991; Shneiderman, 1992). Figure 4.49 is a
screenshot of File System Analyzer, showing a tree map view of 5633 files and 666
folders under the papers directory on my computer.

4.7.7 OmniViz

OmniViz, Inc.[22] was founded in 2000 as a subsidiary of Battelle Memorial Institute.
It offers a number of visualization and decision support products to the life
science, healthcare and chemical industries. OmniViz uses some of the widely
known visualization techniques developed at PNNL, such as GalaxyView and
ThemeView. Unlike hyperbolic views and tree map visualizations, OmniViz's products are designed to deal with unstructured data, which are not necessarily a tree
structure.

On July 29, 2003, Thomson ISI ResearchSoft and OmniViz announced a visualization tool RefVizTM. RefViz allows users to explore bibliographic data and move
between RefViz and other products from ISI ResearchSoft, for example, EndNote®.
The stated goal is to enable users to find major themes and topics in reference
literature.

---

[17]http://www.ilog.com/products/visualization/
[18]http://www.ilog.com/products/jviews/
[19]http://www.ilog.com/products/jviews/graphlayout/
[20]http://www.ilog.com
[21]http://www2.ilog.com/preview/Discovery/
[22]http://www.omniviz.com

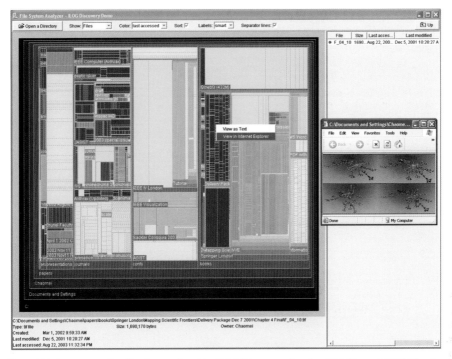

Figure 4.49 A tree-map visualization produced by ILOG Discovery, showing 5633 files and 666 folders in the *papers* directory on my desktop computer. Recently accessed files are in brighter colors. Files can be viewed either as text or with Internet Explorer.

RefViz is designed as text analysis and visualization software. Figure 4.50 is a screenshot of RefViz 1.0. Its user interface consists of a visualization window, a keyword analysis window, and a reference window. I tested it on a data set of 1,463 bibliographic records on visualization. RefViz provides two options for visualizing these records: Galaxy and Matrix. Records are lumped into groups based on the similarity of their words. There are three ways to select records in the Galaxy display: (1) mouse click on individual items, (2) cast a rectangle capturing area, and (3) use quick search. Selected items appear in the reference window, including their group numbers and other standard bibliographic information. Keywords used in these items are displayed in three lists: primary, secondary, and other descriptive terms. The groups are determined by the primary and secondary keywords. Although access is relatively easy and the software is responsive, the galaxy overview does not seem to be powerful enough to reveal trends and associations in references. There are at least two issues RefViz needs to resolve: (1) Bibliographic records are too short as source text. As a result, the binding power based on term similarity is weak. (2) The vocabulary of keywords appears to be too large, which may further reduce the discriminating power. For example, as shown in the figure, terms such as technique, computer, method, user, information, result, new, data, study, technology, analysis are too broad to mean much to the user in a science and technology context. Nevertheless, this is an impressive start and it has a huge population of potential users. Given the amount of effort in information visualization research, the commercialization rate still appears to be lower than one would expect. If RefViz can

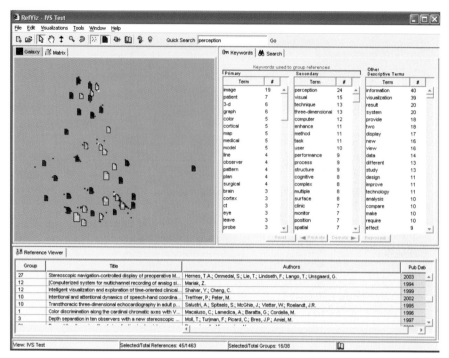

Figure 4.50 RefViz 1.0. The upper left window shows a galaxy visualization. The upper right window shows three lists of keywords, among them the first two lists of keywords determine the groupings of bibliographic records. The lower window lists the selected records, which are also highlighted in the galaxy view.

improve its techniques and capitalize on its unique market position, it may just realize its full potential in the near future.

4.7.8 Grokker™

Sometimes more is less, and some other times less is more. The whole, as it quite often turns out, is more than the sum of its parts. To a Gestalt psychologist, this is Gestalt; to a philosopher, this is holism. In Robert Heinlein's 1961 science-fiction novel *Stranger in a Strange Land*, Grok is a Martian word. To grok something is to look at everything from a holistic perspective, so much so that the observer eventually becomes part of the observed. This was what motivated the development of Grokker™ – the knowledge mapping and information visualization tool by Groxis, Inc.[23] The company was founded in 2001. It currently offers a 30-day free trial of Grokker 2.0. Its purchase price is $49.

Grokker is a Java program, so it works across Windows and Apple systems. It organizes and displays search results in recursively embedded layers of circles and squares. Grokker automatically categorizes individual items into categories. Circles are categories of items, which may be circles of categories themselves further down

---
[23]http://www.groxis.com

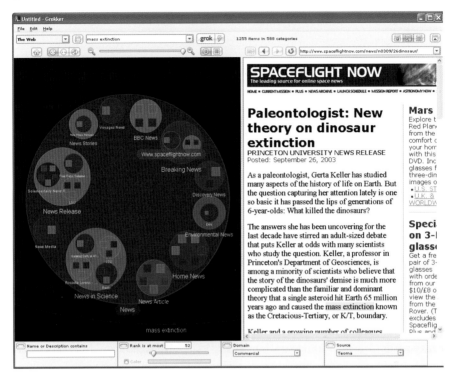

Figure 4.51 Searching the web with *Grokker2* on mass extinction – breaking news, one of the 1255 items in 588 categories made by *Grokker*.

or squares of files. Categories and items have labels. One can drill down by clicking within a circle, or step back by clicking outside the circle. A square is a dead-end. Grokker 2.0 can search the web, the Amazon bookstore, and the local computer.

Figure 4.51 is a screenshot I took as I grokked with the web for "mass extinction". I first drilled down to the Breaking News and then jumped back to its parent category News. Placing various webpages into clearly labeled category circles certainly makes the search easier than scrolling down a list of uncategorized items, although zooming out from a crowded layer of circles could be adventurous – it may take a split of second to locate where you were a moment ago and it would be more comfortable if you could see your own footprints. It harnesses hierarchical structures simply and clearly, but what happens to those horizontal hyperlinks? Probably no one ever wants to see spaghettis of hyperlinks anyway, but someone like me might be obsessed to know what happens to them: whether they are evaporated, absorbed, or still out there? Nevertheless, Grokker 2.0 is an impressive product. It is scalable and fun to use. The best feature I like about Grokker is its incremental filing. Category circles are being filled as new items arrive so that the user can see right away as the overview map evolves.

Rivadeneira and Bederson (2003) reported a controlled experiment, in which fifteen subjects used three interfaces for typical search tasks: Grokker, Grokker Text, and Vivisimo's textual clustering product. All participants were students at the University of Maryland. One example search in the experiment was: "Find in which city and on what date was the Super Bowl played for the 1998 season." Their

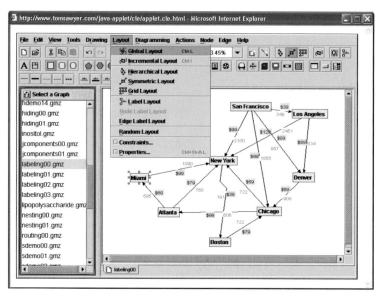

Figure 4.52 Tom Sawyer Software's Graph Editor Toolkit for Java.

experiment identified some very interesting issues. No significant differences were found for performance measures in terms of efficiency and accuracy. Some of Grokker's design problems became apparent; for example, because a visited circle is not marked, subjects tended to make unnecessary revisits to the same clusters. And the meaning of a circle's color was also found to be a mystery. More interestingly, participants' preferences, satisfaction, and sense of accomplishment were strong enough to distinguish the three. Vivisimo was the favored choice. Given that users' preferences and satisfaction tend to play a greater role in the success of a commercial product, formal empirical evaluations can identify deficiencies that may hinder the success of commercialization.

4.7.9 Tom Sawyer Software

Tom Sawyer Software[24] is a long-established provider of graph visualization products. Its products are used by Global 2000 companies to build applications in a variety of industries including bioinformatics, engineering design, intelligence, and networking.

The Graph Editor Toolkit product allows the user to customize both the display and the interactive behaviors of an application using industry standard components, such as toolbars, menus, and mouse-event handling. The Graph Editor Toolkit class libraries are also a valuable resource. The Graph Layout Toolkit product provides portable and flexible components that can be integrated with database, display, and graphics software. Figure 4.52 shows Graph Editor Toolkit for Java.

---

[24]http://www.tomsawyer.com/

Compared to ILOG's products, including JViews and the Graph Layout package in particular, Tom Sawyer Software continues its traditional specialization in graph visualization; all its products are graph-centered. In contrast, ILOG's visualization suites have a broader range of tools such as maps and charts as well as databases. Maps and charts are among the most widely used information representations. In today's competitive world, ILOG's approach may have a better chance to reach more potential customers. Recently, a number of remarkable open source graph visualization projects began to emerge, especially TouchGraph as we mentioned in Chapter 3. If the commercialization follows a similar pattern to tree visualization systems, we can expect to see an increase of commercial systems for graph visualization.

In summary, we may observe what these contemporary information visualization systems have in common and how they differ. In general, the majority of successful and widely accepted commercial systems are designed for general-purpose applications in which core tasks are numeric and statistical analysis. Tree visualizations are the most mature in information visualization research, so it is no surprise that they also dominate the commercialization. Visualizations of less structured data such as graphs have also seen some promising open source projects. We expect these open source projects will lead to further commercialization.

Empirical studies of information visualization have been underrepresented. Evaluations of commercial systems are even rarer. Further to his study of three commercial visualization systems in 2001 (Kobsa, 2001), Kobsa recently reported a study of five tree visualization systems with Windows Explorer as a baseline system (Kobsa, 2003). The five systems he used are Maryland's Treemap 3.2, SequoiaView 1.3, BeamTrees, Star Tree Studio 3.0, and TreeViewer. The results of his study suggest that none of the systems significantly improved user performance beyond the baseline set by Windows Explorer. Integrating into the existing work environment is regarded as a crucial factor that has to be taken into account. This is in line with our analysis of earlier commercial systems in that they are all well integrated into work environments. New commercial systems need to take integration into account.

4.8 Online Resources

The major sources of information visualization literature include the IEEE symposium and conferences on information visualization. The publications of the ACM, especially SIGGRAPH, SIGIR, and SIGCHI, include the most influential works in this field.

There are a number of excellent websites focusing particularly on information visualization. For example, the Atlas of Cyberspaces[25] is a website maintained at the Centre for Advanced Spatial Analysis (CASA), University College London (UCL). It was launched as a dissemination project in spatial analysis, and provides a wide range of reference information and image galleries on information visualization.

The On-line Library of Information Visualization Environments[26] (Olive), created by a class of students at the University of Maryland, includes comprehensive bibliographical information, as well as brief summaries of various techniques.

---

[25]http://www.cybergeography.org/atlas/atlas.html
[26]http://www.otal.umd.edu/Olive/

A comprehensive literature review of 3D information visualization was given by Peter Young (1996) on the web. This review is a technical report of the Department of Computer Science at the University of Durham.

4.9 Summary

This chapter has introduced a number of information visualization systems with applications in several categories. It has drawn attention to how a particular information visualization mechanism can be adapted to meet various requirements from users. For example, cone trees have been used in several systems with different design rationales, such as LyberWorld, Cat-a-Cone, and Hyperbolic 3D.

One section has been devoted to the design of systems based on a spatial metaphor. This metaphor will form the basis for further discussions in subsequent chapters on virtual environments. An extended example of visualizing the literature of hypertext was used to demonstrate the flexibility and extensibility of the methodology of GSA.

One key feature that distinguishes works such as Social Web and Collaborative Browsing from general-purpose chat rooms or even virtual-reality-based environments is the motivation of gathering together. In Social Web, visitors are interested in the co-presence of others, because it is the topical content that attracts these people to visit a web page in the first place. In these cases, the motivation is social navigation – to follow like-minded people. In contrast, the lack of depth in many chat rooms and 3D virtual environments probably results in differences in the dynamics and structures of social interaction.

Before we continue to explore how social navigation and virtual environments may converge in Chapter 7, Chapter 6 will focus on the role of human factors in the use of information visualization techniques. Three empirical studies will investigate the impact of individual differences on information retrieval and foraging with spatial metaphors. Cognitive factors such as spatial ability and associative memory are explored. In Chapter 5, we introduce an emerging area of research where the unit of analysis could be a topical area itself or even an entire discipline.

Chapter 5
Knowledge Domain Visualization

A rock pile ceases to be a rock pile the moment a single man contemplates it,
bearing within him the image of a cathedral.

Antoine de Saint-Exupery

The unit of analysis essentially determines the kind of questions one would ask. So far, our discussion has essentially focused on individual documents in an existing collection, a web locality, or a set of search results. In this chapter, we present examples that focus beyond the role of documents as a bag of words. In some examples we will see, the unit of analysis could be a scholar in a scientific field. In other examples, the unit of analysis could be a specialty behind a moving cluster of documents. Now we are not merely interested in the tasks of finding a document relevant to a query; rather, we are more interested in the movement of intellectual groupings of documents in a broader context and over a longer period of time.

In Chapter 4, we have seen the thematic spaces can be characterized by terms found in documents, for example, "oil", "OPEC", and "crisis". An alternative way of identifying thematic trends and predominant research areas in a field is by studying how peer scientists have referenced relevant publications in scientific literature. This is in effect a voting system in which scientists vote by their decisions and preferences reflected in their publications. In this chapter, we introduce the emergent field of Knowledge Domain Visualization (KDViz). We begin with author co-citation analysis (ACA) and demonstrate how ACA can lead to insightful visualizations of the structure of a dynamic research field. Secondly, we explain how document co-citation analysis (DCA) provides a method to capture the dynamics of scientific paradigms.

5.1 Mapping Science

In *The Unfinished Revolution*, Dertouzos (2001) told a story about the troubles encountered by his son when searching the web for information on Vespas, the Italian scooters that conquered Europe in the 1950s – how he had to deal with the 2545 hits returned by the search engine, and how he had to *squint* his eyes and *labor* his brain so he could quickly decide whether to shove away the next item on his hit list. To Dertouzos the shoveling is simply the sum of two faults: the *manual labor fault* and the *information access fault*. The former refers to the lack of automation on today's web and in all of today's computer systems. According to Dertouzos, "We do not yet off-load human brain work and eyeball work onto our machines. We shovel and shovel, doing by ourselves mental labor we shouldn't have to do." The latter refers to our inability to get at the information we need when we need it.

Compared with what scientists have to do with their own fields, Dertouzos's son should consider himself lucky – all he had to do was to shovel 2545 hits once and for all. Imagine the scooter-equivalent search task for a scientist. Suppose our scientist works on the topic of mass extinction, a fascinating topic on which one can argue about almost anything. There are many theories of what caused the mass extinctions in the past. There is a traditional debate between catastrophists and gradualists. The catastrophists believe that a mass extinction was likely to be the result of a catastrophic event, whereas the gradualists believe that Rome is not built in a day and there is evidence that a mass extinction may be a longer term process.

Surrounded by such competing and conflicting theories and various interpretations, in the early years of his career, our scientist must assemble different pieces of existing works in the field into his domain picture, sometimes with conflicting pieces. He would feel lucky if he has a list of item to go through because the field involves several disciplines such as geology, astronomy, and paleontology. The key questions on his mind would be: what has been done in this field and what is new? Several years down the road in his career, he has established a mental picture of the field, but what he wants to know is essentially the same: what is new and has anyone made progress on a particular problem? Given the mass extinction debates, the questions are more likely to be: what is the latest progress from the point of view of a catastrophist?

Our scientist has to deal with the manual labor fault not once, but repeatedly throughout his career as a scientist. Between the two shovel seasons, he wants to know: how does this field differ from the one three months ago? More importantly, he knows that, among other things, science is a social phenomenon in that fellow scientists' views count and peer scientists' recognition matters. No matter whether he is dealing with the three million hits on Google, or 5000 hits in the Web of Science – ISI's web portal for citation indexing databases – one thing is certain: the manual labor fault does not go away and it does not even get better.

Astrophysicists have the Hubble Telescope to study remote stars and galaxies – they are the unit of their analysis. Biologists have the microscope to examine the microcosms – the unit of their analysis. Why do scientists not have a viewfinder to their own fields? Why cannot scientists videotape the evolution of their own fields, their paradigm shifts, the rises of their own stars and the expansion of their own galaxies of intellectual contributions? How can KDViz help? What does a domain roadmap look like? How does KDViz tip the balance between the brain work and the eyeball work?

Indeed, in his *Little Science, Big Science* Derek Price (Price, 1963) suggested that the science of science should learn from thermodynamics. The behavior of gas is influenced by various conditions of temperature and pressure. Thermodynamics is not particularly concerned with the trajectory of a specific molecule; rather, it concentrates on the phenomenon as a whole. Price suggested that one should study science in a similar way in terms of the volume of science, the trajectory of "molecules" in science, the way in which these "molecules" interact with each other, and the political and social properties of this "gas". The seminal work *Networks of Scientific Papers* (Price, 1965) studies the intellectual structure interwoven between scientific papers.

In 1974, Small and Griffith examined issues concerned with identifying and mapping specialties from the structure of scientific literature, especially based on co-citation patterns (Small and Griffith, 1974). In 1977, Small conducted a longitudinal study of collagen research and found that rapid changes of focus took place in this research (Small, 1977). He computed co-citation strengths between pairs of documents and grouped documents into clusters to represent leading specialties, or paradigms. Rapid shift in research focus is evident when a number of key documents abruptly disappear from the leading cluster in one year and they are replaced by a set of new documents in the following year. This is an important type of specialty change, which is an informative indicator of "revolutionary" changes. More recent studies in related areas include Braam et al. (1991a, b), Garfield (1994) and Small (1997, 1999a, b).

In *Mapping Scientific Frontiers* (Chen, 2003), I examined the origin of various visual representations of scientific activities and their profound implications on the quest for knowledge visualization. Through multidisciplinary integrations of information visualization with citation analysis, domain analysis, sociology of science, and philosophy of science, mapping scientific frontiers now becomes a vibrant and promising field. Knowledge Domain Visualization, or KDViz, is a unifying field that addresses generic questions across a wide range of scientific disciplines. In this chapter and later chapters, we demonstrate that scientific disciplines are not only predominated by scientific paradigms that can be detected through citation patterns, but competing paradigms are also an integral part of the evolution of most if not all scientific disciplines. Scientific frontiers are the boundaries between the known and unknown. Controversies, debates, mysteries, and unsolved puzzles are the norm rather than exceptions. KDViz provides an invisible camera to reveal the footprints of such controversies and debates in scientific literature.

5.1.1 Scientific Revolutions

Scientific networks, including scientific collaboration networks, citation networks, research fronts, and knowledge diffusion networks, have been the central subject of several fields of study, notably complex network theory in theoretical physics, scholarly communication and knowledge domain visualization in information science and information visualization. Scientific networks are large, constantly changing, and practically significant: the citation databases compiled by the Institute for Scientific Information (ISI) alone receive one million new publications and 20 million new citations each year; scientific networks evolve in terms of emerging hubs and authorities, competing paradigms, diffusion, and phase transition; and scientific networks have profound connections to a broad spectrum of scientific, technological, social, and economic activities.

The theory of the structure of scientific revolutions by Thomas Kuhn (1962) is one of the most influential works in the 20th century. Before Kuhn's work, philosophy of science was largely predominated by logical empiricism, which emphasizes the logical structure of science rather than its psychological and historical development. Kuhn criticized that the logical empiricism cannot adequately explain the history of science. He claimed that the growth of scientific knowledge is characterized by revolutionary changes in scientific theories.

According to Kuhn, most of the time scientists are engaged in normal science. A period of normal science is typically marked by the dominance of an established framework. The majority of scientists would work on specific hypotheses within such frameworks, or *paradigms*. The foundations of such paradigms largely remain unchallenged until new discoveries begin to cast doubts over fundamental issues. As anomalies build up, attention is suddenly turned to the validity of assumptions that scientists previously took for granted – this marks a period of crises. To resolve the crises, radically new theories with greater explanatory power are introduced. New theories replace the ones in trouble in a revolutionary manner. Science regains another period of normal science. Scientific revolutions, as Kuhn claimed, are an integral part of science and science progresses through such revolutionary changes.

In order to visualize scientific paradigms, we must have a clear understanding of the key characteristics of a paradigm. Margaret Masterman (1970) examined Kuhn's own work and found that Kuhn used the term in several different connotations, including sociological paradigms, metaphysical paradigms, and problem-oriented paradigms. She suggested that problem-oriented paradigms are central to Kuhn's philosophical system.

In Kuhn's theory, a revolution is often associated with a Gestalt switch. A Gestalt switch defines a turning point in a paradigm shift. It is often enlightening if one can see things from a different perspective or a different angle. Thagard (1992) uses the term conceptual revolution to describe structural changes of scientific knowledge.

To Kuhn, paradigm shifts lead to scientific revolutions. As anomalous results accumulate, scientists need to find a better theory of greater explanation coherence (Thagard, 1992). Can we expect to find distinctive traces of conceptual revolutions in scientific literature? If Gestalt switches take place in science, can we identify them in citation networks? Furthermore, can we unfold the evolution of a citation network over time by way of animation and visualization?

5.1.2 Invisible Colleges

Generations of scientists have been influenced by works such as Thomas Kuhn's structure of scientific revolutions (Kuhn, 1962), Paul Thagard's conceptual revolutions (Thagard, 1992), and Diana Crane's invisible colleges (Crane, 1972). Two significant threads of efforts are particularly worth noting here. One is the work of Eugene Garfield and Henry Small at the Institute for Scientific Information (ISI) in mapping science through citation analysis. The other is the work of Michel Callon and his colleges in tracking changes in scientific literature using co-word analysis (Callon, Law and Rip, 1986). In fact, their co-word analysis is designated for a much wider scope – *scientific inscriptions*, which includes technical reports, lecture notes, grant proposals, and many others as well as publications in scholarly journals and conference proceedings. See Chen (2003) for more detailed analysis of these examples. What are the central issues in a prolonged scientific debate? What constitutes a context in which a prevailing theory evolves? How can we visualize the process of a paradigm shift? Where are the rises and falls of competing paradigms in the context of scientific frontiers? What are the most appropriate ways to visualize scientific frontiers?

To apply science on science itself, we need to understand the nature of scientific activities, the philosophy and the sociology of science. The so-called *visualism* in science says that what contemporary scientists have been doing in their daily work is, in essence, to visualize, to interpret, and to explain (Ihde, 1998). What is the metaphor that we can use to visualize scientific frontiers?

There have been persistent efforts to derive a computational mechanism that can help scientists to track down critical changes in the development of scientific knowledge. Paul Thagard (1992) proposed a computational approach to the study of conceptual revolutions. He argued that a finer-grained theory of revolutionary change than Kuhn's theory would avoid the trap of irrationalism, which has been the most vulnerable part in Kuhn's theory. Thagard placed his own approach in the middle of a scale which has the formal approaches of the logical empiricism at the one hand and Kuhn's historical ones at the other. Thagard's computational approach is driven by artificial intelligence. The primary purpose of such approaches is to clarify the structural characteristics of conceptual systems *before*, *during*, and *after* conceptual revolutions.

Thagard's central claim is that it is best to explain the growth of scientific knowledge in terms of what he called *explanation coherence*. The power of a new paradigm must be assessed in terms of its strength in explaining phenomena coherently in comparison with existing paradigms. He explained what happened to the theory of *continental drift* as an example of a conceptual revolution. A concept system represents part-of and kind-of relations between conceptual components at various levels. The continental drift theory is a conceptual revolution that involved structural changes.

5.1.3 Citation Networks

Studies of citation networks can be divided into three categories: (1) pioneering studies of citation networks before the 1980s, (2) emergent knowledge domain visualization studies since the late 1990s, and (3) statistical mechanics studies over the last two years. Although there appear to be an increasing number of studies integrating the first two categories, few studies have addressed fundamental issues concerning a potential cross-fertilization between the last two categories.

Derek Price (1965) found that the more recent papers tend to be cited about six times more often than earlier papers. The citation rate of a paper then declines. He suggested that scientific literature contains two distinct parts, a classic part and a transient part, and that the two parts have different half-lives. The make-up of these two parts varies from field to field; mathematics, for example, is strongly predominated by the classic part, whereas the transient literature rules in physics. Furthermore, he introduced the notion of research fronts – the collection of highly cited papers that represent the frontiers of science at a particular point of time. Based on an examination of citation patterns of scientific papers, he conjectured that it is possible to identify objectively defined subjects in citation networks. He particularly emphasized the significance of understanding the nature of such moving frontiers in the development of a quantitative method for delineating the topography of current scientific literature.

In the 1970s, Small and Griffith examined issues concerned with identifying specialties by mapping the structure of scientific literatures, especially through analyses of co-citation networks (Small and Griffith, 1974). Small subsequently found rapid changes of focus in collagen research (Small, 1977). Documents clustered by their co-citation links can represent leading specialties. The abrupt disappearance and emergence of such document clusters indicate rapid shifts in research focus. By tracing key events through a citation network, Hummon and Doreian (1989) successfully reconstructed the most significant citation chain in the development of DNA theory. Their study has great impact on subsequent studies of citation networks in the graph drawing community (Batagelj and Mrvar, 2001; Brandes and Willhalm, 2002).

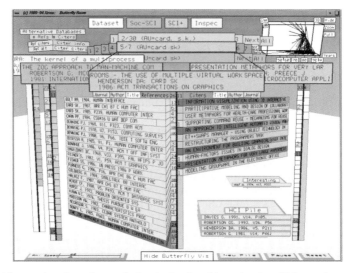

Figure 5.1 The user interface of Butterfly for citation-based browsing (Mackinlay et al., 1995). © 1995 ACM, Inc. Reprinted with permission.

Butterfly is an example of a citation network visualization (Mackinlay et al., 1995). Butterfly was developed at Xerox PARC as a graphical user interface to access bibliographical records stored in DIALOG, and designed to work particularly with bibliographic resources such as Science Citation Index, Social Science Citation Index, and INSPEC. The user interface of Butterfly is shown in Figure 5.1.

The head of the butterfly is the article of the focus. The two wings are associated with two types of citations: the left wing contains the original references cited by the focal article, while the ring wing lists articles that cite the current article. The following examples will show that citation and co-citation indices provide a valuable source for information visualization. The unit of analysis can range from individual documents to people who have contributed to the literature of a subject domain, and emergent patterns may be identified through visualized citation structures.

The number of studies in KDViz is increasing (Chen et al., 2002; Chen and Kuljis, 2003; Chen et al., 2001a; Davidson et al., 1998; White and McCain, 1997, 1998). The basic assumption is that the intellectual structure of a scientific community or a subject domain is identifiable through the dynamics of corresponding citation networks. By modeling and visualizing how citation structures change over time, one can explore and better understand how a knowledge domain evolves. KDViz will enable us to investigate the evolution of a knowledge domain in a much more comprehensive way.

Redner (1998) found a power-law degree distribution, with an exponent of 3, in two large citation networks. He suggested that the citation distribution is an appealing venue for theoretical modeling. Katz (1999) demonstrated that the rich-get-richer phenomenon can be accurately characterized by power laws based on citations as well as on the publishing size of a scientific community. This scale-invariant relationship holds at various levels, from national to institutional and even individual. Katz (1999) demonstrated that the conventional impact indicator gives a distorted view of the UK's science impact and how a power law distribution can help to improve the accuracy of a citation impact indicator. Small-world network properties as well as power-law degree distributions were found in scientific collaboration networks (Newman, 2001b). In a study of the evolution of scientific collaboration networks in physics and biology, Newman (2001a) found that the number of collaborators in common between scientists is a good indicator of the rate of their joint publications, and the more collaborators a scientist has, the more likely it is that they will develop a new one. An et al. (2001) found power-law obeying in-degree citation distributions in three different areas of computer science. Standard graph-theoretic algorithms failed to decompose the citation network because of a large well-connected component. They recommend more sophisticated algorithms such as balanced graph partition algorithms for such large well-connected components (Charles and Mattheyses, 1982; Kernighan and Lin, 1970). They suggested that the evolution of citation networks is a good candidate for predicting research trends and for studying the life span of scientific communities. However, no attempts were made in studies in this category to visualize the citation networks or collaboration networks in question.

The aim of mapping a scientific discipline is to identify sub-fields or specialties of research, and their interrelationships within the scientific discipline (Garfield, 1994). The following examples focus on research areas predominant in the field of hypertext and the use of author co-citation maps to visualize the literature of hypertext. We now need to find out whether author co-citation maps can be used to structure the literature in a similar way to SPIRE's themescape: the visualization is concerned not only with individual documents, but also thematic topics and predominant research areas that may emerge across individual documents.

5.2 Author Co-citation Analysis

Author co-citation analysis focuses on interrelationships among influential authors in the literature, instead of on individual publications. White and McCain (1998) present an extensive author co-citation analysis of information science, based on publications in 12 key journals in information science over a 23-year period (1972–1995). The top 120 authors were selected for the study according to citation counts. Several maps were generated for the top 100 authors in the field, using multidimensional scaling (MDS), and a factor analysis was conducted to identify major specialties in information science, which revealed that information science consists of two major specialties with little overlap in their memberships: experimental retrieval and citation analysis.

Author co-citation is a more rigorous grouping principle than typical subject indexing, because the connectivity is based on repeated and collective views of subject experts expressed in their publications (White and McCain, 1998). Authors cite for a variety of reasons in various contexts. An important hallmark for research is whether or not it can make an impact on researchers in the same field. In addition, author co-citation analysis should help us to interpret and understand computationally constructed visualization structures.

A number of author co-citation analyses have used multidimensional scaling techniques to depict the co-citation patterns. However, this option is often limited by the capacity of multidimensional scaling routines implemented in statistical packages such as SPSS. For example, White and McCain (1998) noted that they had to limit the visualization to the top 100 authors in their study, because 100 is the maximum number of authors that can be handled by multidimensional scaling in the current version of SPSS. In this analysis, we were able to include 367 authors in our map without compromise.

Two sets of data were used in the analysis to delineate both the structure of the hypertext literature and the structure of the hypertext field. First, the structure of the hypertext literature was derived from all the full papers published in the entire ACM Hypertext conference series (1987–1998). Most electronic copies of these papers were available from the ACM Digital Library, and the rest were retrieved from the ACM Hypertext Compendium, which covers the 1987, 1989, and 1991 conference proceedings. The title, the names of authors, and the abstract of each paper were included in the final collection for content-similarity analysis. This collection was automatically analyzed and modeled with generalized similarity analysis tools, particularly LSI and Pathfinder network scaling techniques (Chen, 1998a, b; Chen and Czerwinski, 1998), and the resultant model rendered in VRML 2.0.

The second data set includes author co-citation counts based on all the papers in the conference series (1989–1998), with the exception of the first conference in 1987. In addition to full papers, the second data set also included data derived from short papers. Author co-citation counts were computed for all the authors cited five times or more during the whole period. This selection criterion resulted in a pool of 367 authors for the entire period. In order to discover significant advances and trends in the history of the field, the series of nine conferences were grouped into three sub-periods, each consisting of three consecutive conferences. Author co-citation matrices were generated for the three sub-periods using the same criterion. 196 authors were short-listed for Period I, 195 authors for Periods II and III.

Factor analysis was conducted on SPSS for Unix Release 6.1, because of the size of the overall author co-citation matrix, and the computation-intensive nature of the analysis. Following White and McCain (1998), the raw co-citation counts were transformed into Pearson's correlation coefficients using the factor analysis, which were used to measure the proximity between authors' co-citation profiles. Self-citation counts were replaced with the mean co-citation counts for the same author. In the factor analysis, principal component analysis with varimax rotation was used to extract factors. The default criterion, eigenvalues greater than one, was specified, to determine the number of factors extracted. Missing data were replaced by mean co-citation counts for corresponding authors.

Pearson's r was used as a measure of similarity between author pairs, because, according to White and McCain (1998), it registers the likeness in shape of their co-citation count profiles over all other authors in the set. Pearson correlation matrices were submitted to the GSA environment for processing, including Pathfinder network scaling and VRML-scene modeling. Three sub-period data sets were analyzed with the same methodology.

5.2.1 Author Co-citation Maps

The overall author co-citation map included 367 authors who had made an impact in the field of hypertext over the decade 1989 to 1998. This map is annotated by hand in Figure 5.2, based on automatically displayed node labels. The map is essentially a connected graph, based on various computational algorithms used and our experiences in similar visualization models. For example, a node on the main spine of the map is likely to belong to a much larger number of shortest paths connecting two nodes in the graph than to a leaf node. Thus, a spinal node often

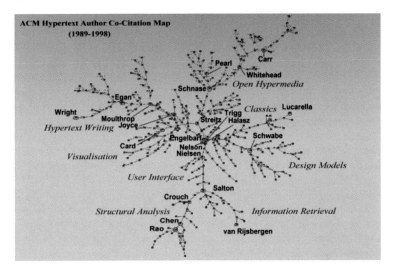

Figure 5.2 An overview of an author co-citation map derived from the ACM Hypertext conference proceedings (1989–1998).

plays a more significant part in mediating different nodes than a leaf node. One may expect to find a highly cited article near to the centre of the map.

Indeed, names such as Engelbart, Nelson, Halasz, Trigg, and Streitz appear near to the centre of the map. Many major groups of authors are connected only because of these centrally positioned authors. For example, if we remove Streitz from the map, many of the insights into the interrelationships among several clusters of authors would be lost. This example also illustrates the role of the triangular inequality condition used in Pathfinder network scaling.

We know that nodes near to the centre of the map are more essential to the field of hypertext in terms of co-citation patterns. Branching nodes are also significant in identifying the sub-fields of hypertext. We particularly verified branching nodes, and used our knowledge about them to suggest the nature of a specialty, which typically includes all the authors in the branch. Eight major specialties can be identified from the map:

- classics
- design models
- hypertext writing
- information retrieval
- open hypermedia
- information visualization
- structural analysis
- user interface.

In Figure 5.2, Salton is at a branching position, via which three branches are connected to the central spine of hypertext. Salton's work in information retrieval and automated hypertext generation is well known in both information science and hypertext. We also checked leaf nodes of these branches, as they represent some unique characteristics. We found that the leaf node of the far right branch is van Rijsbergen, whose name is prominent in information retrieval; it then became apparent that this branch represents a specialty with strong connections with information retrieval, and therefore called the information retrieval specialty.

This map is incorporated into an interactive user interface on the WWW. Users can click on the name of an author in the map and follow links to the corresponding bibliographical entry of the same author. It was actually used in the exploration of the map and verification of various citation details. More thematic groups can be identified and discussed using this method.

The following analysis focuses on the evolution of the hypertext field over three 3-year sub-periods since 1989. The predominant authors in each period are identified, based on author co-citation maps, and patterns are compared across periods.

Figure 5.3 includes three author co-citation maps: Map A for 1989–1991, Map B for 1992–1994, and Map C for 1996–1998. Map A includes 196 authors with five or more citations during the first period. We followed the links from the map to detailed citation information and found that authors were clearly grouped with reference to papers describing hypertext systems, which are all well known today, including NoteCards, Intermedia, KMS, and Microcosm. A specialty of information retrieval was already in place in the first period.

The second period, 1992–1994, is predominated by SEPIA, a collaborative hypermedia system developed at GMD in Germany. The central area of Map B is occupied by six members of GMD. In this map, Pearl became the branching node for the microcosm group. Leggett and Pearl's branches appear on the same major branch. We have identified an open hypermedia specialty in the overall author co-citation map, indicating the emergent open hypermedia specialty. Remarkably, Salton and Croft are not in the same major branch in this map.

The latest period ranges from 1996 to 1998. During this period the WWW has dominated many areas of research and development, including hypertext. We expected author co-citation analysis in this period to reveal an emergent specialty of the WWW, given the apparent influence of the rapid advances of the web and the growth of the WWW as a research field. However, this is not clear from Map C. There may be a number of reasons to explain the absence of a WWW specialty

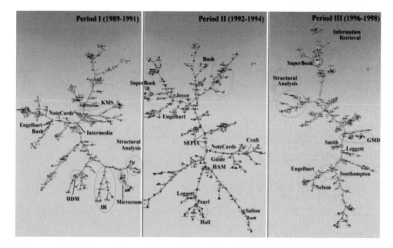

Figure 5.3 Three periodical snapshots of the evolution of the hypertext field: Map A (1989–1991), Map B (1992–1994), Map C (1996–1998).

in the citation data, for instance, the existence of the WWW conferences, and preferences for journal publications. The influence of the WWW is so profound that it may be difficult to single out a specialty in the field of hypertext, and we thus need to examine the citation details more thoroughly. For instance, mapping the literature of related disciplines collectively, such as the WWW and digital libraries, is likely to lead to more insights. The information retrieval specialty is located towards the north of the map, and the structural analysis specialty is located to the west of the map.

5.2.2 A Semantic Space of the Hypertext Literature

Figure 5.4 shows a screenshot of the semantic space derived from 269 full papers published in the ACM Hypertext conference proceedings throughout the decade 1987 to 1998. The latent semantic space was rendered in VRML 2.0. In this VRML model, each sphere represents a paper published in one of the ACM Hypertext conference proceedings. The colors of the spheres indicate the "age" of corresponding papers: those in the earlier years are darker, and those in recent years are lighter. A light-colored cluster of publications may reveal emergent research areas, whereas darker clusters near to the centre of the semantic structure may indicate classic research areas in the field of hypertext.

In addition to the overall semantic space, the example in Figure 5.4 incorporates the results of a search returned by LSI. The search query included three terms: "visualization", "spatial", and "map". The results are represented by red spikes vertical to the global structure. The higher the spike, the more similar the document. The locations of spikes reveal two major clusters of papers relevant to the search. The cluster at the far end is relatively new because it has many recently published

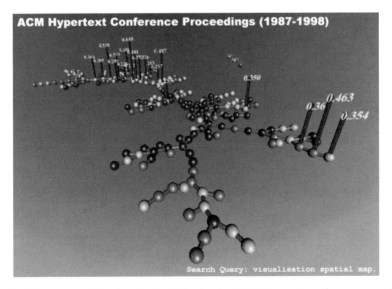

Figure 5.4 A latent semantic network of articles in the ACM Hypertext conference proceedings (1987–1998).

documents (lighter colored ones), whereas the cluster at the near end includes papers published some years ago.

The centre of the semantic structure is occupied by a large number of dark spheres, which indicate papers published in the early years of the ACM Hypertext conference series. Many of them are classic citations in the hypertext literature. This pattern suggests that papers near to the centre of the structure may play an important role in connecting papers across different areas. In the subsequent author co-citation analysis and associated co-citation maps, this pattern becomes even stronger and more intuitive.

Factor analysis extracted 39 factors from the co-citation matrix of 367 authors. These factors explain 87.8% of the variance. The top four factors alone explain 52.1% of the variance. In terms of specialties, these four factors imply some substantial sub-fields of study in hypertext. These specialties will be discussed further with reference to author co-citation maps.

In order to understand the nature of each specialty associated with an identified factor, we rank the authors according to their loadings on each factor, and categorize the corresponding specialty according to the profiles of the top 20 authors. Of course, we could describe a specialty more accurately if we had more detailed information about the nature of a particular co-citation pattern, for example, which particular piece of an author's work was referred to by citing authors.

Based on the list of top 20 authors in each factor, one can further identify the nature of each factor. The names in the Factor 1 column are well known to the hypertext community, and represent the impact of classic hypertext systems. Therefore, we named Factor 1 as "Classics". The nature of Factor 2 is also apparent – we can easily recognize the names of authors whose work was focused on information retrieval, for example, Salton, Crouch, and Sematon. The third factor includes names such as Rao, Pitkow, and Jones. We suggest that this factor is about graphical user interfaces, and probably an information visualization-related specialty. The membership of the fourth factor is clearly about links and linking mechanisms, especially the Southampton group. In the following discussion on author co-citation structures, we will identify further specialties, based on topological patterns suggested by the co-citation maps.

5.3 Tracking the Growth of Knowledge

Incorporating information visualization techniques into the study of scientific paradigms is not only a challenge to information visualization research but also a challenge to the advancement of a range of scientific disciplines. In the following example, we draw upon Kuhn's paradigm shift theory, an understanding of citation networks, and visualization and animation techniques to address the question: how can information visualization techniques help us understand the dynamics of a scientific paradigm? We choose to visualize the development of string theory over the last two decades in an attempt to replicate significant paradigmatic changes in visualization models. String theory, as one of the hottest topics in physics, went through conceptual revolutions twice over the last 20 years: once in the mid-1980s and again in the mid-1990s. We apply various visualization and animation techniques in order to capture the dynamics of the underlying paradigms. For example, several levels of transparency are used to depict the formation of highly influential and strongly connected articles and associated state transition flows. The study shows

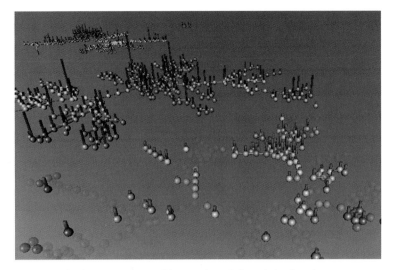

Figure 5.5 A citation landscape is an extensible metaphor of a knowledge domain.

informative and promising results. The work has implications on new ways of studying scientific paradigms and visualizing the evolution of a specialty. Figure 5.5 shows an example of the growing citation landscape metaphor.

5.3.1 Building an Invisible Camera for Invisible Colleges

The problems of scientific communication can be understood in terms of interaction between a complex and volatile research front and a stable and much less flexible formation communication system. The *research front* creates new knowledge; the formal communication system evaluates it and disseminates it beyond the boundaries of the research area that produced it. The research front is continually evolving and developing, which makes it difficult for anyone to keep abreast of new findings in a research area solely through the articles appearing in the formal communication system. In 1972, Diana Crane argues scientific knowledge is diffused through invisible colleges (Crane, 1972). Research has shown that when scientists experience difficulties in finding information through formal communication channels, the lack of contextual knowledge of where a particular piece of information belongs in a relatively unfamiliar area is often the reason. Derek Price was a pioneer in proposing that citation study can establish a conceptual map of current scientific literature (Price, 1965).

String theory, as one of the hottest topics in physics, went through conceptual revolutions twice over the last 20 years: once in the mid-1980s and again in the mid-1990s. We apply various visualization and animation techniques in order to capture the dynamics of the underlying paradigms. We expect that the additional temporal dimension to visualization models of citation networks may better reveal the dynamics of the development of a scientific paradigm.

When the term *information visualization* was coined in 1989, it was inspired by the idea of applying *scientific visualization* techniques to abstract information spaces. Information visualization focuses on the use of interactive techniques that can transform data, information, and knowledge into a form from which the human visual system can easily perceive its meaning (Robertson et al., 1993).

In 2001, *Communications of the ACM* devoted its entire August issue to "Visualizing Everything". In particular, Gershon and Page (2001) echo the issue raised by Robertson in their article "What storytelling can do for information visualization". They described how storytelling might influence the future of information visualization.

Chen (2003) examines the nature of constellations in order to uncover insights into the use of metaphors for information visualization. Some of the questions most interesting to knowledge visualization are: what is the role of mythic stories behind these constellations? How can we connect a story and an image in general? If a picture is worth thousands of words, can an image tell a story all by itself? A real challenge in information visualization is to find an informative metaphor that can serve as a vehicle to transform non-spatial and non-numerical information into an effective visual form (Chen, 1999a).

In information visualization, a few display and organizing metaphors are particularly appealing at the microscopic level, the macroscopic level, or both. For example, there are several widely used spatial metaphors: in a metaphor of the universe, information is organized as galaxies, clusters, or superclusters; in a constellation metaphor, information is structured like a star map; in a landscape metaphor, information is shaped into peaks and valleys. There are also a number of temporal metaphors, such as timeline.

Among these metaphors, the landscape metaphor and the constellation metaphor are by far the most popular choice of designers, although empirical studies are needed to establish which metaphor works for given tasks. For example, a three-dimensional landscape model is widely known through the work of ThemeView™ (Wise et al., 1995). A network representation relies on a more abstract metaphor. Everyone recognizes a landscape, but not everyone can make sense of the meaning of a network or graph easily. The landscape metaphor is good at conveying spatial relationships, whereas the network is appropriate for representing abstract structures.

What is the best metaphor for revealing the structure of knowledge? What works best to represent the growth of knowledge? In the early days of computer graphics, each new rendering algorithm must pass the "teapot" test by rendering the famous teapot data set. In the early days of scientific visualization, it has its own "teapot" – the storm. The storm shows the evolution of a storm. An intuitive hallmark of a good information visualization is the "Ah ha!" effect, which represents the moment when the intended meaning of a metaphor is recognized. What is the teapot for information visualization? Perhaps it is the three-dimensional cone trees; or perhaps it is the three-dimensional hyperbolic trees. Visualizing scientific paradigms is perhaps more closely related to scientific visualization than traditional information visualization in that one expects to see a "storm" more than a "teapot".

An underlying theme in Chen (2003) is mapping scientific frontiers by revealing the dynamics of the development of scientific knowledge. What we are looking for in such scientific frontier maps is the development of a significant line of research. There are three general models of scientific knowledge growth: (1) the cumulative growth model, (2) the random growth model, and (3) the revolutionary model. The cumulative growth model portrays a cumulative progression of new ideas developing from antecedent ideas in a logical sequence. The acceptance of a theory is simple: either in or out, with no room for ambiguity. As a result, there could be no disagreement among scientists. The random growth model, however, suggests that new ideas could sprout anywhere across the entire history of a cultural area. This type of highly unstructured growth is regarded as characteristic of the humanities. The revolutionary model, notably Kuhn's theory, describes the growth of knowledge as periods of continuous cumulative growth interspersed with periods of discontinuity. In Kuhn's terminology, periods of cumulative growth are normal science. The disruption of such cumulative growth is characterized by crisis or revolution.

5.3.2 Visualizing Scientific Paradigms

Until recently, KDViz research has focused on the construction of static snapshots of citation and co-citation structures rendered in a landscape metaphor (Chen and Paul, 2001). The landscape metaphor extends the notion of thematic maps in cartography, where a thematic map consists of a geographic base map and a thematic overlay. The layout of the geographic base map is stable, and so is the thematic overlay. Studying ways in which to depict the growth of scientific paradigms has led us to consider the following three-dimensional model concerning the dynamic and static properties of a visual–spatial model.

A landscape–network model has three degrees of freedom. The structure of the base network can be dynamic or static, depending on whether new nodes and new links can be added to the network. The base network can also be dynamic or static – if the displayed network structure is a function of time. Finally, the citation impact, the shape of the landscape, can be dynamic or static as a function of time. The following formal definitions summarize the structure of our methodology.

Let V, E, T, $Color$, Tr, S_V, S_E, and N denote various sets. In particular, V is a set of vertices; E is a set of edges; T is the time; $Color$ is a set of color values; Tr is a set of transparency levels; S_V is the state space of a vertex, for example if a vertex represents an article, it can go through publication, citation, and co-citation states; S_E is the state space of edges, for example, if an edge represents a co-citation link, it can have states such as pre-citation, pre-co-citation, and co-citation; and finally N is the set of all natural numbers. The $(+)$ operator denotes that one can incrementally add individual components to the main model.

$$\lambda_{Structure}(V, E): V \times E \to V \times E$$
$$\lambda_{Partition}(V, E): V \times E \to (V \times Color) \times E$$
$$\lambda_{Unfold}(t): V \times E \times T \to V \times E$$
$$\lambda_{Transition}(t): (V \times S_V \times Tr) \times (E \times S_E \times Tr) \times T \to (V \times Tr) \times (E \times Tr)$$
$$\lambda_{Citation}(t): V \times T \to N \times Color$$
$$Model = \lambda_{Structure} \oplus \lambda_{Partition} \oplus \lambda_{Unfold} \oplus \lambda_{Transition} \oplus \lambda_{Citation}$$

$\lambda_{Structure}$ denotes a set of structural mapping functions, which transform a theoretical graph to a sub-graph. Examples of such functions include a minimum spanning tree (MST) and Pathfinder network scaling. $\lambda_{Partition}$ denotes a set of functions that divide a graph into a number of regions and color each region using a pre-defined color map. λ_{Unfold} denotes a snapshot function, which generates a snapshot of a graph at a particular time point. $\lambda_{Transition}$ denotes a set of state-transition functions. Transitions of vertices from one state to another are shown through different levels of transparency of these vertices. $\lambda_{Citation}$ is a set of functions for generating citation bars in the visualization.

Structural information can be extracted from a variety of association measures, such as co-citation, co-word, or co-descriptor. In our experience, structural information can be concisely represented as a Pathfinder network, which maintains the strongest connections in the original network. The landscape is shaped by the citation impact of each individual article. The color of each year's section in the citation bar indicates the recentness of citations: the darker the color, the earlier the citations were made. Identifying a landmark in such knowledge landscape becomes a simple task: a tall citation bar with a large number of segments in bright color is likely to be a landmark article in the given knowledge domain. In our approach, the membership of specialty, sometimes also known as a sub-domain, or a theme, is colored according to the results of factor analysis.

Chen (2003) demonstrates the use of citation-based approaches to knowledge domain visualization and presents in-depth analysis of several puzzle-solving cases, in particular, including debates between competing theories on the causes of dinosaurs' extinctions, the power sources of active galactic nuclei, and the connections between mad cow disease and a new variant of human brain disease.

As part of our long-term research, we have conducted a series of studies in an attempt to identify the ways to capture and reveal tell-tale features of the growth of scientific knowledge derivable from scientific literature. We have developed prototypes using color-mapping overlay to reveal the membership distribution of specialties and using animated annual citation bars to depict the growth of citation impact (Chen et al., 2001a, b, 2002; Chen and Paul, 2001).

Currently, all articles above the citation threshold are shown throughout the range of years covered. Similarly all the significant co-citation links selected are shown instantly. Feedback from domain experts and knowledge workers has highlighted some potentially significant improvements over the current design, especially given the perspective of supporting visual exploration of the dynamics of scientific paradigms.

5.3.3 A "Continental Drift" Metaphor

Although animated citation bars vividly represent the growth of citation impact of individual articles, it is of more profound significance if the visualization and animation can depict the dynamics of the development of scientific knowledge at a larger granularity, just as Price suggested the behavior of gas in thermodynamics rather than the trajectories of individual molecules. In other words, it would be much more challenging but rewarding if we could see the forest out of individual trees. The thematic overlay provides limited mechanisms towards this goal. Now the question is: can we do better to uncover underlying groupings in an intuitive and meaningful way?

The refinement of our landscape model of knowledge growth is based on an analogue of Wagner's continental drift. Predicting what is the next discovery has always been a fascinating idea, but rarely practical. Instead, we choose a retrospective approach to look at the immediate past of science advancements. If our strategy works, then we can do it frequently and repeatedly so as to proximate as closely as possible to what the contemporary scientific literature conveys.

Figure 5.6 is a sketch of our strategy. As scientific paradigms grow, clusters of articles appear as if they form an intellectual continent. The changing course of a

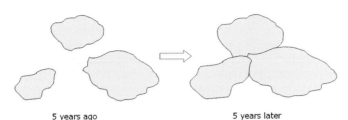

Figure 5.6 Intellectual continental drift? A visualization of scientific paradigm should depict the evolution of a paradigm over time in an intellectual context. Source: Chen and Kuljis (2003).

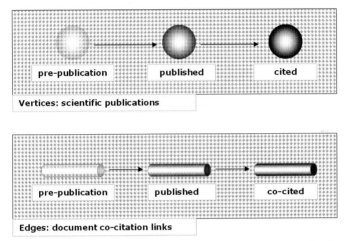

Figure 5.7 Visual attributes are designed to convey the status of a publication. The earlier the status of an article in the historical scene, the more transparent it is rendered in the virtual reality scene. Source: Chen and Kuljis (2003).

paradigm would be best depicted by a sequence of pictures of the intellectual world across a time interval. A very useful feature of Pathfinder networks is that the most significant and relevant work tends to be located in the center of its Pathfinder network representation, whereas other relevant but less predominant work appears at the outskirts of such networks.

The key to our refined visualization and animation is the use of transparency-based encoding in order to represent transitions between various states of citation and co-citation of articles in the scene. Each article in the scene can go through three states: prepublication, publication, and first citation (Figure 5.7). Similarly, a pair of articles also have three related states: one article in the pair cited, both articles get cited but may not be co-cited, and the two articles are co-cited.

5.4 Case Study: String Theory

String theory is one of the most active areas of research in physics. In string theory, the traditional notion of a point particle is replaced with a string, which is either a line segment or a circle. Strings can be open or closed loops. The vibrations of strings and their interactions with the topology of the space where they exist dramatically simplified the representations of various particles. Scientists are very interested in string theory because it provides a promising vehicle to study bosons, which are the particles that carry forces, and fermions, which are the particles that make matter. The trajectory of a particle is a worldline in spacetime, whereas the trajectory of a string is a worldsheet in spacetime. String theory requires a Minkowski space of 10 or more dimensions.

5.4.1 Two Superstring Revolutions

It has been recognized that there have been two superstring revolutions over the last two decades. The first superstring revolution took place between 1984 and 1985. The second superstring revolution started in 1995. See Schwarz (1996) for a historical account.

In 1997, *Science Watch*® selected the top ten most cited physics papers in its November/December issue. Four of them are about string theory (Mitton, 1997). Edward Witten, of the Institute for Advanced Study, Princeton University explained to *Science Watch* the significance of these string theory papers. For example, by mid-1995 it had become clear that a new kind of miniature black hole called a Ramond-Ramond (RR) charge was important in the general understanding of string theory. Joe Polchinski's paper (Polchinski, 1995), ranked as the number two of the top ten physics papers, solves two significant problems at once: the inclusion of RR states in string theory and the interpretation of RR charged solitons arising in the context of string duality. Polchinski's paper quickly received many citations. By August 1997, *Science Watch* found 167 citations, which is quite high for a purely theoretical paper.

In Witten's own paper, ranked as number 6, he used the new understanding from Polchinski to address an important question in type IIB superstring theory, and introduced gauge theory techniques. This paper has led to much activity on the role of black holes in string theory as well as renewed vigor in the attempt to understand string theory as a theory of quantum gravity.

In 1999, *Science Watch* produced another report (Mitton, 1999). Once again, four of the top ten most cited physics papers are string theory papers. The impact of the second superstring revolution is evident even more strongly in the second round of ranking, which shows that theorists in physics are now deeply involved in a new superstring revolution. For example, papers ranked at the sixth and ninth positions both deal with Dirichlet brane (D-brane) descriptions of black holes. These two papers are the first to explore the relation between two very different descriptions of how D-branes stack up. It is an important step towards showing that the two are different descriptions of the same object.

The tenth paper is on M-theory. There used to be five string theories before the second superstring revolution. Later on, theoretical physicists discovered that what they once thought were completely different theories are in fact different ways of looking at the same theory. The "Holy Grail" for string theory is to unify all theories into one theory. The theory behind all five string theories is called M-theory. As for what M stands for, it is intentionally left open, for example, M as in the mother of all theories, magic, and matrix.

The Scientist's predictions based on their citation analysis was that if the Nobel Prize were awarded for work on the string theory, the prize could be shared by Michael B. Green of Queen Mary College in London, John H. Schwarz of the California Institute of Technology in Pasadena, and Edward Witten of Princeton.

Green and Schwarz are often recognized for having revitalized string theory. Two of their influential and highly cited papers appeared in the mid-1980s (Green and Schwarz, 1984, 1985). Witten, as the leading proponent of the superstring theory of unification, is the most cited physicist in terms of total citations for the period 1981–1988.

The history of string theory has many "bizarre twists and turns" (Schwarz, 1996). String theory arose in the late 1960s in an attempt to describe strong nuclear forces. It was active for about five years before it ran into theoretical difficulties, and QCD came along as a convincing theory of the strong interaction.

In 1971, it was discovered that the inclusion of fermions – particles that make matter – requires word-sheet *supersymmetry* (Ramond, 1971). This led to the development of space-time supersymmetry, which was eventually recognized to be a generic feature of consistent string theories, hence the name "superstring".

Strings can join and split. There is a massless string state that has spin too. In 1974, Joël Scherk and John Schwartz showed that this particle interacts like a graviton, which opened up string theory to include general relativity. Instead of throwing this massless particle out, they realized that they could touch the problems of string theory and turn them into "gold" – now string theory can possibly achieve much more than was originally expected as a theory of hadrons (Scherk and Schwarz, 1974).

We choose string theory in this study because it is a good candidate for us to detect the presence or absence of a Gestalt switch in the meaning intended by Kuhn in visualization models. As a result, this Gestalt switch has reduced the magnitude of the characteristic size of a string by the order of 20 to the Planck length L_{PL}.

The First Superstring Revolution (1984–1985)

In 1983, Alvarez-Gaumé and Witten (1983) identified a mathematical problem called *anomalies* in high-dimensional supersymmetric theories. If string theory wanted to survive, it had to resolve the anomalies. In 1984, Green and Schwarz demonstrated that the anomaly in superstring theory could be avoided (Green and Schwarz, 1984). String theory was saved. Many physicists were attracted to string theory. Schwarz put it (Schwarz, 1996): "Almost overnight, the subject was transformed from an intellectual backwater to one of the most active areas of theoretical physics, which it has remained ever since." They were convinced that superstring theory was a very promising approach to unification.

The most significant advance in the first revolution was that there were five different superstring theories, type I, type IIA, type IIB, $E_8 \times E_8$ heterotic (HE), and SO(32) heterotic (HO), each requiring ten dimensions (nine space and one time).

The Second Superstring Revolution (1994 – Present)

Dualities and D-branes are the two cornerstones that sustain the second superstring revolution. Dualities had led to one of the most profound breakthroughs in the second revolution. Given different conditions, water can turn into ice or stream. However, to scientists they are different phases of the same thing, H_2O. Before the second superstring revolution, there were five different string theories. The most remarkable achievement in the second revolution is the recognition that the five theories indeed have something fundamentally in common. It turned out that the five theories are five perturbative expansions of a single underlying theory about five different points! This is a breakthrough. Scientists are over the moon.

Another breakthrough has made it possible to compute non-perturbative solutions using perturbative methods. This is significant because now theorists can use the good old tools to tackle the new, non-perturbative phenomena. At the center of this breakthrough was a special class of p-branes known as Dirichlet p-branes or simply D-branes. D-branes have been studied for a number of years, but their significance was not clear until Polchinski's landmark contribution (Polchinski, 1995). D-branes have many interesting applications, but most remarkably in the study of black holes (Strominger and Vafa, 1996).

As we examined some historical accounts of the superstring revolutions, it became clear that string theory would be an excellent subject to take for a test drive with Kuhn's philosophical and historical framework of scientific revolutions and our citation-driven paradigm shift detectors. We expected that at least one revolution would become evident in our newly enhanced animated domain visualizations.

5.4.2 Revealing Revolutions

Now we take string theory as the subject of our visual exploration for paradigm shifts. We first searched the Web of Science (1981–2002) for articles on the topic string theory. To simplify the search, we searched for records in which the topic field contains the term "string theory" or "superstring". We also imposed global restrictions on the search; for example, articles must be published in English.

A total of 3708 citing articles were located in this way. These articles have cited a total of 137,655 references. Figure 5.8 shows the occurrence rates of terms before and after the second superstring revolution.

First of all, references cited 35 times or more over the period 1981–2002 were selected. This resulted in a total of 375 unique references, which included monographs, journal papers, conference papers, and technical reports. We then

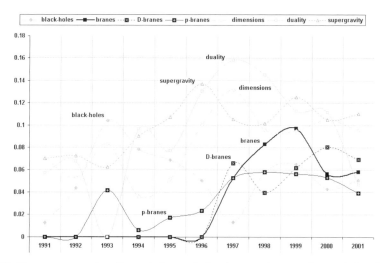

Figure 5.8 The occurrence rates of terms before and after the second superstring revolution. Source: Chen and Kuljis (2003).

extracted a 375×375 document co-citation matrix $\{cc_{ij}\}$. The co-citation count cc_{ij} is defined as the number of articles among the 3708 that have cited both references d_i and d_j. This co-citation matrix was subsequently transformed to Pearson's correlation coefficient matrix $\{r_{ij}\}$. The new matrix represents 62,588 pairs of co-citation connections, which is 89% of the density of a complete matrix of this size. Pathfinder network scaling ($q = N - 1$, $r = \infty$) was applied to the correlation matrix so as to reduce its complexity. As a result, a Pathfinder network of 375 nodes and 381 links was produced.

In parallel, principal component analysis (PCA) was applied to the correlation matrix in order to identify predominating specialties reflected through the citing behavior of this sample of 3708 articles. A total of 18 components were extracted using the conventional 1.0 as the eigenvalue threshold. Altogether these 18 components accounted for 95% variances in the co-citation data, although 66% of the variances were explained by the largest three components.

The animated visualization model consists of a base map and a thematic overlay. The base map is the Pathfinder network. There are several layers of the thematic overlay. First, the distribution of specialties was rendered as a color map of specialties based on factor loading coefficients produced by PCA. We used the RGB color scheme. The largest component, or factor, was assigned to red; the second to green; and the third to blue. This is a reasonable color mapping scheme, which projects each individual article to the first three factors, or the first three dimensions of an 18-dimensional space, albeit the largest three (66% of variance). If a reference's color is white or something close to white, it means that the three largest factors are equally important for this reference as far as the citing articles are concerned. On the other hand, if a reference's color is black, then it means that the first three dimensions do not adequately capture the essence of this reference. A series of our studies have shown that references with strong colors tend to appear towards the center of the Pathfinder network. The annual citation counts were added on top of the Pathfinder network, i.e. the base map, as the second thematic layer. The growth of citations year by year was animated so that users can see directly how many citations are received each year for a particular article.

As explained earlier, in order to identify and visualize scientific paradigms clearly, we introduced the use of transparency as a new visual attribute in our animated visualization system. Transparencies of various levels are used to denote state transitions concerning the citation history of an article as well as the co-citation history of all the articles involved. Articles at earlier states of the citation history are displayed highly transparent, whereas articles at later states are shown as opaque, smooth, and shiny. Links of the underlying Pathfinder network step through transparency-encoded state transitions similarly. Having drawn upon early studies, the sign of a new paradigm is expected to be the rise of a cluster's overall citation counts (Chen and Carr, 1999b; Chen and Paul, 2001; Small, 1977, 1986). By visualizing and animating such state transitions, we expect that the new visualization and animation model would be able to spot the sign of a new paradigm.

5.4.3 The Formation of Co-Citation Clusters

As we know, the resultant landscape should feature at least three predominant clusters of articles, namely the red cluster, the green, and the blue. By visually exploring the shape, the color, and the transparency of these clusters in the context of other

Figure 5.9 The landscape of string theory: the predominance of the green cluster. Source: Chen and Kuljis (2003).

Figure 5.10 The landscape of string theory: the continuous growth of the green cluster and the build-up of the blue cluster. However, the red cluster is essentially underneath the "water". Source: Chen and Kuljis (2003).

clusters, our subsequent analysis focuses on chronological implications of these visual–spatial attributes, which in turn should lead to insights on the development of scientific paradigms.

Figures 5.9 to 5.11 are three instances of the string theory landscape. Figure 5.9 corresponds to the early years in string theory. The most predominant cluster of articles, the green cluster, is located at the far end of the view. There are many isolated scientific articles scattered here and there. Furthermore, many articles are almost invisible due to the highly transparent rendering, indicating that the majority of these articles were not yet published at that time. There is a trace of the sign that the blue cluster towards the east of the scene would emerge soon.

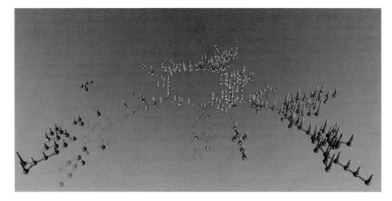

Figure 5.11 The landscape of string theory: the era of a red-cluster predominated landscape started. Source: Chen and Kuljis (2003).

Figure 5.10 shows the string theory landscape a few years later. Although the basic shape and structure of the landscape are essentially the same as the one in Figure 5.9, the green cluster now has consolidated itself with more articles appearing in bright green and taller citation bars. In addition, the blue cluster has emerged and expanded inwardly to the central ring of the underlying Pathfinder network. However, much of the center ring and a large area of articles are still essentially transparent. The appearances of these almost invisible articles make them look as if they were underneath the surface of water. Tides of new articles are about to emerge, and they would represent the red cluster.

In Figure 5.11, articles rapidly appear in areas that are deemed to be the red cluster. Their citation rates grew quickly as transparent articles turned into solid and shiny articles with a considerable number of citations. According to our design principle, the red cluster represents the most salient and predominant specialty. As will become clear in the following text, the late arrival of the most salient specialty in string theory highlights the major force behind the second superstring revolution. In fact, the green cluster corresponds to the first revolution.

5.4.4 Specialties

The landscape of string theory conveys some useful information about the field. Not only can we track the chronological order of individual articles as they enter the knowledge domain, but also the collective chronological order of a cluster as a whole. Animated visualizations of citation and co-citation patterns vividly replay the historical landmarks in terms of publication, citation, and co-citation. Now let us examine the nature of each cluster with reference to the first-hand historical account of string theory. A total of 18 components, also known as factors, are extracted. The first three components account for 66% of variances (See Table 5.1).

In order to identify the nature of each individual specialty, especially the highly cited ones, we ranked references by factor loading. The higher the score, the more representative it is to the specialty. The nature of each specialty is identified by extracting the most common terms used in the titles of the top ten articles ranked by factor loading. This method is illustrated in Table 5.2. The most frequently occurred

Table 5.1 Total variance explained

Component	Total	% of Variance	Cumulative %
1	**125.749**	**33.533**	**33.533**
2	**68.127**	**18.167**	**51.700**
3	**53.980**	**14.395**	**66.095**
4	28.848	7.693	73.788
5	15.908	4.242	78.030
6	14.726	3.927	81.957
7	12.218	3.258	85.215
8	9.897	2.639	87.854
9	6.677	1.781	89.635
10	4.275	1.140	90.775
11	3.794	1.012	91.786
12	2.723	.726	92.512
13	2.355	.628	93.141
14	1.978	.527	93.668
15	1.661	.443	94.111
16	1.544	.412	94.522
17	1.081	.288	94.810
18	1.016	.271	95.081

Table 5.2 Title words frequently used by the top ten articles in each of the first three specialties

	Factor 1		Factor 2		Factor 3
Name	D-branes	Name	Anomaly cancellations	Name	Black holes
Freq.	Phrases	Freq.	Phrases	Freq.	Phrases
4	Dirichlet branes (**D-branes**)	4	superconformal field-theories	5	**black-holes**
2	Born-Infeld action	4	string theory	3	string theory
2	p-branes	2	moduli	2	Dilaton

title phrase is Dirichlet branes, also known as D-branes, which occurred in four of the top ten articles with the highest factor-loading ranking. D-branes therefore will be chosen as the heading of the specialty. One can name specialties algorithmically based on this strategy. The third specialty is named as "black holes" because it was the most frequently used in the titles of the top ten articles. However, we didn't identify the second specialty as "superconformal field-theories" as the simple frequency counts suggest. Instead, we chose to identify the second specialty as one of the top ten articles entitled "anomaly cancellations" because it was this article that had sparked the first superstring revolution.

Table 5.3 shows the largest specialty, the D-branes. Interestingly, two of the top ten most cited physics papers by *Science Watch* 1997 are also included in the table. This indicates that citation ranking shares some insights with co-citation-based clustering.

In 1983, Alvarez-Gaumé and Witten (1983) showed that higher dimensional supersymmetric theories suffered from mathematical disasters called *anomalies*.

Table 5.3 Factor 1: D-branes. Polchinski (1995) on Physical Review Letters has been regarded as the landmark paper responsible for the second superstring revolution

Factor loading	Publications
0.946	Callan, CG (1998). Brane dynamics from the Born-Infeld action. *Nuclear Physics B*, **513**(1–2), 198–212.
0.941	Polchinski, J (1996). HEPTH9611050.
0.940[1]	Witten, E (1996). Bound states of strings and p-branes. *Nuclear Physics B*, **460**(2), 335–350.
0.939	Strominger, A (1996). Open p-branes. *Physics Letters B*, **383**(1), 44–47.
0.934	Douglas, MR (1995). HEPTH9512077.
0.934[2]	Polchinski, J (1995). Dirichlet branes and Ramond-Ramond charges. *Physical Review Letters*, **75**(26), 4724–4727.
0.915	Banks, T, Fischler, W, Shenker, SH, and Susskind, L (1997). M theory as a matrix model: A conjecture. *Physical Review D*, **55**(8), 5112–5128.
0.908	Douglas, MR, Kabat, D, Pouliot, P, Shenker, SH (1997). D-branes and short distances in string theory. *Nuclear Physics B*, **485**(1–2), 85–127.
0.905	Tseytlin, AA (1996). Self-duality of Born-Infeld action and dirichlet 3-brane of type IIB superstring theory. *Nuclear Physics B*, **469**(1–2), 51–67.
0.890	Green, MB, Harvey, JA, and Moore, G (1997). I-brane inflow and anomalous couplings on D-branes. *Classical and Quantum Gravity*, **14**(1), 47–52.

[1] Number 6 in the top ten most cited physics papers ranked by *Science Watch* in 1997.
[2] Number 2 in the top ten most cited physics papers ranked by *Science Watch* in 1997.

Table 5.4 Factor 2: Anomaly cancellations and five string theories

Factor loading	Publications
0.857	Green, MB, and Schwartz, JH (1984). Anomaly cancellations in supersymmetric D = 10 gauge theory and superstring theory. *Physics Letter B*, **149**, 117–122.
0.817	Cecotti, S, Ferrara, S, and Girardello, L (1989). Geometry of Type-II Superstrings and the Moduli of Superconformal Field-Theories. *International Journal of Modern Physics A*, **4**(10), 2475–2529.
0.817	Seiberg, N (1988). Observations on the moduli space of superconformal field-theories. *Nuclear Physics B*, **303**(2), 286–304.
0.806	Scherk, J (1979). How to get masses from extra dimensions. *Nuclear Physics B*, **153**(1), 61–88.
0.783	Narain, KS (1986). New heterotic string theories in uncompactified dimensions less than 10. *Physics Letters B*, **169**(1), 41–46.
0.777	Witten, E (1982). Constraints on supersymmetry breaking. *Nuclear Physics B*, **202**(2), 253–316.
0.764	Narain, KS (1987). *Nuclear Physics B*, **279**, 369.
0.749	Dine, M, Huet, P, and Seiberg, N (1989). Large and small radius in string theory. *Nuclear Physics B*, **322**(2), 301–316.
0.739	Candelas, P, Delaossa, XC, Green, PS, and Parkes, L (1991). A pair of Calabi-Yau manifolds as an exactly soluble superconformal theory. *Nuclear Physics B*, **359**(1), 21–74.
0.738	Sagnotti, A (1992). A Note on the Green-Schwarz mechanism in open-string theories. *Physics Letters B*, **294**(2), 196–203.

Table 5.5 Factor 3: Black holes

Factor loading	Publications
0.894	Gibbons, GW, and Maeda, K (1988). Black-holes and membranes in higher-dimensional theories with Dilaton fields. *Nuclear Physics B*, **298**(4), 741–775.
0.891	Garfinkle, D, Horowitz, GT, and Strominger, A (1991). Charged black-holes in string theory. *Physical Review D*, **43**(10), 3140–3143.
0.887	Shapere, A, Trivedi, S, and Wilczek, F (1991). Dual Dilaton dyons. *Modern Physics Letters A*, **6**(29), 2677–2686.
0.872	Maharana, J, and Schwarz, JH (1993). Noncompact symmetries in string theory. *Nuclear Physics B*, **390**(1), 3–32.
0.869	Horowitz, GT, and Steif, AR (1990). Spacetime singularities in string theory. *Physical Review Letters*, **64**(3), 260–263.
0.866	Gibbons, GW (1982). Anti-gravitating black-hole solitons with scalar hair in N = 4 supergravity. *Nuclear Physics B*, **207**(2), 337–349.
0.863	Hassan, SF, and Sen, A (1992). Twisting classical-solutions in heterotic string theory. *Nuclear Physics B*, **375**(1), 103–118.
0.819	Susskind, L, and Uglum, J (1994). Black-hole entropy in canonical quantum-gravity and superstring theory. *Physical Review D*, **50**(4), 2700–2711.
0.807	Holzhey, CFE, and Wilczek, F (1992). Black-holes as elementary-particles. *Nuclear Physics B*, **380**(3), 447–477.
0.800	Kallosh, R, Linde, A, Ortin, T, Peet, A, and Vanproeyen, A (1992). Supersymmetry as a cosmic censor. *Physical Review D*, **46**(12), 5278–5302.

In 1984, Green and Schwarz discovered that in superstring theory, there was a way to avoid the anomaly (Green and Schwarz, 1984). The mainstream physics community finally accepted string theory. This anomaly cancellation calculation has been regarded as the beginning of the first superstring revolution.

The most significant advance in the first revolution was that there were five different superstring theories, type I, type IIA, type IIB, $E_8 \times E_8$ heterotic (HE), and SO(32) heterotic (HO), each requiring ten dimensions (nine space and one time).

5.4.5 Visual Attributes of Scientific Paradigms

Once we have identified the nature of the major specialties, it is desirable to see if the new visualization may lead us to new insights into the structure of scientific paradigms. Figure 5.12 shows a snapshot of the landscape just before the second superstring revolution. The use of transparency appears to be very informative as well as intuitive. Before the second revolution, key papers were yet to be published. The transparency-encoded rendering mechanism makes these unpublished papers look as if they were underneath the surface of water. Transparency is a good visual attribute. On the one hand, it provides distinct placeholders for papers to appear. On the other hand, it provides non-intrusive and consistent state transitions between various stages of a paper.

The fact that the red cluster appears after the green and blue clusters is also a significant message to scientists. Because the red cluster corresponds to the largest specialty, it is reassuring to know that string theory is still evolving.

The details of the scene before and after the second revolution are shown in Figures 5.13 and 5.14. In the animated version, the rapid growth of relevant areas in the scene becomes clear and easy to follow.

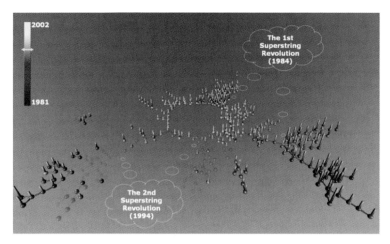

Figure 5.12 The new landscape view accommodates the history and future at a given point. Source: Chen and Kuljis (2003).

Figure 5.13 This frame reflects the dynamics of superstring research before the second revolution. The red arrow in the scene points to Polchinski's 1995 paper on D-branes. Source: Chen and Kuljis (2003).

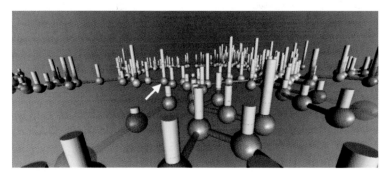

Figure 5.14 Citations grew rapidly in the most predominant specialty. Most publications have gained substantial citations, although some papers are yet to be co-cited. Source: Chen and Kuljis (2003).

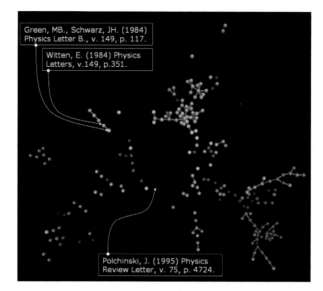

Green, MB., Schwarz, JH. (1984)
Physics Letter B., v. 149, p. 117.

Witten, E. (1984) Physics
Letters, v.149, p.351.

Polchinski, J. (1995) Physics
Review Letter, v. 75, p. 4724.

Figure 5.15 An overview of the intellectual landscape in the making. Green and Schwarz's paper and Witten's paper belong to the first superstring revolution, whereas Polchinski's paper belongs to the second revolution.

Visualizations in study have shown the position of the second revolution in string theory before and after the revolution took place (Figure 5.15). The first revolution is not as evident as the second one within the limited scope of the sample period (1981–2002). Transparency-based encoding has enriched the meaning of visual–spatial models. This method has demonstrated its potential for visually exploring scientific paradigms and conceptual revolutions. We strongly recommend that the modeling and visualization techniques experimented with in this study should be consolidated and integrated into methodologies for the study of the dynamics of a scientific paradigm.

5.5 Summary

KDViz has a promising future as a continuous line of multidisciplinary research. Researchers in the future should address theoretical as well as practical issues concerning the quality of investigations utilizing visualization tools, such as the coverage of the data, the scope of the topic, the interpretation of results, and triangulations with domain experts through longitudinal and multidisciplinary studies.

Visualizing scientific paradigms in particular needs to address issues concerning philosophical implications. For example, what happens after a scientific revolution? Will the winning paradigm dominate the landscape? Shall we let the losing paradigm disappear from the scene? We need to constantly update our knowledge of philosophy of science and related subjects to ensure a sound modeling and visualization methodology. Such questions may lead to further refinements of the theoretical model so as to provide a useful vehicle for philosophers of science as well as others to examine scientific revolutions in new ways.

The starting point of our methodology is the search of articles based on user-chosen keywords. To generate informative visualizations, one needs to choose such search terms carefully so that they are broad enough to cover the different paradigms involved. One of the future research questions is how to facilitate the user to choose such terms.

In conclusion, the refinements and the new developments of our visualization techniques have produced some promising results. The formation of specialties is visually represented and accessible for repeated inspections. Chronologically accurate visualizations and animations make it possible for us to study the emergence of a new scientific paradigm in a meaningful context. These visualizations and animations also have educational values – one can replicate the citation history of an unfamiliar field and get to know its key players and major milestones. Such visual images can provide a useful starting point for learners to establish their own mental image of a scientific field. We began to understand some of the important characteristics of a citation-based image of a scientific paradigm. The visualization and animation sequences provide an easy way to communicate and replay the conceptual revolutions in a visual form. This will make it possible to convey the dynamics of scientific revolutions to a wider audience so as to foster further studies of this topic. We will revisit the string theory case in Chapter 8 in a search for intellectual turning points.

Chapter 6
Empirical Studies of Information Visualization

The farther back you can look, the farther forward you are likely to see.
Winston Churchill

The purpose of an empirical study is to discover and explain facts and factual relationships. The dictionary defines the term "empirical" as meaning "relying on or derived from observation or experiment". In philosophy of science, inductivism refers to the belief that scientific knowledge is derived from the facts of experience acquired by observation and experiment, and that science is objective (Chalmers, 1982). This view first became popular due to the Scientific Revolution in the 17th century, especially the work of great pioneering scientists such as Galileo and Newton. The foundation of inductivism – the nature of observation – has been studied and challenged by philosophers over the past few hundred years. Chalmers describes the problem with inductivism as: "two normal observers viewing the same object from the same place under the same physical circumstances do not necessarily have identical visual experiences, even though the images on their respective retinas may be virtually identical." In other words, our visual experience is influenced by our past experience, our knowledge, and our expectation. This in part explains why Galileo's rivals could not see through Galileo's telescope what Galileo could see, and why an X-ray expert could tell much more than a novice student from the same X-ray photograph of a patient. Modern philosophy of science has advanced much further beyond inductivism in understanding the nature of scientific knowledge and scientific methods. Interested readers are recommended to plunge into the vast literature ocean of philosophy of science. In this chapter, we will restrain ourselves and focus on empirical studies of information visualization. A study is counted as an empirical study if it explores and analyzes data associated with the use of information visualization functions as well as systems. Until recently, the number of empirical studies of information visualization techniques and applications has been rather small in comparison to the overall growth of the field, but the situation is changing.

6.1 Introduction

The 1990s witnessed leaps and bounds in the field of information visualization with increasingly powerful techniques and visually appealing information visualization artifacts (Card et al., 1999; Chen, 1999a; Ware, 2000; Spence, 2001). Research in information visualization has been traditionally dominated by sophisticated and eye-popping innovations of visual representations and technical mechanisms. In contrast, empirical evaluations of information visualizations are often overshadowed by the enthusiasms for what can be done rather than for what should be done.

George Robertson, the inventor of the classic Cone Trees (Robertson et al., 1991), raised the issue in his keynote speech at the 1998 IEEE Information Visualization Symposium. Evaluations of information visualization techniques began to emerge, but the pace needs to be faster and the probe needs to be deeper. In 2000, I and Mary Czerwinski guest edited a nine-article special issue on empirical evaluations of information visualizations in *International Journal of Human–Computer Studies*, featuring two thematic streams: (1) evaluations of classic information visualization techniques and (2) applications of information visualization techniques in practical settings. Also in 2000, we guest edited another special issue in *Journal of the American Society for Information Science* on individual differences in virtual environments.

For a fast-advancing field like information visualization, empirical evaluations are particularly important. Empirical evidence is an integral part of our domain knowledge, especially on what works, what failed, or what remains unknown. This is also a good opportunity for a fast-expanding field to incorporate valuable experiences and adapt established methodologies from such relevant disciplines as Human–Computer Interaction (HCI) and psychology. Indeed, a substantial proportion of empirical studies have appeared in HCI-related journals and conferences. Obviously, the home discipline of an application domain should always get involved.

In this chapter, we introduce some of the most representative empirical studies of information visualization, not only to outline the proven knowledge of the domain, but also to stimulate more empirical evaluations of information visualizations. Every empirical study addresses issues concerning users, tasks, visualization designs, and the visualized information, although individual studies may differ in terms of their focus and approaches. The organization of this chapter essentially follows this sequence:

1   Users, including cognitive factors such as spatial ability, spatial memory, and associative memory, as well as the effects of gender and prior knowledge.
2   Tasks, including visual search tasks, visual scanning, detecting shortest paths, judging visualized quantitative information.
3   Visual Features, including focus + context views, 2D versus 3D.
4   Visualized Information, including hyperlinks of a website and networks of documents.

Figure 6.1 is a co-citation network derived from empirical studies of information visualization between 1993 and 2003. The visualization was generated by CiteSpace (see Chapter 8). A few pivot points in the network are worth noting. The Cone Trees paper by Robertson et al. (1991) is located in the center of the map, joining networks from four of the six time slices. Shneiderman's 1992 tree maps paper is also a pivot point, connecting three slices since 1990. Chernoff's (1973) paper connects two slices. So do Inselberg and Dimsdale's 1990 paper on parallel coordinates and LeBlanc, Ward, and Wittels 1990 paper. Tufte's 1990 book connects three time slices between 1997 and 2002. Such images filtered by citation and co-citation strengths directly reflect where the focus of empirical studies has been.

We begin with a meta-analysis of empirical studies of mainly visual information retrieval tasks, followed by more generic perceptual tasks. We attempt to maintain focus on such tasks as the starting point of each empirical study. Non-experimental studies are also introduced in this chapter. The intended message is that empirical studies should take a broader view.

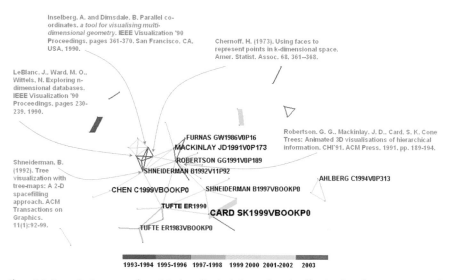

Figure 6.1 A co-citation map of empirical studies in information visualization based on a sequence of two-year time slices (1993–2003).

6.2 Meta-analysis

A number of fundamental issues must be addressed for the further development of the information visualization field. What is the central research question that most studies aim to address? What is the optimal task–feature taxonomy for information visualization design? What is the most commonly used experimental design? Is there any consensus that one can draw from the existing empirical findings in the literature? What is the most powerful visualization feature for a given task? To what extent are the current empirical findings consistent across different studies?

The subsequent meta-analysis used the same methodology as the meta-analysis of hypertext systems (Chen and Rada, 1996). This meta-analysis focuses on the field of information visualization. A comprehensive report of the meta-analysis can be found in (Chen and Yu, 2000). As we will see, this is only the first step to building a task–feature taxonomy that can accommodate empirical evidence concerning various information visualization technologies.

6.2.1 Sampling Empirical Studies

The meta-analysis focuses on experimental studies that include at least one of the three types of independent variables, users, tasks, and tools. User-related variables are mainly represented by individual differences in terms of cognitive factors; tool-related variables include a variety of information visualization features. Measures to do with users include several cognitive factors such as associative memory (MA), spatial ability (VZ) and visual memory (MV). However, because of the small number of papers that directly address these cognitive factors, they are excluded from the meta-analysis. Instead, we will discuss some of these studies in the second half of this chapter.

Table 6.1 A classification of meta-analytical methods

	Diffuse		Focused	
	Significance Level	Effect Size	Significance Level	Effect Size
Compare	A	B	C	D
Combine	E	E	F	F

The meta-analysis is concerned with two broadly defined types of dependent variables: *accuracy* and *efficiency*. Accuracy measures typically include precision, error rate, the average number of incorrect answers, and the number of correct documents retrieved. Efficiency measures typically include the average time to completion, and the performance time. In terms of tools, interfaces that support visual–spatial features, such as cone trees, information landscape, associative networks and multidimensional scaling solutions, are valid candidates.

Table 6.1 shows a classification of six meta-analytical methods. A meta-analysis is determined by three factors. A diffuse study formulates and tests a null hypothesis, whereas a focused study tests not only a hypothesis of significant difference, but also the direction of the difference. A focused study requires a better understanding of the underlying relationship to formulate the more specified hypotheses.

Since a combining meta-analysis does not distinguish diffuse and focused studies, there are a total of six ways to conduct a meta-analysis: (A) comparing diffuse studies of significance testing, (B) comparing diffuse studies of effect size estimation, (C) comparing focused studies of significance testing, (D) comparing focused tests of effect size estimation, (E) combining studies of significance testing and (F) combining studies of effect size estimation.

The aim of the meta-analysis of information visualization studies is to find invariant patterns in the existing body of empirical evidence. It focuses on the combined findings concerning the following hypotheses.

- H1 – Effects of users' cognitive ability:
  - Users with stronger cognitive ability perform more accurately with information visualization systems than users with weaker cognitive ability.
  - Users with stronger cognitive ability perform more efficiently with information visualization systems than users with weaker cognitive ability.
- H2 – Effects of information visualization:
  - Users perform better, in terms of accuracy or efficiency, with interfaces with visualization components than with interfaces without such features.

Studies were selected from the results of a comprehensive bibliographic search on published studies indexed by keywords such as visualization, image, graphics, evaluation, empirical and experiment. The following journals and conferences were searched in particular:

- *Communications of ACM*
- *ACM Transactions on Computer–Human Interaction*
- *ACM Transactions on Information System*
- *ACM Transactions on Computer System*
- *ACM Transactions on Design Automation of Electronic System*
- *ACM Transactions on Database System*

- *IEEE Computers*
- *Journal of American Society for Information Science*
- *IEEE Information Visualization Symposium* (1995–1999)
- *IEEE International Conference on Information Visualization.*

Each located study must meet the following selection criteria:

- The study must include an experiment design.
- The study must include at least one experimental condition in which a visual–spatial component appears in the user interface.
- The study must include at least one dependent variable on accuracy or efficiency.
- The study must report its results in sufficient detail, including F-test, t-test, correlation coefficients or p levels.

The search located 35 evaluative studies published between 1991 and 2000. In particular, 32 studies (91%) were published between 1996 and 2000, indicating that the empirical evaluation of information visualization is still in its early stage.

An array of information was coded for each study: independent variables, dependent variables, sample sizes, methods of assigning subjects, the background of the researchers, visual–spatial components used, the year of publication, tasks and statistics of significance tests. Among the 35 studies, eight studies were excluded in the first round. Seven studies were further removed because they only reported standard deviations and means. For studies that only report group means and standard deviations, the significance levels can be calculated as paired t-tests. However, it was decided that such studies should not be included. Eventually, six fully qualified studies entered the meta-analysis, investigating two broad types of causal relationships:

1   Effects of visual–spatial interfaces on information retrieval.
2   Effects of cognitive ability of users on information retrieval.

Effects are measured by two categories of dependent variables: accuracy and efficiency.

The magnitude of a specific relationship between two variables is often estimated by an effect size r, which can be calculated from a given one-tailed p value and the corresponding sample size. Tests of significance alone are not informative enough for practitioners and designers of visualization systems to judge the usefulness of a visualization feature. A meta-analysis typically compares and combines effect sizes and significance levels in the form of Fisher's standard score z_r and the standard normal deviate score Z.

An effect size r is transformed to Fisher's z_r. For instance, an effect size r of 0.30 corresponds to Fisher's z_r of 0.31. Z scores can be obtained from reported one-tailed p values of significance tests according to cumulative distribution functions, such as CDF and FCDF.

Effect sizes in Fisher's z_r can be combined using standard formulae, which can be found in textbooks on meta-analysis (e.g. Rosenthal, 1987). The Z scores can be combined using Stouffer's method (see Rosenthal, 1987). These two procedures of combination are recommended for their computational simplicity. Finally, the results of the combination need to be converted back to a correlation coefficient r as the combined effect size and a one-tailed p value as the combined significance level.

For studies that only reported group means and standard deviations, the significance levels can be calculated as paired t-tests. However, it was decided to keep the simple selection criteria and not to involve data that require additional processing at this stage. If results were reported as non-significant, a p value of 0.50 and a Z of 0.00 were coded.

The heterogeneity test verifies whether a group of variables indeed represent the same underlying factor. A large heterogeneity implies a grouping that may not capture the variance of a group of results. According to Rosenthal (1987), the heterogeneity of a set of effect sizes refers to fluctuations from the average of the group. It follows a distribution of χ^2 with $K - 1$ degrees of freedom, where K is the number of studies. The heterogeneity of significance levels has the same distribution.

Chen and Yu (2000) grouped a number of accuracy measures, such as the average number of incorrect documents retrieved, and recall. The measures of efficiency such as the completion time, performance time, response time and search time, were lumped into another group.

6.2.2 Effects of Individual Differences on Accuracy

Individual differences refer to users' experience and their ability to use various visualization tools and their cognitive abilities in general. The synthesizing hypothesis states that users with stronger cognitive abilities, for instance, high VZ scores for spatial ability or high MA scores for associative memory, will benefit significantly more from visual–spatial interfaces than those with weaker cognitive abilities. The results from three studies were compared and combined.

The combined effect size of cognitive abilities on accuracy is 0.60, which is usually regarded as a medium-to-large effect size. The combined significance level Z is 6.66 and this is statistically significant ($p = 0.001$).

Comparing the significance levels of diffuse studies yielded a statistically significant χ^2 ($\chi^2 = 15.99$, df $= 2, p = 0.001$). Comparing the effect sizes of diffuse studies was also found statistically significant ($\chi^2 = 9.71$, df $= 2, p = 0.0078$). These results have confirmed that the meta-analysis hypothesis, i.e. users' cognitive abilities, have effects on accuracy with visualization interfaces.

Comparing focused studies did not find a statistically significant linear trend associated with the degree of visual–spatial features in interfaces. Contrast weights were assigned to MDS, Aspect window, and NIRVE (globe) on comparing focused tests are ($Z_{\text{focused-contrast-linear-test}} = 0.9822, p = 0.16$) and ($Zr_{\text{focused-contrast-linear-test}} = 0.5, p = 0.28$).

6.2.3 Effects of Cognitive Abilities on Efficiency

The meta-analysis hypothesizes that users with stronger cognitive abilities will perform more efficiently than users with weaker cognitive abilities. This hypothesis was supported by all the results from studies. Results supporting the hypothesis were assigned positive signs, and the negative signs indicate findings in the opposite direction.

The combined effect size of users' cognitive abilities is 0.59, which is statistically significant ($p = 0.005$, one-tailed). The combined significance level Z is 6.66, which is also statistically significant ($p = 0.005$, one-tailed). The significance levels in comparing diffuse studies are heterogeneous according to the heterogeneity test

($\chi^2 = 13.69$, df $= 2$, $p = 0.0002$), which means that these findings are essentially different from each other.

On the other hand, the heterogeneous test of effect sizes in diffuse studies is not statistically significant ($\chi^2 = 3.9$, df $= 2$, $p = 0.14$), which means, in terms of effect sizes, that these findings are similar to each other. There is a statistically significant linear tread in terms of effect size across this set of studies. Effect sizes on visual–spatial interfaces towards the high end tend to be smaller than those on visual–spatial interfaces towards the lower end ($Zr_{\text{focused-contrast-linear-test}} = 1.36$, $p = 0.0043$). These results suggest that given the same level of cognitive ability, users tend to perform better on less-sophisticated visualization interfaces. For example, users with MDS are likely to outperform their counterparts with NIRVE.

6.2.4 Effects of Visualization on Accuracy

The meta-analysis considered five studies that tested the effects of visualization. The hypothesis was that users perform better with visual–spatial information-retrieval interfaces than traditional retrieval interfaces. This hypothesis was supported by four out of the five studies.

The combined effect size is small ($r = 0.089$) according to Cohen (1977), but this is not statistically significant ($p = 0.234$). The individual effect sizes significantly differ from each other. The combined significance level ($Z = 2.11$) is also not statistically significant ($p = 0.05$).

Statistically significant discrepancies were found among both significance levels and effect sizes ($\chi^2 = 39.89$, df $= 4$, $p = 0.000$ and $\chi^2 = 64.12$, df $= 4$, $p = 0.000$, respectively). The results of linear trend tests in focused studies did not show a statistically significant linear trend across the range of visual–spatial interfaces ($Zr_{\text{focused-contrast-linear-test}} = -0.464$, $p = 0.32$, one-tailed). For example, users did not perform increasingly better from MDS to the Data Mountain.

Major conclusions from the meta-analysis can be summarized as follows.

- Empirical studies of information visualization are still very diverse and it is difficult to apply meta-analysis methods.
- Individual differences, including a variety of cognitive abilities, should be investigated systematically in the future.
- Given the same level of cognitive abilities, users tend to perform better with simpler visual–spatial interfaces.
- The combined effect size of visualization is not statistically significant. A larger homogeneous sample of studies would be needed to expect conclusive results.

This is the first attempt in raising the awareness that it is crucial to conduct empirical studies concerning information visualization systematically within a comparable reference framework. As the number of studies on similar visualizations increases, we expect that regularly conducted meta-analyses would be particularly useful to help us to improve our understanding of the empirical aspect of the field as a whole.

The meta-analysis eliminated many studies because they failed the conventional selection criteria for a meta-analysis one way or the other. In order to improve the quality, clarity and comparability of experimental studies of information

Table 6.2 A list of empirical studies of information visualization

Study	Year	Users	Tasks	Visualizations
Cleveland and McGill	1984		Reading quantitative information	Framed-rectangle charts
Hollands et al.	1989		Trip planning with subway networks	Fisheye view
Ware and Franck	1994		Manipulating, moving or rotating, graphs	2D vs. 3D
Stanney and Salvendy	1995	Spatial ability	Accessing a hierarchical information structure	
Sutcliffe and Patel	1996			2D vs. 3D
Darken and Silbert	1996		Navigating in virtual reality	Landmarks as navigational cues
Schaffer et al.	1997		Path finding in hierarchically clustered graphs	Fisheye view vs. full zoom views
Chen and Czerwinski	1997	Spatial ability	Searching documents	Pathfinder networks of documents
Robertson et al.	1998	Spatial memory	Long term spatial memory of manually placed document icons	Data Mountain planar surface with passive landmarks on landscape texture
Chen and Yu	2000	Meta analysis	Meta analysis	Meta analysis
Purchase	2000		Identifying nodes and edges that are necessary for keeping a graph connected	Graph drawing aesthetics
Chen	2000	Spatial ability, associative memory, spatial memory	Searching documents	Pathfinder networks of documents
Risden et al.	2000		Searching files/ directories	Hyperbolic 3D vs. hierarchical browser
Stasko et al.	2000		Searching files/ directories visualized by space-filling algorithms	Treemap vs. Sunburst
Westerman and Cribbin	2000		Searching information nodes	2D vs. 3D MDS
Cockburn and McKenzie	2002	Spatial memory		2D vs. 3D physical vs. virtual
Cockburn and McKenzie	2001		Storing and retrieving web page thumbnail images	2D vs. 3D Data Mountain
Cockburn and McKenzie	2000		Searching hierarchies of files and directories	Cone Tree vs. standard tree browser
Goguen	2001			
Kobsa	2001			
Chen et al.	2001		Searching documents	Pathfinder networks of documents
Czerwinski et al.	2002	Women		Wide field of view with a large display
Ware et al.	2002		Finding shortest paths	Smoothness of a path
Pirolli et al.	2003		Browsing a tree structure	Hyperbolic view

visualizations, future experimental studies of information visualizations should carefully take into account the following six aspects of an experimental design:

1 The use of standardized testing information.
2 The clarity of descriptions of visual–spatial properties of information visualizations.
3 The use of standardized task taxonomies for activities such as visual information retrieval, data exploration and data analysis.
4 The focus on the task–feature binding to be investigated in experimental studies.
5 The use of standardized cognitive ability tests.
6 The level of details in reporting statistical results.

Some of the resources are available and some are yet to be developed to enable us to carry out experimental studies at a larger scale of consistency and comparability. For example, many experiments have already made use of the data collections prepared by NIST for the TREC Conference series. These collections include not only documents but also pre-defined queries and relevance judgments given by domain experts. Factor-Referenced Cognitive tests have been widely used to measure individuals' cognitive abilities. Conventions of reporting statistical results should become a part of the standard instructions for authors in key journals and conferences in the field, for example, use $p = 0.078$ rather than $p < 0.1$.

The more challenging issue is the design of realistic and practical tasks that can really put specific features of information visualization to the test. The provision of more task–feature taxonomies is certainly desirable so as to widen the range of our options in designing experimental studies. The development of task–feature taxonomies relies on a better understanding of how users make use of given visualization functions. To a large extent this is an adaptation process between users, available visualization functions and their tasks at hand; there is always more for us to find out.

The above guidelines are recommended for reporting empirical findings in a more consistent and comparable manner. As a result, we will be able to utilize analysis and synthesis tools such as meta-analytical methods more effectively. We will be able to make sense of diverse and possibly conflicting empirical findings more confidently and systematically. Table 6.2 lists a collection of empirical studies. In the subsequent sections of this chapter, we will discuss some of the studies, although it is not feasible to cover all the studies in one place.

6.3 Preattentive and Elementary Tasks

One way to categorize empirical studies is by the granularity of tasks performed by subjects. At the highest level, subjects may perform monolith and highly application-oriented tasks using a dedicated computer system which has an information visualization component, for example, using a cone tree visualization to find PDF files that are related to *IEEE Visualization* 2003. In contrast, at a lower level, subjects may perform atomic and application-neutral tasks which may or may not directly involve an information visualization feature at the system level, for example, given a group of shapes on the screen, identifying the odd one out. Currently, there is still a huge gap between the two extremes in the literature of information visualization.

One of the major challenges facing empirical studies of information visualization is the lack of a clear understanding of how people react upon various visual and spatial cues at the application level and how such cues are translated into

Figure 6.2 A filled circle can be preattentively detected in the left image, but not in the right one.

observable actions. The best starting point is the lower level elementary tasks. Once we have a good understanding of how we perform elementary tasks, we may find ways to break down more complex tasks into elementary sub-tasks, or at least isolate the crucial element of a given task.

6.3.1 Preattentive Processing

Human eye movements take about 200 milliseconds to initiate. Perceptual tasks that can be performed in less than this amount of time are called *preattentive*, because such tasks ought to be effortless for us to perform. This is about the amount of information that a single glimpse can pick up. A small number of visual properties are known to be preattentive and they can literally be spotted at a glance.

Spotting an odd object from similar ones is a typical preattentive task. If the target object has a unique visual feature, then we can easily tell its presence or absence at a glance. In contrast, if the target object does not have a unique visual feature, then we have to perform a more detailed visual scan to determine whether the target is there or not. Searching for a filled circle in the left-hand side of Figure 6.2 is a preattentive task, whereas the same task is not preattentive to the right-hand side of Figure 6.2.

Healey et al. (1996) collected a list of 2D visual features that can pop out during visual search. For example, the list includes studies by Juléz and Bergen (1983) on various elements in preattentive vision and perception of textures, and by Triesman (1985) on preattentive processing in vision. Table 6.3 is a list of preattentive visual features compiled by Healey et al. (1996).

6.3.2 Change Blindness

Change blindness is a phenomenon in visual perception in which very large changes occurring in full view in a visual scene are not noticed (O'Regan, 2001). Change blindness is likely to occur if the changes are arranged to occur simultaneously with some kind of irrelevant, brief disruption in visual continuity, such as the large retinal disturbance produced by an eye saccade, a shift of the picture, a brief flicker, an eye blink, or a film cut in a motion picture sequence. These phenomena are attracting an increasing amount of attention from experimental psychologists and philosophers, because they suggest that humans' internal representation of the visual world is much sparser than usually thought.

Change blindness was first noticed in an experiment by McConkie and Currie (1996), which focused on the role of eye movements. In their experiment, observers viewed high-resolution, full-color everyday visual scenes on a computer monitor.

Table 6.3 Preattentive visual features
(Healey et al., 1996).

Feature
Line (blob) orientation
Length
Width
Size
Curvature
Number
Terminators
Intersection
Closure
Color (hue)
Intensity
Flicker
Direction of motion
Binocular luster
Stereoscopic depth
3D depth cues
Lighting direction

Their eye movements were measured. The computer could make changes in the scene as a function of where the observer looked. For example, when the observer looked from the door of a house to the window, the window changed in some way: it could disappear, be replaced by a different element, change color, or change position. When the change occurred *during* an eye movement, surprisingly large changes could be made without being noticed by observers. Elements of the picture that occupied as much as a fifth of the picture area would not be seen. At first, the phenomenon was assumed to have something to do with the mechanisms the brain uses to combine information from successive eye fixations to form a unified view of the visual world. In particular, every time the eye moves, the retinal image shifts. Some mechanism in the brain may correct for such shifts in order to create a stable view of the world. However the mechanism could be imperfect and not take into account certain differences in the visual content across the shift, thereby explaining why changes made during saccades might sometimes go unnoticed.

Further research has revealed that the change blindness phenomenon was not specifically related to eye movements. Instead of focusing on an eye movement, Rensink, O'Regan, and Clark (1997) introduced a brief flicker between successive images. For example, one picture was first shown for 250 ms, followed by a brief blank screen for about 80 ms before a modified picture was shown. The 80 ms is about the same duration of an eye movement. Observers were told that something was changing in the picture every time the flicker occurred, and they were asked to search for it. Under conditions where no flicker was inserted in between the pictures (A-B-A-B-...) the change was immediately visible and totally obvious (Figure 6.3).

However, with the flicker it was often much more difficult to locate the change, especially for changes that were not of "central interest" in the scene. For example,

Figure 6.3 Can you see the difference between the two pictures? (O'Regan, 2001). Reprinted with permission of J.K. O'Regan.

the reflection of houses in a lake scene, though occupying a very large part of the picture, would not be considered to be what the picture was about. Observers sometimes were unable to see such changes at all, even after searching actively for as long as one minute. On the other hand, the changes were perfectly visible once they were pointed out to observers.[1]

The flicker technique shows that change blindness could occur without synchronizing the change with eye movements. This observation led to the re-examination of earlier experiments where changes *were* synchronized with eye movements. Once it was realized that change blindness was not specifically related to eye movements, but to the brief disruption that is inserted between the two versions of the picture, a large number of follow-up experiments were performed, mainly concerning three categories of disruptions: global disruptions, local disruptions, and progressive changes (Simons and Levin, 1997).

Global disruptions are the ones that cover the whole area of the picture. The flicker experiments are global disruption experiments, since the blank displayed briefly between original and modified images covers the whole picture. Other global disruption examples are eye blinks, picture shifts, and film cuts. An additional, amusing, variant of the experiments with global disruptions are experiments in which the change occurs in real life. In a typical scenario described by Simons and Levin (1998), the experimenter stops a person in the street and asks for directions. While the person is speaking to the experimenter, workers carrying a door pass between the experimenter and the person, and an accomplice takes the place of the experimenter. The person usually goes on giving directions after the interruption, and very often does not notice that the experimenter has been replaced by a different person. Local disruptions are limited to five or six small, localized disturbances superimposed on the picture, just like mud splashes on a car windscreen (O'Regan et al., 1999). The disturbances can be small in comparison to the size of the change and they may have nothing to do with the location of the change. Slow changes involve no local or global disruption at all. Slow changes are hard to detect.[2]

Nowell et al. (2001) illustrated the change blindness problem with information visualization in SPIRE when users were using the Time Slicer. Users found

---

[1]http://nivea.psycho.univ-paris5.fr/ECS/kayakflick.gif
[2]http://nivea.psycho.univ-paris5.fr/ECS/sol_Mil_cinepack.avi

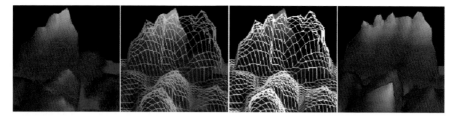

Figure 6.4 Changes from one time slice to another were aided with wireframes and variable translucency (Nowell et al., 2001). The figure was produced at the Pacific Northwest National Laboratory, which is managed and operated by the Battelle Memorial Institute on behalf of the United States Department of Energy. © 2001 IEEE. Reprinted with permission.

themselves unable to identify what had changed from one time period to the next. And they were unable to remember what was different in the previous slice. Nowell et al. used a white wire-frame for the emerging contours to highlight the change. Simultaneously, the opacity and color saturation of the vanishing contours was reduced. The emerging contours gradually changed their translucent color to become brighter and less translucent (Figure 6.4).

6.3.3 Elementary Perceptual Tasks

Good empirical studies are built on solid theoretical foundations. The absence of good empirical studies in a field could be the sign that the field lacks theoretical foundations. As early as 1975, Kruskal (1975) identified the lack of theoretical foundations in the study of graphical methods: "in choosing, constructing, and comparing graphical methods we have little to go on but intuition, rule of thumb, and a kind of master-to-apprentice passing along of information ... There is neither theory nor systematic body of experiment as a guide." Until recently, this would not have been a bad description of the empirical frontiers of today's information visualization field.

An intriguing exemplar of a good empirical study is due to Cleveland and McGill (1984). Not only is its very methodology applicable to studying today's information visualization artifacts, but it also demonstrates how often we are trapped by ideas that are too familiar to us. Cleveland and McGill had a simple goal of finding out how accurately people perform a number of basic tasks for extracting quantitative information from graphs (Cleveland and McGill, 1984). For example, which task is simpler and more accurate: reading time from a digital clock display or reading time from an analog clock display? Similarly, we can compare the accuracy of such tasks as comparing positions on a common scale and comparing angles or color saturations. Cleveland and McGill illustrated the profound difference between reading from a bar chart and reading a pie chart. In a bar chart, judging position along a common scale is the primary task, whereas the primary task in a pie chart is judging angles, arc lengths, and areas of pie slices. It may be intuitive to us that the bar chart reading task is probably more accurate than the pie chart reading task, but how do we find out for sure and how do we extend such comparisons to a wider range of information visualization designs? Cleveland and McGill's study provides an excellent example.

Cleveland and McGill argued that once an elementary perceptual task is empirically proven to be more accurate than others, it becomes possible to design a graphical representation such that people will interact with the graphical representation through more accurate tasks. The Cleveland–McGill study ranks ten elementary perceptual tasks as follows, 1 being the most accurate, and 6 the least:

1   Positions along a common scale.
2   Positions along non-aligned scales.
3   Length, direction, angle.
4   Area.
5   Volume, curvature.
6   Shading, color saturation.

What is the basis of this ranking? In fact, they used power laws of theoretical psychophysics (Stevens, 1975) – if p is the perceived magnitude and a is the actual magnitude, then p is related to a by $p = ka^\alpha$. If a_1 and a_2 are two such magnitudes and p_1 and p_2 are corresponding perceived values, then $p_1/p_2 = (a_1/a_2)^\alpha$. The value of α is therefore an indicator of the accuracy of the perception. When α is 1, the perceived scale is the same as the actual physical scale. The closer α is to 1, the more accurate the perceived value. Baird (1970) reviewed a large number of experiments in an attempt to determine the value of α. It was discovered that values of α tend to be reasonably close to 1 for length judgments, smaller than 1 for area judgments, and even smaller for volume judgments. This means that people tend to judge lengths accurately, underestimate areas, and even more underestimate volumes.

Cleveland and McGill tested their ranking system in two experiments. They asked subjects to estimate the percentage that one value represents of a larger value. Such values were depicted as lengths, positions, and angles. Their experiments found that position judgments were the most accurately performed, followed by length judgments and angle judgments. More specifically, position judgments were between 1.4 and 2.5 times as accurate as length judgments, and 1.96 times as accurate as angle judgments.

The main message of their study is: graphs should engage users in elementary tasks as high in the accuracy ranking as possible. They demonstrated how this principle can be applied to bar charts, pie charts, and statistical maps with shading. They recommended dot charts, dot charts with grouping, and framed-rectangle charts as alternative representations. In fact, framed-rectangle charts are one level higher in the accuracy ranking hierarchy, and they lead to more accurate estimates. They went into further details to demonstrate how a framed-rectangle chart solves a serious problem of shade- or color-coded statistical maps, such as the 1978 murder rate map of Gale and Halperin (1982). The primary elementary task for understanding Gale and Halperin's murder rate map is mainly shading perception and comparison (Figure 6.5). The accuracy of shading-based judgments is at the bottom of the Cleveland–McGill accuracy ranking hierarchy. The goal was to transform the lower ranking task to a higher ranking task. Framed-rectangle charts are a better alternative because they require perceptual tasks based on judging position along a common scale, which can be performed more reliably (Figure 6.6).

Cleveland and McGill cautioned that the accuracy criterion should be taken into account in a broader context – the power of a graphical representation is its ability to reveal patterns and structures not readily shown by other means.

One of the most promising approaches to studying elementary perceptual tasks is eye tracking. Although eye tracking itself is by no means easy enough to be integrated into every empirical study of information visualization, it has the potential to identify the source of attraction from our information visualization design

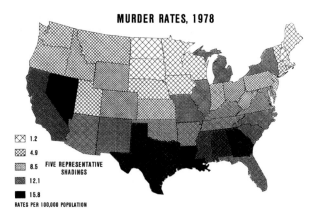

MURDER RATES, 1978

Figure 6.5 The shade-coded murder rate map (Gale and Halperin, 1982). Reprinted with permission from the American Statistician. © 1982 by the American Statistical Association. All rights reserved.

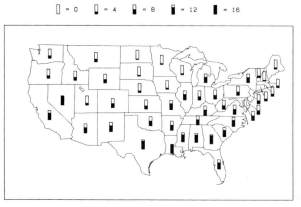

Figure 6.6 A framed-rectangle rework of the murder rate map (Cleveland and McGill, 1984). Reprinted with permission from the Journal of the American Statistical Association. © 1984 by the American Statistical Association. All rights reserved.

and track ultimately what types of visual attributes attract the most attention. Figure 6.7 shows an example of what the eye fixation-worn photograph can tell us about where viewers were paying attention.

6.3.4 Semiotics and Semiology

Moving from elementary perceptual tasks to application-oriented tasks requires a careful mapping between visual representations of information and how they may be interpreted by human users. Research in semiotics is one of the most relevant areas, although much has to be done to incorporate semiotics into empirical studies of information visualization.

Figure 6.7 Titanic. © 2003 Tobii Technology (www.tobii.se). Reprinted with permission of Henrik Eskilsson.

Semiotics and semiology are closely related to each other but distinct. Semiotics is essentially due to the American philosopher, mathematician, and logician Charles Saunders Peirce, whereas semiology is primarily developed by the Swiss linguist Ferdinand de Saussure. What distinguishes the two schools of thought is the concept of interpretant, which is from Peirce's model.

In de Saussure's linguistically oriented semiology, a sign – a word – is fixed by the text in which the word occurs. In semiology, two things are involved with the sign: the *signifier* and the *signified*. This approach is particularly suitable for a linguistic sign, but becomes problematic for a visual sign. Unlike a linguistic sign, a visual sign does not usually have an immediate and explicit context; therefore, a visual sign may appear as context *independent*. In other words, a visual sign is subject itself much more to changes in its implicit context. Peirce added the concept of interpretant to resolve the problem. Peirce's work is regarded as the best source to develop a design or visual communication theory on semiotics.

Codes are not only one of the fundamental concepts in semiotics, but also a sense-making framework in which signs become meaningful. The framework serves as interpretative devices. Scholars in semiotics distinguish social codes, textual codes and interpretative codes. Within a code there may also be "subcodes": such as stylistic and personal subcodes (or idiolects). Some codes are fairly explicit; others are much looser, called "hermeneutics" by Guiraud.

Semiotics believes that a sign does not have an "absolute" value in itself; rather, its value is dependent on its relations with other signs within the signifying system as a whole. When looking at a cave painting, or the Pioneer's plaque, how is the viewer supposed to understand and interpret what they see?

To be able to understand the message, the viewer needs to have prior knowledge of conventions on what a sign means and what a signifier connects to a particular domain.

Information visualization is particularly in need of a generic theory that can help designers and analysts to assess information visualization designs. Goguen (2000) developed a computational theory called semiotic morphisms on preserving the meaning of signs in translating symbol systems. He demonstrated the potential of semiotic morphisms in identifying defects of information visualization.

From the semiotic mapping point of view, fundamental issues in information visualization can be understood in terms of *representation*: a visualization is a representation of some aspects of the underlying information; and the main questions are *what* to represent, and *how* to represent it. Information visualization needs a theory of representation that can take account not just of the capabilities of current display technology, but also of the structure of complex information, such as scientific data, the capabilities and limitations of human perception and cognition, and the social context of work.

However, classical semiotics, which studies the meaningful use of signs, is not good enough, because it has unfortunately not been developed in a sufficiently rigorous way for our needs, nor has it explicitly addressed representation; also, its approach to meaning has been naive in some crucial respects, especially in neglecting (though not entirely ignoring) the social basis and context of meaning. This is why semiotics has mainly been used in the humanities, where scholars can compensate for these weaknesses, rather than in engineering design, where descriptions need to be much more explicit. Another deficiency of classical semiotics is its inability to address dynamic signs and their representations, as is necessary for displays that involve change, instead of presenting a fixed static structure, e.g. for standard interactive features like buttons and fill-in forms, as well as for more complex situations like animations and virtual worlds.

Goguen's initial applications of semiotic morphisms on information visualization have led to several principles that may be useful in assessing a range of information visualization design (Goguen, 2000). He suggested three rules of thumb:

- Measuring quality by what is preserved and how it is preserved.
- It is more important to preserve structure than content when a trade-off is forced.
- The need to take account of social aspects in user interface design.

The semiotics morphisms methodology is not just algebraic but also social. More in-depth studies are needed to verify the power of this approach.

6.4 Interacting with Trees

Browsing a tree structure and finding an item in a hierarchy are the tasks by far the most extensively supported by the arsenal of information visualization. The most widely known information visualizations include cone trees, hyperbolic views, tree maps, and fisheye views. See Chapter 4 for a detailed description of each individual visualization. Since they support similar tasks, a typical empirical study in this group compares a visualization interface with the standard tree browser, namely the File Explorer in Windows on a personal computer.

6.4.1 Cone Trees

Cockburn and McKenzie (2000) compared cone trees and an Explorer-like browser for exploring hierarchical data structures. In their test, the branching factors of cone trees were limited to 20 or less in order to avoid cluttered cone trees. The original upper limit of a branching factor of 30 was noted in Robertson et al. (1991). They compared the performance of users browsing documents through a 3D cone tree interface and a normal tree browser. Browsing tasks were further divided into shallow browsing and deep browsing. Subjects in their experiment followed the paths more quickly with the normal tree browser than the 3D cone tree browser. Not surprisingly, it took longer to complete a deep browsing than a shallow browsing. As expected, it also took longer to follow paths in densely populated data structure.

Despite the less efficient performance with the 3D interface, Cockburn and McKenzie noted possible reasons in subjects' reports. For example, the 3D interface made it easier to see the structure and the search space. Subjects also felt that their lack of familiarity with the 3D cone tree interface affected their completion times, and they believed they would be able to become much more efficient with more experience. The relatively lower fidelity of the cone tree interface was also noted as a possible confounding factor.

This study illustrates a challenging issue that empirical studies of innovative information visualization must address. Prior knowledge and practical experience are among the most predominating compounding factors. Longitudinal studies may resolve some of the problems. The challenging issue is also related to the granularity of the tasks studied. Browsing hierarchically organized files is a task that is so familiar to us, it becomes difficult to break away from the routine and think of how the work can be done differently. This is a general problem with the empirical study of information visualization. The 1984 Cleveland–McGrill study brilliantly demonstrates a potentially generic approach that can be adapted for the empirical study of today's information visualization.

6.4.2 Tree Maps

The *TreeMap* visualization technique is another classic technique that supports browsing hierarchically organized files on computer (Johnson and Shneiderman, 1991; Shneiderman, 1992). TreeMap utilizes a space-filling algorithm that fills recursively divided rectangle areas with components of a hierarchy.

One of the most remarkable facts about tree maps is their continuous growth since the original design. It is both intriguing and informative to look at the evolution of tree maps in a broader context. Researchers at the Human–Computer Interaction Lab (HCIL) at the University of Maryland have done enormous innovative and stimulating work in information visualization, notably dynamic queries, tree maps, and zoomable user interfaces. The *Maryland way* to information visualization has several unique characteristics. Their vibrant approaches have been driven by a strongly user-centered philosophy, from direct manipulation, dynamic queries, to Shneiderman's information visualization mantra. Important design decisions are made based on what users need. Another unique character of HCIL's approaches is their emphasis on rigorous scientific methods. Every technical innovation comes with a series of persistent empirical evaluations and continuous refinement studies. Since the original tree map design in the early 1990s, the use, evaluation, and refinement of tree maps have led to a continuous stream of systems such as ordered tree maps and quantum tree maps. Research in zoomable user interfaces at HCIL has led to widely used toolkits such as Jazz and Piccolo.

The Craft of Information Visualization, written and edited by Bederson and Shneiderman (2003), features 38 seminal publications from their lab over the last two decades in information visualization. More importantly, it sets these seminal contributions to information visualization in the broader context of the field as a whole. Instead of attempting a partial coverage of the influential topics in this book, the reader is recommended to read *The Craft of Information Visualization* thoroughly. In this section, we start with an empirical study of TreeMap and SunBurst visualizations, followed by an example from HCIL on improving tree maps, namely ordered tree maps and quantum tree maps. We end this section with an empirical study of SpaceTree, also from HCIL. Although SpaceTree per se does not belong to the tree map family, its empirical evaluation reflects valuable insights into the visualization of hierarchical data structures.

Stasko et al. (2000) compared TreeMap and SunBurst visualizations of hierarchies of computer files and directories. Both TreeMap and SunBurst can be regarded as space-filling visualizations. TreeMap fills a rectangle area completely (Figure 6.8), whereas SunBurst fills a circular area partially (Figure 6.9).

In SunBurst, the top of the hierarchy is at the center of the visualization, whereas deeper levels of the hierarchy fan out away from the center and sub-directories are confined by their parent directories' radial boundaries. The effects of the two visualization browsers on time to complete browsing tasks were tested on two hierarchies

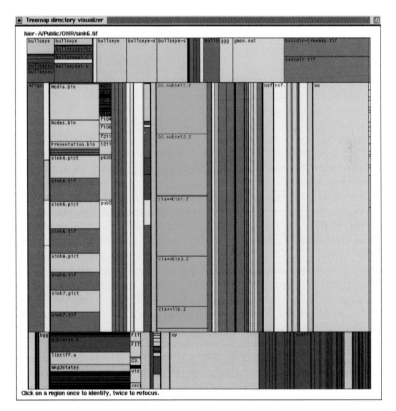

Figure 6.8 TreeMap visualization (Stasko et al., 2000). Reprinted with permission of John Stasko.

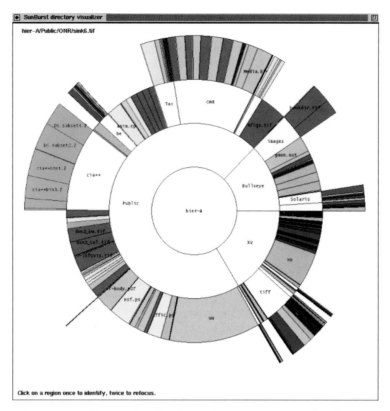

Figure 6.9 SunBurst visualization of a file directory's structure. Reprinted with permission of John Stasko.

of about 500 nodes each in the first experiment and about 3000 nodes each in the second experiment. The second independent variable *phase* was the order of two 16-task blocks.

When tested with the smaller 500-node hierarchy in the first experiment, a main effect of browsers on task correctness was found, but the phase has no main effect and no interaction was found either. When tested with the larger 3000 node hierarchy in the second experiment, on the other hand, no main effect of browsers was found.

Bederson et al. (2001) described the design of ordered and quantum treemaps in attempts to resolve some of the problems identified with earlier treemap designs. Rectangles are the building blocks of a treemap. Very thin rectangles tend to cause users problems. In general, a rectangle with a shape closer to square is easier to see from the user's point of view. Therefore, balancing the aspect ratios of rectangles in a treemap has been proposed so as to avoid ultra-thin rectangles in a treemap. However, this solution introduces a new problem: it may no longer preserve the order of the underlying data and its stability is not guaranteed. The intrinsic order of data items is often an important clue in identifying visual patterns; for example, preserving the chronological order is an important requirement for an analysis of maturity and interest rate of bonds. In order to resolve this dilemma, the ordered treemap algorithms, including strip and pivot algorithms, provide a trade-off solution. Ordered treemaps maintain the original order to an extent in treemaps while minimizing the presence of ultra-thin rectangles. As a result, ordered treemaps are characterized by layouts of partially ordered and close to square rectangles.

Bederson et al. (2001) reported an interesting user study of ordered treemaps. They compared how long it took users to find specific rectangles among 100 rectangles mapped by different treemap algorithms, including squarified, pivot, and strip treemap algorithms. In terms of completion time measures, the expectation was that the fastest would be layouts created by the strip algorithm, then the pivot one, and finally the squarified algorithm. Although the results did not identify a clear winner between the strip and pivot maps, there was an indication of a trend consistent with the expectation: the strip was the fastest, followed by the pivot, which was in turn followed by the squarified. They went on to develop another improvement of treemaps called quantum treemaps. The reader is referred to *The Craft of Information Visualization* for detailed descriptions. As concrete exemplars, such a series of development, evaluation, and refinement efforts has practical implications on empirical evaluations of information visualization. It clearly shows the integral role of empirical evaluation and how it may become an indispensable component of a development methodology.

We end this section with another example from HCIL. Plaisant et al. (2002) reflect on the evolution of the design of SpaceTree and a controlled experiment in which SpaceTree was compared with Microsoft Explorer and the hyperbolic view visualizations. Empirical evaluations of hyperbolic views are discussed in the next section. SpaceTree is not a space-filling algorithm like treemaps, but it addresses another type of space-filling questions. SpaceTree was directly motivated by the feedback from users on semantic zooming versus geometric scaling. One question is to do with geometric scaling when some of the fonts become too small to be readable: to show or not to show visible but unreadable texts? Instead of showing the unreadables, SpaceTree truncates unreadable levels of a hierarchy into expansible icons. In a way, this is in the same spirit of the way hyperbolic views treat items in surrounding areas. Earlier user studies of hyperbolic views found that a radical change of spatial configuration in hyperbolic geometry can cause disorientation problems. The need to re-focus when each time the display is updated is not a trivial cognitive burden. SpaceTree's design particularly aims to maintain a stable and consistent layout.

A controlled experiment was undertaken with 18 subjects working with a tree of more than 7,000 nodes visualized by Microsoft Explorer, Hyperbolic views, and SpaceTree, respectively. The test tasks were node search (e.g. find kangaroo), return to previously visited nodes (e.g. go back to kangaroo), and questions concerning the topological structure of the tree (e.g. given a branch find three nodes with more than 10 children nodes). The results indicate a substantial role of individual differences in terms of individuals' performance and their preferences. For example, subjects found the Hyperbolic Browser was more "cool" than Explorer and SpaceTree, but preferred to use SpaceTree. Similar findings have been reported in the literature – people may be more impressed by a 3D interface, but prefer to use a 2D version nevertheless. Exactly what does it take to make something cool also something usable and vice versa? This is a generally recognized issue, but there is no readily convincing answer. Empirical studies at finer granularity are certainly necessary.

In terms of performance measures, Explorer was the fastest in the first kangaroo-finding tasks. Learning was expected to be a factor as SpaceTree became the fastest in the third task. Explorer was the winner in the returning-to-kangaroo tasks, followed by SpaceTree; the Hyperbolic Browser took the longest time. SpaceTree was significantly faster than Explorer on topological tasks; the Hyperbolic Browser was in between. Examples in this section and indeed examples in this chapter highlight the challenging nature of empirical evaluation of information visualization. It would be much informative if a performance difference can be traced back to the original design decision and a problem can be resolved at the early stage. The crucial role of a user-centered philosophy is evident in the two examples from HCIL, which also confirms how much one can learn from the field of human–computer interaction along the way of empirical evaluation of information visualization. Users perform better with a stable layout, items in preserved orders, shapes that are easily readable, and many more. As one of the most widely tried visualizations, treemaps have the valuable opportunity to gather feedback from a wide range of users. The open source policy and the wide availability of treemap algorithms have also contributed to their proliferation and healthy improvements.

6.4.3 Hyperbolic Views

Two empirical studies are highlighted below for the widely known focus + context views. Risden et al. (2000) compared two conventional 2D hierarchical browsers and a browser with an interactive 3D hyperbolic view. They demonstrated where focus + context views might become particularly useful for experienced users. Their results suggested that 3D interactive techniques might best be introduced alongside more familiar 2D visualizations so that the user can integrate interaction strategies.

Empirical evidence so far appears to suggest a neck-and-neck situation in the 2D versus 3D studies, if not a winning 2D. Some of the empirical studies are discussed in earlier sections of this chapter. On the other hand, it should be noted that one should carefully examine the existing evidence and bear in mind the large amount of known and unknown confounding factors. One possibility is that file management tasks with 2D and 3D may require different perceptual and cognitive processes altogether at this level; therefore, it may be necessary to investigate tasks of much finer granularity.

Some of us strongly believe that 3D visualizations should ultimately outperform their 2D counterparts. This is indeed a challenging and complex question, and it may never have a clear cut answer. Nevertheless, whenever there is a negative result to 3D, we are tempted to explain away the finding with confounding factors.

The complexity of the issue is clear in a number of empirical studies associated with the evaluation of hyperbolic view browsers. Neither Lamping et al. (1995) nor Czerwinski and Larson (1997) find significant task performance improvements with a hyperbolic tree browser. However, when competing with other browsers in two competitions, the hyperbolic tree browser was the winner twice. Such mismatches between laboratory studies and field tests motivated a recent study by Pirolli et al. (2003). They studied the effects of information scent on visual search with a hyperbolic tree browser.

Pirolli et al. (2003) introduced the concept of information scent into the race. Information scent is task-relevant display cues, such as node labels on a tree structure. At the beginning of this chapter we distinguish two types of tasks: visual–spatial tasks and semantic tasks, which are further refined to Type I and Type II tasks when dealing with graphs. Information scent can be seen as the symbolic reinforcements of spatial references. As a result, we can expect that such symbolic reinforcements will make Type II tasks easy to perform. Therefore, if one performs Type II tasks with an interface, then information scent should make a difference. In this context, what Pirolli and his colleagues did becomes apparent. Information scent was quantified as an empirical *accuracy of scent* (AOS) score. Such AOS scores were used to characterize tasks to be performed. Task performance with different AOS scores was compared across a hyperbolic tree browser and the Microsoft Windows File Explorer. Two experiments were conducted.

Although the first experiment found no overall difference in task completion time between the two browsers, there was an interesting finding: subjects performed better with the hyperbolic browser on high AOS tasks, whereas subjects performed better with the Windows File Explorer on low AOS tasks. Does it suggest that low AOS tasks are equivalent to Type I tasks? In other words, does it mean the Windows File Explorer works best with hierarchical organizations of straightforward symbolic references?

The second experiment studied retrieval tasks only, and the analysis was enhanced by eye-fixation data. Hyperbolic tree users examined more nodes and visually searched through the tree hierarchy faster than users of an interface similar to the Windows File Explorer. Two factors affected visual search in the hyperbolic display: strong information scent improves visual search, and the density of a target region hinders visual search especially when information scent is weak.

Earlier in this chapter, the Cockburn–McKenzie study found that an increased density in 3D cone trees makes tasks more difficult. Now similar results were found in 3D hyperbolic trees. There is at least one method that can definitely reduce the local density of a tree display, no matter in a Euclidean space or a hyperbolic space – using a fisheye view.

6.4.4 Fisheye Views

Schaffer et al. (1997) compared fisheye views to traditional zooming on a hierarchically clustered network. Subjects were first asked to find a broken telephone line in a hierarchically clustered network and repair the broken phone line. Broken phone lines were displayed visually as red lines. The interface has a main effect on times for completing each task. People performed the task much faster when using fisheye views. In addition, subjects used zooms much less frequently with the fisheye view interface than with the full zoom interface. The significantly fewer number of zooming requests suggests that the problems associated with the density of tree visualization could indeed be resolved by a fisheye view.

Hollands et al. (1989) compared task performance using fisheye and scrolling views. Subjects were asked to plan a trip with a subway map. Tasks involved locating stations, selecting optimal routes, and constructing optimal itinerary between stations on a subway network. The results slightly favored fisheye views. One of the problems with the fisheye viewer used in the study was that it moves the focal point to the center of display in an abrupt motion that caused disorientation. Carpendale et al. (1997) particularly addressed such disorientation problems. Users often experience disorientation when viewing distorted displays, such as fisheye views and hyperbolic views. Carpendale and her colleagues proposed to use visual cues such as shading and grid lines to help users correctly interpret the distortions. However, so far we are not aware of any comprehensive empirical studies that compare fisheye views with other types of information visualizations.

It is clear that more empirical evaluations of information visualizations are needed to address issues regarding the reliability and efficiency of individual visualization features. On the other hand, alternative research methods should be encouraged.

6.5 Interacting with Graphs

One of the single most important ingredients for an empirical study is tasks. Tasks are not only an integral part of an empirical investigation, but also the key to understanding an empirical study as a whole. At the highest level, all interactions between users and information visualization can be characterized by the level of information that users act upon. Sometimes recognizing visual patterns may be all it takes to understand the visualized information. Sometimes, however, one has to dig deeper and think harder to make a connection and interpret what a visual representation means. We distinguish tasks involved in such situations by calling the former visual–spatial tasks, and the latter semantic tasks. Although in information visualization, tasks often go beyond the visual–spatial level, semantic tasks do not necessarily follow a visual–spatial task. Here we define two more specific types of tasks concerning graphs.

One may perform two types of tasks when dealing with a graph, Type I and Type II. Type I tasks are purely concerned with topological properties of the graph, whereas Type II tasks are concerned not only with the topology, but also with the connections to the underlying phenomenon from which the graph is abstracted. Some typical examples of Type I tasks are: is the graph connected? Or, is node n_i reachable from node n_j? In contrast, examples of Type II tasks could be: what is Arnold Schwarzenegger's Kevin Bacon number in the Hollywood movie stars network? Or, what rewiring can be done to make the North American electrical grids more resilient to a massive blackout?

6.5.1 Aesthetics and Legibility

Until recently graph drawing algorithms have been evaluated exclusively in terms of their computational efficiency. Through a series of empirical studies, Helen Purchase, now at the University of Glasgow, Scotland, is pursuing a unique route to investigate the effects of various graph drawing aesthetics on human performance from a user-centered perspective (Purchase, 2000, 2002). Purchase primarily investigated Type I tasks in her studies. And she called these tasks *relational*, as opposed to *interpretative* Type II tasks.

Purchase (2000) reported two experiments to study the effects of various graph drawing aesthetics on the error rates and the time to completion of subjects. In the first experiment, hand-drawn graphs were used with carefully varied graph drawing aesthetics as the independent variables. In the second experiment, graphs were drawn by algorithms. Five common graph drawing aesthetics were used in the first experiment (Purchase, 2000):

- *minimize bends* – minimize the total number of bends in polyline edges (Tamassia, 1987);
- *minimize edge crossings* – minimize the number of edge crossings in the display (Reingold and Tilford, 1981);

- *maximize minimum angles* – maximize the minimum angle between edges extending from a node (Coleman and Parker, 1996; Gutwenger and Mutzel, 1998);
- *orthogonality* – fix nodes and edges to an orthogonal grid (Tamassia, 1987; Papakostas and Tollis, 2000);
- *symmetry* – display a symmetrical view of the graph if possible (Gansner and North, 1998).

Purchase tested the five primary hypotheses associated with these aesthetics. In addition, Tukey's WSD pairwise comparison procedure (Gottsdanker, 1978) was used to determine if there were significant understandability priorities between the aesthetics. She found a significant effect of bends on errors, but not on response time; edge-crossing on both measures; angles on none; orthogonality on none; and symmetry on response time, but not on errors. More specifically, her results suggest that edge-crossing becomes particularly problematic when there are a large number of crossed edges.

Her second experiment compared the error rates and response times on graphs drawn by eight graph layout algorithms, including Fruchterman and Reingold's force-directed placement algorithm (Fruchterman and Reingold, 1991), and Kamada and Kawai's layout algorithm (Kamada and Kawai, 1989). The main effect of the algorithms was statistically significant for errors, although not significant for response time. Kamada and Kawai's algorithm has the lowest error rates. It also has the second lowest response time, but the difference is not statistically significant.

Purchase (2002) compared 11 algorithms with respect to their measured presence of seven aesthetics, according to metric formulae, rather than based on human judgments. The 11 algorithms include spring-based algorithms and grid-based algorithms. All algorithms implicitly minimize the number of edge crosses. Spring-based drawings are straight-line drawings, and they also implicitly favor symmetric layout structures. Grid-based drawings perform better than spring algorithms on the symmetry aesthetic.

6.5.2 Continuity as an Extrinsic Criterion

The validity of graph drawing aesthetics are often taken for granted, rather than being derived from empirical evidence and theoretical foundations. Purchase (2000) identified edge crossings as the most important aesthetic based on two hand-drawn graphs, one with many crossings and one with few. Why are edge crossings bad? Are there more profound reasons behind the edge-crossing problem?

These questions have not been empirically addressed, except by a recent study published in the new journal *Information Visualization* (IVS). In this strongly cognitive-flavored study, Ware et al. (2002) closely examined the role of good continuity in understanding a graph and began to explain why edge crossings are not only aesthetically unpopular, but they also slow down the speed of our visual search.

Our perception seeks visual patterns no matter whether the perceived patterns are intended or not. When we see a group of nearby stars, we think of a constellation. When we see a few stars in a row, our mind draws a line to join them. Gestalt laws are concerned with our pattern perception. Gestalt laws determine whether we see something as a *figure* as opposed to *ground*. Ware's book *Information Visualization* is a good source on this topic. The principle of good continuation is one gestalt law that is especially relevant to graph drawing. It suggests that we will more easily see smooth continuous contours than jagged ones. It also suggests that we will be able to interpret graphs that use smoothly curved lines more easily than grid layout graphs, because the continuous lines are more likely to "pop out" as perceptually complete objects (Ware et al., 2002).

As defined by Ware et al. (2002), a graph has a good continuity if multi-edge paths in the graph are drawn as straight as possible; in other words, if each path as a whole is close to a smooth line as much as possible. The dependent variable was the time to perceive the shortest path between two nodes specified in a spring layout graph. A regression model was built based on a number of independent variables of topological and aesthetic properties. The primary variables are summarized as follows:

- Node continuity – given a node, the continuity is measured as the degrees of the angular deviation from a straight line of the two edges on the shortest path through the node.
- Path continuity – the sum of node continuity measures for all nodes on the path. The best possible path continuity is 0 degree.
- Number of crossings – the number of crossings on the shortest path.
- Average crossing angles – the average cosine angles of each edge crossing. Acute angles were expected to be more disruptive than more perpendicular angles.
- Number of branches – the degree of each node on the shortest path minus two, i.e. branches that are not part of the shortest path. Judging a path with more such branches can be expected to be more difficult.
- Length of the shortest path – self-explanatory.

The total number of edge crossings in the entire graph was also recorded, mainly for comparison purpose as this measure was used by Purchase (2000). Test graphs contained 42 nodes and the degree of each node was randomized between 1 and 5. The length of a target shortest path was between 3 and 5.

The findings are intriguing. The path length has the strongest effect on the perception time. Since the path length is determined by the graph itself, continuity is the graph drawing aesthetic property that has the strongest effect on finding shortest paths. Furthermore, the regression mode makes it possible to estimate cognitive costs associated with various factors. For example, 100 degrees of continuity on a path add 1.7 seconds to the time spent on finding the shortest path, and each edge crossing adds 0.65 seconds. This is equivalent to saying that the cognitive cost of a single edge crossing causes about the same amount of trouble as 38 degrees of continuity. As a result, a graph drawing algorithm may consider a new strategy for drawing easy to understand graphs by increasing the path continuity as well as reducing the number of edge crossings.

The study also confirms that the total number of edge-crossings in the entire graph is not a significant indicator of response time. Instead, what really matters for this type of task is the number of edges that cross the shortest path itself. This is an intuitive finding. It should be noted that the shortest path tasks here are different from tasks tested by Purchase (2000). In the 2000 study, the tasks were identifying nodes and edges that hold a graph together as a single piece. It would be even more interesting if the two experiments were more comparable to each other.

The Cleveland–McGill (1984) study and the Ware et al. (2002) study are different in many ways, but they have something fundamental in common – both of them established an interrelationship between perceptual tasks and the way that the information is displayed. Cleveland and McGill focused on the accuracy of perceptual tasks, whereas Ware et al. focused on the time efficiency. Cleveland and McGill studied tasks of comparing values, whereas Ware et al. studied tasks of finding shortest paths.

6.6 2D versus 3D

It doesn't seem to matter whether we perform our 3D tasks well or not; many of us like 3D visualizations anyway. Interestingly, many of us do not like 3D by instinct. Human beings are creatures who live in a 3D world. Many people enjoy 3D video games and immersive virtual reality, and yet many people equally enjoy the simplicity and clarity of 2D space. A 3D world gives us an extra degree of freedom, but sometimes the extra degree of freedom also leads to confusions and complications. Researchers are puzzled by the seeming mismatch between 3D's appeal and 3D's performance, as we shall see in the empirical studies explained in this section. Shneiderman (2003) recently questioned whether the richness of 3D reality is necessarily a good model after all. He quoted evidence such as disorientating navigation and annoying occlusions from the real world to highlight the potential pitfalls of 3D interface designs, and emphasized that to go beyond merely mimicking reality advanced designs we need to support the following three important features:

- rapid situation awareness through effective overviews;
- reduced number of actions to accomplish tasks; and
- prompt, meaningful feedback for user actions.

One of the practical questions is: how much of the 3D attraction can be translated into improved performance scores and more enjoyable experience? Designers may ask themselves whether they have turned over every stone, or more precisely, pushed the right buttons, used the right colors, the right shapes, and so on.

The notion of Type I and Type II tasks in information visualization can be useful in organizing various empirical findings regarding the 2D versus 3D debates. Recall that Type I tasks are only concerned with visual–spatial properties, while Type II tasks involve a deeper understanding of the underlying meaning which may or may not be fully revealed by such visual–spatial properties.

An increasing number of empirical studies began to address the potential gains by the extra dimension of display. We will see quite a few of them in this section. Do we have sufficient empirical evidence to settle the 2D versus 3D debates? Is a 3D visualization always better than its 2D counterpart? Is this merely a question about an extra dimension of freedom? The following empirical studies illustrate some of the major concerns, what has been done so far, and what might be done in the future.

6.6.1 Spatial versus Symbolic References

In an earlier study Jones and Dumais (1986) assessed the accuracy of spatial versus symbolic references in three experiments of news article reading and filing. In the first experiment, performances with spatial references were not only poor in comparison to the symbolic references, but also deteriorated more rapidly than symbolic references as the number of articles increased. In the second experiment, a 2D space was used with an office metaphor, induced by landmarks such as a desk, a table, and filing cabinets. In the third experiment, subjects placed objects in an actual 3D mock office. However, neither of these enhancements significantly improved the accuracy of spatial reference; in fact, the performance remained below what was achieved by symbolic references in the first experiment.

Jones and Dumais suggested that the formation of spatial memory in many situations is essentially effortless; however, this is not necessarily the case in a computer filing situation. Furthermore, because spatial references with a computer seemed to entail higher costs than symbolic references, and the immediate benefits of such high-cost actions may not always be clear, users may choose symbolic references over the spatial ones. They also suggested that news articles filed in the experiments do not especially lend themselves to a spatial organization. Given the popularity of spatial models and their applications to visualizing news article collections and webpages a decade after these experiments, for example, *ThemeView* and *Data Mountain*, this is indeed a challenging empirical question that the information visualization community must answer.

6.6.2 Understanding 3D Structures

Westerman and Cribbin (2000) examined information search tasks in 2D and 3D multidimensional scaling (MDS) maps and particularly focused on the extent to which 2D and 3D MDS maps differ in terms of semantic richness and cognitive demands. They compared the amount of additional semantic information that a 3D MDS map conveys with the increased cognitive demands, and concluded that the gain is insignificant as compared to the loss.

From Cleveland and McGill's study of the elementary perceptual tasks, we know that some tasks tend to be performed more accurately than others, depending on the way quantitative information is depicted. When dealing with MDS maps, a basic perceptual task is to judge the distance between two objects. Judging such distances in MDS can be a challenging task, especially in 3D MDS maps. This leads to the question about graphs: is this low cost-effect ratio also true for 2D and 3D graphs, where the distance between two objects is represented by explicit links?

The first quantitative estimate of the benefits of 3D stereo viewing for perceiving graphs was made by Ware and Franck (1996) in their study of how people understand 3D graphs presented in 2D and 3D displays. They found that people performed significantly better in 3D than in 2D conditions. The task was to determine if there was a path of length 2 between two highlighted nodes in a graph (Figure 6.10). In Ware and Frank's study, the 3D condition allowed users to move and rotate the graph. Indeed, motion and rotation may be the key to the superior 3D performance.

6.6.3 Data Mountain

Robertson et al. (1998) described the design of Data Mountain, an inclined plane in a 3D desktop virtual environment for users to place icons of documents at arbitrary positions in the plane. Data Mountain uses a manual layout to exploit spatial memory for long-term use. The Data Mountain study also reminds us of the Jones–Dumais study of spatial versus symbolic references, such as the spatial placement of document icons and the reference to the spatial memory of users.

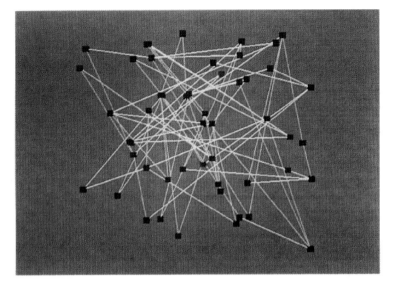

Figure 6.10 Graph containing 78 nodes and 104 edges. The subject's task was to determine if there was a path of length 2 between the two red nodes (Ware and Franck, 1996). © 1996 ACM, Inc. Reprinted with permission.

Data Mountain uses a plane tilted at 65 degrees for a user to place web pages anywhere on the mountain. The landscape texture in Data Mountain provides passive landmark references, but the landmarks themselves have no special meaning. The design of Data Mountain values the serendipity of its layouts: as long as a layout means something to whoever created it, anything goes. The empirical evidence suggested that it took less time to retrieve web pages from Data Mountain than from a standard tree browser. The improvement was attributed to the provision of both spatial and symbolic cues in Data Mountain. With reference to the Jones–Dumais study (1986), this is probably the strongest positive evidence for a combination of spatial and symbolic references.

Cockburn and McKenzie conducted a series of empirical studies concerning the effects of 2D and 3D interfaces, especially with designs that closely mimic Data Mountain. Two of their recent studies are of particular interest. Cockburn and McKenzie (2001) compared the effects of 2D and 3D Data Mountain-like interfaces for placing and retrieving webpage thumbnails. Two independent variables were included: (1) *interface type* – 2D and 3D, and (2) *data density* – sparse, medium, and dense, implemented as 33-, 66- and 99-thumbnail displays respectively. Subjects placed webpage icons through Data Mountain interfaces and retrieved these webpages. The mean task completion time was measured as the dependent variable.

There were no statistically significant differences between the 2D and 3D interfaces, but there was a significant preference for the 3D interfaces. On the other hand, the main effect of data density was statistically significant, and there was no interaction between the two factors.

In an even more interesting study, Cockburn and McKenzie (2002) compared not only the dimensionality factor, but also a realism factor, which was a rare effort in empirical studies of visualization interfaces. They used a $2 \times 3 \times 3$ mixed factorial analysis of variance (ANOVA). The dimensionality factor has three levels: 2D, $2\frac{1}{2}$D,

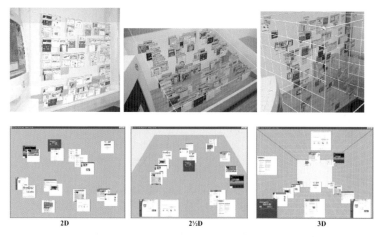

2D   2½D   3D

Figure 6.11 Physical and virtual interfaces used by Cockburn and McKenzie (2002). © 2002 ACM, Inc. Reprinted with permission.

and 3D, whereas the realism factor is between physical and virtual versions. Fishing lines were used in their physical interfaces to hold webpage printouts in place. Data density was once again included, like their 2001 experiment: sparse, medium, and dense. A total of six interfaces were used in their experiment (Figure 6.11).

Although the empirical studies discussed so far in this section used the term *spatial memory*, they were not related to psychometric tests of spatial memory. In the second half of the chapter, we will see empirical studies that specifically measured spatial memory as a cognitive ability.

The second Cockburn–McKenzie study found the main effect of dimensionality – it took increasingly longer to retrieve pages from interfaces of higher dimensions. The results were confirmed by the decreasing effectiveness reported by the subjects.

In summary, empirical evidence appears to suggest that simply increasing an interface from 2D to 3D is unlikely to be enough to boost the task performance unless additional functions are provided so that users can have greater controls of objects in 3D interfaces.

6.7 Cognitive Abilities

Take a look at a user satisfaction survey of an empirical study of information visualization, and you will quickly find out that there will always be some users who will reportedly like the spatial metaphor of an interface, and there will always be others who will tell you they don't. A more interesting fact is that sometimes our preferences appear to have little to do with how well or how badly we tend to perform with our favorite interfaces anyhow. In contrast, there are indeed situations in which we excel if we have in hand our favorite tools. How do we know what we will be good at? And if we don't know, how do we find some ways to compensate our potentially disadvantaged cognitive appetite? These are the questions that research in individual differences can help us to answer.

Individual differences have been a unique area of study in such disciplines as psychology and human computer interaction. Individual differences refer to relatively stable personal and cognitive traits. It is believed that a wide range of cognitive abilities of individuals can be accounted for by a relatively fewer number of cognitive factors. Some factors may be more relevant to information visualization than others. For example, spatial ability, spatial memory, and associative memory are among the ones that are more likely to be relevant. Individual differences are just one aspect of the dynamics of using information visualization and virtual environments. Social and ecological dimensions are equally important in understanding how people perceive and behave in a virtual environment. These dynamics in virtual environments will be discussed in Chapter 7.

There are two general views on individual differences. One believes that the differences can be reduced through education and training, while the other believes that these differences are difficult to change, but may be accommodated through the use of specially designed tools. The 2000 special issue on *Individual Differences in Virtual Environments* in the *Journal of the American Society for Information Science* (Chen et al., 2000) features a number of articles on this topic.

Empirical evidence in situations similar to the use of information visualization systems suggests that spatial ability, associative memory, and visual memory should be a good starting point (Benyon, 1993; Carroll, 1993; Dahlbäck et al., 1996; Dillon and Watson, 1996; Höök et al., 1996; Vicente and Williges, 1988). The first example is an empirical study focusing on spatial ability and visual information retrieval. The second example is focusing on associative memory and visual memory, and the third is the most extensive experimental study of the three, focusing on the role of both spatial ability and associative memory in visual information retrieval.

6.7.1 Cognitive Factors

Methodologically, an introduction to factor-referenced cognitive tests in Eckstrom et al. (1976) is the first step. Is it sensible to test an information visualization design with the whole range of cognitive factors? Is it a practical starting point to establish a baseline of representative information visualization design? Can factor-referenced cognitive tests provide researchers and designers with common ground for analyzing and comparing the effects of different information visualization options in comparable cognitive tests?

The first comprehensive introduction of individual differences into human–computer interaction (HCI) is Egan's seminal work (1988), which has inspired many studies in the field. According to Egan (1988), differences between users can be in the staggering order of 20:1 for common computing tasks, such as programming and text editing. More importantly, such differences can be understood and predicted, as well as modified through design.

The most influential and updated work on the study of individual differences in psychology is presented by Carroll (1993). Cognitive factors are grouped into a three-level hierarchy: general intelligence (g) is at the top level, eight ability categories reside at the second level, and first order factors derived from these general ability types are at the third level. In particular, the eight second-level general ability categories are:

- crystallized intelligence
- fluid intelligence
- general memory and learning
- broad visual perception

- broad auditory perception
- broad retrieval ability
- broad cognitive speed
- processing speed.

At the third level, each of these general ability types is split into first order factors; for example, memory becomes associative memory, visual memory, episodic memory, and memory span. This hierarchical organization is regarded as the standard conceptualization (Kline, 1994; Dillon and Watson, 1996).

Dillon and Watson (1996) presented a thought-provoking review of the study of individual differences, and its position in the field of HCI. According to Dillon and Watson, a core number of basic cognitive abilities have been reliably and validly identified, as influencing the performance of specific tasks in predictable ways. Several areas are potentially fruitful for HCI. They recommend that psychological measures of individual differences should be used as a basis for establishing context, and achieving a greater degree of generalisability of HCI findings.

The subsequent empirical studies investigate the relationship between individual differences and information foraging within a semantically organized virtual world. This virtual world is constructed automatically, based on the results of information visualization. Three cognitive factors are specifically examined in the use of the semantically organized virtual world: spatial ability, associative memory, and visual memory. Studies of these not only illustrate a generic methodology for evaluating the usefulness of information visualization design, but also highlight cognitive factors that may lead to insights into information visualization design itself.

Spatial Ability

Spatial ability, also known as visualization ability, is the ability of an individual to manipulate or transform the image of spatial patterns into other arrangements (Eckstrom et al., 1976). The role of spatial ability in navigating through information structures has received much attention over the past decade, ranging from large file structures and database systems, to hypermedia, and virtual reality-based spatial models. For example, Vicente and Williges (1988) found that spatial ability affected the user's ability to navigate a large file structure. Campagnoni and Ehrlich (1989) reported that users with good visualization ability used the top-level table of contents less frequently than users with lower visualization ability, suggesting that a good spatial ability may help in memorizing how the information is organized. Dahlbäck et al. (1996) found a strong correlation between users' spatial abilities and their task completion times. The fastest subject completed tasks 19 times faster than the slowest subject. The study suggested that solving problems in the real world and solving problems in a virtual world involve different spatial abilities.

Our 1996 meta-analysis of empirical studies of hypertext found a number of large effects that are relevant to cognitive abilities (Chen and Rada, 1996). The meta-analysis found that the complexity of tasks has the greatest effect size on effectiveness measures, such as accuracy and error rate measures ($r = 0.63$), followed by graphical maps ($r = 0.38$). More interestingly, the strongest effects on efficiency measures are due to spatial ability of individuals ($r = 0.45$) and the complexity of tasks ($r = 0.58$). These are large effect sizes according to the guidelines of Cohen (1977) – one should take these factors seriously.

The relationship between spatial ability and visual navigation in a virtual reality-based spatial user interface was studied by Chen and Czerwinski (1997). Spatial ability, measured by paper-folding tests (VZ-2) included in Eckstrom et al. (1976), was strongly correlated with the accuracy of sketches made by subjects after they searched through a semantically organized spatial model. The spatial ability was positively correlated with the differences between the main structure in the spatial layout and the sketches made by individuals (Spearman's $r = 0.774$, $p = 0.004$, one-tailed). Similarly, a strong correlation was found between spatial ability and the secondary structures in the spatial layout, and structures memorized by individuals (Spearman's $r = 0.591$, $p = 0.036$, one-tailed).

Associative Memory

Sometimes we learn two things together, despite they have nothing to do with each other otherwise. We may associate one thing with another in this way. Associative memory is our ability to recall one part of the relationship when seeing the other part (Carroll, 1974). This factor involves the storage and retrieval of information from intermediate-term memory. Individual differences observed in such conditions may be largely due to the successful use of strategies such as rehearsal, and using mnemonic mediators.

In the following examples, a document in a spatial model of a semantic network is shown as a colored sphere labeled by the initials of authors. An interesting question is what role is played by associative memory in visual navigation. Can we build a mental map based on spatially associated graphical and textual cues? If we can develop an effective mental map, presumably we should be able to find the information more efficiently.

Visual Memory

Visual memory is the ability to remember the configuration, location, and orientation of figural material, another potentially useful cognitive factor for the use and evaluation of a virtual environment, based on a spatial metaphor (Eckstrom et al., 1976). Visual memory involves different cognitive processes from those used in other memory factors. A good visual memory should enable users to memorize and locate local structures more efficiently; thus more effective information search and information foraging is possible.

The three empirical studies summarized below tested the effects of individual differences on visual search and navigation. Individual differences were measured by factor-referenced cognitive tests (Eckstrom et al., 1976). Spatial ability is measured by VZ-2 scores, associative memory by MA-1 scores, and visual memory by MV-1 scores.

The search space consisted of a document similarity network of 169 papers published in three ACM SIGCHI conference proceedings between 1995 and 1997. The document similarity networks were in fact Pathfinder networks derived from inter-document similarities determined by latent semantic indexing (LSI) (Deerwester et al., 1990). The document network was rendered in virtual reality modeling language (VRML) 2.0. Users can walk and fly through the semantic space. The screen is split into two frames: the semantic space is displayed as a virtual world in the left-hand side frame. Document spheres were color coded by the year of their publication: 1995 papers in red, 1996 in green, and 1997 in blue. Each sphere is labeled with the initials of authors of the paper. Clicking on the sphere will load the abstract into the right-hand side frame. The technical background for LSI and Pathfinder network scaling is described in Chapter 2. Readers may also consult the original publications such as Chen (1998a,b) and Chen and Czerwinski (1998).

6.7.2 Study I: Spatial Ability

The first study focuses on correlation relationships between spatial ability and visual navigation. Eleven subjects performed search tasks through the VRML-based interface. Moving the mouse cursor over a sphere would pop up the paper's title. Clicking on the sphere would display the abstract in the right-hand side frame. All the movements on the computer screen were videotaped and subsequently analyzed. Users can zoom in and out to obtain an overview of the entire structure or a detailed view of specific areas. The user interface also allows tele-porting-like instant zoom right in to the front of a sphere.

Subjects' spatial ability scores were collected through a standard paper-folding test (Eckstrom et al., 1976). The paper-folding test requires subjects to answer multiple-choice questions about the consequence of punching a hole in a paper folded in a particular way. A spatial ability score ranges from 0 to 20. This study has the average score of 10 and a standard deviation of 3.91.

The tasks were finding papers on particular topics and saving relevant papers to a local directory on their PC. In the first task, subjects were told to find as many papers as they could about a topic, whereas in the second task, they were told to find the five most relevant papers on a different topic. The 169 papers fall into three categories of relevancy: (1) the most obvious ones – their relevance is clear from their titles; (2) the intermediate ones – their relevance is not clear from their titles alone, but clear enough if you read their abstracts; and (3) the least obvious ones – reading the full text is necessary. For example, if we look for papers on *visualization*, it is immediately clear by just reading the titles that papers 1 and 2 below are relevant, but the relevance of paper 3 is less obvious:

- Paper 1. Tilebars: visualization of term distribution information in full-text information access.
- Paper 2. Visualizing complex hypermedia networks through multiple hierarchical views.
- Paper 3. An organic user interface for searching citation links.

There were 24 relevant papers for Task 1, and 18 for Task 2. Having completed Task 1, subjects sketched the structure of the visualized semantic space as best they could from memory. Research has shown that if we engage ourselves more deeply in the study of an object, then we tend to recall more details (Craik and Lockhart, 1972). In this case, since subjects engaged in visual search, such sketches should reveal to which parts of the semantic space they directed most attention.

Subjects performed a categorization and abstraction task after Task 2 – they gave names to clusters of papers in the visualized semantic space. This task was designed to find out whether subjects could summarize groups of papers associated with distinctive structural patterns, and what naming schemes they would use. Such input can be used as semantic labels, landmarks, and signs. However, some subjects found this task very difficult; some could not even complete it. Some wanted to check particular spheres again before they could provide a name for the given structures.

Task performance scores were measured as the number of times that a subject read an abstract, the number of saved abstracts, and the number of relevant abstracts saved. The entire session lasted approximately 30 minutes. Task performance scores were split into a high spatial ability group (A) and a low spatial ability group (B). The high spatial ability group saved more than twice as many abstracts as the low spatial ability group in Task 1, and slightly more in Task 2. Group A also found about twice as many relevant abstracts as Group B. Spatial ability was positively correlated with recall scores in both Task 1 and Task 2 ($r = 0.42$ and 0.37, respectively), but were negatively correlated with precision scores in Task 1, and to a lesser degree in Task 2 ($r = 0.53$ and 0.18, respectively). The total number of abstracts viewed was not correlated with spatial ability in Task 1 ($r = 0.07$), but negatively correlated in Task 2 ($r = 0.43$). The number of saved abstracts was positively correlated with spatial ability in both Task 1 and Task 2 ($r = 0.45$ and 0.27, respectively).

The results suggested that subjects did well if relevant papers were located in structurally significant areas of the user interface, especially at nodes with high degrees. However, subjects were less successful on the outskirts of the structure. Subjects typically examined key positions such as branching points or central points in their first few moves.

The videotapes recorded a number of interesting search strategies. First, most subjects started their search from the central circle structure, and they ignored the outskirts of the central circle during their initial search. Next, subjects would check a number of positions on the circle, especially points connecting to branches. Over time, they would gradually expand their search space outwards, to reach nodes farther away from the central area. An interesting observation was that after a few visits to a target document, subjects appeared to suddenly decide the document was relevant after all and would save it immediately. This implies that subjects continuously adjust their relevance criteria. Some subjects hopped from one cluster to another in long jumps, whereas others carefully examined each node along a path, according to the virtual semantic structure. Subjects who made longer jumps apparently realized that they might be able to rely on the structural patterns to help with their navigation. Navigational patterns also highlighted the special role of distinctive structural patterns such as circles, stars, and long spikes, as we expected from earlier research (Chen, 1998a, b).

Some people only realized that they could benefit from the structure during the second half of their session. The spatial memory test highlighted the need for reinforcing strategically significant points, or structural hotspots, as well as larger structural patterns in the virtual environment. Strong stimuli (e.g. landmarks or signs) should be recommended, to reinforce users' cognitive map of the virtual space. For example, an animation of how papers were organized would help users to understand the nature of the organization. This notion awaits further user interface design work.

Correlation between spatial ability and user behavior was computed for a number of different tasks. Although we found that recall was positively correlated with spatial ability, as were a number of other measures, the overall impact of spatial ability was not straightforward. Sometimes the direction of the correlation was unexpected. A few aspects of the design of this study could be improved in future research, to help clarify the impact that spatial ability might have on the usability of such information visualizations. For example, the entire task session was very limited in terms of time, especially for subjects who had not used the VRML viewer prior to the test session. The sample size should be increased to minimize variability in the data resulting from extreme combinations of spatial ability and experience with computers.

On the other hand, the spatial memory test and the categorization task turned out to be very informative. We recommend usability studies on visualization-based information systems to include such tasks.

6.7.3 Study II: Associative Memory and Visual Memory

The second study focuses on the effects of associative memory and visual memory on visual navigation performance with the same interface as in Study I. Ten subjects participated in this study. Associative memory scores (MA-1) and visual memory scores (MV-1) were obtained one day before search sessions.

Subjects sketched the spatial layout of the search space at the end of the first block of search tasks. When subjects completed the second block of tasks, they were asked to name the cluster of papers in the semantic space. The recall and precision scores were calculated based on the underlying latent semantic indexing techniques. We used the keywords appearing in the task descriptions to formulate the search. The top 20 papers returned by the LSI were regarded as the short-listed documents for the given topics. Because the semantic space was generated on the basis of the LSI modeling, it is reasonable to use the results of LSI on the same document collection to measure the relevance. Correlations were computed between task performances and subjects' memory scores.

The number of abstracts saved by each individual was positively correlated with the memory associated test in Task 1. As predicted, subjects with better memory performed better. However, the number of saved abstracts was negatively correlated with both memory tests in Task 2. The possible reason for this could be that in Task 2 it was difficult to search for a specific topic. Subjects would need to explore the content of the paper more deeply, especially those without background in this area. The use of more general content papers could solve this problem. Associative memory was strongly correlated with the mean recall scores of Task 1 ($r = 0.855$, $p = 0.003$), whereas visual memory was negatively correlated with the mean recall scores of Task 2 ($r = 0.649$, $p = 0.041$).

All the subjects included a central circle in their sketches. However, the detailed structures vary. Figure 6.12 includes four sketches of the spatial layout of the underlying search space, made by subjects who had the highest performance scores, as well as the ones who had lowest performance scores.

In sketch (a), the subject who scored high in both recall and precision accurately depicted most details about the surrounding branches and strokes inside the central circle. The sketch in (b) was very interesting: most links were omitted, but it still gave an accurate outline of the structure. This sketch shows the branches that the subject visited several times in greater detail. In sketch (c), although the overall recall was not as accurate as (a) and (b), the subject depicted the branches that he searched, especially the branch he started with. Finally, sketch (d) was the least accurate by a subject with the lowest recall score for the first topic.

With little knowledge of the underlying structure, many users adopted a brute-force search strategy; much of their initial inspection relied on mouse hovering and title pop-ups. People with stronger memory abilities were expected to perform better. In fact, a strong positive correlation was found between associative memory and task performance for Task 1 ($r = 0.855$, $p = 0.003$). However, visual memory was negatively correlated for Task 2 ($r = 0.649$, $p = 0.041$).

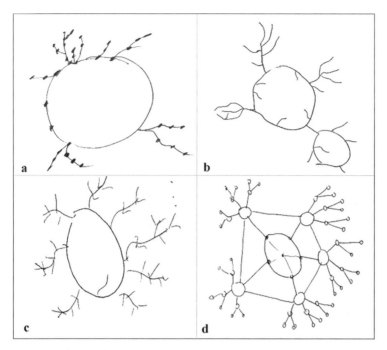

Figure 6.12 Subjects' sketches of the semantic space they searched. Source: Chen and Czerwinski (1997).

6.7.4 Study III: Associative Memory and Spatial Ability

The third study further explores the effects of cognitive factors on visual navigation performance. It was a within-subject design. Scores of spatial ability (VZ-2)
and associative memory (MA-1) were obtained from a pretest. Two user interfaces
were used in each session: one was spatial, and the other was textual. The search
task was to find as many papers as possible relevant to four topics. Twelve subjects
were scheduled according to a Latin-Square design. Subjects searched in one user
interface for two topics, and then switched over to the other interface for the
remaining two topics. Ten minutes were allocated for each topic.

To compensate for the less familiar search topics, the relevance of a document
was calculated based on pooled answers among subjects. If two or more subjects
marked a document as relevant to a given topic, then it would be treated as relevant. The recall and precision were calculated as usual. Spearman's correlation
coefficients were computed between subjective ratings, and both spatial ability and
associative memory scores. Unless stated otherwise, all the statistical significance
was one-tailed at the conventional 0.05 level. Higher spatial ability scores and
higher associative memory scores were associated with the positive direction.

Spearman's correlation coefficients reveal a negative correlation between associative memory and the usefulness rating on the textual user interface (Spearman's
$r = 0.597, p = 0.020$), implying that a user with a good associative memory is more
likely to favor the spatial user interface, rather than the textual one. There was a

positive correlation between spatial ability and associative memory (Pearson's $r = 0.581, p = 0.024$).

A negative correlation was found between associative memory and precision in the spatial user interface (Pearson's $r = 0.544, p = 0.034$), and a negative correlation between spatial ability and precision in the textual user interface (Pearson's $r = 0.553, p = 0.031$). Both correlations are statistically significant, and the magnitudes can be regarded as medium or large.

In general, subjects performed slightly better with the textual interface than the spatial one. General factorial analysis and linear regression analysis were used to analyze the multivariate effects on the overall information foraging performance. Spatial ability scores (VZ-2) and associative memory scores (MA-1) were used as covariants in these models. A dummy variable S was also assigned, to indicate whether the spatial user interface was used before the textual one.

There was a strong effect of associative memory on precision ($F(1, 10) = 6.69$, $p = 0.027$), which explains 40% of the variance. However, the main effect of associative memory on recall was not statistically significant ($F(1, 10) = 0.672, p = 0.431$). Stepwise linear regression analysis yielded a single predictor model for both precision and recall. Associative memory explained more than 70% of the variance ($R^2 = 0.731$, Adj. $R^2 = 0.707$). Spatial ability (VZ-2) and the dummy variable S were excluded from the model. Similarly, associative memory remained the best predictor for recall, explaining 59% of the variance according to the adjusted R^2.

In summary, associative memory appears to be a good predictor of task performance with the spatial user interface, whereas spatial ability seems to be overshadowed by the cognitive factor of memory. The first study found a strong correlation between spatial ability and the accuracy of a sketch task. The second study extended its scope to the two cognitive factors, associative memory (MA-1) and visual memory (MV-1). A strong positive correlation was found between associative memory and overall recall. Finally, the third study compared the same spatial user interface and a textual user interface in a within-subject Latin-Square experimental design. Precision with the spatial user interface was negatively correlated with associative memory, whereas precision with the textual user interface was negatively correlated with spatial ability.

6.8 Summary

In this chapter, we have discussed a variety of empirical studies concerning various aspects of information visualization, ranging from the usage of classic information visualization designs such as cone trees and hyperbolic view browsers to individual differences in terms of spatial ability, associative memory, and visual memory.

Much of the existing empirical studies can be divided into ones that deal with lower-level elementary perceptual tasks or higher-level application-related tasks. Although information visualization can no doubt benefit from all empirical studies, the crucial and profound understanding at this stage is more likely to come from the study of lower-level tasks. Many application-oriented empirical studies have generated valuable insights into the complex relationship between tasks and visual cues. On the other hand, the empirical link between visual attributes and perceptual tasks is still missing in many areas of information visualization.

Chapter 7
Virtual Environments

All that is valuable in human society depends upon the opportunity for development accorded the individual.

Albert Einstein

What is a virtual environment? What is special about a collaborative virtual environment? Who is using them? What do they have to do with information visualization? Why do we care about them from the perspective of information visualization? We will address these questions in this chapter.

A study of a virtual environment typically focuses on issues such as: how is it constructed, and how is it used? Now information visualization introduces an interesting spin. What are the roles that information visualization can play in the construction of a virtual, collaborative environment? How do people interact with visualized information in such environments?

Traditionally, a virtual environment does not necessarily need to have the presence of a two- or three-dimensional spatial model to make it a virtual environment; indeed, many earlier virtual environments are text-based. On the other hand, a virtual environment with a spatial–visual interface is more likely to make a lot of difference. Researchers distinguish collaborative virtual environments (CVEs) from general multi-user virtual environments, or distributed virtual environments, by stressing their built-in facilities for various social activities.

Boyd and Darken organized a workshop at CHI '96 with more focused themes on psychological issues (Boyd and Darken, 1996), and identified some major human aspects of virtual environment (VE) interaction, in particular the psychological difficulties encountered when using them. Here are some examples:

- Spatial orientation and wayfinding in virtual worlds.
- Designing the virtual world to relate to human perceptual abilities, not just striving for photo-realism.
- Means of traveling from one virtual location to another, directed or browsing, and for acting in the environment.
- Designing the controlling inputs to take advantage of human physical abilities, and adapting to disabilities.
- Evaluating VE interfaces, experiences with usability testing of whole systems.
- Appreciating the interdependence between task features and interface design.
- Understanding the dimensions of usefulness and complexity for VE interfaces.

A workshop even more directly related to social interaction was held in Stockholm in March 1998,[1] organized by IFIP working group WG13.2 and the Navigation SIG of Esprit's I³-net (Information Intelligence Interfaces). The focus of the Stockholm workshop was personalized and social navigation in information space.

---

[1]http://www.sics.se/humle/projects/persona/web/

7.1 Social Dimensions of Information Spaces

Virtual environments incorporate a broad range of information and communication systems for both individual and social use. These systems are often characterized by the use of virtual reality, multimedia, 3-dimensional graphics, computer networks, and various communication facilities. Virtual environments can be categorized along two dimensions concerning the role of a spatial metaphor: spatial representation and spatial semantics. Spatial representation refers to the use of textual, graphical, multimedia, or virtual reality. Spatial semantics refers to the extent to which the meaning of spatial configuration is related to the information needs of users.

Traditional chat rooms involve little or no spatial configuration. As a result, their rating on the semantic dimension is low. The Palace inherits the meaning of places in the physical world, using photo-realistic images to convey its spatial organization, such as a bar or the beach. The design and use of these virtual environments will be described further. Although media spaces and collaborative virtual environments had little overlap in terms of their evolution until recently, they do have some profound connections. In fact, they can be seen as two different approaches to the same problem: to facilitate informal collaboration between people separated by geographical distance. Therefore, media spaces are considered of considerable significance to the design of new virtual environments.

7.1.1 Mutual Awareness and Contextualization Cues

Informal communication is an important part of collaborative work (Kraut et al., 1988; Whittaker et al., 1994). According to Kraut et al. (1990), informal communication tends to be brief, frequent, and unplanned, and physical proximity is a good predictor of scientific collaboration. Much attention has been given to the notion of proximity and its role in mediating informal communication. Proximity is fundamental to structuring and visualizing a semantic space for informal communication and social construction of knowledge.

Media spaces are distributed electronic environments designed for supporting both the social and task-oriented aspects of collaborative work. The principal design rationale is that work is fundamentally social (Bly et al., 1993). In geographically distributed groups, informal interaction is particularly important (Bly et al., 1993).

Several methodologies from sociology, anthropology, and linguistics are potentially useful for exploring the structure of social interaction, and how it reflects the influence of a meaningful context. Two concepts are particularly concerned with structures of social contexts: the concept of *contextualisation cues* from linguistics (Gumperz, 1982) and the concept of *frames* from sociology (Goffman, 1974). The following review is partially based on Drew and Heritage (1992).

Sociolinguistics had initially treated context in terms of the social attributes that speakers bring to talk – for example, age, class, ethnicity, gender, geographical region, and other relationships. Studies of data from natural settings have shown that the relevance of these attributes depended upon the particular setting in which the talk occurred, and also upon the particular speech activities or tasks that speakers were engaged in within those settings.

The dynamic nature of social contexts and the importance of linguistic details in evoking them have been studied in Gumperz (1982). He shows that any aspect of linguistic behavior may function as a contextualization cue, including lexical, phonological, and syntactic choices, together with the use of particular codes, dialects, or styles. These contextualization cues indicate which aspects of the social context are relevant in interpreting what a speaker means. By indicating significant aspects of the social context, contextualization cues enable people to make inferences about each other's communicative intentions and goals.

The notion of contextualization cues offered an important analytical way to grasp the relationship between language use and speakers' orientations to context and inference making. There is a significant similarity between the linguistic concept of contextualization cues as outlined by Gumperz (1982), and the sociological concept of frames developed by Goffman (1974). The notion of frames focuses on the definition which participants give to their current social activity – to what is going on, what the situation is, and the roles which the participants adopt within it. These concepts both relate specific linguistic options to the social activity in which language is being engaged.

Conversation analysis (CA) is one of the most influential analytical tools in the study of talk-in-context (Drew and Heritage, 1992). It focuses on the contextual sensitivity of language use in everyday conversations. CA has been frequently used in the study of ordinary talk between people in a wide variety of social relations and contexts. The combination of virtual environments and online discussion facilities in our approach enables researchers to study discourse structures in a new environment. We will analyze dialogues in our virtual environment using a number of analytical techniques, including conversation analysis.

The organization principle of our shared three-dimensional semantic space is based on an enriched spatial model. The intention is to provide additional resources that stimulate participants to question, interpret, and discuss the meaning of the underlying spatial metaphor. The spatial model therefore invites people to discuss their own understanding of the semantic structure and of the implications of the presence of such a structure on the appropriateness of interactive behavior and discourse structures.

7.1.2 From Proximity to Mutual Awareness

When people are near to each other in the physical world, they may become interested in knowing what others are doing. As the distance between them becomes less, they may start to talk to each other. Proximity-triggered communication mechanisms are essentially based on a similar scenario. They have been adapted in distributed computer environments to deal with the need for mutual awareness and direct communication. Relevant empirical data are yet to be available for us to understand fully the underlying mechanisms that transform the need of mutual awareness into direct interaction and how we can effectively support such transitions in distributed collaborative systems.

SEPIA is a cooperative hypermedia authoring environment (Haake and Wilson, 1992). It is a good example of incorporating the idea of proximity in a collaborative environment. SEPIA uses three modes to model the degree of interdependency among the participants of a collaborative system: (1) the independent mode, in which participants use the system as individuals; (2) the loosely-coupled mode (LC), in which participants maintain minimum mutual awareness; and (3) the tightly-coupled mode (TC), in which participants collaborate with each other fully.

SEPIA aims to track and facilitate interactions among co-authors. The proximity between co-authors is measured in terms of the distance between their positions in SEPIA's activity spaces. If one user opens a composite node that is currently being used by someone, then the two users transit from an independent mode to an LC mode. The structure of communications is strongly influenced by the structure of the underlying activity spaces. And such activity spaces are in fact a type of collaborative virtual environment.

Interestingly, many have considered using proximity as an indicator of mode transitions. Mode transitions triggered by proximity prompt people to communicate with each other if they move close enough to each other. This is different from problem-driving mechanisms; for example, in Montage, the need for communication is characterized in terms of the arrival of a problem (Tang et al., 1994). In this chapter, we are interested in how users navigate in groups in a virtual environment, how they communicate with each other, and the impact of information visualization on group dynamics.

7.1.3 Gidden's Structuration Theory

Studies of earlier media spaces have led to an interesting finding – a media space evolves as people use it. This is particularly interesting; given the close connection between a media space and a virtual environment, one may explore the counterpart of this phenomena in virtual environments, especially those predominated by 2D or 3D information visualization artifacts. As people interact through visualization-empowered virtual environments, is there a meaningful way in which the underlying virtual environment can transform and adapt itself to its users" needs and preferences?

The theory of structuration (Giddens, 1984) addresses the interdependent relationship between human action and social structure. Structures are composed of *rules* and *resources*. Rules and resources provide contextual constraints that individuals draw upon when acting and interacting. The interplay between structure and action produces and reproduces social systems. This is what has been experienced in the evolution of media spaces, such as the Palo Alta-Portland link (Bly et al., 1993).

Interactionism emphasizes the *social* impact on the creation and interpretation of meanings, as opposed to the *objective* meanings of reality upheld by system rationalists (Kling, 1980). To interactionism, collaboration is the process in which people establish a mutual understanding of meanings in a specific context. The term *infrastructure* refers to resources, procedures, and institutionalized values for providing these supporting resources, including organizational plans, definitions of roles, and documentation.

If rules and resources are so important to the creation and interpretation of meanings in a socio-collaborative setting, to what extent is information visualization playing its role in the establishment of a mutual understanding of meanings?

7.1.4 Social Episodes

The study of social episodes has been strongly influenced by the landmark work of Forgas over the last two decades, notably Forgas (1979) and Forgas et al. (1984). The strong influence is reflected in more recent studies of social episodes and social cognition, such as Rooney and Schmelkin (1996). A distinguishing significance of the work of Forgas is that it has established an effective way of studying a wide variety of aspects of the so-called social episodes, based on multidimensional scaling techniques. A key focus of such analytical studies is on what people perceive, and how they interpret what they see of complex social, cultural, and ecological activities.

The reasons for introducing the study of social episodes here are two-fold. First, social episodes are traditionally studied in real-world behavior settings. We knew little about social episodes in a virtual environment until relatively recently, despite the fact that many virtual environments are based on real-world settings and scenarios. There is a wide spectrum of virtual environments in which the dynamics and structures of social episodes are likely to be different, but associated with what people do in the real world. The study of social episodes, therefore, is a potentially valuable source of knowledge for the design of virtual environments, and for the understanding of social interaction in new settings.

The second reason is the need for effective analytical and modeling methodologies that are easy to understand and which can be adopted by researchers and practitioners who might not have experiences in social psychology. There are some intrinsic connections between techniques in the multidimensional scaling family and the visualization techniques that we have described earlier in this book.

The term "social episodes" is used in a number of different senses in many areas of social science, such as sociology, social psychology and linguistics. What is common among these different uses is that "episode" always refers to a unit of social interaction. Similar concepts of a unit of social interaction include a "situation", an "encounter", or even a "performance". Episodes are the smaller building blocks of larger and more complex social situations. A dinner party, as a social situation, can be divided into a number of social episodes, such as arrival and greetings, drink and chat before dinner, and the dinner (Argyle, 1976). The problem with such perspectives is that situations and episodes may not always be clearly distinguished consistently.

Alternatively, the term "episode" is also regarded as a generic label of goal-directed recurring interaction sequences with a culturally determined meaning. It is argued that the study of formal, explicitly regulated, episodes may provide the clue to the understanding of naturalistic episodes.

In the study of social episodes, environments are distinguished as macro- and micro-environments. In a macro-environment, the scene is usually landscape, streets, and whole institutions, whereas a micro-environment typically involves a room, the equipment of a room, or a shop. Canter and his colleagues explored the relationship between the person and the environment in a series of studies (Canter et al., 1974, 1985). The study of social episodes in a virtual environment seems likely to be a fruitful area of research, which may lead to useful insights into the role of abstract information spaces in stimulating and fostering social interaction.

7.2 Online Communities

Currently, surfing on the web is largely an individual experience. Users cannot tell from their browsers whether other people are visiting the same web page at the same time. The invisible nature of browsing is a feature that distinguishes a multiple user system from a collaborative one.

To solve this problem, Donath and Robertson at MIT Media Lab have developed a Sociable Web, consisting of a modified web server and browser. On the Sociable Web, users have access to a list of people concurrently browsing on the same web page. Concurrent visitors communicate with each other using a tool called WebTalk, sharing, for example, URLs, sounds, and graphics. In fact, the user does not even have to hang around the same page to "stay tuned" to a group of people.

Social Web explores several interesting concepts: visibility among web users on the same page, synchronous collaboration among web users, and the sharing of URLs for a group of people to browse together. However, the system relies on a modified server and browser, which may prevent Social Web from being widely accessed and integrated into the current web infrastructure.

An increasingly popular approach to the development of a virtual place for people to meet and chat is to use open standards such as VRML, and to incorporate the capabilities of Java-enabled applications or simply Java applets, tiny programming components that can be easily sent through computer networks.

Several front-runners in virtual reality-based multi-user environments include Online Community from blaxxun interactive, Community Place from Sony, and ActiveWorlds from The Circle of Fire Studio. The first two are VRML-based. Active-Worlds is built on a format called Renderware, which only recently started to enable some basic VRML features.

In these virtual worlds, users are represented as some form of 3D graphical icon known as an avatar. People use various avatars, from human figures, to birds, sharks, and dinosaurs. A potentially useful feature of avatar-based user interfaces is that one can see the movement of an avatar and follow the trail of it, which fosters an intuitive metaphor of social navigation. In addition to the visual effects in virtual reality applications, people visiting the same virtual environment can communicate with other people via chat facilities.

An important insight from the social navigation trends is that like-minded people may form a group or even a crowd as they are attracted by the content of a web page. In social navigation, people gather together because they are all interested in a particular topic. This distinguishes the concept from traditional chat rooms, where a considerable number of people come, just for the sake of talking to someone.

This contrast leads to a far-reaching question: if the reality-based virtual environment can bring like-minded people together on topical subjects in a given domain, will that enable people to experience more engaging and more focused social interaction? If so, such virtual environments might bridge the gap between chat- and collaboration-oriented virtual environments. Collaborative virtual environments have a wide range of applications, such as distance learning, digital libraries, and online communities.

Pioneering media spaces are typically equipped with video and audio channels connecting groups of people across geographically separated sites. Media spaces integrate video, audio, and computer media to help individuals and groups to work together, despite being spatially and temporally distributed (Mantei et al., 1991).

Figure 7.1 A naturalistic landscape in ActiveWorlds.

Famous media spaces include Xerox's Palo Alto-Portland link (Bly et al., 1993), CAVECAT (Mantei et al., 1991), and Virtual Windows (Gaver et al., 1995).

The evolution of a media space has been characterized by the interplay between the design and how people actually use it. A variety of metaphors have been used in the design to help users to interact and communicate. For example, in order to provide a sense of proximity for distributed groups, Tang et al. (1994) developed a media space called Montage, where people can make momentary, reciprocal "glances" among networked workstations. This is a lightweight approach: when people have encountered problems, they can quickly and easily find out whether colleagues who might be able to help are available.

Bly et al. (1993) have grouped distinguishing characteristics of media space design into three major points of reference: spatial, object, and figural. The notion of media space is associated with a mapping from abstract electronic space to abstract physical space. Spatial models and metaphors have been increasingly popular in collaborative systems. Many media-space systems are designed to reflect the structure of the physical world. Offices, hallways, conference rooms, and design studios have frequently appeared in media spaces and collaborative virtual environments using spatial metaphors.

Media spaces and collaborative virtual environments have some subtle but fundamental differences. For example, media spaces normally involve both real and virtual worlds, known as hybrid spaces (Harrison and Dourish, 1996), whereas a virtual environment gives users the freedom to do things that might be impossible in a real world setting. The power of information visualization techniques can largely strengthen and augment users' abilities.

ActiveWorlds,[2] presented by the Circle of Fire, is a generic platform for creating and exploring virtual worlds. Registered users can build their own properties as well as visit gardens, parks, and houses built by others. There are hundreds of virtual worlds in ActiveWorlds, ranging from the Yellowstone National Park to Mars, and the system is featured in Damer's book on avatars (1998). Figure 7.1 shows

---

[2]http://www.activeworlds.com/

Figure 7.2 Blaxxun's online communities.

a scene from ActiveWorlds. People's avatars gathered around the ground zero – the entry point to the virtual world, and users can chat with other visitors to the virtual world using a textual chat dialogue window.

A rival virtual world platform is provided by blaxxun interactive. Its online community[3] accommodates 3D interactive VRML worlds, based on a client-server architecture on the Internet. The online community client browser is a VRML plug-in for both Netscape and Internet Explorer. blaxxun's VRML browser is one of the few VRML browsers that work with both VRML 2.0 and 1.0 worlds. The blaxxun community server allows users to build and support their own 3D interactive VRML worlds. One major advantage of using VRML in online community is that it allows users to integrate existing VRML worlds into a multi-user virtual environment. Chat is supported by textual dialogue windows on the client browser.

The spatial metaphor is often intended to resemble the physical world. Figure 7.2 is a screenshot of a scene near to the ground zero, i.e. the entry point, of the Activity World. This virtual world is organized on an abstract spatial model. However, chatting and dialoguing in this type of virtual world did not seem to develop into deeper and more engaging conversations, despite the fact that engaging conversations do arise in chat rooms. Can we facilitate and promote the transition from an informal chat to a productive conversation through the design of a virtual environment?

Gopher VR – a spatial interface to GopherSpace – was developed to create a publicly accessible 3D space (McCahill and Erickson, 1995). Thomas Erickson's publication list[4] includes additional interesting articles about the design of Gopher VR.

The design of Gopher VR focuses particularly on the design issues raised by 3D spatial interfaces. Most 3D spatial interfaces to information spaces are in research laboratories. Gopher VR aims to enable a broad range of people to access a large public information space. Two potential advantages of 3D interfaces are specifically

---

[3]http://www.blaxxun.com/
[4]http://www.pliant.org/personal/Tom_Erickson/TomsPubs.html

pursued in the design of Gopher VR: compact and natural 3D representations of high dimensional information and meta-information, and, in the long run, use of the information space as a social space, with 3D serving as a natural framework for supporting social interaction (Erickson, 1993).

The design of Gopher VR is also driven by problems identified with the existing Gopher user interface. Erickson lists the following problems (McCahill and Erickson, 1995):

The "Lost-in-Space" problem: users may feel lost in their navigation, and have difficulty remembering where they found an interesting article. The "lost-in-hyperspace" problem is well known in hypermedia. This problem is due in part to the absence of any global representation of the information structure, and in part to the path followed by a user often being invisible for them to trace back. Users need an overview of Gopher Space, within which they can see their locations and the paths they have followed.

The grouping problem: within a directory, it is difficult to show relationships between items represented in a linear list. A similar problem is seen in the lists of results generated by search engines. The results are typically sorted by document–query relevance, but the user interface does not convey their relative relevance effectively. Ideally, both relevance to the search query and "closeness" to other documents should be clear to the user at a glance.

The browsing problem: it is difficult to browse, because the names of documents reflect so little of their content. The user has to open the document – often a time consuming process in itself – and read the document. Users need to see more information about the content of a document, without there being so much that they are unable to compare different documents.

In addition to solving these problems, there are a number of intriguing prospects which a new interface should consider:

Interaction traces: users browsing a large information space could benefit from the activities of previous visitors. For example, users are often interested in knowing about the relative popularity of documents, as judged by the frequency with which they are viewed or copied. The idea behind interaction traces is to reflect this in the visual appearance of the document's icon. Researchers have explored ways in which visible representations of computational objects can reflect the ways in which users have interacted with them, for example, "read wear" and "edit wear" (Hill et al., 1992, 1995).

Providing a sense of place by customisation: Gopher Space is generic: any gopher directory looks like all the others, regardless of where it is or what it contains. Gopher VR wants to reflect its contents, and something about those who construct it and maintain it. As information spaces develop their own sense of place, it seems likely that users will begin to recognise places and regions; and, while users may still get lost, they may begin to develop a sense for where they are lost (McCahill and Erickson, 1995).

Transforming information spaces into social spaces: asking someone directly for information is often the easiest and the most efficient way. In fact, sometimes people search for documents so that they can find out about their authors, to whom they then direct their queries (Erickson and Salomon, 1991). Much information access is part of a larger, often collaborative task: people seek information because they are trying to solve a problem, test a theory, understand a concept, or communicate their understanding to others. All this suggests that information access should not be isolated from other activities.

The increasing popularity of MUDs for supporting conversation, teaching, and other group activities, demonstrates that virtual spaces – even those that are purely textual – can serve as frameworks for a broad range of collaborative activities (Curtis and Nichols, 1993; Dieberger, 1997; Erickson, 1993, 1996, 1997). The design of Gopher VR is to explore expanding Gopher Space into a social space supporting a broad range of activities that complement information browsing and access.

Figures 7.3 and 7.4 show how the results of a search are organized as a spiral in Gopher VR. The spiral has a family resemblance to the circular arrangement: it defines an enclosed area with a centre point. Furthermore, the open and dynamic shape of the spiral reflects the transitory nature of most queries. A spiral provides a natural ordering of search results. The more relevant the documents, the closer they are to the root of the spiral. A search that returns a large number of very relevant documents will have a tightly coiled spiral, whereas one with few relevant items will have a very loose spiral.

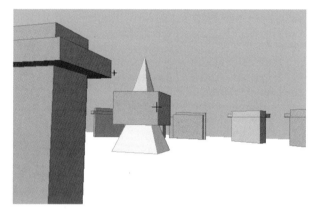

Figure 7.3 GopherVR allows the user to get a sense of the overall arrangement of the neighborhood. Reprinted with permission of Thomas Erickson.

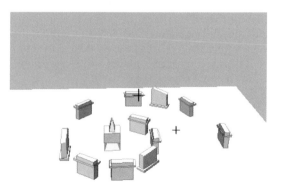

Figure 7.4 Search results are show in a spiral pattern in GopherVR. Reprinted with permission of Thomas Erickson.

7.2.1 Collaborative Virtual Environments

According to Benford et al. (1997), Collaborative Virtual Environments (CVEs) aim to provide a shared virtual space that can afford collaboration. It becomes possible to study interrelationships between documents, mutual awareness, coordination, and cooperation. VR-VIBE was developed at Nottingham University, UK to support the cooperative browsing and filtering of large document stores (Benford et al., 1995). VR-VIBE extends an information visualization system – VIBE – into three dimensions. The essence of VR-VIBE is that multiple users can explore the results of applying several simultaneous queries to a corpus of documents. Cooperative browsing is supported by directly embodying users, and providing them with the ability to interact over live audio connections, and to attach brief textual annotations to individual documents.

Users specify keywords that they wish to use to generate the visualization, and place these keywords in 3D space. Representations of the documents are then displayed in the space, according to how relevant each document is to each of the keywords. The relevance is based on a simple keyword-matching model. The position of a document to a given keyword is proportional to the relative importance of the keyword to the document.

VR-VIBE was used in an example of searching a CSCW bibliography of 1581 entries and five keywords; some other users browsing the information space were also visible. Only documents with sufficiently high relevance ratings are displayed; less relevant documents are not displayed.

We are interested in a semantically organized virtual space, and how such spatial organization shapes the cognition, interpretation, and the interaction of users. We also need to compare our approach with the valuable lessons learned from the use of previous media spaces, and how people work in distributed groups. We would like to explore how information visualization and semantic space modeling techniques can be utilized in the design of new media spaces, and more generally, whether media spaces and collaborative virtual environments work in harmony, in order to augment our working environments more effectively.

MASSIVE (Greenhalgh and Benford, 1995) is a well-known virtual space for distributed multi-user interaction. It uses a spatial model of interaction. Participants' awareness of each other, and opportunities for interaction, are supported through spatial extensions of their presence – "aura", attention – "focus", and influence – "nimbus". These mechanisms have been designed using real-world patterns of awareness and interaction in these virtual spaces.

MASSIVE is a collaborative virtual environment designed for teleconferencing (Greenhalgh and Benford, 1995). Multiple users may use the system simultaneously to communicate using arbitrary combinations of media, especially audio, graphics, and text, over computer networks. The MASSIVE system is built on a spatial model, incorporating a fundamental concept of awareness. Users' positions and orientations with reference to other users are represented on the basis of this spatial model.

The ultimate goal of a media space is to help people to transcend the limits of the physical world, and work harmoniously and productively. Informal communication has been recognized as one of the most crucial elements in successful collaborative work. A challenging issue in the design of collaborative environments that support informal communication has been to facilitate seamless transitions from accessing information individually to engaging social interaction. The use of spatial models in previous collaborative virtual environments has been criticized as oversimplifying the issue of structuring interactive behavior. In this chapter, we describe a novel approach to the design of a three-dimensional virtual environment, focusing on the role of an enriched spatial metaphor, in which the underlying semantics of a subject domain are reflected through the structure of the virtual environment. We show that this approach offers a framework that naturally unifies spatial models, semantic structures, and social interactive behavior within the virtual environment. By offering users a wider range of choices in sharing and experiencing this semantically organized virtual place, this approach has both theoretical and practical implications on the design of media spaces.

The Distributed Interactive Virtual Environment (DIVE) is an Internet-based multi-user VR system (Carlsson and Hagsand, 1993). DIVE supports the development of virtual environments, user interfaces and applications, based on shared 3D synthetic environments. It is especially tuned to multi-user applications, where several networked participants interact over a network.

Participants navigate in 3D space, and interact with other users and applications. It is integrated with the WWW. DIVE reads and exports VRML 1.0 and several other 3D formats, and its applications and activities include virtual battlefields, spatial models of interaction, virtual agents, real-world robot control, and multi-modal interaction.

7.2.2 Spatial, Semantic, and Social Navigation

Dourish and Chalmers (1994) emphasize the profound implications of enabling integrated spatial, semantic, and social navigation in an information space. A few studies in collaborative virtual environments (CVEs) investigated related issues such as movements in virtual environments and related graph dynamics (Greenhalgh, 1997; Tromp et al., 2003). A typical collaborative virtual environment in these studies would inherit a metaphor of an architectural design, an urban design, or a natural world design. What about other overarching design metaphors? A particularly interesting type of virtual environment is Collaborative Information Visualization Environments (CIVE). The spatial configuration of a CIVE is predominated by an information visualization model. CIVE offers unique opportunities for developing an integrative framework that can incorporate these intriguing ideas with quantitative as well as qualitative methods.

Spatial metaphors have been increasingly popular in the design of collaborative systems over the past few years. The following description from Tolva (1996) reflects how natural a spatial metaphor can be when describing our way of thinking:

> "the model of the intersecting sheets of paper – parallel, interpenetrating planes connected by zero-length 'worm holes' – is one way of visualizing link-rich text. Physicists call such a thing 'multiply connected surfaces'; we call it hypertext."
>
> (Tolva, 1996, p. 67)

Kaplan and Moulthrop (1994) have explored some trends in hypermedia towards modeling hypermedia as extended or global spaces. In this approach, nodes and links acquire meaning in relation to the space in which they are deployed. As echoed in the title of their article, "Where no mind has gone before: ontological design for virtual spaces", they pointed out that familiar metaphors drawn from physics, architecture, and everyday experience have only limited descriptive or explanatory value for this type of space.

The notion of virtual spaces shifts the focus from an external to an internal perspective, and highlights the need for a more sophisticated approach to hyperspace. A hyperspace is more than an architectural model of an information space – it must have its own semantics.

Kaplan and Moulthrop also considered an analogy between the semantic space of hypermedia and the interstellar spaces in science fiction:

> "To imagine journeys beyond the solar system, science fiction writers have to invent methods of faster-than-light travel. These inventions often involve discontinuities in the space-time continuum: wormholes, trans-dimensional portals, or the solution most familiar to addicts of American TV, the 'warp field effect', in which vessels bend or fold space around themselves. … We are concerned here only with the analogy between Roddenberry's famous 'final frontier' and another imaginary space, the semantic domain in hypermedia. Both are in a crucial sense elastic – spaces in which dimensional properties like distance and contiguity can be easily annulled."

Kaplan and Moulthrop highlight the distinctive difference between navigating floating vessels and traveling through spaces in a starship. The spacecraft of Star Trek and other starships move by distorting the space–time continuum. Instead of propelling through a medium, like aircraft or boats, they warp or wrap space around themselves, or teleport themselves. Similar ideas are found in ancient Chinese classic novels: zero-time travel was described as if one can shrink the large distance so that the destination comes to meet the starting point.

Dillon et al. (1993) suggest that the precise nature of the representation is less important to workers in the field of interactive technology than the insights any theory or model of navigation provides. They propose that landmarks, routes, and surveys should be considered as instantiation of basic knowledge in the design of electronic information spaces. They call for better spatial metrics and metaphors for hypermedia. Kaplan and Moulthrop emphasize that on the one hand, semantic and architectonic spaces cannot be perfectly reconciled, but on the other hand, we should aim for systems that accommodate the two in harmony as well as possible, given the contingent nature of any such harmony.

The appeal of a spatial model is rooted in its simple and intuitive association with our experience in the physical world. Conference rooms, virtual hallways, and virtual cities are examples of the impact of architectural and urban design on electronic worlds. Users feel familiar and comfortable with systems based on such spatial models. From the point of view of a designer, it is a natural choice to build an electronic environment similar to the real world, so that users can easily adopt and transform their interactive behavior, styles, and patterns, from the physical world into virtual ones.

The spatial organization of a virtual environment is a good starting point for understanding the profound relationship between information visualization and virtual environments. A virtual environment can strengthen and deepen the impact of an information visualization display, for example, by enhancing users' sense of immersion and presence. Not only can users engage themselves with visualized information in a virtual environment, but also interact with other concurrent users and reflect on other users' trails in the environment. Indeed, the spatial organization of a virtual environment can make the environment much more meaningful.

The use of spatial models in the design of previous collaborative virtual environments has been criticized as oversimplifying the issue of structuring interactive behavior (Harrison and Dourish, 1996). An inspiring, stimulating, and collaborative environment needs more than just a spatial model. People need additional resources to derive a sense of *context,* to adapt and organize their course of action and conversation.

The use of spatial models in previous collaborative virtual environments has been criticized as oversimplifying the issue of structuring, or framing, interactive behavior. Harrison and Dourish (1996) examined the notions of space and spatial organization of virtual environments and called for a re-examination of the role of spatial models in facilitating and structuring social interaction. Furthermore, they argue that it is the sense of place – instead of space – that frames interactive behavior.

Designers search for a critical property that can facilitate and shape interactive behavior in a distributed working environment. Harrison and Dourish (1996) refer to such critical properties as *appropriate behavioral framing,* which provides a reference framework for users to judge whether their behavior is appropriate. In their opinion, spatial models alone are inadequate for people to adapt their behavior; rather, it is a sense of place and shared understanding about behavior and action in a specific culture that determines how people interact and communicate (Harrison and Dourish, 1996).

Activity Theory is originated in Vygotsky's work (1962). It conceptualizes human cognition as an adaptation to ecological and social environments; furthermore, human cognition is mediated by cultural signs, including languages and tools. What is the role of a virtual environment as a medium that shapes a discourse?

Erickson (1997) analyzed how people communicate in Café Utne, one of the busiest web conferencing communities on the Internet. Café Utne is built on a metaphor of a place where people come, and find conversations concerning their interests. Erickson found that the social pressures for participation, often found in face-to-face participation, are missing in the virtual discourse medium, and therefore mutual awareness would be essential (Erickson, 1997).

In this chapter, we describe a novel approach to the design of a three-dimensional virtual environment. We will focus on the role of an enriched spatial metaphor, in which the underlying semantics of a subject domain are reflected through the structure of the virtual environment. We show that this approach offers a framework that naturally unifies spatial models, semantic structures, and social interactive behavior within the virtual environment. By offering users a wider range of choices in sharing and experiencing this semantically organized virtual place, this approach has both theoretical and practical implications for bringing media spaces and collaborative virtual environments closer.

Social navigation differs from both spatial and semantic navigation by drawing various navigational cues from usage signs (e.g. read-wear and edit-wear (Hill et al., 1992), footprints (Wexelblat, 1999; Wexelblat and Maes, 1997), dog-ears (Dieberger, 1997)), the gathering and movement of fellow tourists at the same attraction site, or the behavior of fellow users of the same information space (Crossley et al., 1999). Interpersonal relationships in two- and three-dimensional virtual worlds have been an important issue. Examples in this area include (Crossley et al., 1999; Erickson, 1993; Fry, 2003; Greenhalgh and Benford, 1995; Jeffrey and Mark, 1998). The concept of constrained navigation environments has been studied by Hanson et al. (1997). Constrained navigation appropriately restricts the user's degree of

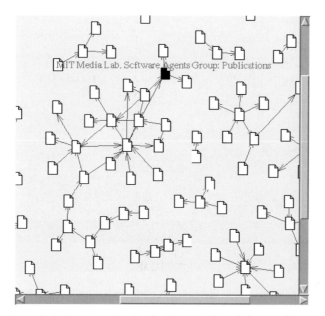

Figure 7.5 Browsing paths in Footprints. Reprinted with permission of Alan Wexelblat.

freedom when there is a mismatch between the goal of navigation and the user'
search knowledge of the exploration domain. Social dynamics in virtual worlds
has been studied from the perspectives of linguistics and small group behavior
(Tromp et al., 1998). A recent study by Börner and Penumarthy (2003) visualizes
the growth of virtual worlds along with an analysis of social diffusion in the virtual
worlds; furthermore, they define a measure of group dynamics in order to
characterize groups as focused, unfocused, expanding, shrinking, or any time
sequence of these characteristics. However, the virtual world in their study did
not incorporate semantic aspects; therefore, a study of semantic navigation was
not possible.

The Footprints system was developed at MIT Media Lab (Wexelblat, 1999).
It visualizes the paths of users moving from one document to another on a web
server (Figure 7.5). The Footprints system includes only documents that have been
visited at least once. The visualization is useful for system administrators to help
spot broken links or other problems which could otherwise be hard to detect.

Collaborative Browsing (CoBrow)[5] is a joint European project between the
University of Ulm, the University of Lancaster, and the Swiss Federal Institut of
Technology in Zurich (ETH). Its aim is to encourage and enhance communication
and collaboration using the web, by establishing a new form of collaborative work
on the Internet and transforming the web into an environment where people meet,
share information, collaborate, and perform other social activities. Figure 7.6 is the
screenshot of a CoBrow prototype created by Klaus Wolf and Holger Boenisch,
which presents a graphical representation of a number of web pages linked by
hypertext links. Each sphere represents a document, and the sphere is wrapped by
a miniature image of the document as a texture map.

---

[5]http://www.tik.ee.ethz.ch/~cobrow/

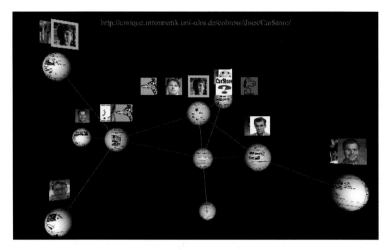

Figure 7.6 CoBrow. Reprinted with permission of Klaus Wolf and Holger Boenisch.

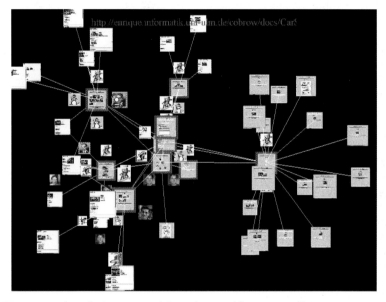

Figure 7.7 Document icons in CoBrow are miniature images of the corresponding pages. Hypertext links are also shown. Reprinted with permission of Klaus Wolf and Holger Boenisch.

Figure 7.7 shows another example from CoBrow. Edges in the 3D graph represent hypertext reference links provided by each web page. One of CoBrow's unique features is to use miniature images as document icons, to allow users to determine whether or not to pursue a particular page.

However, it is not clear how CoBrow would pursue its goal for people to meet and interact with each other, although one obvious option is to use multiuser virtual environments as a vehicle for social interaction.

Our research in knowledge domain visualization has gone beyond providing an interface for visual information retrieval; rather, the more ambitious goal is to enable users to understand not only a static structure of a knowledge domain, but also how it grows and where the research frontiers are. The design of such collaborative information visualizations needs to be augmented by a deeper understanding of how such visualization models may influence the performance as well as the experiences of users.

7.3 The StarWalker Virtual Environment

The StarWalker virtual environment is designed to maximize the role of implicit semantic structures in the structuration process of social activities within a virtual environment (Chen et al., 1999). The principle design rationale is that if the virtual environment can reflect the underlying semantic structure of an abstract information space, then users may develop more engaging social interactions.

As noted by Harrison and Dourish (1996), what distinguishes a space and a place is whether people can derive various contextual cues from the resources available. The appropriateness of interactive behavior in a particular multi-user virtual environment is subject to the interpretation of individual participants. Such interpretation may be regarded as a type of social construction of knowledge (Hjorland, 1997). It is such collective sense-making that actually transforms a space into a place. Dieberger (1997) referred to the construction of such a sense of a place and how it shapes the behavior of users in a MOO[6] environment, as social connotation.

7.3.1 The Background

StarWalker is a multiple user, domain-specific, three-dimensional virtual environment. People can meet and talk in this virtual environment, with direct reference to the scholarly literature of a specific subject domain. Users can explore domain-specific knowledge structures as a virtual reality world.

The first prototype of the StarWalker virtual environment is based on the semantic space extracted from the ACM SIGCHI conference proceedings (1995–1997). More recently, spatial models of other semantic spaces have been generated and become available for the StarWalker virtual environment, for example, the ACM Hypertext conference proceedings (1987–1998) (Chen, 1999b; Chen and Carr, 1999b; Chen and Czerwinski, 1998).

The StarWalker virtual environment is based on a client-server architecture, to maintain communication and coordination among multiple users. The design emphasizes that a virtual environment must integrate semantic, spatial, and social structures in order to foster social interaction in a scholarly environment.

A key element of the StarWalker virtual environment is the visualization of an abstract information space. The visualization highlights the underlying semantic structure associated with the information space, derived using latent semantic indexing and Pathfinder techniques.

---

[6]MOO: Multiuser Object-Oriented.

This unique approach is a natural integration of latent semantic indexing (LSI) and Pathfinder network scaling (Chen, 1998a, b; Chen and Czerwinski, 1998). The latent semantic space is modeled and simplified as a Pathfinder network. The resultant Pathfinder network becomes the blueprint of a virtual reality scene in VRML. These virtual reality models can be integrated into the design of a user interface, accessible through our familiar web browsers. As with other virtual worlds, users are able to explore the information space in a variety of intuitive ways, such as walking, flying, and rotating.

A significant part of the work is a combination of the visualization of an abstract information space with a multi-user chat environment. The combined virtual environment presents a new metaphor of social interaction. Multiple users can explore the same semantic space. Furthermore, the spatial and semantic implications of the new metaphor provide a concrete test bed in which one can observe and make sense of the dynamics of social interaction, especially social navigation. Users cannot only see how others navigate in a three-dimensional virtual world, but also talk to them, using multi-user chat facilities.

Figure 7.8 illustrates the overall architecture of the StarWalker virtual environment. The web is the major source of data. Domain specific corpuses are selected from the ACM Digital Library, which contains more than 15,000 scientific articles published by the ACM. In particular, our focus is on two subject domains: human–computer interaction (HCI) and hypertext. Two examples demonstrate how the underlying structures can be derived and represented as the backbone of the StarWalker virtual environment.

The first example derives content-based information structures. These structures are extracted using latent semantic indexing and Pathfinder network scaling techniques. The result is a network of documents linked according to the strongest semantic relationships. The second example derives reference-based information structures. Author co-citation analysis generates the strengths between each pair of authors who have published in the field. Pathfinder network scaling is also used in generating a network of authors. These associative networks are rendered in VRML, which is then embedded as a part of a multi-user virtual environment, so that it can be accessed from the WWW.

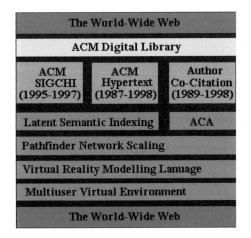

Figure 7.8 StarWalker's architecture.

The initial prototype of the StarWalker virtual environment relies on the blaxxun's online community client-server architecture. Users access the StarWalker virtual environment on the Internet through the blaxxun's online community client browser. This browser supports a text-based chat facility, along with a virtual reality scene written in VRML. Many of these virtual worlds are seamlessly integrated with the World Wide Web (WWW). Virtual worlds provide a convenient gateway to access documents on the web. The user can "beam" to an avatar, and invite the other person for a private chat. Alternatively, one may simply watch how other avatars travel through semantic space and how they interact with each other.

A screenshot of the StarWalker client user interface is shown in Figure 7.9. The semantic model in the background is based on a semantic space derived from the ACM SIGCHI proceedings. On arrival, users will see the landscape scene in front of them. The night sky color implies that this is an unlimited space – users can go wherever they like.

The underlying semantic structure is rendered as a star constellation. It is tempting for users to question the nature of the model, the meaning of the links, and why they are placed in a shared virtual environment. In fact, these have been the most frequently asked questions when a new visitor arrives in the StarWalker. Do these questions lead to more specific questions about the spatial model and, more importantly, the underlying subject domain? The design of StarWalker aims to provide a virtual environment where conversations and other social interaction can be triggered by the semantic implication of a spatial metaphor.

In fact, visitors frequently asked about the semantic structure embedded in the StarWalker virtual environment, instead of the overall spatial metaphor. In our experience, StarWalker has given users a strong feeling that it is considerably different from other virtual worlds that they have visited – most of them are based on buildings, cities, and other familiar landscapes.

The StarWalker virtual environment introduces new social structures appropriate to a specific online community. The design principle is that if a virtual environment

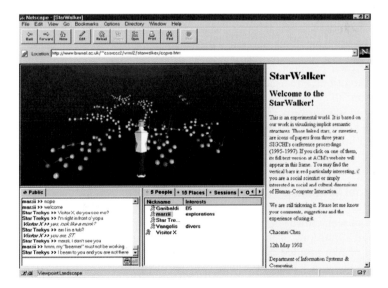

Figure 7.9 Users can explore the semantic space and interact with others in StarWalker.

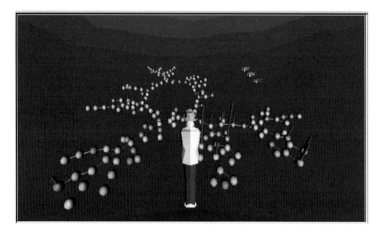

Figure 7.10 This is the scene at the entry point to the virtual environment.

reflects the knowledge structure of a subject domain, it will shape the structure of social interaction to a considerable extent. A particularly interesting area is the development of semantically organized virtual environments where people can not only chat, but also develop deep conversations about specific subjects.

Users visiting the StarWalker virtual environment are able to perform the following tasks:

- talk in public or private
- walk or fly through the virtual world
- beam to other avatars
- reposition to a predefined viewpoint in the virtual world
- view the full text version of a paper in HTML
- move to other virtual worlds
- search (restricted access at the moment).

Upon entering the virtual world, the visitor will see a landscape view of the semantic structure (Figure 7.10). There are seven viewpoints currently available for users to change their perspectives, including an overview, several landscape views from various directions, and a galaxy view to reinforce the new paradigm of interaction.

Users are able to watch the movement of the avatars of other users. Because the topology is semantically significant, the movement of avatars may also be meaningful. In Figure 7.11 we can see an avatar, a car, approaching the area with a number of landmark poles. Such awareness could be useful; for example, the person is probably interested in topics discussed by papers in that area.

7.3.2 Social Navigation

We have all seen crowds of people gathered at scenery viewpoints, around popular exhibits in a museum, or in front of a classic painting in a gallery. Such clustering behavior of like-minded people is a common source of reference for judging the value of a place or a point of interest. Social navigation is a counterpart of such referencing strategies and searching heuristics in abstract information spaces. Social navigation has drawn the attention of researchers from a diverse range of

Figure 7.11 A visitor, in an avatar of a car, flying through the virtual galaxy.

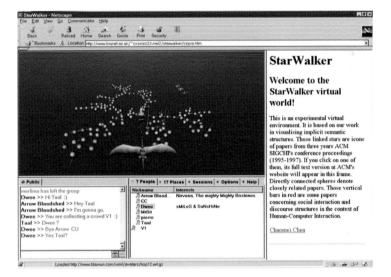

Figure 7.12 Seven people visiting StarWalker.

interests (Dieberger, 1997; Dourish and Chalmers, 1994; Erickson, 1996, 1997; Harrison and Dourish, 1996; Jeffrey and Mark, 1998; Pedersen and Sokoler, 1997).

To make social navigation possible, one needs not only a virtual place where people can meet and talk, but also a virtual place that has meanings and values, so that people can associate themselves with various places accordingly. In Star-Walker, since the latent semantic structure is reflected in the spatial configuration of the virtual environment, the positioning, movement, and groupings of avatars in such space becomes significant and meaningful to the peer participants at the time. Mutual awareness in such environments becomes semantically interpretable. Browsing semantics of concurrent users become visible and meaningful.

The trajectory of an avatar can reflect the nature of interaction between a user and the virtual environment. It is interesting to see that the movement of avatars seems to be associated with the landmarks in the scene, i.e. the vertical red poles, which may lead to more chances for avatars to *meet* each other (see Figure 7.12).

Figure 7.13 Two avatars exploring the central circle in StarWalker.

Figure 7.14 More avatars arrived in StarWalker.

Figures 7.13 to 7.15 are three consecutive snapshots taken from the StarWalker client screen. Upon arrival, the user will face the landscape model. Going forward is a natural step: it brings the user closer to the model. Therefore, avatars seem to follow an invisible avenue. In the second snapshot, more avatars arrive in StarWalker, and their positions clearly reflect their initial choice. In the third snapshot, avatars spread out to explore various locations, but mainly around the areas with distinctive landmarks – the red, spiky search bars.

Embedding information visualization into an organizing spatial model introduces a number of advantages that enrich the virtual environment. New types of interactive behavior become appropriate and meaningful. For example, the spatial model visualizes the semantic space, based on all the papers published in the proceedings of ACM conferences on Hypertext between 1987 and 1998.

This semantic world not only provides a valuable gateway to access a large amount of scholarly articles in the same subject domain, but also presents users with an initial cognitive map that they can extend, modify, and transform, as they learn more about the subject domain. In other words, the semantic world is more

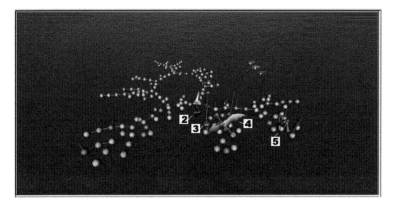

Figure 7.15 Positioning, movement, and social groupings of avatars are shaped by the spatial–semantic backdrop within StarWalker.

than a tool for information retrieval; it can support learning and knowledge management.

A virtual environment should enable users to adapt the virtual space according to their own interests. Users should be able to personalize a sub-space, and re-structure it to meet their own needs. For example, researchers can use their own publications to extract related papers in the shared environment. The persistent nature of StarWalker allows people to access such resources as an integral part of their distributed collaborative environment. In this way, a media space and a collaborative virtual environment can be merged and integrated. Users can explore and share their interpretation of knowledge structures more effectively.

In order to find out special characteristics of social interaction in the virtual world of StarWalker, we include the following examples of virtual meetings on topics specifically related to the design of StarWalker to topics inspired by the metaphor of the StarWalker. In this chapter, we focus on two aspects of social interaction within the virtual world:

- the dynamics of the discourse
- a mutual coupling between the discourse and the spatial structure of the virtual world.

The analysis of the dynamics of the discourse is largely based on the interaction process analysis (IPA), which tracks down transitions between task-oriented and socio-emotional episodes in face-to-face meetings of small groups. We need to find out how conversations in a virtual world such as StarWalker differ from conversations in the real world, or in other virtual worlds. If the IPM model can characterize the discourse of an engaging and balanced conversation, then a balanced discourse structure of a virtual meeting may lead to insights into how engaging conversations differ from casual and passing conversations. Furthermore, we would like to find out how conversations are related to the spatial structure of the virtual world, in particular, the influence of the constellation metaphor on perspectives that people choose to adopt in their conversations.

The first analysis of discourse structures is based on a virtual meeting between the author and a domain expert in distributed virtual environment systems. The domain expert was invited to join the session from a remote site. The meeting lasted about an hour and half in a private mode – other visitors to the virtual world could not take part in the meeting. The analysis focuses on the following two questions:

1   How did the discourse proceed alternatively between task-oriented and socio-emotional episodes in the virtual meeting?
2   Were these changes triggered by the spatial structure of the virtual world?

In the following transcript, speaker A denotes the author, and speaker B denotes the domain expert.

As noted in Bowers et al. (1997), users in embodied virtual environments were found to co-ordinate their avatars so that they could see each other in the conversation. Similar movements and adjustments were also found in our virtual meeting: the two users moved about their avatars until they could see each other:

A: Hello?
B: Hi there – where did you go?
A: I was facing the world.
B: Ah – so it's probably behind me now?

This episode suggests that there is a strong connection between users and the positions of their avatars in the virtual world. In many virtual worlds, it is common to see the following dialogue:

A: Is there any way to beam to an object here?
B: No – you would have to set a viewpoint in the VRML world.

Users in the virtual world are able to seek instant help from each other.

7.3.3 Transitions between Episodes

According to Bales' IPA model, a face-to-face small group meeting tends to switch between task-oriented episodes and socio-emotional ones. In several cases, a transition from a task-oriented episode to a socio-emotional one can be clearly identified.

A: I probably should set a meeting point in the central circle.
B: Yes and some images for the sides, top and bottom to help orientation.
A: Good points.
B: I wrote about that in my paper for the VR journal.
A: I saw your ad for a PhD a while ago – very interesting.
B: Thanks – we've found a student too.

The focus of the conversation smoothly drifts from specific design options to a wider, social, and institutional point of view. The following socio-emotional episode highlights a photo-taking event in the virtual world, and a consequence of the overlapped "talk" towards the end.

A: Can you move to the highest red bar?
B: I'll try …
A: I'd like to take a photo of you in the virtual world.
B: Okay, I'm next to one of the tall, red bars.
A: See you now.

B: I'm saying "cheese".
A: Click.
B: I hope you got my good side.
A: The scale of the world looks too big.
B: I need to take some pictures too, for a poster session.
A: The radius of a sphere is 4 meters …
B: Also, is the data spread in the vertical plane?
A: Okay, where do you want me to stand?
B: For the photo – it's in a different world.
B: I might ask you to volunteer another time.

Two strands emerged after the "photo" was taken in the virtual world (line 8 above:) speaker A started to talk about technical details of the design (line 9), indicating a transition back to a task-oriented episode, while speaker B continued the original theme about taking pictures in virtual worlds (line 10). The development of parallel strands is mainly due to the delay in receiving the text from the remote server. This is a known problem with textual-based virtual worlds. Higher-quality audio and video communication channels help to alleviate this, such as NetMeeting and CuSeeMe. The snapshot in the virtual meeting is shown in Figure 7.16, in which speaker B was standing at the foot of a very tall red pole.

The next episode is an example of a *Social–Task* transition, which was proceeded by talks about research systems and their developers. A task-oriented episode was clearly marked by a specific technical question from speaker B as follows:

A: Yes, I am not good at people's names.
B: Okay, can you tell me what the semantic relationship is between the balls in the scene?

This question contains three definite references to the spatial structure visualized in the virtual world: *the* semantic relationship, *the* balls, and *the* scene. The scene and the visualized structure were shared between the two speakers within the virtual world. A similar question would have been much longer and more complex, if the spatial structure was not available to the speakers. The virtual world

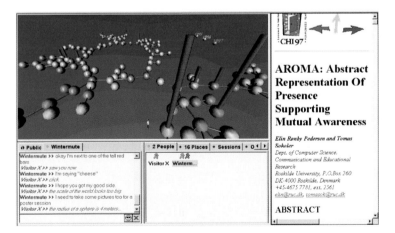

Figure 7.16 The snapshot taken in the virtual meeting. Speaking B was standing by a red pole.

therefore provides visual contextualization cues that can help speakers to understand and interpret their context.

7.3.4 Chat in StarWalker

The second analysis focuses on casual talks in the virtual world of StarWalker. In these cases, users have a diverse range of backgrounds and interests. It has been noted that people do experience engaging conversations in primitive virtual worlds (Damer, 1998). The aim of the preliminary analysis is to find out to what extent the content of a conversation is triggered and shaped by the spatial structure.

The analysis particularly focuses on the following questions:

1   Why do people visit the StarWalker virtual world?
2   What do they talk about in StarWalker?
3   What do they think of the overall organization of the StarWalker virtual world?
4   What is the most interesting feature to them?
5   What do they think of the semantic network?

Most visitors have been regular users of the blaxxun's online communities. They tend to be interested in meeting people, and curious to explore a new virtual world (Figures 7.17 and 7.18). The following examples partially explain why they came:

- Hello ... don't remember seeing this world before ...
- I saw it on the list and never been here.
- StarWalker sounded interesting.

The spatial metaphor of StarWalker evoked several episodes with the familiar question-and-answer pattern. The following example, in which A and C have not previously met, is a typical example:

C: As I look at this it looks more like a star map.
A: Yeah?
A: It would be nice if each node had music...
C: Yes, if you put our galaxy center in the center ... well, you know.
A: Do you know where I can get a gift for that?
C: Well, you really can't get one of our galaxy.
A: Hi, MAD660.
C: Mankind has not been that far yet.
MAD660: For what?
C: Foto [photo] of our galaxy.
C: ?
A: To get a glimpse of our galaxy.
C: We can only view the edge.
A: As a backdrop of this world?
C: Oh, cool.
C: Go to nasa.gov.
C: Hubble ST [space telescope] has all kinds of good stuff.

In many virtual worlds, people often feel free to ask for help. Such requests were quite common in StarWalker, with users asking, for example, how to configure preferences of a browser plug-in, and how to open audio channels along with the built-in textual interface.

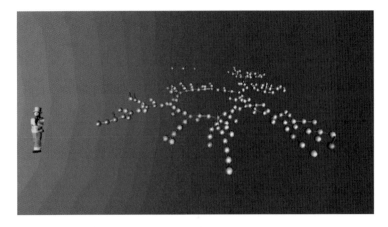

Figure 7.17 Exploring the virtual space alone.

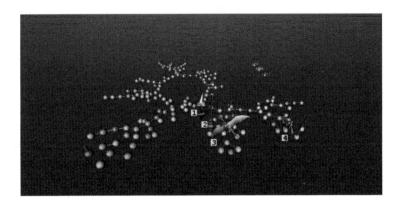

Figure 7.18 Exploring the virtual space in groups.

Users also talked a lot about the spatial layout and its meaning. Many people thought the semantic model was a molecule. One visitor said, "Ahaa, I see now. It is the DNA for me as an avatar and the vr-universe!" Some users thought it was a star map, others thought it was to do with Star Trek or spaceships.

It is clear from the transcripts that StarWalker gave users a strong feeling that it is considerably different from other virtual worlds they had visited. Most of them are based on buildings, cities, and other familiar landscapes. Note, in the following example, that visitor OML referred to the place as an inner space.

OML: I saw it on the list and never been here.
OML: StarWalker sounded interesting.
OML: But instead of going to outer space I came into inner space.

Here is another interesting example. One visitor asked if this place was only for "trekkies". Looking at this example again, users were concerned whether their social behavior would fit the constraints implied by the StarWalker spatial metaphor.

Marzii: Only trekkies allowed?
Star Trekys: Depends, Mar.
Marzii: (De)pends on what?
Star Trekys: Are you a trekkie?
Star Trekys: Treky.
Marzii: Not a trekky – more like an observer.
Star Trekys: You are here right?
Marzii: Correct.
Star Trekys: Since you are, you must be allowed.
Star Trekys: Or you couldn't be here.
Marzii smiles at Star Trekys.
Marzii: Aha – logic.

The unique feature of the StarWalker virtual world was a recurring subject in dialogues in StarWalker. One user said:

- "I have not seen any multiuser environment this abstract before …"
- "I always thought the communities look too much like the 'real' world …"

   Much of the conversation in the public session was related to the semantic or spatial organization of the StarWalker. In parallel, participants' interests were discussed in an informative way. In contrast to the invited meeting with the domain expert, the overall spatial metaphor played an important role in maintaining an interesting and considerably focused conversation between two people who had never met each other before.

7.3.5 Dynamics of Social Interaction

In this chapter, we have introduced a novel approach to the development and study of virtual environments, based on a notion of structural duality and a semantically enriched spatial metaphor in StarWalker. Users clearly noticed the uniqueness of StarWalker in terms of its spatial metaphor, and the semantics conveyed through the virtual environment as a whole. Will they interact and communicate differently with each other in StarWalker?
   We have analyzed conversations from StarWalker in an attempt to identify links between social interaction and the contextual role of the specialized semantic space. Our initial experiences suggest that StarWalker provides a flexible platform for shared intellectual work in specific subject domains, as well as for social interaction in general. Based on our experiences with StarWalker, we can draw the following conclusions:

- Incorporating information visualization components into a virtual environment leads to a flexible virtual environment, not only for social interaction, but also for shared intellectual work.
- The notion of social navigation fits the new metaphor very well; the combination of spatial, semantic and social navigation results in a coherent and intuitive means of interaction.
- The concept of structural duality turns out to be a thought-provoking way of approaching a better understanding of social dynamics in virtual environments.

It has the potential of functioning as a reference framework to unify inter-disciplinary approaches addressing some challenging issues raised in computer mediated social interaction, and collaborative work.

StarWalker demonstrates a generic approach to the development of virtual environments, with potential applications in areas such as shared digital libraries, collaborative learning, and virtual conferences for special interest groups and virtual communities.

Who will benefit from this type of virtual environment? Given that the semantic space is restricted to a specific subject domain, researchers, practitioners, and students are likely to benefit most. Special interest groups and virtual communities may also use virtual environments similar to StarWalker to create a persistent place to meet and collaborate.

The preliminary results of this investigation into the relationship between discourse and the contextual role of the visualized semantic space indicate that the virtual environment may accommodate more focused and deeper social interaction than that fostered by general-purpose virtual worlds currently available on the Internet.

7.4 Group Tightness

A major challenge in the study of group dynamics is to find a generic methodology that is not only applicable to a wide range of realistic scenarios, but also capable of capturing the dynamics of a group as they interact with a virtual environment. Collaborative learning, distance learning, social networks, collaborative information visualization, and digital libraries are among areas that are likely to excel. A quantitative approach to the study of group dynamics in such environments may provide a fresh angle for us to understand what is going on in a virtual environment.

The spatial-semantic impact of a collaborative information virtual environment on group dynamics is a relatively new topic. Now we will take a closer look at the spatio-temporal aspects of group dynamics as people interact with abstract visualization structures in a virtual environment. We begin with the concepts of *spatial tightness* and *semantic tightness* of a group.

In this section, we introduce a set of metrics for the analysis of different aspects of collaborative navigation. In particular we define a set of quantitative measures of the *spatial tightness* and the *semantic tightness* of a group.

7.4.1 Defining Group Tightness

Spatial tightness, semantic tightness, and overall group tightness measures are defined as follows.

Spatial Tightness (δ)

The spatial tightness of a group is defined as the ratio between the mean distance between group members over the entire session and the total distance traveled by the group as a whole. This definition is to compensate groups with members who traveled a large amount of virtual mileages. We are not interested in the extreme scenario in which no one would ever make a move in an entire session.

A generic definition of the spatial tightness δ is given as follows. Given a group of N members, if the total distance traveled by each member is d_{m_i}, and the total amount of distance traveled by a group is $\Sigma_{i=1}^{N} d_{m_i}$, then the average of the total distance traveled is

$$\frac{\sum_{i=1}^{N} d_{m_i}}{N}$$

At time t, the distance between group members i and j is denoted by $d_t(m_i, m_j)$. The group diameter at time t is the mean of member–member distances

$$\frac{\sum_{i,j}^{N} d_t(m_i, m_j)}{N}$$

The average of group diameter across the entire time series gives the overall group diameter; if T denotes the length of the time series, then the overall group diameter is

$$\frac{\sum_{i,j}^{N} d_t(m_i, m_j)}{N \cdot T}$$

The spatial tightness of the group is therefore given by the following formula:

$$\delta = 1 - \frac{\dfrac{\sum_{i,j}^{N} d_t(m_i, m_j)}{N \cdot T}}{\dfrac{\sum_{i=1}^{N} d_{m_i}}{N}} = 1 - \frac{\sum_{i,j}^{N} d_t(m_i, m_j)}{T \cdot \sum_{i=1}^{N} d_{m_i}}$$

Note that this definition is applicable to single-person groups as well as for groups of two or more members. All groups participating in this study had two members.

Semantic Tightness (σ)

The semantic tightness of a group measures the proximity between the group as a whole and the visualization models. Given a group of N members to search for O relevant target documents, or other types of targets, calculate the distance at time t between the group and the set of search targets; this is simply the shortest distance between any group member and any target object at time t $\min_{i \in N, j \in O} d_t(m_i, o_j)$.

This shortest distance measures the proximity between the group and the most relevant objects as far as the search tasks are concerned. Finally, average the shortest
distance time series over the entire session. We refer to the average shortest distance as *the group-to-target distance*. The semantic tightness is derived from the
ratio between the group-to-target distance and the average of group travel distance.

$$\sigma = 1 - \frac{\displaystyle\sum_{t}^{T} \min_{i \in N, j \in O} d_t(m_i, o_j)}{\displaystyle\frac{\sum_{i=1}^{N} d_{m_i}}{N}} = 1 - \frac{N \cdot \displaystyle\sum_{t}^{T} \min_{i \in N, j \in O} d_t(m_i, o_j)}{T \cdot \displaystyle\sum_{i=1}^{N} d_{m_i}}$$

Given the same amount of total group travel distance, a group is semantically tight
if it has a relatively small group-to-target distance; the opposite is obviously a
semantically loose group. Like spatial tightness δ, the semantic tightness σ is also
applicable to single-user groups as well as groups of two or more users.

Overall Tightness (Σ)

The overall tightness of a group combines the spatial tightness δ and semantic
tightness σ with an emphasis to the semantic tightness. More precisely, the impact
of spatial tightness is reduced to the square root of its original value.

$$\Sigma = \frac{\sigma \sqrt{\delta}}{\sqrt{\sigma^2 + \delta}}$$

Given the same semantic tightness σ, a group with higher spatial tightness will also
have a higher overall tightness measure. Similarly, given the same spatial tightness
δ, the higher overall tightness goes with the semantically tighter group.

These definitions are also consistent with our general observations. The majority of existing studies of CVEs emphasize the necessity of spatial proximity in
maintaining effective collaborations. However, CIVEs may lead to a different scenario in which the superiority of spatial proximity may be overridden by semantic
tightness. Being spatially farther apart in a virtual world does not necessarily indicate a loosely coupled group. When two friends are connected by their cellular
phones, they could be miles and miles away geographically but maintain an instant
communication bond. Similarly, if a group as a whole can manage to stick to the
vicinity of the most relevant part of the virtual world, then they don't have to maintain their spatial proximity. In fact, one may even argue if the semantic navigation
is so strong, it shows a better quality of the group if they are loosely coupled spatially, but tightly coupled semantically. At least in the setting of our study, the need
of spatial proximity is no longer the predominant navigation concern.

In summary, an ideal group would be able to maintain a relatively small semantic distance to the visualization models while they enjoy the freedom of traveling
over large spatial distance without worrying too much about spatial proximity to
their own members; and obviously, they need to find all the right answers as well.

7.4.2 The Construction of the CIVE

The following experiment was part of a joint work between Drexel University and Indiana University (Chen and Börner, forthcoming). The visualized network structures were derived from a bibliographic collection of documents published between 1983 and 2003 relevant to the topic of information visualization. Each bibliographic record contains a list of documents that it referenced to, or cited. The collection itself was generated by searching all articles cited Edward Tufte – of which more shortly.

The visualization models used in this study are an extension of typical Pathfinder networks: both document co-citation links – which form links of Pathfinder networks – and the citation history of an individual document are depicted. The visualization models were designed to capture the structure of their own field – information visualization, which has grown considerably over the last decade. In order to investigate the evolution of the citation networks, we evenly divided the entire 20-year time interval of the dataset into two sub-periods. Two visualization models were produced: one for the period between 1983 and 1992, and a second for the period between 1993 and 2003.

Figure 7.19 shows a screenshot of one visualization model. The network was rendered as interconnected spheres. Spheres denote documents, and cylinders connecting spheres denote the strongest co-citation links between them. The visualization only shows Pathfinder network links for simplicity and clarity. The poles stemming out of the spheres represent the citation history of individual documents. The entire height of a pole is proportional to the total amount of citations to the corresponding document accumulated over the entire period. The higher a pole, the more popular the document has been. Figure 7.20 is a screenshot from ActiveWorlds.

These visualization models use two sets of color coding schemes to provide finer details of visual attributes. The color of a sphere represents the result of principal component analysis (PCA) as part of the modeling procedure. Briefly speaking, co-citation data corresponds to a sub-set of a high-dimensional space. PCA is a commonly used method for dimensionality reduction (Jolliffe, 1986; Thurstone, 1931). It can characterize the original dataset with fewer dimensions, or factors.

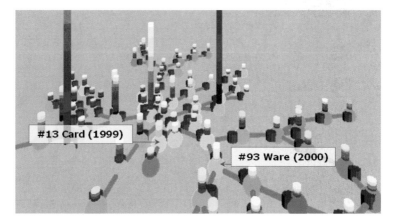

Figure 7.19 A visualization model of citation patterns.

Factor loading coefficient, representing the magnitude of each document projected on each dimension of the lower dimensional space, can be regarded as a quantitative measure of the extent to which a document is defined by the given dimension. A document with a large factor loading coefficient tends to be one of the most distinguished representatives of an underlying dimension. Researchers in information science have used this mechanism to identify specialties, or subfields of a discipline, as the groups of documents that have much in common in this sense.

We used the factor loading coefficients of the largest three factors to color the spheres to color code the groups of similar documents in terms of the way they were cited. For example, spheres in red or colors close to red would be documents from the largest specialty, or the mainstream of the field; spheres in green or nearly green would identify the second largest specialty; spheres in blue or similar colors would identify the third. Any colors in between are due to the combination of the three basic colors; for example, a white or gray colored sphere would be a document that is almost equally recognized by all three major specialties. In other words, specialties are not mutually exclusive.

A citation pole, representing the number of citations received by the base document, usually consists of a number of segments in different colors. The entire sample period was mapped to a spectrum of colors with the earlier years in darker colors and later years lighter colors. Along with the total height of a citation pole, the color spectrum of a citation pole is designed to give the viewer a glimpse of the citation history. For example, an all-time popular document would be shown as the tallest citation pole with an almost evenly distributed color band, whereas a

Figure 7.20 Viewing the visualization in ActiveWorlds.

rising-star document would have a considerably larger portion of its citation colors in light colors as it must have attracted many citations in a relatively short and recent period of time.

The first period (1983–1992) was predominated by the highly cited Tufte's books, Bertin's *Semiology of Graphics*, and Cleveland's several articles as statistical graphics. The citation visualization also featured documents on graphical data analysis and Exploratory Data Analysis (EDA). In essence, the second period (1993–2003) echoed the emergence of information visualization as an independent field. Tufte's books still attracted by far the highest citations. New documents with high citation rates in the second period included Robertson, Card, and Mackinlay's classic article on information visualization (Robertson et al., 1993) and Cleveland's *Visualizing Data*. The single most noticeable trend between the two citation landscapes would be the emerging documents on information visualization and the receding of statistical graphics from its prominent position in the 1980s.

Subjects, students at Indiana University, took part in the experiment in groups. They performed collaborative search tasks in group sessions. Each subject first completed a pretest questionnaire on simple demographics, including age, sex, and their experience in using three-dimensional virtual worlds, using computers in general, and the knowledge of the subject of information visualization. After a five-minute practice task, each pair of subjects had 40 minutes to collaboratively examine the two visualization models in order to answer ten questions. Feedback on search strategies and encountered problems was collected from a post-test questionnaire.

Ten questions were given to the subjects. Subjects were instructed to search through the Data Set 1 (1983–1992) model for the first five questions, and the Data Set 2 (1993–2003) model for the second five questions. Subjects were instructed to answer the retrieval questions by filling in the identification numbers of corresponding documents.

Q1.–Q5. Go to Data Set 1 (1983–1992)

Q1. Find Tufte, E. R. (1983) and Tufte, E. R. (1990). #: _____ #: _____
Q2. Find at least two entries of Bertin, J. #: _____ #: _____
Q3. Find an entry on Exploratory Data Analysis. #: _____
Q4. Find Chernoff, H. (1973). # _____
Q5. Open-end questions: Can you identify the common themes of documents colored in red, green, and blue?

Q6.–Q10. Go to Data Set 2 (1993–2003)

Q6. Find Tufte's three books #: _____ #: _____ #: _____
Q7. Find two most highly cited and recently published papers, one was published in 1999 and the other was published in 2000. #: _____ #: _____
Q8. Open-end questions: Can you identify the common themes of documents colored in red, green, and blue?
Q9. Open-end question: What was new in the second period?
Q10. Open-end question: Can you identify any 1st-period topics that subsequently disappeared in the 2nd period?

The ten questions varied in terms of the level of difficulty and the amount of information to be gathered. The simplest questions required the subjects to identify

Edward Tufte's three books. All his three books have the highest citations in both periods, so they can be easily spotted in the virtual world. A more difficult question required the subjects to find at least two documents from another prominent figure, Jacques Bertin, but no other clues were given. A tougher question required the subjects to find two recently published and highly cited documents. The clue to this question was in the color patterns of their citation poles: their citation poles should be covered by bands of light colors because of the recent publication years, and the height of these poles should be the tallest among poles with similar color patterns. To answer this question, the subjects would have to compare the visual–spatial patterns carefully. An even tougher question was for the subjects to identify the nature of document groupings according to their sphere colors. To answer this question, the subjects would have to compare and examine documents of similar colors and identify patterns. The most difficult question was about the major differences between the two periods. This question would entail the most extensive search and comparison between the two models at the global level.

Usage data and the configurations of the virtual worlds of information visualization were cross-referenced and plotted in a set of chat maps and trail maps. These maps provide a visual summary of the history of a group exploring and interacting with the virtual worlds.

7.4.3 Group Dynamics

The tightness metrics were incorporated into the analysis of the spatial-semantic impact of a CIVE on group dynamics. Table 7.1 summarizes the performance scores and movement measures of all four groups. Definitions are repeated in the table for convenience. Details of the results are further explained subsequently.

Task Accuracy

Factual search questions were scored as recall – the percentage relevant answers found in the total number of relevant target documents. Open-end questions were

Table 7.1 Performance scores and group dynamics measures

Group	Recall (Qs:1–4, 6–7) excluding open-end questions	Total distance traveled by individual max d_{m}	Total distance traveled by individual min d_{m}	Average total distance traveled $\dfrac{\sum_{i=1}^{N} d_{m_i}}{N}$	Group diameter $\dfrac{\sum_{i,j}^{N} d_t(m_i, m_j)}{N \cdot T}$	Group-to-target distance $\dfrac{\sum_{t}^{T} \min_{i \in N, j \in O} d_t(m_i, o_j)}{T}$
1	0.36	68868.19	6579.76	37723.98	1746.78	5261.93
2	0.46	18072.38	11189.53	14630.96	3225.29	6081.48
3	0.47	29645.03	5555.89	17600.46	842.61	5397.32
4	0.52	22851.16	20929.50	21890.33	2821.77	6417.49
Mean	0.45	34859.19	11063.67	22961.43	2159.11	5789.56

assessed but not scored. Group 4 has the highest recall score; Group 3 the second; Group 2 the third; and Group 1 the lowest.

Travel Distance

Group 1 has by far the largest group travel distance, the third largest group diameter, and the smallest group-to-target distance. In contrast, Group 2 has the least amount of combined travel distance, the largest group diameter, and the second largest group-to-target distance. Not surprisingly, according to these measures, Group 2 was loosely coupled semantically and spatially.

Group Diameter

The group-to-target distance is the semantic distance between a group and a visualization model. Group 1 has the smallest group-to-target distance, and Group 2 has the second smallest measure. We incorporated the group-to-target distance sequence into a display of the sequence of chat utterances. Substantial changes of such distances may be the sign of significant transition positions in chat sequences.

Group Tightness

Table 7.2 lists the spatial, semantic and overall tightness for all four groups. Remember that the tightness coefficients range between 0 and 1. The value of 1 indicates a tightly coupled group, whereas the value of 0 indicates a loosely coupled group. If two groups have the same level of spatial tightness, the one with a stronger semantic coupling is tightly coupled overall.

Group 1 has the strongest overall tightness (0.646), whereas Group 2 has the weakest (0.487). Group 3 and Group 4 have similar values. The spatial couple of Group 1 is the strongest, whereas Group 2 is the weakest. The difference between Group 3 and Group 4 in their spatial tightness was reduced in the overall tightness measure because they have very similar semantic tightness.

Group Tightness Space

Two factors influence the tightness of a group: the total distance traveled (α) and its overall diameter (β). The two factors can be used to characterize various tightness

Table 7.2 Three tightness measures of groups

Group	Spatial tightness (δ)	Semantic tightness (σ)	Overall tightness (Σ)
1	0.954	0.861	0.646
2	0.780	0.584	0.487
3	0.952	0.693	0.565
4	0.871	0.707	0.563
Mean	0.889	0.711	0.565

properties of groups in an abstract space, called the "group tightness space", as shown in Figure 7.21. Each point g in the space represents a group with its dynamics characterized by a set of five values, namely $g = (\alpha, \beta, \delta, \sigma, \Sigma)$. The horizontal dimension represents the distance traveled by a given group. The length of the distance increases from the left to the right. The vertical dimension represents the diameter of a group; its value increases from the top to the bottom. Given a point in the tightness space, its spatial tightness δ, semantic tightness σ, and overall tightness Σ can be calculated. The three values determine the color of the group on the plane. Thus we can see the distribution of group dynamics over a wide variety of scenarios. We can find not only the positions of the groups in our experiment, but also patterns of how the tightness measures can be influenced by the two factors.

Four major areas can be distinguished based on the strength of the spatial- and semantic-coupling of groups. The upper left area contains groups that have tight coupling both spatially and semantically; the upper right area contains groups with strong semantic-coupling but weak spatial-coupling. Groups in lower left areas have strong spatial tightness, but are weak in semantic-coupling. Groups in lower right areas are weak in both spatial- and semantic-coupling. In general, the closer a group is to the upper left corner, the stronger its tightness; one may expect to find a highly focused and experienced group in this area. In contrast, the closer a group to the lower right corner, the weaker it is coupled. We can imagine a diffused social gathering in a virtual world with no central attraction objects, and no semantic attachments would be positioned in this area.

The group tightness space gives us a generic framework to identify the position of a particular group in the context of other groups performing similar tasks. The four groups in our study are all located in the upper left region because their spatial and semantic tightness measures are all greater than the dividing threshold of 0.5. The positions of the four groups are marked by the contour belts. Points on the same belt represent groups, including hypothetical groups, that have the same spatial and semantic coupling strengths but might differ in their group travel distances and group diameters. For example, the particular group dynamic of Group 1 is just one among many possibilities – a different point on the contour line represents the same group tightness level as Group 1, which may come from the same

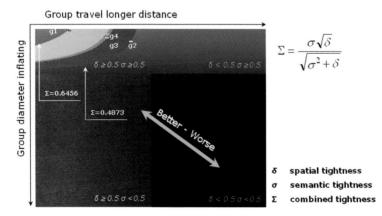

Figure 7.21 Group tightness space, colored by tightness measures (Chen and Börner, forthcoming).

group performing the same experiment, or even a different group. The diagram shows that it is possible for a group to demonstrate the same degree of tightness if it maintains a shorter traveling distance even if its group diameter is larger. Group 1 has the best tightness measures in this study followed by Groups 4, 3, and 2.

7.4.4   Semantic-Indentation Chat Display

The semantic-indentation display was developed to show intuitively how far away the group was from the visualization model when chat utterances were made. It displays chat utterances in the original sequence, but the amount of space indented from the left margin is proportional to the shortest semantic distance at the time of the current utterance. If the position of an utterance was shifted to the right, then it implies that the subject was moving away from the relevant target area.

The semantic distance of a group contains important clues for detecting the boundaries of individual episodes in a chat sequence. In Figure 7.22, the first significant increase of the group-to-target distance shown was linked to the utterance: "Should we concentrate on answering the rest of Data Set 2 questions for now?" In Figure 7.23, the first major semantic distance increase was linked to a similar utterance of a suggestion: "[let's look for] more Tufte." The group subsequently switched their search to a different area.

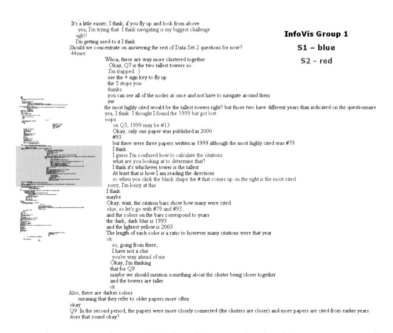

Figure 7.22 The chat sequence of Group 1 is indented in proportional to their group-to-target distance. Sudden changes of the group-to-target distance may be associated with potentially interesting transitions of the discourse. An overview map of the complete chat log is given on the left. Highlighted is the enlarged text given on the right (Chen and Börner, forthcoming).

7.4.5 Clock-Face Maps

Clock-face maps are a Java-driven interactive interface for examining various connections between chat sequences and the spatial configuration of the virtual worlds. A clock-face map displays one utterance at a time in the sequence of the original chat; in addition, the appearance of the utterance is cross-referenced to the spatial position in the virtual world. Utterances made at different times may be linked by straight lines on the clock-face map if their timestamps were close enough to each other; therefore, it is possible to trace the movement of a subject by following such straight-line trails. These interactive maps give us the greatest flexibility in examining all details associated with a chat session.

A clock-face icon in such maps visualizes the temporal position of an utterance in a given session. A clock face shows the time swept from the beginning of the session. Utterances within the same temporal neighborhood would have similar patterns on their clock faces. As shown in Figure 7.24, Group 3 worked on the upper cluster in the first part of the session, and then in the lower cluster towards the end of the session. The lines connecting utterances in the visualization highlight the utterances made within a short interval; in this study, linked utterances were made less than 25 seconds apart from each other.

Figure 7.25 shows a more detailed analysis of the collaborative search session of Group 3. Significant episodes of the chat sequence were identified by extracting sub-sequences of utterances that were within each other's temporal vicinity. The shading of each cluster was added by hand. An episode typically began with a question or a suggestion, especially questions and suggestions associated with

Figure 7.23 The chat sequence of Group 3 is indented in proportional to their group-to-target distance. The significant jump corresponded to the search for the second half of the questions, marked by Subject 5: "[let's look for] more Tufte" (Chen and Börner, forthcoming).

Figure 7.24 The clock-face visualization of the timing and the locations of individual utterances (Chen and Börner, forthcoming).

substantial changes of semantic distance. In addition, the temporal clusters of utterances may also identify an episode. We successfully identified some interesting episodes using the 25-second silence margin. For example, a short tutorial episode started with the question "How did you get up so high?", which was followed by a number of chat exchanges as one subject was learning from the other subject how to navigate in ActiveWorlds. The concentration of clock faces in Figure 7.25, just below the cluster of small rectangle objects, indicates that the subjects spent a considerable amount of time in the vicinity of the visualization model.

We also explored the chat sequences using a longer silence margin and actually found a different type of episode. These episodes consisted of a substantial period of silence during which no chat communications were made; the 25-second silence margin would separate the utterances before and after the silence into two different

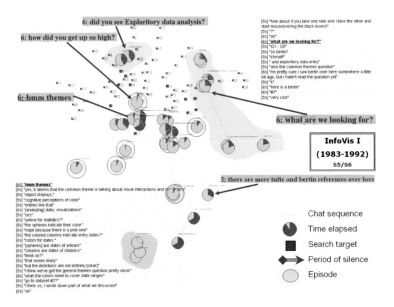

Figure 7.25 Episodes of collaborative search by Group 3 (Chen and Börner, forthcoming).

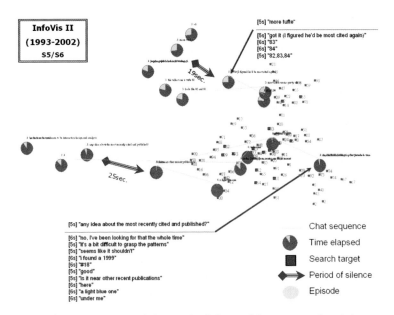

Figure 7.26 Episodes containing extended intervals of silence while group members being engaged in individual search (Chen and Börner, forthcoming).

episodes. However, we considered them as utterances from the single episode if we could infer from the utterances that subjects were still engaged in the same task. Figure 7.26 is an example. During the silent interval, the subjects apparently went to search and resumed the chat only after they had found something. The "bridge" between the opening line of such an episode and the main body of the episode could be as long as 25 seconds as shown in the middle of Figure 7.26. The episode was opened with a question: "[Do you have] any idea about the most recently cited and published [documents]?" There was a 25-second silence in the chat window before the other subject responded: "No. I've been looking for that the whole time." Both subjects subsequently moved from their original positions to the cluster of objects where the target documents reside.

During the silent interval, the first subject did not even ask the other one to clarify the status of their collaboration mode. We are interested in how representative this case is. We might consider this phenomenon as a series of transitions of collaboration mode, from a tight mode to a loose mode, and then back to a tight mode.

7.4.6 Reflections

We have developed a number of techniques for visualizing and analyzing group dynamics as well as various activities in CIVEs. The development of the quantitative measures of spatial and semantic couplings in this study is an important step towards the establishment of analytical and modeling methods for understanding group dynamics by taking into account the impact of information structures intrinsic to a CIVE. Furthermore, the methods are generally applicable to a wide range of CIVEs. Various visual analysis methods we have used in this study are generic in nature; they are readily adaptable for analyzing a variety of chat logs in 2D and 3D virtual environments. The ability to detect significant transition points in a discourse is also an important addition to the toolkit of analysts. These methods will considerably strengthen the connection between information visualization and CIVEs in terms of cross-domain collaboration and applications.

The simple experiment has generated a lot of interesting and practically meaningful data. Cross-referencing the chat log, the spatial configuration of the virtual world, and the trails of users has enabled us to examine group dynamics from several perspectives in a novel CIVE. The initial results are particularly encouraging as we move towards the establishment of a generic framework for the study of the spatial–semantic impact of CIVEs on group dynamics. Our ultimate goal is to understand not only how people navigate in existing virtual worlds, but also how we may draw insightful feedback from quantitative measures of group dynamics as they interact with CIVEs so that we can specifically tailor the design of CIVEs and make it a better place for future visitors.

This experiment has already generated some interesting ideas on refining the collaborative information visualizations. For example, all the citation details of documents in the experiment were available from the single HTML document. The chat log implies that some subjects might have taken advantage of this design; instead of conducting a visual search in the spatial interface, one can answer at least the first few questions by a text search in the HTML. In the new design, each bibliographic record will be isolated from the rest of records to ensure that visual search is used.

Some interesting feedback also drew our attention to the overall design of the virtual environment, namely, the general support for information search and more specific supports for carrying out in-depth analysis of patterns and trends. In the former, examples include making the clickable anchor objects in the scene larger and/or higher so that one can easily select them and click for further details.

In addition to being able to click objects in a visualization model and examine further details outside the spatial interface, subjects also expressed the desire to be able to click the HTML back into the visualization model. Both spatial and textual interfaces need to be integrated more tightly.

A tougher challenge is to facilitate users to perform tasks involving in-depth analysis beyond an individual document. More challenging and potentially more rewarding facilities would be a search mechanism that integrates visual–spatial properties with semantic properties of the underlying information space; for example, "give me a list of all documents on data layout shown in red" or "show me where the documents on data layout in red from the first period are located in the second model". In the current experimental setting, these facilities are not available to users, which in part explained the difficulties experienced by the subjects in searching for answers to the last few questions. This experiment has provided valuable input concerning how to further investigate and improve the match between tasks for users and facilities available in the virtual environment. This is also a necessary step to incorporate information visualization into collaborative virtual environments in practical applications such as distance learning, digital libraries, and online scientific communities.

7.5 Summary

In this chapter, we have introduced a number of virtual environments and the design rationale underlying them. We have focused on the role of information visualization techniques in the development of dynamic and evolving virtual environments, and have emphasized the notion of social navigation as one of the most fundamental organizational principles for a virtual environment.

We have described a novel approach to the development of semantically organized virtual environments, illustrating the design rationale and theoretical issues through the experimental virtual environment of StarWalker, and have also focused on how semantically-enriched spatial models mediate the interactive behavior of users in a domain-specific context.

Our experience with StarWalker is encouraging – many visitors to the virtual environment have shown interest in the organization principle, and some engaging conversations have taken place. This approach can be incorporated with techniques developed in media spaces. The enriched spatial model may play a significant role in attracting people to visit, to interact, and to adapt it into their distributed working environments.

We have addressed the major challenges: (1) establishing an integrative methodology to the quantitative analysis of spatial navigation, semantic navigation, and social navigation, and (2) incorporating visualization and analysis tools into the study of virtual environments.

Introducing information visualization into the design of multi-user virtual environments has profound and far-reaching implications to both fields of study. Virtual environments will be enriched by the incorporation of information visualization components, by becoming more interactive and intuitive, to fulfill the mission of providing a medium for social interaction across geographical distance. At the same time, virtual environments play a contextual role in highlighting the usefulness of information visualization techniques, and in giving more insights into visual navigation in a wider context, such as information foraging.

There seem to be two broad avenues to pursue: individual differences, and social dynamics in semantically organized virtual environments. In fact, these avenues may lead to two new frontiers in the research of information visualization and virtual environments, given their theoretical and methodological roots in multiple disciplines – psychology, HCI, sociolinguistics, ethnomethodology and computer-supported co-operative work. Chief among the issues we have identified for further study is the problem of accommodating both social interaction and individual requirements within the same virtual environment. Will it be a fruitful route to pursue the convergence of information visualization and virtual environments at a deeper level?

The design and initial use of StarWalker has led to theoretical, empirical and engineering issues regarding the development and use of virtual environments for social interaction. It would seem sensible to review discourse analysis techniques more critically in further studies. IPA, for example, distinguishes only task and social–emotional discourse, and yet even in the small examples discussed here, it is clear that situated social action often falls outside these categories. The nature of a dialogue must be understood in its context. Further work on social episode and work domain analysis could strengthen the study of the relationships between situational context and dialogue structure.

The more recent study of group tightness is an important step towards the development of a methodology that can quantitatively as well as qualitatively investigate the interrelationship between group dynamics and the contextual environment provided by information visualization.

A recurring theme in this chapter is the interplay and convergence between information visualization and virtual environments. Both of the fields are interdisciplinary in nature. Fostering focused social interaction provides a good point for us to articulate various theories and methods into a cohesive whole, and also provides a test bed for the development of an integrative paradigm to advance information visualization and virtual environments. The ultimate goal of these studies is to augment reality and make our social and intellectual interaction more efficient, natural, and enjoyable.

Chapter 8
Detecting Abrupt Changes and Emerging Trends

Distinguishing wiggles from genuine turning points is a serious
and difficult problem.

Arthur M. Okun (1960)

Various changes can be broadly categorized as gradual changes or abrupt changes. A gradual change may take millions of years in examples such as human evolution and the expansion of the universe. An abrupt change can occur within days, hours, or seconds in examples such as avalanches, volcano eruptions, a stock market crash, or the spread of epidemic diseases. Whether a change is gradual or abrupt is determined within the contextual scale of specific subject domains. For example, on the scale of history, the industrial revolution and scientific revolutions are regarded as abrupt changes. On the other hand, the Chicago Fire and Hurricane Isabel were certainly abrupt change on a much smaller time-scale. It may take months to recognize a recession formally, but investors on the stock market may have to deal with the abrupt changes in stock prices. In general, abrupt changes are harder to deal with than gradual changes.

The question whether it is possible to predict changes is as old as our civilization. To be able to predict the future is part of our dream. In many situations, we wish we could get hold of a crystal ball to see the future. Among various characteristics of changes, we are particularly interested in the beginning and the end of a change – turning points.

This chapter addresses three major examples that illustrate the detection and visualization mechanisms underlying the detection of changes, namely how economists detect turning points that lead in and lead out of a recession in the economy, how text retrieval researchers detect emerging thematic patterns in text documents, and how knowledge domain analysts may use progressive visualization techniques to identify intellectual turning points that trigger scientific revolutions.

8.1 The Complexity of Abrupt Changes

Abrupt climate changes, natural disasters, and diseases are among the major forces that brought down several ancient civilizations. The complexity of the dynamics behind profound changes is illustrated in the following examples. The Anasazi civilization's collapse and the Lost Colony mystery shed some light on understanding important characteristics, especially for detecting abrupt changes and emerging trends.

Las Vegas, Nevada, is the fastest-growing metropolis in the USA. Its population has increased sharply in recent decades; for example, its population of 273,000 in 1972 was almost tripled in 1986 to 608,000. The growth of Las Vegas can be seen in Landsat images (Figure 8.1).

Figure 8.1 Landsat image of Las Vegas: (left) September 10, 1986, (right) September 13, 1972. http://edcwww.cr.usgs.gov/earthshots/slow/LasVegas/LasVegas. Credit: USGS EROS Data Center.

One can only imagine how large-scale prehistoric changes took place, especially when changes were abrupt. Historians and archaeologists have to examine every piece of evidence and trace each trail of clues. In many cases, the magnitude and rapidity of changes and their impact are so drastic and profound that they may lie beyond our comprehension. The two examples below are by no means rare in the realm of science. Rather, almost every scientific discipline has something as complex and intriguing as these are.

8.1.1 The Anasazi Civilization's Collapse

One of the great prehistoric puzzles is the collapse of the Anasazi civilization because of its completeness and rapidity.[1] The Anasazi, also known as the Ancient Pueblo peoples, were ancestors of today's Pueblos, Zunis, and Hopis of New Mexico and Arizona.[2] The word Anasazi means *enemy ancestors* in Navajo. Some may regard Anasazi as a racist term, but we use it as it is a well-defined term in the scientific literature.

The Golden Age of Anasazi was between about 900 and 1130 AD. One of Anasazi's most remarkable achievements was Pueblo Bonito, the largest single building that housed over 1000 residents in more than 600 rooms. But by 1130–1150, many of the Anasazi towns were deserted. Chaco Canyon was a deserted ruin by the 13th Century. At Sand Canyon, evidence suggests that people didn't even take their belongings. What happened? What made families abandon their homes in such a haste?

Human bones found in the ruins suggest that the Anasazi had been suffering from malnutrition. An early theory suggests that a prolonged dry spell called the Great Drought was the primary cause. Dendrochronologists, who study tree rings, found from the tree rings in that area that very little rain fell in 1125–1180, 1270–1274, and 1275–1289. Until the 1990s, the Great Drought Theory represented the trend of explaining the Anasazi collapse with a single factor.

The Great Drought Theory was challenged in the early 1990s, when Carla Van West (1991) reported her tree-ring study, which showed that even during the great drought it was still possible to grow enough corn to support the population. The initial emphasis on the environment as the single determining cause of the collapse

---

[1]http://www.cpluhna.nau.edu/People/anasazi_collapse.htm
[2]http://www.augustachronicle.com/stories/051897/fea_floyd.html

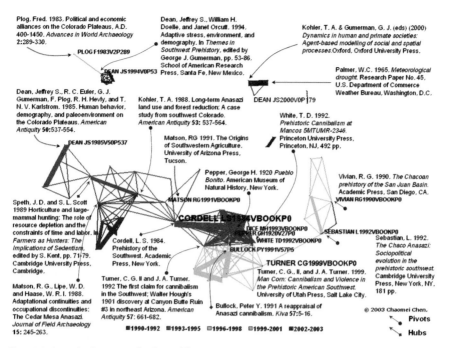

Figure 8.2 A co-citation network of 68 publications on Anasazi. WOS: 1990–2003.11. See section 8.5 for technical details of the mapping.

was replaced by a stronger emphasis on social and religious reasons. More factors must be considered!

It was believed that the Anasazi went through a catastrophic spiritual crisis. Evidence suggests that the Anasazi probably abandoned their religion once they migrated elsewhere because of the lack of traditional ceremonial structures such as kivas in their new homes. An abrupt climate change may have been a factor, but scientists began to extend their search to more indirect consequences. For example, disrupted rainfall patterns shown by tree-ring evidence might have destroyed the Anasazi faith in their old religion. The debate will continue. Drought, violence, culture, and religion may have all contributed to the collapse of the once prosperous civilization.

The multiple time-sliced co-citation map in Figure 8.2 shows the major articles and their groupings. The most interesting ones in the map are pivot points and hubs – the concepts are explained further in later sections of this chapter. Pivot points in this map include Matson et al. (1988) on adaptation, Turner and Turner (1992) and White (1992) on prehistoric cannibalism, Sebastian (1992) on social-political evolution, Vivian (1990), and Dean et al. (1994) on adaptive stress, environment, and demography. Palmer's (1965) *Meteorological Drought* is one of the most cited articles over the past two years.

8.1.2 The Lost Colony Mystery

The earliest English colony in the New World started on Roanoke Island in North Carolina. The disappearance of Roanoke Island colonists and the later Jamestown

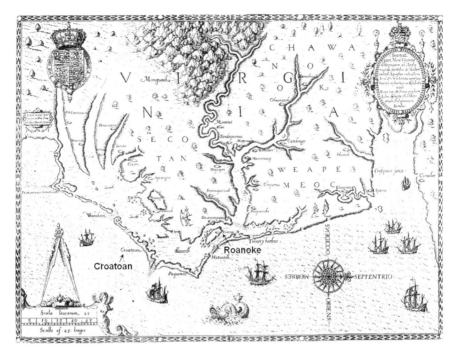

Figure 8.3 White-De Bry Map of Virginia (1590) map. Roanoke Island and Croatoan Island are marked for readability. http://www.nps.gov/fora/whitede2.htm

colony is the most enduring mystery of American history (Stick, 1983; Bosco, 1984). An interesting account of the mystery is in *Historical mysteries: Indian tribe was remarkably European.*[3] Another good website is *Roanoke Colony: Prelude to Jamestown?*[4]

In 1585, the first group of English colonists arrived at Roanoke Island and they built a settlement called Fort Raleigh after Sir Walter Raleigh, who masterminded the expedition. In 1586, the colonists abandoned the fort and returned to England. Fifteen men were left on the island as a holding force.

In July 1587, a larger group of men, women, and children under the governorship of John White arrived at Roanoke Island; the 15 men were not there any more. White had the settlement started in Fort Raleigh. On August 27 he returned to England for supplies and left other settlers on the island. Before his departure, White instructed that should the remaining colonists be forced to leave the settlement in his absence, they were to inscribe their destinations in an obvious place.

White was not able to return until two years later in August 1590.[5] The fort was deserted, the entire population was vanished, and the only trace left by the colonists was a word *croatoan* carved on a fort post and the letters *C R O* carved on a tree. White thought that the colonists might have moved to Croatoan Island, an island about 50 miles away, but he was prevented by storms from further search before returning to England. Both Croatoan and Roanoke Islands are shown in Figure 8.3.

---

[3]http://www.virginiaplaces.org/settleland/roanokecolony.html
[4]http://wvwv.essortment.com/anasaziculture_rcvi.htm
[5]John White's own writing: http://www.webroots.org/library/usahist/rtr00000.html

Historians have long wondered about the fate of those colonists, who became known as the Lost Colony of Roanoke. What happened to them? Were they killed by pirates or Spanish soldiers? Did they simply move to Croatoan Island?

Some anthropologists believe Roanoke's settlers simply joined a local tribe in order to survive, and they became the ancestors of the fair-skinned, blue-eyed Indians. According to the legend,[6,7] in the 18th century, a tribe of Indians was found along the Lumber River in North Carolina, and they spoke English and wore European-style clothes, lived in multiroom dwellings and were familiar with whiskey and the English language. These Indians identified themselves as *Croatoans*. On the other hand, the overall picture of the Roanoke Colony's fate is not conclusive, even though it was probably not as complicated as the Anasazi's collapse.

The Jamestown colony was founded in 1607 but suffered an appallingly high death rate in 1609 and 1610 – historically known as "the starving time". According to historians, in June of 1610 there were 350 colonists, but 43% of them were dead by the end of that summer.

A joint research article published in *Science* (Stahle et al., 1998) shed some light on the kind of environment faced by these colonists. They studied tree rings of baldcypress trees (*Taxodium distichum*) in the area and found that the most severe season drought and the most severe three-year period of drought in 800 years coincided with the disappearance of the Roanoke Island colonists.

Every year trees grow two layers of wood cells in the growth season. The earlier, thin-walled layer of cells is called earlywood, whereas the later, thicker-walled layer of cells is called latewood. The difference between the two layers is the tree ring. A tree usually stops growing at the end of fall. The width of the tree ring tells us how much the tree has grown in a particular growth season. All trees in the same area will show the same pattern of rings. Dendrochronologists – scientists who study tree rings – can establish the climate of hundreds or even thousands of years into the past in a region. This method is generally accurate to one year and, in certain instances, it can even determine the season.

The tree rings revealed two severe droughts in the Tidewater region: one in 1587–1589 near Roanoke and the other in 1606–1612 near Jamestown (Figure 8.4). The three-year Lost Colony drought was the worst of the past 800 years. The seven-year Jamestown drought was the all-time worst between 1215 and 1984. It was the same time that the English colonists tried to settle in Roanoke and Jamestown. What a coincidence!

Research continues. Historians, archaeologists, and climatologists have worked together and identified various pieces of the puzzle. The complexity involved in solving the puzzle is enormous. Researchers must comb through a wide variety of evidence and clues not only in the fields of history, archaeology, and climatology, but also other fields to identify missing pieces and missing links.

What has all this to do with information visualization? What are the key challenges? And what are the implications of considering such challenges on advancing information visualization? The Anasazi example and the Lost Colony example illustrate the consequences of profound changes in the past. Scientists are still in the quest for convincing and conclusive explanations of what happened. We want to learn from the past so that we may be able to handle catastrophic situations in better and wiser ways in the future. There are two major roles that information

---

[6]http://www.augustachronicle.com/stories/051897/fea_floyd.html
[7]http://si.unm.edu/si2002/NICOLE/TIM_0004/ROA_000C.HTM

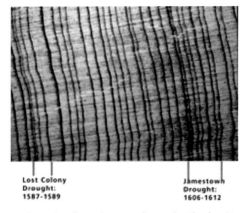

Lost Colony
Drought:
1587-1589

Jamestown
Drought:
1606-1612

Figure 8.4 These tree rings indicate that the settlements of Roanoke Island and Jamestown coincided with respectively the worst three-year and seven-year period of the past 800 years. http://www.wm.edu/wmnews/042398/drought.html

visualization can play. At the microscopic level, information visualization may enhance the ability of scientists to identify potentially important clues and reconstruct the ecological environment and a variety of underlying factors. At the macroscopic level, information visualization may help scientists to monitor the research fronts across a wide range of relevant disciplines.

On the one hand, monitoring the growth of a large city over decades has become increasingly easier and straightforward, as shown in the satellite photos of Las Vegas. On the other hand, the Anasazi and Roanoke examples also indicate that it is less likely that the fate of a complex system is solely determined by a single factor. Is it even possible that one can take all the significant factors into account?

Research in the Anasazi civilization's collapse and the lost Roanoke colony appears to go through a similar pattern. Researchers started with the search for a single cause, whether the Great Drought drove Anasazi people away from their home, what happened to the Roanoke settlers. Subsequent theories often do not replace the earlier ones; rather, they undermine the predominant positions of theories that attribute profound changes to a single event. Similar patterns can be found in other scientific fields, for example, the mass extinction debates (Chen, 2003). The impact theory suggests that an asteroid or a comet hit the earth and consequently wiped out all the dinosaurs 65 million years ago. Given that five mass extinctions happened on the earth, scientists want to find out whether there is a common explanation for these extinctions. A theory that can explain all five extinctions is certainly more valuable than a theory that can only explain one extinction. Similarly, a theory that can explain the collapses of various civilizations is more fundamental than a theory that can only explain the collapse of a particular civilization, which would be a remarkable achievement in its own right. In this sense we all have a long way to go!

The behavior of a complex system may be controlled by a number of parameters. When a parameter exceeds a threshold, things are different. For example, by raising or lowering the temperature one can melt ice or freeze water. However, there are complex systems, in fact, many of them in our everyday life, whose behavior is an intrinsic property of their dynamics. In other words, there may not be an apparent trigger event or a trigger mechanism to be responsible of abrupt changes. There may be no apparent threshold crossing behavior. Instead, tiny vari-

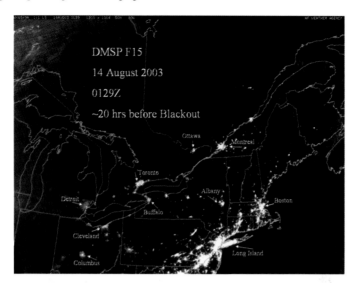

Figure 8.5 DMSP satellite image of the north-eastern United States approximately 20 hours before the August 14, 2003 blackout. Credit: Air Force Weather Agency. http://www.globalsecurity.org/eye/black-out_030814_dmsp-01an.htm

ations, rather than violent shocks, may lead to categorical changes. This is in essence what is called the butterfly effect. Self-organized Criticality (SOC) is a generic approach to this type of complex systems.

8.1.3 Self-organized Criticality

The Great Northeast Power Blackout in North America on August 14, 2003 affected approximately 52 million people from Detroit to New York and Canada, and more than 240,000 square kilometers of the United States and Canada. The cost of the blackout was estimated to be $800 million in New York City alone. The impact of the massive blackout can be seen on images by the orbiting Defense Meteorological Satellite Program (DMSP) satellite (Figures 8.5 and 8.6). On November 19, 2003, a report by the US Department of Engergy and Canadian authorities concluded that the blackout was largely preventable and sharply critized the Ohio-based power company FirstEnergy Corp for violating industry standards. The report identified a series of faults that led to the massive blackout. The blackout began when three FirstEnergy transmission lines in the Cleveland area failed because of tree limbs which the company had not trimmed. The failure of those lines then overloaded neighboring transmission lines, triggering a domino effect. Another factor was that FirstEnergy's emergency warning system was down and operators in the control rooms did not react to other clues that their warning system was not working properly. When they responded over an hour later, it was too late. One line after another went down, overloading ever fewer lines and causing them to shut down. It took only seven minutes for the blackout to reach Ontario and most of the northeast. The report said that control room operators had no experience with major outages, nor had they been trained for them.

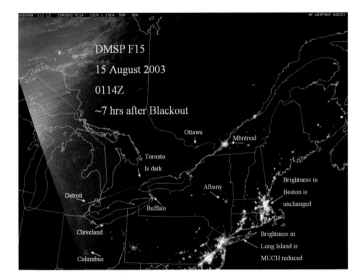

Figure 8.6 DMSP satellite image of the north-eastern United States approximately 7 hours after the blackout. The cities of Ottawa, Toronto, Detroit, Cleveland, Columbus and Buffalo virtually disappeared, while the Greater New York City area is much darker! Credit: Air Force Weather Agency. http://www.globalsecurity.org/eye/black-out_030814_dmsp-02an.htm

In 1987 Per Bak et al. introduced self-organized criticality theory (SOC) to model *critical* phenomena precisely like this – the state of complex systems swings between stability and chaos. Such systems can reach a *critical point* by their intrinsic dynamics without apparent control parameters. There is no simple causality; a seamingly trivial change may or may not cause a dramatic effect. In such a critical state, the propagation of the interactions among the components of the system is inversely proportional to its frequency $1/f$ with the functional relationship of a power law. Here is how the *American Heritage Dictionary* defines the concept of critical point:

1 *Physics* The temperature and pressure at which the liquid and gaseous phases of a pure stable substance become identical.
2 *Mathematics* **a.** A maximum, minimum, or point of inflection of a curve. **b.** A point at which the derivative of a function is zero, infinite, or undefined.

The archetype model of such a system is the so-called sand-pile model. Sand grains are dropped on the top of a pile of sand one by one. Most of the time, a dropped grain has little global impact on the sand pile. However, dropping a sand grain does cause a sand avalanche once in a while. Because its behavior follows a power law, the larger an avalanche, the more rarely it happens. The impact of dropping the next sand grain on a pile of sand is not predictable. What Benjamin Franklin (1706–1790) wrote more than 200 years ago amusingly illustrates SOC:

> For want of a nail a shoe was lost,
> for want of a shoe a horse was lost,
> for want of a horse a rider was lost,
> for want of a rider an army was lost,

for want of an army a battle was lost,
for want of a battle the war was lost
for want of the war the kingdom was lost,
and all for the want of a little horseshoe nail.
                              Maxims prefixed to Poor Richard's Almanac, 1757

The description also applies to a stock market crash, an electronic power grid black-out, the climate, and probably the collapse of a civilization, and a scientific paradigm shift. The latter two are untested but they are of particular interest to information visualization, especially knowledge domain visualization (Chen, 2003).

Carreras et al. (2000) examined blackouts in the North American power trans-mission grid from 1984 to 1998 and found a striking similarity between blackout sizes and avalanche sizes in a sand pile. The blackout size time series is statistically indistinguishable from the sand pile avalanche size time series. In other words, the global complex dynamics of power systems may be governed by SOC dynamics. Information on blackouts in North America can be downloaded from the NERC website at http://www.nerc.com/dawg/database.html.

Research in paleontology has shown a power law relationship between the fre-quency of species extinction events and the size of the extinction impact. Krink and Thomsen (2001) designed an extinction model based on spatial SOC to char-acterize the critical state between chaos and stability. From time to time, spatial disaster zones are generated in which all individuals are substituted by new indi-viduals. In their study, an avalanche would be an incidence of extinction. Most of the time there are no extinctions, except a few individuals die. However, their model always allows the best individual to survive extinction events and repro-duces the extinct individuals with the genome of the surviving individuals. The SOC spatial extinction model was found to outperform two other non-SOC mod-els. They conclude that extinction is an integral part of evolution.

Figure 8.7 shows a co-citation network of research in SOC. The technical details of the mapping can be found in section 8.5 in this chapter. Hubs and pivot nodes are important in the network.

The third example is the ongoing research in whether there will be an abrupt cli-mate change (Alley et al., 2003; Adams and Foote, 2003). The Ocean Studies Board, Polar Research Board, and Board on Atmospheric Science and Climate published a report in 2002, entitled *Abrupt Climate Change: Inevitable Surprises*. Most of the studies and debates on potential climate change have focused on a gradual increase of global warming. But this report drew a considerable amount of attention to a possible turn of climate change that few people would expect from global warm-ing. The future climate may suddenly switch from the current global warming to a global ice age.

The *Abrupt Climate Change* report calls for more research into past abrupt events and ways in which the oceans and the atmosphere interact with one another. One of the striking pieces of evidence in the past is related to what is known as the Younger Dryas cooling period 12,000 years ago. Younger Dryas are arctic wildflower remains found in northern European sediments. During the Younger Dryas, global temperatures fell sharply by as much as 16 degrees within a decade and rainfall reduced by 50%. The period lasted more than 1000 years. The climate had changed abruptly before, and it will happen again. What was the cause of the Younger Dryas cooling?

By examining tree rings and gas bubbles trapped in ice cores, scientists have dis-covered patterns of especially large and abrupt climate changes in the past. Recent

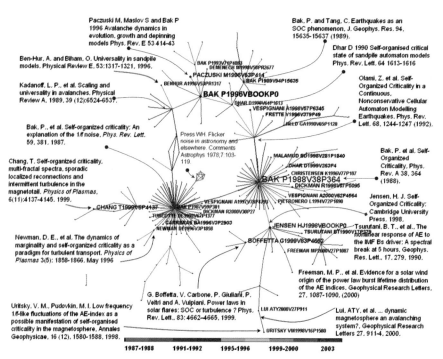

Figure 8.7 A co-citation network of self-organized criticality across time slices shows the diversity of SOC systems, including earthquakes, solar flares, magenetosphere, and evolution and growth models.

evidence demonstrates that Earth's climate changed abruptly over the last 100,000 years. Earth's climate is a typical self-organized criticality system. Certain characteristics have to be met for a mechanism to cause abrupt climate change:

- A trigger or a chaotic perturbation that causes a threshold crossing.
- An amplifier to intensify and spread the influence of small or local change.
- A source of persistence, allowing the altered climate state to last for up to centuries or millennia.

The warmer climate melts more ice and the fresh water from melting ice may trigger a sudden switch from global warming to global ice age. Scientific evidence shows a steady freshening of the Atlantic water over the last 40 years at a rate of 0.01 per decade. A 0.04 freshening over 40 years is equivalent to adding an additional source of fresh water 3–4 meters thick down to depths of 2–3 km over a broad area of the northern North Atlantic. Scientists believe such increase of fresh water can make the climate system unstable. Like a self-organized criticality examples such as sand piles, the climate can dramatically change within periods of as short as ten years.

8.2 Detecting Abrupt Changes

The detection of abrupt changes has many applications. As we have seen in this chapter, abrupt changes are not necessarily large. In fact, many change detection problems are concerned with the detection of small changes. In their *Detection of Abrupt Changes*, Basseville and Nikiforov (1993) discuss mathematical statistics of change detection.

8.2.1 Statistical Approaches

The detection of abrupt changes aims to prevent failures or catastrophic events. Basseville and Nikiforov (1993) formalize the detection of abrupt changes as follows. Let $(y_k)_{1 \leq k \leq n}$ be a sequence of observed random variables with conditional probability density function $p_\theta(y_k | y_{k-1}, \ldots, y_1)$. Before the unknown change time t_0, the conditional probability parameter equals to θ_0. After the change, the parameter equals to θ_1. The goal is to detect the occurrence of the change as soon as possible. A certain false alarm rate before t_0 is acceptable. The estimation of the parameters θ_0 and θ_1 is not necessary, but can be useful. It is also assumed that changes occur sequentially such that one can consider only one change at a time, as opposed to changes occuring simultaneously. The detection algorithm has two constraints: the *delay for detection*, which indicates how soon the algorithm can set an alarm when a change actually occurs, and the *mean time between false alarms*, which indicates how frequently false alarms are made. Usually the goal is to shorten the delay given a fixed false alarm rate.

Consider two hypotheses on the condition probability distributions: one when no change happens (H_0), the other when a change occurs at time t_0 (H_1). Given a finite sample $y_1, \ldots, y_N$, test between

$$H_0: \quad \text{for } 1 \leq k \leq N: p_\theta(y_k | y_{k-1}, \ldots, y_1) = p_{\theta_0}(y_k | y_{k-1}, \ldots, y_1)$$

$$H_1: \quad \text{there exists an unknown } 1 \leq t_0 \leq N \text{ such that:}$$

$$\text{for } 1 \leq k \leq t_0 - 1: p_\theta(y_k | y_{k-1}, \ldots, y_1) = p_{\theta_0}(y_k | y_{k-1}, \ldots, y_1)$$

$$\text{for } t_0 \leq k \leq N: p_\theta(y_k | y_{k-1}, \ldots, y_1) = p_{\theta_1}(y_k | y_{k-1}, \ldots, y_1)$$

This approach does not require the estimate of exactly when the change time t_0 is. The key requirement is a sensitive detection below given false alarm rates. The standard strategy is to maximize the probability of confirming H_1 when H_1 is actually true, subject to the constraint of the probability of false alarms $p(H_1 | H_0)$. Basseville and Nikiforov suggested five intuitive performance indexes for designing and evaluating change detection algorithms:

1 mean time between false alarms;
2 probability of false detection;
3 mean delay for detection;
4 probability of non-detection;
5 accuracy of the change time and magnitude estimates.

Obviously, the smaller the mean time between false alarms, the better; the lower the false alarm probability, the better; the shorter the mean delay, the better; the lower the non-detection probability, the better; and the more accurate the estimates, the better.

Let E_{θ_0} and E_{θ_1} denote the expectations of the random variables under the two distributions p_{θ_0} and p_{θ_1}, respectively. The log-likelihood ratio – the logarithm of the likelihood ratio – is defined as follows:

$$s(y) = \ln \frac{p_{\theta_1}(y)}{p_{\theta_0}(y)}$$

A useful property of the log-likelihood ratio is that $E_{\theta_0}(s) < 0$ and $E_{\theta_1}(s) > 0$. In other words, a change in the parameter θ is reflected as a change in the sign of the mean value of the log-likelihood ratio. This property indicates whether the change is detectable. $K(\theta_1, \theta_0) = E_{\theta_1}(s)$ is known as the Kullback information K. The difference between the two mean values is as follows:

$$E_{\theta_1}(s) - E_{\theta_0}(s) = K(\theta_1, \theta_0) + K(\theta_0, \theta_1) > 0$$

Therefore, a detectable change can also be defined in terms of the Kullback information between the two models before and after change.

Quality control, also known as continuous production monitoring, is one of the earliest change detection applications. The quality control problem can be simplified as a two-state system: the in-control state and the out-of-control state. When a process moves from in-control to out-of-control, it is called a disorder. An ideal quality control solution is the quickest detection of the disorder with the least number of false alarms. In reality, the best solution is a trade off between the two potentially conflicting criteria.

Basseville and Nikiforov (1993) included a few examples of change detection applications, for example, navigation systems, signal segmentation, and vibration monitoring. Detecting abrupt changes in navigation systems such as radio navigation systems and global satellite navigation systems focuses on the detection of faulty sensors. The same criterion of quick detection with the least number of false alarms applies. A quick detection is particularly important as the longer the delay of the detection, the more severely the navigation will be off track. Signal segmentation gives another example. A segmentation algorithm splits the signal into homogeneous segments, in terms of the mean level or spectral characteristics. Signal segmentation is useful in automatic analysis of continuous speech signals and various biomedical and geophysical signals, for example, electrocardiograms. The desirable criteria are essentially the same as earlier examples. On the other hand, signal segmentation is often merely the first step of a recognition process. Additional criteria may be imposed accordingly with reference to subsequent analysis. False alarms and errors at the segmentation stage can often be easily recognized and corrected at later stages. Vibration monitoring represents another class of change detection applications. Complex mechanical structures, such as bridges, buildings, dams, and rotating machines, such as turbo-alternators and gearing systems, need to be monitored for vibrating characteristics in non-intrusive ways.

8.2.2 Economic Turning Points

The dot-com bubble finally burst in 2000. That year, Yahoo! was down more than 85%, Amazon.com down more than 75% and Intel Corp. more than 55%. The Nasdaq composite index tumbled nearly 50% from its peak in March 2000. And yet, the telecom bubble-burst of 2002, pales the dot-com bubble burst. *Wall Street Journal* reported scandals of many telecom executives who sold their stock before the telecom market finally fall apart, and left investors with huge, unprecedented losses. If timing is everything, was there something the insiders knew about the state of the industry that the general population of shareholders didn't? In stock market jargon, a bull market is a period in which stock prices rise across the board, and a bear market is a period in which stock prices drop, normally by 15% or more in major stock averages such as the Don Jones Industry Average (DJIA) and the S&P 500 Index. Economists, fund managers, and individual investors have been searching for a crystal ball that can tell them the swings between a bull market and a bear market.

Economists have developed a wide variety of techniques to detect and monitor changes in economic activities. A basic concept is *business cycles*. Burns and Mitchell (1946) defined the concept as fluctuations in the aggregate economic activities of a nation. A business cycle includes a period of expansion, followed by recessions, contractions, and revivals. Three important characteristics are used when identifying a recession: duration, depth, and diffusion – the three Ds. A recession has to be long enough, from one year to ten years; a recession has to be bad enough, involving a substantial decline in output; and a recession has to be broad enough, affecting several sectors of the economy. The NBER Business Cycle Dating Committee determines recession and expansion dates essentially based on this definition. The committee aims to identify recessions, rather than predict recessions. It is not uncommon for an official announcement of a recession to come a few months after the economics went into recession. No wonder people say that economists are the last to recognize a recession.

Arthur Okun uses two types of turning points in real GDP to define the beginning and the end of a recession. A *peak* in real GDP is the beginning of a downturn GDP. If the downturn lasts for two consecutive quarters or longer, then the peak at the beginning of the decline is dated as the beginning of a recession. The end of a recession is similarly defined by a *trough* if it is followed by two consecutive quarters of growth (Del Negro, 2001). Policymakers and investigators are obviously eager to know if there are ways that can reliably predict each turn of the economy.

Del Negro (2001) presents a very informative introduction to the state of the art in turning point forecasting. There are two major approaches: the leading indicator approach and the econometric approach. The leading indicator approach is the most well known. Leading Economic Indicators (LEI) were originally proposed in 1938 by Burns, Mitchell, and their colleagues at the NBER (Mitchell and Burns, 1938). An advantage of using leading indicators is its simplicity and easily interpretability. The inclusion of a series in the index is based on its ability to predict *past* recessions. Whether the leading indicators are able to predict future recessions is a different matter. In fact, the list of leading indicators is periodically revised. The Leading Economic Indicators Index is a weighted average of all leading indicators. The index of LEI currently includes average weekly hours, average weekly initial claims for unemployment insurance, manufactures' new orders, building permits, stock prices, interest rate spread, index of consumer expectations, and a few other measures. Forecasters pay particular attention to turning points in the index, although it is still not always easy to recognize turning points.

The detection of a turning point is often based on a so-called three-consecutive-declines rule (3CD): three consecutive declines in LEI index mark a turning point – an imminent downturn in economic activity. On the other hand, Diebold and

Rudebusch (1989) find the sequential-probability-of-turning-point approach overperforms the 3CD rule in predicting post-war US recessions.

The econometric approach contains two types of modeling strategies. One way is to build generic statistical models that predict turning points as well as other daily forecasting. There are three types of such models: (1) the structural models, (2) the vector autoregression (VAR) models, and (3) the dynamic factor models (Del Negro, 2001). Structural models include the Penn-MIT model, the Fair model, and the Macro-Advisors model. The vector autoregression (VAR) models include Bayesian VARS. All these models have a common assumption that the underlying structure of the economy does not change from a recession to an expansion. A recession is regarded as a shock that hit this underlying structure.

The Markov-Switching regime model was introduced by James Hamilton (1989). Having observed that such time series frequently exhibit shifts in mean, Hamilton's original idea was to model these non-stationary time series by using a piecewise stationary linear process. It is often assumed that the observed time series are approximated by an autoregressive process, whose parameters evolve through time. Moreover, their evolution is ruled by an unobservable variable which in turn follows a first order K-state Markov chain, independent of past observations on the observed time series.

The Markov-Switching models have been extensively used in practice. Anas and Ferrara (2002) present a review of applications in the macroeconomic field. The Markov-switching process of Hamilton, $(Y_t)_t$, in the case of a VAR(p) process, is given by the following equations:

$$Y_t - \mu(S_t) = \sum_{j=1}^{p} \Phi_j(S_t)(Y_{t-j} - \mu(S_{t-j})) + \varepsilon_t$$

where $(\varepsilon_t)_t$ is a Gaussian white noise process with finite variance $\sigma^2(S_t)$ and where the unobservable variable $S_t = 1, \ldots, K$ is supposed to represent the current state of the economy. This is known as the mean adjusted form of the Markov-Switching(K)-VAR(p) model.

In a fundamentally different view, turning points are not simply regarded as the result of a large negative shock in the underlying economic structure; instead, they indicate profound shifts in the economic behavior of agents. Therefore, good predictors of routine fluctuations may not be of much use in predicting rare business cycle episodes such as recessions. After all, predicting turning points may be a completely different business altogether from predicting the economy between turning points.

Given that recessions are rare, an alternative way is to build models that specifically aim at predicting turning points. A different approach, originally developed in the early 1990s, models the probability of a recession using a *probit* model (Estrella and Mishkin, 1998). The probit form is determined by the fact that we are only interested in two possible states of the economy – whether it is or is not in a recession. The model is defined as follows:

$$y_{t+k}^* = \beta' x_t + \varepsilon_t'$$

where y_t^* is an unobservable variable that determines the occurrence of a recession at time t, k is the length of the forecast horizon – usually the number of quarters ahead, β is a vector of coefficients, x_t is a vector of values of the independent variables, and ε_t is a normally distributed error term. If $y_t^* > 0$, then there is a recession, $R_t = 1$; otherwise, no recession, $R_t = 0$. The task now is to estimate the probability of $R_{t+k} = 1$ within the next k quarters. The estimation is based on the following equation:

$$P(R_{t+k} = 1) = F(\beta'x_t)$$

where F is the cumulative normal distribution function corresponding to $-\varepsilon$. The model is estimated by maximum likelihood, with the likelihood function L defined as:

$$L = \prod_{R_{t+k}=1} F(\beta'x_t) \prod_{R_{t+k}=0} (1 - F(\beta'x_t))$$

In practice, the standard NBER recession dates are used as the recession indicator:

- $R_t = 1$, if the economy is in recession in quarter t;
- $R_t = 0$, otherwise.

As Del Negro (2001) explains, unlike econometric models such as VAR models, probit models do not distinguish between policymakers' actions and shocks coming from elsewhere in the economy. Since policymakers need to have an idea how their actions may influence the likelihood of a recession, this is one of the major weaknesses of probit models.

In Del Negro's comparison, econometric models such as the Bayesian VAR model (BVAR) outperformed the three-consecutive-decline rule (3CD). In addition to visual inspection of the turns of curves, two quantitative measures were used to compare predictive abilities. The two measures are called (1) the quadratic probability score (QPS), and (2) the log probability score (LPS)

$$QPS = \frac{1}{T}\sum_{l=1}^{T} 2(P_l - R_l)^2$$

where P_l is the probability given by the model in question and R_l is the recession indicator, which equals to 1 if a recession is occurring within the next eight quarters and 0 otherwise. If the model is right all the time, the QPS is 0; if the model is wrong all the time, the QPS is 2.

$$LPS = -\frac{1}{T}\sum_{l=1}^{T} \left[(1 - R_l)\ln(1 - P_l) + R_l \ln(P_l) \right]$$

In essence, the QPS is proportional to the sum of squared errors, whereas the LPS penalizes large errors more heavily. The QPS scores of BVAR and 3CD are 0.37 and 0.67. The LPS scores are 0.59 and 2.32. Furthermore, in a comparison between BVAR and the Estrella–Mishkin probit model, the probit model outperformed the BVAR model (QPS = 0.19 and 0.31 respectively; LPS = 0.32 and 0.95 respectively). Given the results, Del Negro's conclusion is that one should supplement the BVAR with a turning point model such as the Estrella–Mishkin model.

Economic turning points, civilization collapses, abrupt climate changes, and lost colonies are only a glimpse into a diverse range of practical problems. They are distinct from one another in so many ways. Self-organized criticality is one way to explore the profound dynamics in complex systems. These examples are more illustrative in nature at this stage. Indeed, many of them are yet to draw enough attention from the mainstream of information visualization. If the first generation of information visualization is characterized by the success in revealing salient information structures, then the second generation of information visualization should go beyond the structuralism and explore more fundamental dynamics that govern the formation and evolution of information structures. From this perspective, a better understanding of abrupt changes is certainly a necessary starting point. Detecting turning points and triggers is a challenging and risky route, but it is also potentially rewarding to the healthy development of information visualization as it extends its principles and strengths to broader areas of practical situations.

8.3 Topic Detection and Tracking

Topic Detection and Tracking (TDT) projects aim to develop and evaluate technologies required to segment, detect, and track topical information in a stream consisting of news stories. TDT has five major task groups: (1) story segmentation, (2) topic detection, (3) topic tracking, (4) first story detection, and (5) story link detection. Topic detection focuses on discovering previously unseen topics, whereas topic tracking focuses on monitoring stories known to a TDT system. First Story Detection (FSD) is particularly relevant to the theme of this chapter. FSD aims to detect the first appearance of a new story in a time series of news associated with an event. Roy et al. (2002) presented methodologies for trend detection. Kontostathis et al. (2003) gave a comprehensive survey of emerging trend detection in textual data mining in terms of four distinct aspects: (1) Input Data and Attributes, (2) Learning Algorithms, (3) Visualization, and (4) Evaluation. Table 8.1 lists the TDT systems in the survey.

8.3.1 First Story Detection

In 1993 terrorists drove a truck packed with 1100 lbs of explosives into the basement parking garage at the World Trade Center. Six people were killed and 1000 injured. The towers were repaired, cleaned, and reopened in less than a month. In 1995, a massive bomb inside a rental truck exploded outside the nine-story Murrah Federal Building in downtown Oklahoma City. Mass media provided continuous coverage of the two events: the World Trade Center bombing and the Oklahoma City bombing. The goal of First Story Detection algorithms is to identify the beginning of the streams of news reports about an event like this.

TDT projects typically test their systems on TDT data sets, which contain news stories and event descriptors. The assessment of the performance of a TDT algorithm is based on *Relevance Judgment*, which indicates the relevancy between a story and an event. Take the event descriptor *Oklahoma City bombing* as an example. If a matching story is about survivors' reaction after the bombing, the relevance judgment would be *Yes*. In contrast, the relevance judgment of the same story and a different event descriptor *US Terrorism Response* would be *No*.

Allan et al. (1998) presented a single pass clustering algorithm, in which the entire content of each story is represented as a query. A newly arrived story is compared with all the existing stories. If the new story is similar enough to one of the

Table 8.1 TDT systems featured in the Kontostathis et al.'s survey

System	Year	Bibliography
ThemeRiver™	2002	Havre, S, Hetzler, E, Whitney, P, and Nowell, L (2002). ThemeRiver: Visualizing thematic changes in large document collections. *IEEE Transactions on Visualization and Computer Graphics,* **8**(1), 9–20.
CIMEL	2001	Blank, GD, Pottenger, WM, Kessler, GD, Herr, M, Jaffe, H, Roy, S, Gevry, D, and Wang, Q (2001). *Cimel: Constructive, collaborative inquiry-based multimedia e-learning.* Proceedings of the 6th Annual Conference on Innovation and Technology in Computer Science Education (ITiCSE), June 2001.
HDDI™	2001	Pottenger, WM, Kim, Y, and Meling, DD (2001). HDDI(TM): Hiarachical distributed dynamic indexing. In R Grossman C Kamath, V Kumarand and R Namburu (Eds), *Data Mining for Scientific and Engineering Applications.* New York: Kluwer Academic Publishers.
TimeMines	2000	Swan, R, and Jensen, D (2000). *TimeMines: Constructing timelines with statistical models of word usage.* Proceedings of the 6th ACM SIGKDD International Conference on Knowledge Discovery and Data Mining.
New Event Detection	1998	Allan, J, Papka, R, and Lavrenko, V (1998). *Online new event detection and tracking.* Proceedings of ACM SIGIR. pp. 37–45.
PatentMiner	1997	Lent, B, Agrawal, R, and Srikant, R (1997). *Discovering trends in text databases.* Proceedings of 3rd International Conference on Knowledge Discovery and Data Mining. California.
TOA	1995	Porter, AL, and Detampel, MJ (1995). Technology opportunities analysis. *Technological Forecasting and Social Change,* 49, 237–255.

existing ones, then to the algorithm, it is really nothing new. In contrast, if no match is found between the new story and existing stories, then the newly arrived story is marked as something completely new. It was reported that the single pass algorithm can distinguish the Oklahoma City bombing stories from the earlier stories on the Word Trade Center bombing. However, their algorithm could not distinguish OJ Simpson trial stories from other court cases.

Swan and Allan (1999) constructed a statistical model that can detect the arrival of significant information. For a collection of time-stamped documents such as email or news, tokens refer to the words in such documents. This is very similar to a standard time series data, except each time point is associated with a bag of tokens. The arrival of these tokens can be modeled as discrete events of a random process with an unknown distribution. In other words, tokens are emitted by a random process. Such random processes are assumed to be stationary, meaning that they do not vary over time. In addition, tokens' arrivals are completely independent from one another. A 2 by 2 contingency table of token by time is modeled by a χ^2 distribution with one degree of freedom. A token ω has two conditions, either presence or absence; time τ also has two conditions, a time point t or else. The independence assumption implies $P(\omega_i) = P(\omega_i|\omega_j)$. Similarly, another 2 by 2 contingency table of co-occurrences of two tokens ω_i and ω_j also follows a χ^2 distribution with one degree of freedom. The key to their approach is to use a χ^2 distribution to identify the probability of a single random word passing the χ^2 test and thereby to determine whether the appearance of a feature is purely by chance or not.

Their approach was tested with a sub-set of the Topic Detection and Tracking (TDT) pilot study's corpus, which contains CNN broadcast news and Reuters

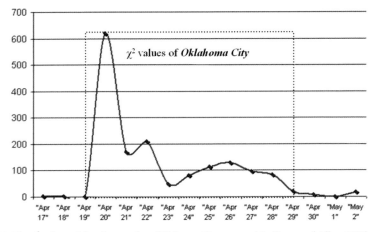

Figure 8.8 The χ^2 values of the phrase token Oklahoma City reported in (Swan and Allan, 1999).

newswires. For each token and each date, they calculated the χ^2 value. If the value is above 7.879, which means statistically significant at the significance level of 0.005, then the token was flagged as having a significant appearance on that day and it was subsequently tracked. The χ^2 values of the phrase token *Oklahoma City* are shown in Figure 8.8.

The Swan–Allan method requires preprocesses such as extracting named entity features and noun phrases. Many stories change over time. Showing how the information evolves over time is one of the most challenging and significant tasks. It is also where information visualization has a major role to play, especially given the promising work such as *ThemeRiver* and others.

Allan et al. (2000) showed that simple parameter tuning is unlikely to bring significant improvements to the TDT research community. Instead, new approaches should be developed beyond the current tracking models, especially by taking into account task-specific information and how new topics and events are related and defined.

8.3.2 Burst Detection

An interesting observation of news stories is that events are often reported in burst. Yang et al. (1998) depicted a daily histogram of story counts over time. News stories about the same event tend to appear within a very narrow timeframe. The gap between two bursts can be used to discriminate distinct events. More recently, Jon Kleinberg (2002) developed a burst detection algorithm and applied it to the arrivals of email and words used in titles of articles.

The idea of burst detection is to find a sudden increase in the use of some words in a sequence of documents. Kleinberg was originally motivated by the need to filter his email. He expected that whenever an important event occurs or is about to occur, there should be a sharp increase of certain words that characterize the event. He called such sharp increases *bursts*. He quoted E.M. Forster (1927) that "when we look at our past it does not stretch back evenly but piles up into a few notable pinnacles, and when we look at the future it seems sometimes a wall, sometimes a cloud, sometimes sun, but never a chronological chart".

Essentially, Kleinberg's burst detection algorithm analyzes the rate of increase of word frequencies and identifies the most rapidly growing words. He tested his algorithm on the full text of all the State of the Union addresses since 1790. The burst detection algorithm identified important events occurring at the time of some of the speeches. For example, *depression* and *recovery* were bursty words in 1930–1937, *fighting* and *Japanese* were bursty in 1942–1945, and *atomic* was the buzz word in 1947 and 1959. What makes this interesting is that such trends may be obvious to people, but not to a computer, which lacks the knowledge of history. One of the implications is that one may use this method to narrow web searches with the clustering effect of bursts. One may identify emerging trends by monitoring the growth rate of words.

Kleinberg's burst detection differs from the Swan–Allan approach. The Swan–Allan approach is essentially a threshold-based detection in that once the arrivals of a word token exceed a predefined threshold, the token will be tracked until its prevalence drops below the threshold. The duration in which the token stays above the threshold corresponds to a single episode of an underlying event. In contrast, Kleinberg's burst detection algorithm aims to detect an episode that may last months and even years, and during such a long period of time, it is quite common for a thematic token to fall below a constant threshold. In addition, it is also interesting to detect bursts embedded within bursts. It is difficult to handle these kinds of scenarios with a threshold-based approach.

Instead of focusing on the elevation level of a token, an alternative way is to model the gaps between the arrival times of such tokens. For example, we are more likely to receive email messages relating to a given topic separated by hours or days, than with gaps of months and years. An exponential distribution is one of the simplest models of such phenomena. Suppose the probability of observing a temporal gap t between the arrival times of two consecutive messages follows an exponential distribution:

$$f(t) = \alpha e^{-\alpha t}$$

The expected gap value is α^{-1}; hence, α is called the rate of message arrivals. The burst detection is now formulated as a Markov source model that can emit messages at certain arrival rates, and the change of arrival rates can be modeled as a state transition. For example, before the beginning of a burst period, the messages can be seen as emitted from a low state with a rate α; a burst is defined as a sequence of messages that are emitted at a higher arrival rate s_α $(s > 1)$. Before the emission of each message, the probability of changing from one state to another is p. This model can be generalized to represent states that correspond to arbitrarily small gaps with rates increased by a factor of s. Kleinberg proved that this model can be reduced to a finite-state system because the maximum likelihood state sequence involves only k stats, where k is bounded by a combined factor of the length of the time window, the minimum gap, and the acceleration rate s. Eventually the task becomes to look for those longest state sequences above certain levels of emission rates.

The major advantage of Kleinberg's approach is that it can handle multiple levels of bursts. There are alternative approaches, such as wavelet analysis, Hidden Markov Models (HMMs), and machine-learning and other data mining and knowledge discovery algorithms. Data mining and knowledge discovery algorithms provide a rich source of resources that can be used to enhance information visualization. Algorithms that can detect abrupt changes with the least number of false alarms are certainly useful to filter out noises from the original data so that subsequent modeling and visualization can produce much improved and sharp focused information visualization.

8.3.3 Fraud Detection

A significant application of abnormality detection is fraud detection. Example applications include detecting telephone frauds, money laundering, network intrusion, and potentially counter-terrorist activities. The major challenge of any fraud detection is to discover fraudulent activities in a large amount of legitimate ones. The normal and abnormal cases are extremely unbalanced. Stolfo et al. (1997) described an approach to credit card fraud detection. They worked on a half million credit card transaction record database from a member of the Financial Services Technology Consortium (FSTC). Among the 500,000 records, 20% were labeled by the banks as fraudulent transactions, but the true fraud rate is a closely guarded industry secret. The best overall performance was achieved by combining different machine-learning algorithms into a meta-classification hierarchy, although it is still not clear about the characteristics of component algorithms for the best meta-classifier.

Burge and Shaw-Taylor (1997) described a differential analysis of detecting fraudulent use of mobile phones, i.e. cellular phones based on behavior profiling. Their approach belongs to a class of so-called unsupervised learning algorithms. A shorter sequence of current behavior profile (CBP) and a longer sequence of behavior profile history (BPH) are considered in their approach as finite length queues. The fraud detection is done by examining a metric called the Hellinger distance, d_H, which is a natural measure to compare two probability distributions of the shorter-term and longer-term profiles CBP and BPH. A zero value of d_H means the two distributions are the same, whereas the maximum of 2 means the two distributions are completely different.

$$d_H = \sum \left(\sqrt{\mathrm{CBP}_i} - \sqrt{\mathrm{BPH}_i} \right)^2$$

Whenever the d_H is above a threshold, an alarm is raised for fraud inspection. Burge and Shaw-Taylor (1997) illustrated an acceptable behavior and a possible fraudulent behavior. If someone who used to make international calls did not make international calls, but if supplementary services such as voice mail and call forwarding were used, then it might be considered as acceptable or legitimate behavior. However, if the lack of international calls comes with a sudden drop of supplementary services as well, then an alarm should be raised because a possible scenario would be a handset theft where the thief is unlikely to use the voice mail service of the owner.

8.4 Visualizing Temporal Patterns

The examples so far in this chapter are essentially outside current mainstream information visualization research and practice. We expect that these examples will provoke some reflective thinking on information visualization itself and hope that a new generation of information visualization will go beyond the structure-centric first generation. Researchers are increasingly interested in visualizing emerging patterns in association with evolving information structures, using tools such as Disk Trees and Time Tubes (Chi et al., 1998) and Botanical Trees (Kleiberg et al., 2001). In the following sections, we focus on works within the information visualization community, especially in terms of visualizations of temporal patterns.

8.4.1 The Storm

Evolution of a Numerically Modeled Severe Storm was a five-minute movie that showed the evolution of a 140-minute storm (Wilhelmson et al., 1990). The supercomputer-visualized storm is a classic of scientific visualization. The original visualization was later redesigned by Edward Tufte and Colleen Bushell and others. The design principles are explained in Tufte's book *Visual Explanations* (1997). He maintains that although cartography and statistical graphics have routinely used the fundamentals of scale, orientation, and labels, they are often missing from the colorful computer visualizations. He examined 134 color images of supercomputer scientific animations and found 65% of them had no scales or labeled dimensions at all, 22% had partial scales or labels, and only 13% had complete labels and scales. Tufte regarded this as a dequantification problem. And the goal of the redesign was essentially to restore the lost quantification fundamentals.

In *After the Storm*, Baker and Bushell (1995) explained how the thunderstorm visualization was redesigned. Several design ideas in the new version of the Storm are generically applicable in visualizations involving patterns evolving over time. For example, the new design drew the viewer's attention to the cloud and the once strong grid in the original design faded into the background (Figure 8.9). The

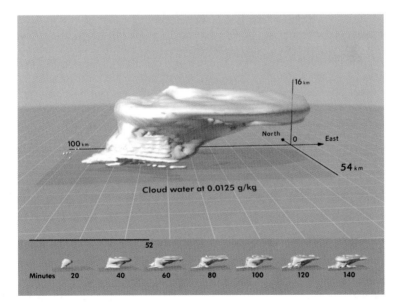

Figure 8.9 The new design of the storm (Baker and Bushell, 1995). http://www.ncsa.uiuc.edu/~baker/Images/stormTimeline.jpg

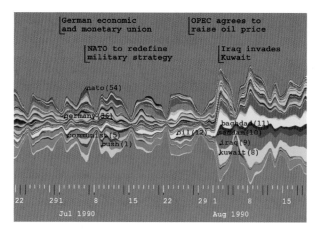

Figure 8.10 ThemeRiver visualization of Associated Press news wire stores from July and early August 1990 (Havre et al., 2002). The figure was produced at the Pacific Northwest National Laboratory, which is managed and operated by the Battelle Memorial Institute on behalf of the United States Department of Energy. © 2002 IEEE. Reprinted with permission.

new design improved the amount of quantitative information displayed in the visualization.

8.4.2 ThemeRiver

ThemeRiver (Havre et al., 2002) is a visualization system that uses the metaphor of a river to depict thematic flows over time in a collection of documents. The thematic changes are shown along a time line of corresponding external events. A thematic river consists of frequency streams of terms; the changing width of a stream over time indicates the changes of term occurrences (Figure 8.10). The occurrence of an external event may be followed by sudden changes of thematic strengths. On the one hand, searching for an abruptly widened thematic stream is a much more intuitive task to detect a new story than text-based TDT systems that can only report changes in terms of statistics. On the other hand, ThemeRiver does not incorporate additional data filters that would make changes in thematic patterns easy to detect. The lack of a dedicated data filter is common in the current generation of information visualization. In part, this is due to an overly emphasized reliance on perceptual and cognitive abilities of human beings. Powerful data modeling techniques can make salient patterns clearer and in sharper contrast. This is one of the areas to which information visualization should pay substantial attention in the future.

8.4.3 Disk Trees and Time Tubes

Some of the major technical problems are how to make the changes over time easy to understand and how to preserve the overall context in which changes take place. Web ecology is concerned with relationships among users and their information environment, and its evaluation over time in terms of the content, the topological properties, and the usage (Chi et al., 1998). Disk Tree represents the

Figure 8.11 A disk tree of the XeroX website (Chi et al., 1998). © 1998 ACM, Inc. Reprinted with permission.

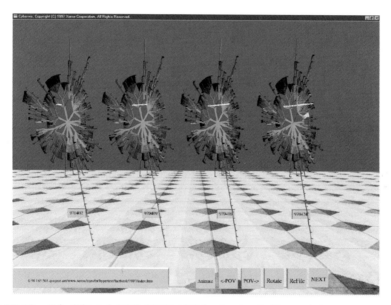

Figure 8.12 Time Tube (Chi et al., 1998). © 1998 ACM, Inc. Reprinted with permission.

hyperlink structure of a website (Figure 8.11). It uses a breadth-first search (BFS) algorithm to extract a tree structure from the original network, and then visualizes the tree structure. Time Tube shows an array of disk trees to show the evolution of a website (Figure 8.12). They are designed to support tasks such as comparison and trend detection. Disk Tree and Time Tube were tested on the website of XeroX, www.xerox.com, over a 30-day period.

The major advantage of Time Tube is its simplicity. Disk Trees in the Time Tube are similar to an array of snapshots taken at different times. Similar to the

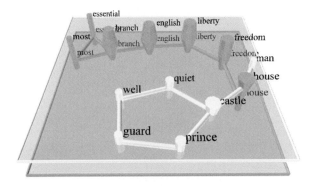

Figure 8.13 Semi-transparent layers pile up to depict the evolution of a discourse structure (Brandes and Corman, 2003). © 2003 Palgrave-Macmillan. Reprinted with permission.

ThemeRiver approach, Disk Tree does not contain a dedicated component that can either filter out noises or amplify signals in the original data.

8.4.4 Network Evolution

Detecting and visualizing changes in an evolving network presents significant challenges to the current arsenals of information visualization. Incremental graph drawing provides a unique perspective to the understanding of the challenge of comparing different networks (North, 1995). The graph drawing community has also contributed ways to match the layout of a graph and the mental map of a user (Misue et al., 1995). Large-network analysis and visualization software Pajek supports a function called timed networks for the user to step through a network at consecutive time points (Batagelj and Mrvar, 1998).

One way to visualize temporal dynamics of networks is to use multiple time planes. Each time plane depicts a snapshot of the underlying network. A chronological sequence of time planes is then used to reveal temporal patterns. Recent studies of temporal graph visualization include Brandes' work (Brandes and Corman, 2003) and the TGRIP system (Erten et al., 2003, 2004). Brandes and Corman (2003) used semi-transparent layers one on another to display the progress of a discourse (Figure 8.13).

Erten et al. (2003) reported an interesting example of temporal graph visualization of papers in ACM conference proceedings. The evolution is visualized through a sequence of graphs, G_1, G_2, ..., G_n, one for each year in a given time period. Particular attention was paid to maintain a user's mental map between two adjacent graphs in the sequence. Each individual graph was visualized in a two-dimensional layout. An aggregated graph $G_{1...n}$ was created, containing vertices from all time-sliced graphs $G_1, G_2, ..., G_n$. In addition, the same vertices in adjacent graphs were connected by extra edges explicitly. Finally, the combined-graph $G_{1...n}$ was drawn using a modified version of a force-directed graph drawing algorithm. The visualized graph can be animated through time.

Erten et al. used their technique to visualize category graphs derived from the categorization of papers in ACM conference proceedings (Figure 8.14). The

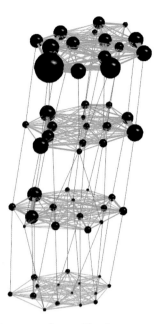

Figure 8.14 Each vertex represents a research area. The size represents the concentration of work in that area. Two areas are connected by a heavy edge if they are well related. Four time-slices from bottom to top: (1981–1985), (1986–1990), (1991–1995), (1996–2000). (Erten et al., 2003). Reprinted with permission.

category graph for a given time period is an undirected graph. Vertices represent categories and edges represent categories that co-occurred in these conference papers. The weight of a node represents the concentration of research on a category. The weight of an edge represents the strength of the relationship between two categories.

Chen and Morris (2003) demonstrated an animated visualization technique that can display the process of network evolution. A Pathfinder network version and a minimum spanning tree (MST) version were compared in a study of co-citation networks over a time span of nearly 60 years. Although the MST version contained many hubs, the animation revealed that the Pathfinder version maintained the local accuracy of network evolution in a much better way (Figures 8.15 and 8.16).

Before we leave the topic of visualizing temporal patterns, we want to note that searching for new metaphors of visualization has been a persistent challenge that the information visualization community must face. Searching for a metaphor that can grow in an organic way is certainly an even tougher challenge. Fractals and trees are two promising candidates for growth visualization. One of the most intriguing studies of the relationship between fractals and networks is due to Pickover (1988). Figure 8.17 shows a 2D stability plot of a network. The resultant plots are fractals.

Diffusion Limited Aggregation (DLA), a fractal generation model, has several practical implications. DLA generates a fractal based on a diffusion process. Particles are launched one after another. Each particle randomly wanders around in a two-dimensional plane. An aggregate is a set of stationary particles in the plane. If a moving particle is in touch with the aggregate, it will stick to the aggregate and becomes part of it. A particle can wander off and it will simply disappear. The

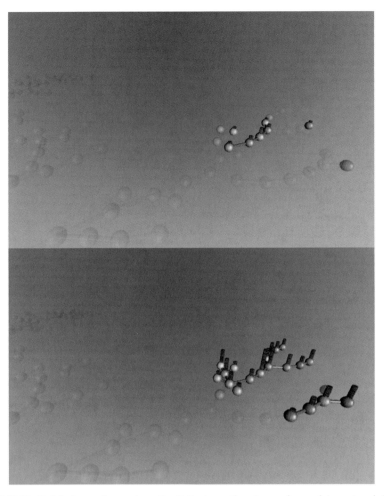

Figure 8.15 The Pathfinder version captures the distinct growth patterns of an evolving network (Chen and Morris, 2003). © 2003 IEEE. Reprinted with permission.

aggregate generated in such diffusion processes is a fractal. DLA aggregates have some interesting properties. For example, a diffusing particle is more likely to attach to the outskirts of the aggregate than to inner areas. Particles are independent of each other. The attachment does not depend on any assumptions of inter-particle relationships.

Chen and Lobo (2003) explored the potential of using DLA as a new organizing metaphor. The traditional diffusion process is modified so that the attachment of a particle is determined probabilistically based on the semantic similarity between the moving particle and the nearest particle in the aggregate. The more frequently two articles are co-cited, the more likely the attachment when one is the moving particle and the other is the nearest aggregate particle. Hence, the process is called semantically modified DLA. The modified DLA not only maintains the fractal structure of DLA, but also organizes particles according to their intrinsic relationships (Figure 8.18).

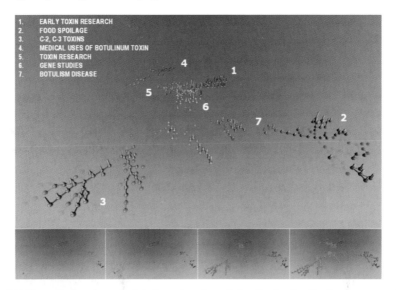

Figure 8.16 The evolution of a network is shown in animated visualization. Smaller figures are snapshots from the animation sequence (Chen and Morris, 2003). © 2003 IEEE. Reprinted with permission.

Figure 8.17 A 2D stability plot of a network. Such plots are fractals, or self-similar structures. Source: Pickover (1988). © 1998 ACM, Inc. Reprinted with permission. See also: www.pickover.com

Tree-rings occur in several examples earlier in this chapter. Tree-rings help scientists to reconstruct the climate in the past. We experiment a tree-ring visualization of citations. Imagine an article is a tree. The citation tree grows by adding a layer of citations each year, instead of a layer of wood cells. If we look at the tree rings of such an article tree, we will see rings of annual citations. By studying the

367-Author Co-Citation Network   10,000-Particle DLA   1,250-Article Co-Citation SM-DLA

Figure 8.18 An author co-citation network and a DLA aggregate have a striking resemblance. The SM-DLA maintains the fractal structure (Chen and Lobo, 2003). © 2003 IEEE. Reprinted with permission.

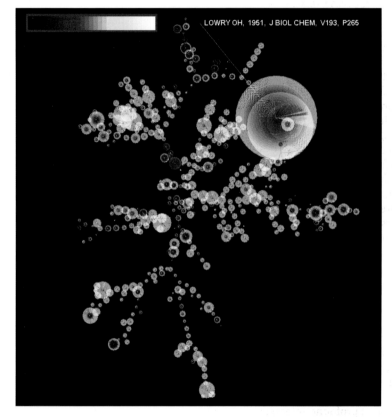

Figure 8.19 Tree rings of citations. Each article grows like a tree by adding a layer of annual citations.

widths of these citation rings one can tell not only whether an article is a citation classic, but also specific years in which the article was highly cited. This is an alternative metaphor to the three-dimensional landscape metaphor. A relevant metaphor would be the botanic tree visualization (Kleiberg et al., 2001), although botanic tree visualizations were not designed to capture temporal patterns. Figure 8.19 shows an example of tree ring visualization of a co-citation network.

8.5 Intellectual Turning Points

Each scientific discipline has its unique unit of analysis. Particle physicists are interested in various properties and behavior of particles. Cosmologists are concerned with the universe as a whole: how it began and how it evolved. In functional analysis, mathematicians study a space of functions. Philosophers of science study the nature of scientific branches. In information retrieval, the focus is on a space of documents.

Visualizing the evolution of a scientific discipline needs a perspective from 64,000 miles above. Although thematic turns detected in document streams are important indicators of the evolution, they do not explicitly carry an endorsement of domain experts or fellow scientists. In contrast, citations of a scientific publication provide indirect measures of impact. A related concept is the impact factor of a journal. Seeing through a pair of citation glasses prompts us to ask questions about the evolution of a discipline as a whole. Where are its frontiers? What are the most significant turns it has ever made? What was it like before and after a scientific revolution?

In this section we introduce a novel method that can progressively visualize the evolution of a knowledge domain's co-citation network over time. The method, called progressive knowledge domain visualization (P-KDViz), produces a panoramic view of co-citation patchworks across a sequence of time slices. Critical transitions from one slice to another are shown as points with visually salient properties, especially in terms of topological properties and other intrinsic properties of a co-citation network. More interestingly, the method demonstrates the potential benefits of transforming the search for intellectual turning points into an intuitive search for visually salient representations of articles in the literature visualization.

The P-KDViz method is applied to a co-citation study of the superstring field in theoretical physics so as to demonstrate that a search for intellectual turning points can be narrowed down to visually salient nodes in the visualized network. The study focuses on the search of articles that triggered two superstring revolutions. An earlier version of the work is described in Chen (2004).

8.5.1 Progressive Visualization

The most widely known model of science is Thomas Kuhn's *Structure of Scientific Revolutions* (1962), in which science is characterized by transitions from normal science to science in crisis, and from crisis to a scientific revolution. Kuhn's theory suggests that scientific revolutions are a crucial part of science. The notion of paradigm shift is widely known in virtually all scientific disciplines. Kuhn's model has generated profound interest in detecting and monitoring paradigm shifts through the study of temporal patterns in co-citation networks. Small (1977) identified and monitored the changes of research focus in collagen research in terms of how clusters of most co-cited articles change over consecutive years. Small's study predated many modern visualization techniques. However, the representations of co-citation clusters were isolated from one year to another; significant temporal patterns or transitions may go unnoticed if they fall between the clusters from different years.

Researchers have been persistently searching for underlying mechanisms that may explain various changes and patterns in scientific networks. On the other hand, this is an ambitious and challenging quest because of the scale, the diversity, and the dynamic nature of scientific networks that one has to deal with. The P-KDViz method is designed to reduce some of the complexities associated with identifying key changes in a knowledge domain. The method is applied to co-citation networks, although it is applicable to a wider range of networks.

The P-KDViz method draws its strengths from a divide-and-conquer strategy. It slices a given time interval into a sequence of segments. A snapshot of the underlying co-citation network is taken for each time slice. The time series of these network snapshots are merged into patchworks. Major changes between adjacent slices are highlighted in a panoramic visualization of the merged network. The ultimate goal is to simplify the search for significant papers in a knowledge domain's literature so that one can search for visually salient features, such as landmark nodes, hub nodes, and pivot nodes, in a visualized network. The entire progressive visualization process is streamlined and implemented in a computer system called *CiteSpace*.

Chen and Kuljis (2003) introduced animated visualization techniques to re-construct citation and co-citation events in their chronological order so that one can examine the growth history of a domain in a broader context in a similar way to how we play a video in a fast-forward mode. The animated visualization revealed paradigm-like clusters of co-cited articles corresponding to significant changes in the field of superstring – the same topic to be visualized with the P-KDViz method below, but the visual features of some of the groundbreaking articles were not distinct enough to lend themselves to a simple visual search. Mechanisms such as time slicing, multiple thresholding, and merging were not incorporated into an integrated methodology. Now we are interested in visualization techniques that can give groundbreaking articles some distinguishable visual features.

A research front consists of transient clusters of most recently cited works in the literature of a scientific field (Price, 1965). A research front represents the state of the art of a field. Research fronts move along with the underlying scientific field as new articles replace existing articles. If we visualize the evolution of co-citation network from one time slice to another, are we going to see the movement of a research front? What will they look like? More importantly, can we easily spot intellectual turning points like those that triggered superstring revolutions?

Much of the existing approach to visualizing the evolution of a network falls into one of the two categories: the *slide-show* approach and the *panorama* approach. Just as in a slide show, the former aims to highlight the changes as the viewer moves forward, sometimes back and forth, in a time series of snapshots. The latter aims to pack synthesized temporal changes into a single image.

The slide-show approach has several advantages, including being easy to implement and flexible to use. This approach often provides additional visual aids to help viewers identify changes between adjacent snapshots. In earlier sections, we have introduced examples of visualizing how a discourse evolves as a network of words and how semantic structures are visualized across different time planes. However, research in perceptual cognition has shown that comparing two images back and forth could be a very cognitively demanding task and prone to errors.

The panorama approach aims to depict temporal as well as spatial changes in such a way that viewers can detect a trend or a pattern by studying a single image. This approach could minimize the disturbance to the viewer's mental model. Related work in this area includes incremental graph drawing and the timed network display function in Pajek. Our earlier work on using animated visualization techniques to depict temporal changes in a co-citation network also belongs to this category (Chen and Kuljis, 2003).

A progressive visualization method aims to visualize the evolution of a network over time. The following three issues need to be addressed for visualizing time sliced networks:

1 Improving the clarity of individual networks.
2 Highlighting transitions between adjacent networks.
3 Identifying potentially important nodes.

The first issue is concerned with the clarity of individual networks' representations. One of the major aesthetic criteria established by research in graph drawing is that link crossings should be avoided whenever possible. A network visualization with the least number of edge crossings is regarded as not only aesthetically pleasing, but also more efficient to work with in terms of the performance of relevant perceptual tasks. The number of link crossings may be reduced by pruning various links in a network. Minimum spanning trees and Pathfinder network scaling are commonly used algorithms. The major advantages and disadvantages of these scaling techniques are further analyzed in the following subsection.

The second issue is concerned with progressively merging two adjacent networks so that one can identify which part of the earlier network is persistent in the new network, which part of the earlier network is no longer active in the new network, and which part of the new network is completely new. Much of the novelty of our method is associated with the way we address this issue.

The third issue is concerned with the role of visually salient features in simplifying search tasks for intellectual turning points. Visually salient nodes include landmark nodes, pivot nodes, and hub nodes.

Issue 1: Improving the Clarity of Networks

Co-citation networks often have a vast number of links, and displaying links indiscriminately is the primary cause of clutter. There are two general approaches to reduce the number of links in a display: a threshold-based approach and a topology-based approach. In a threshold-based approach, the elimination of a link is purely determined by whether the link's weight exceeds a threshold. In contrast, in a topology-based approach, the elimination of a link is determined by a more extensive consideration of intrinsic topological properties; therefore, such approaches tend to preserve certain topological intrinsic properties more reliably, although the computational complexity tends to be higher.

Pathfinder network scaling was originally developed by cognitive scientists to build procedural models based on subjective ratings (Schvanevedlt, 1990; Chen, 1998a,b; Chen and Paul, 2001; Chen, 2003). It uses a more sophisticated link elimination mechanism as compared to MST. It can remove a large number of links and retain the most important ones. Given a network, one can derive a unique Pathfinder network that contains all the alternative MSTs of the original network.

The goal of Pathfinder network scaling is, in essence, to prune a dense network. The topology of a Pathfinder network is determined by two parameters, r and q. The r parameter defines a metric space over a given network based on the Minkowski distance so that one can measure the length of a path connecting two nodes in the network. The Minkowski distance becomes the familiar Euclidean distance when $r = 2$. When $r = \infty$, the weight of a path is defined as the maximum weight of its component links, and the distance is known as the maximum value distance.

Given a metric space, a triangle inequality can be defined as follows:

$$w_{ij} \leq (\Sigma_k w^r n_k n_{k+1})^{1/r}$$

where w_{ij} is the weight of a direct path between i and j, $wn_k n_{k+1}$ is the weight of a path between n_k and n_{k+1}, for $k = 1, 2, ..., m$. In particular, $i = n_1$ and $j = n_k$. In other words, the alternative path between i and j may go all the way round through nodes $n_1, n_2, ..., n_k$ as long as each intermediate link belongs to the network.

If w_{ij} is greater than the weight of the alternative path, then the direct path between i and j violates the inequality condition. Consequently, the link $i - j$ will be removed because it is assumed that such links do not represent the most salient aspects of the association between the nodes i and j.

The q parameter specifies the maximum number of links that alternative paths can have for the triangle inequality test. The value of q can be set to any integer between 2 and $N - 1$, where N is the number of nodes in the network. If an alternative path has a lower cost than the direct path, the direct path will be removed. In this way, Pathfinder reduces the number of links from the original network, while all the nodes remain untouched. The resultant network is also known as a minimum-cost network.

The strength of Pathfinder network scaling is its ability to derive more accurate local structures than other comparable algorithms such as multidimensional scaling (MDS) and minimum spanning tree (MST). However, the Pathfinder algorithm is computationally expensive; the published algorithm is in the class of $O(N^4)$. KDViz approaches built on the Pathfinder network scaling algorithm have a potential bottleneck if one needs to deal with large networks. The maximum pruning power of Pathfinder is achievable with $q = N - 1$ and $r = \infty$; not surprisingly, this is also the most expensive one because all the possible paths must be examined for each link. In addition, the algorithm requires a large amount of memory to store the intermediate distance matrices. This is the first of the three issues our new method is to deal with.

Issue 2: Merging Heterogeneous Networks

The second issue identified above is concerned with progressively merging two temporally adjacent networks. Depending on the nature of a knowledge domain, networks to be merged could be heterogeneous as well as homogeneous in terms of intrinsic topological properties and additional attributes of nodes and links. For example, intellectual structures of a knowledge domain before and after a major conceptual revolution are likely to be fundamentally different as new theories and new evidence become predominant. Co-citation networks of citation classics in a field are likely to differ from co-citation networks of newly published articles. The key question is: what is the most informative way to merge potentially diverse networks?

A merged network needs to capture the important changes over time in a knowledge domain's co-citation structure. We need to find when and where the

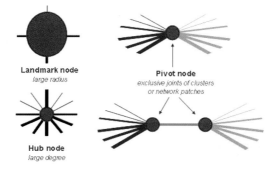

Figure 8.20 Three types of visually salient nodes in a co-citation network (Chen, 2004). © 2004 PNAS.

most influential changes took place so that the evolution of the domain can be characterized and visualized. Few studies in the literature investigated network merge from a domain-centric perspective. The central idea of our new method is to visualize how different network representations of an underlying phenomenon can be informatively stitched together.

Issue 3: Visually Salient Nodes in Merged Networks

The third issue is concerned with the identification of potentially important articles in a co-citation network. The importance of a node in a co-citation network can be quickly identified by the local topological structure of the node and by additional attributes of the node. We are particularly interested in three types of nodes: (1) landmark nodes, (2) hub nodes, and (3) pivot nodes (see Figure 8.20). The visually salient properties of these nodes are the key to the switch from overloaded brain work to more intuitive eyeball work.

A landmark node is a node that has extraordinary attribute values. For example, a highly cited article tends to provide an important landmark regardless how it is co-cited with other articles. Landmark nodes can be rendered by distinctive visual–spatial attributes such as size, height, or volume. A hub node has a relatively large node degree. A widely co-cited article is a good candidate for significant intellectual contributions. A high-degree hub-like node is also easy to recognize in a visualized network. Both landmark nodes and hub nodes are commonly used in network visualization. Although the concept of pivot nodes is available in various contexts, the way they are used in our method is novel. Pivot nodes are joints between different networks. They are either the common nodes shared by two networks, or the gateway nodes that are connected by internetwork links. Pivot nodes have an essential role in our method.

8.5.2 CiteSpace

CiteSpace is a streamlined system that supports the following procedural steps, namely time slicing, thresholding, modeling, pruning, merging, and mapping. Although pruning is not always necessary, it is a potentially valuable option when dealing with a dense network. The input to *CiteSpace* is a set of bibliographic data files in the field-tagged ISI Export Format. The outputs of *CiteSpace* include visualized co-citation networks. Each network is shown in a separate interactive window interface.

Time Slicing

The entire time interval can be sliced into equal-length segments. The length of each segment can be as short as a year or as long as the entire interval. If appropriate data become available, it is possible to slice it thinner to make monthly or weekly segments. Currently, sliced segments are mutually exclusive, although overlapping segments could be an interesting alternative worth exploring.

Thresholding

Citation analysis and co-citation analysis typically sample the most highly cited work – the cream of crop – with a single constant threshold. However, a single constant threshold is a crude sampling mechanism if the citation patterns over an extended period of time are being considered. By default, both citations and co-citations are calculated within each time slice, as opposed to across all time slices.

Time slicing provides the flexibility to tailor a threshold more closely to the characteristics of citation and co-citation activities in each individual time slice. This flexibility is expected to reduce the bias associated with a single one-size-fits-all threshold. One can even compare and merge two very different networks within this framework, for example, a network of articles from Nobel Prize winning scientists, and a network of technical reports. The key questions are: what is the common ground between two networks? How can one extract insights into the internetwork relationship from such common ground? A flexible threshold configuration can find a common ground more easily.

The co-citation network in a given time slice is determined by three thresholds: a citation threshold (c), a co-citation threshold (cc), and a cosine coefficient threshold (ccv). In *CiteSpace*, the user needs to select desired thresholds for three specific time slices, namely the beginning, the middle, and the ending slices. *CiteSpace* automatically assigns interpolated thresholds to the remaining slices. In practice, the user starts with an arbitrary threshold configuration and then adjusts thresholds accordingly based on the reported statistics such as the citation population, the numbers of nodes and links in a network.

In the citation world, articles are not created equal. Some articles have for more than their fair share of citations, some have less, and some have none at all. Citations depend on many underlying factors. For example, success breeds success. A highly cited article is likely to receive more citations than a currently less frequently cited article. In order to detect intellectual turning points, we are particularly interested in articles that have rapidly growing citations. In the following superstring example, we use a simple model to normalize the citations of an article within each time slice by the logarithm of its publication age – the number of years elapsed since its publication year. The rationale is to highlight articles that increased most in the early years of their publication. More sophisticated models can be derived based on citation distribution models of a given dataset and a model of the growth and decay of scientific citations. Building such models is significant and challenging in its own right.

Modeling

By default, co-citation counts are calculated within each time sliced segment. Co-citation counts are normalized as cosine coefficients, $cc_{cosine}[i, j] = cc[i, j]/sqrt$ $(c[i], c[j])$, where $cc[i, j]$ is the co-citation count between documents i and j, and $c[i]$ and $c[j]$ are their citation counts, respectively. The user can specify a selection threshold for co-citation coefficients; the default value is 0.15.

Alternative measures of co-citation strengths are available in the information science literature, such as Dice and Jaccard coefficients. In earlier studies, we used Pearson's correlation coefficients. Recently, researchers began to examine the nature of how Pearson's correlation coefficients transform the underlying structure of a co-citation network (Ahlgren et al., 2003), but available evidence is still inconclusive (Chen and Morris, 2003; White, 2003a). The impact of various co-citation metrics on the resultant network visualizations is worth pursuing.

Pruning

An effective pruning can reduce link crossings and improves the clarity of the resultant network visualization. *CiteSpace* supports two common network pruning algorithms, namely Pathfinder and MST. The user can select to prune individual networks only, or the merged network only, or prune both. Pruning increases the complexity of the visualization process. In the following section, visualizations with local pruning and global pruning are presented.

To prune individual networks with Pathfinder, the parameters q and r were set to $N_k - 1$ and ∞, respectively, to ensure the most extensive pruning effect, where N_k was the size of the network in the kth time slice. For the merged network, the q parameter was $(\Sigma N_k) - 1$, for $k = 1, 2, \ldots$

Merging

The sequence of time sliced networks is merged into a synthesized network, which contains the set union of all nodes ever to appear in any of the individual networks. Links from individual networks are merged based on either the earliest establishment rule or the latest reinforcement rule. The earliest establishment rule selects the link that has the earliest time stamp and drops subsequent links connecting the same pair of nodes, whereas the latest reinforcement rule retains the link that has the latest time stamp and eliminates earlier links.

By default, the earliest establishment rule applies. The rationale is to support the detection of the earliest moment when a connection was made in the literature. More precisely, such links mark the first time a connection becomes strong enough with respect to the chosen thresholds.

Mapping

The layout of each network, either individual time sliced networks or the merged one, is produced using Kamada and Kawai's (1989) algorithm. The size of a node is proportional to the normalized citation counts in the latest time interval. Landmark nodes can be identified by their large discs. The label size of each node is proportional to citations of the article, thus larger nodes also have larger-sized labels.

The user can enlarge font sizes at will. Both the width and the length of a link are proportional to the corresponding co-citation coefficient. The color of a link indicates the earliest appearance time of the link with reference to chosen thresholds.

Visually salient nodes such as landmarks, hubs, and pivots are easy to detect by visual inspection. CiteSpace currently does not include any algorithms to detect such nodes computationally. Instead, the visual effect is a natural result of slicing and merging, although additional computational metrics may enhance the visual features even further. A useful computational metric should reflect the degree of a node, and it should also take into account the heterogeneity of the node's links. The more dissimilar links a node connects to others, the more likely the node has a pivotal role to play. In the following example we only consider nodes that have a degree of 10 or higher for visual inspection.

8.5.3 Superstring

Two superstring revolutions are documented over the last two decades: one in the mid-1980s and one in the mid-1990s. We reported animated visualizations of the superstring co-citation networks using a single constant citation threshold, and Pearson's correlation coefficients were used to measure the strength of each co-citation link. The changes of the co-citation network were animated by the growing height of a citation bar and as a state transition process. Although key articles to the revolutions were identifiable in the resultant animations, they did not quite lend themselves to a simple visual inspection. We expect that the progressive visualization method can make it more easily to identify intellectual turning points by visual inspection. The superstring data set in this study is updated to include citation data between 1985 and 2003.

Visualized networks were validated by the leading scientists in the field of superstring. We showed the merged map, without pruning, to John Schwarz at CalTech and Edward Witten at Princeton University. Schwarz was the co-author of the article that triggered the first superstring revolution. Witten has a number of highly cited articles on superstring. He is also the top ranked physicist in a list of the 1000 most cited physicists between 1981 and 1997. The list was compiled by the Institute for Scientific Information (ISI). They were asked to explain the nature of intellectual contributions identified by pivot points and hubs in the networks.

The 19-year time interval was sliced into six 3-year segments, starting from 1985–1987 and ending at 2000–2002, plus a one-year segment for 2003. Two sets of results were generated from two separate runs. One used relatively higher threshold settings, which resulted in small networks. The other used lower threshold settings for larger networks. Two versions of the larger network are shown, unpruned and pruned. Links were color-coded by the earliest establishment rule. Darker colors indicate links from earlier time slices, whereas lighter colors indicate links from more recent slices. Networks in individual time slices are not shown due to the page limitation.

8.5.4 Maps of Intellectual Turns

Table 8.2 shows the size of the citespace and details of individual networks and the merged network. The size of the cite space in a given time slice is the number of articles that have at least one citation within the given time slice. The size is generally

Table 8.2 Higher threshold settings for small networks

Time slices	f_c	f_{cc}	Citespace size	Top cited	Sample %	cc (cosine $\geqslant$ 0.15)
1985–1987	3	1	604	16	2.65	58
1988–1990	10	3	2,740	15	0.55	30
1991–1993	50	7	12,214	18	0.15	62
1994–1996	60	10	16,147	19	0.12	53
1997–1999	80	10	19,716	20	0.10	60
2000–2002	85	15	22,449	20	0.09	54
2003	25	10	9,594	13	0.14	34
Total			83,464	121	Mean 0.54	Total
(Unique)				(82)		351

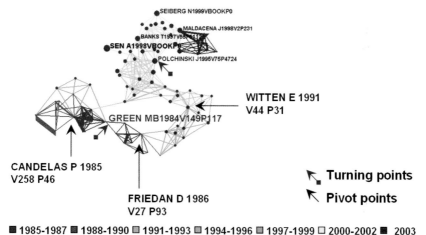

Figure 8.21 The small network of 82 articles, containing both turning points (Chen, 2004). © 2004 PNAS.

increasing over time. The size for 2003 is smaller because the 2003 data is still incomplete. The merged network contains 82 articles. Various pivot points are evident at a glance (Figure 8.21).

Table 8.3 shows the threshold setting for a sequence of larger networks. The co-citation network in each time slice represents approximately the top 1% most cited articles. The merged network contains 647 unique articles, which collectively made 1097 appearances in these time slices. In other words, 41% of articles appeared in more than one time slice.

The locally pruned version of the merged network is shown in Figure 8.22; the globally pruned version is shown in Figure 8.23. Color-coded links in effect partitioned the merged network into several major clusters of articles. Clusters of the same color represent co-citations made within the same time slice. More importantly, within-cluster co-citation links are evidently more common than between cluster links. A strongly clustered network also makes it easy to identify pivot

Table 8.3 Threshold settings for larger networks

Time slices	f_c	f_{cc}	Cite space size	Top cited	Sample %	cc (cosine $\geqslant 0.15$)
1985–1987	2	1	604	39	6.46	229
1988–1990	4	3	2,740	114	4.16	283
1991–1993	15	7	12,214	200	1.64	1263
1994–1996	20	10	16,147	229	1.42	895
1997–1999	25	10	19,716	223	1.13	956
2000–2002	30	15	22,449	180	0.80	486
2003	10	10	9,594	112	1.17	131
Total			83,464	1097	Mean 2.4	Total
(Unique)				(647)		4243

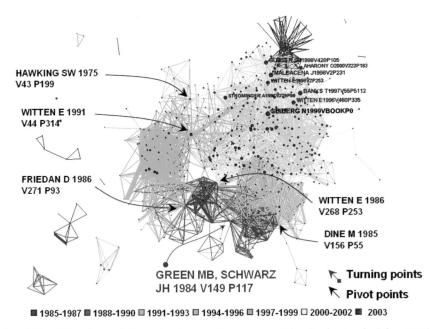

Figure 8.22 A 624-node co-citation network merged across seven time-sliced networks (Chen, 2004). © 2004 PNAS.

nodes and between-cluster links. Six structurally strategic nodes are identified in Figure 8.22, including the 1984 Green–Schwarz article, which triggered the first superstring revolution. However, the 1995 Polchinski article that triggered the second superstring revolution was not obvious in the dense visualization. Polchinski introduced the fundamental concept of D-branes in that article.

The 1984 Green–Schwarz article is a typical pivot node – it is the only contact point between two densely connected clusters in blue (1985–1987). It was this article that sparked the first superstring revolution – the famous 1984 Green–Schwarz anomaly cancellation paper. Friedan's 1986 article is a distinct pivot node connecting a blue cluster (1985–1987), a pink cluster (1988–1990), and a green cluster

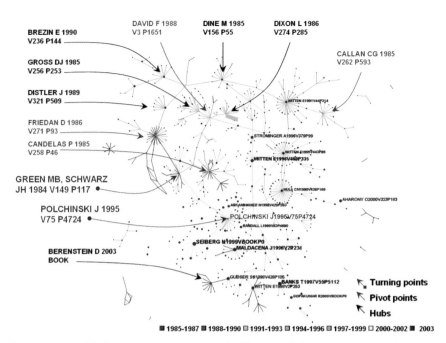

Figure 8.23 The Pathfinder version ($q = N - 1, r = \infty$) of the network shown in Figure 8.22 (Chen, 2004). © 2004 PNAS.

(1991–1993). Witten's 1986 article is a pivot between a blue cluster (1985–1987) and a yellow cluster (2000–2002). Figure 8.22 also contains a couple of smaller clusters that are completely isolated from the main super cluster. Small clusters in red (2003) indicate the candidates for emerging clusters. We were able to find Polchinski's 1995 article in a smaller sized merged network, but the article must be overwhelmed by the 4000 strong links of the larger network. Nevertheless, the quality of the visualized network is promising: intellectually significant articles tend to have topologically unique features.

Some articles have so many citations that their labels are even readable at this resolution, for example, articles by Maldacena, Witten, and Gubser-Klebanov-Polyako located towards the top of the major network component; they were all published in 1998. When we asked Witten to comment on an earlier version of the map, in which citation counts were not normalized by years since publication, he indicated that the Green–Scharwz article is more important to the field than the three top cited ones, and that the earlier articles in the 1990s appeared to be under-represented in the map. The apparent mismatch between citation frequencies of nodes and their importance judged by domain experts was partially corrected in the new version. Witten's comments raised an important question: is it possible that an intellectually significant article may not always be the most highly cited?

Figure 8.23 shows the merged network pruned by Pathfinder. The pruned version contains fewer links than the version in Figure 8.22. Much of the within-cluster links are reduced to links between cluster centers and other cluster members. Links between non-center members are essentially removed. The overall structure is simpler and easier to explore. In addition, the number of link colors attached to

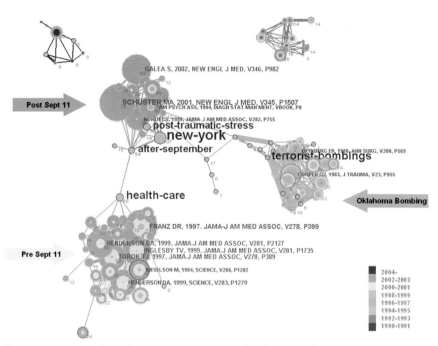

Figure 8.24 Transient information structures can be visualized to reveal the impact of abrupt changes. This phrase-and-article map shows how citing patterns in terrorism research changed over time after major terrorism events. Predominant themes before and after the September 11 terroist attacks in New York and the earlier Oklahoma city bombing are captured in three major clusters. Pink circles are sharply increased phrases found in citing articles' titles or abstracts. Multi-color treerings are articles cited over the years. The "after September 11" cluster shows a strong emphasis on post-traumatic stress disorders (PTSD), whereas the "before" cluster focuses on health care issues in the context of bioterrorism threats. The size of labels is proportional to the frequency of their use.

a node distinguishes a pivot node from a non-pivot node. If a node connects to other nodes through links in a single color, then it is not regarded as a pivot node because it does not imply intellectual transitions over time. In contrast, if a node joins several different colored links, then it is a good candidate for an intellectual turning point – because if paths connecting articles in different clusters must go through a pivot point, the pivot point is likely to have a unique position in the literature.

The Green–Schwarz article is located towards the center of the visualization; it joins links from four different time slices. The 1995 article by Candelas et al., is similar in terms of the link colors. According to ISI's Science Citation Report (1981–1998), Candelas et al.'s article has a total of 1538 citations during that period and its average annual citation is 110. The 1995 Polchinski article can be easily found at the lower center of the map; according to Schwarz, it explained the concept of D-branes, a crucial ingredient in almost all modern string theory research. It appears to be more of a hub than a pivot node – connected by links of only two colors – brown (1997–1999) and yellow (2000–2002). To the left of Polchinski's article is a cluster centered by the 1998 Maldacena article. Schwarz noted that in this article Maldacena made a major new discovery that in certain circumstances relates string theories to quantum field theories.

The comments from domain experts have confirmed that both versions of the merged network indeed highlight significant articles. And these articles tend to have unique topological properties that distinguish themselves from other articles. The globally pruned version is easier to explore than the local pruning only version.

The presence of pivot nodes enables us to narrow down the visual search quickly to a small number of good candidate nodes for intellectual turning points. An easy identification of such turning points is an important and necessary step towards an effective detection of paradigmatic changes in a knowledge domain. The small network is particularly clear, containing both turning points. The larger network without pruning is cluttered, although it is still possible to identify several pivot points. The interpretation and validation of the visualizations have greatly benefitted from the help from leading scientists in the knowledge domain. The work has also shown that using a variable threshold could be a potentially good practice for citation analysis in general.

The P-KDViz method produces more distinct visual features for key articles. More importantly, such visual features appear to be independent of the number of citations of a node. In other words, a lower citation rate is not necessarily preventing a node from having salient visual features, suggesting that co-citations must have played a greater role. Pivot nodes can be identified even if they have relatively fewer citations. This could be a particularly useful feature for the detection of significant articles that could be easily overlooked by falling below a single high citation threshold.

The 1984 Green–Schwarz article for the first revolution is a typical pivot node, whereas the 1995 Polchinski article for the second revolution is more of a hub than a pivot node. This finding suggests that before we have further evidence, it would be sensible to examine both types of visualizations, pruned and unpruned, in a study of intellectual turning points.

The progressive visualization method introduced here has practical implications. It provides scientists with a roadmap of their own field. A long standing challenge is to be able to visualize co-citation networks of a domain as quickly as new bibliographic data become available so that one can monitor the changes of a domain more closely on a monthly or even a weekly basis. The approach provides a practical starting point. Users have the flexibility to slice a time interval into smaller segments as well as larger ones.

A challenging issue is concerned with the detection of abrupt changes in citations within a short period of time. We normalized the citations of an article by its publication age. Additional metrics of pivot nodes should augment the power of visual inspection even further. Knowledge discovery and data mining techniques, such as Kleinberg's burst detection technique, could play a more substantial role in identifying temporal and spatial patterns in sharper contrast. See Figure 8.24 for example.

Finally, the role of domain experts in KDViz needs to be further investigated. Experts in the fields are the best sources to seek validations and interpretations. On the other hand, one should also use domain visualizations with caution; and it should be made clear that algorithmically generated domain visualizations, however crafted, merely portray the complexity of an underlying domain from a limited perspective. If KDViz can stimulate scientists to look at their own field from a different perspective and pose new questions about the evolution of their domain, then KDViz will ultimately become a practical tool to study science itself.

8.6 Summary

In this chapter, we started with a number of examples outside the mainstream information visualization to illustrate the complexity of detecting abrupt changes in phenomena such as the collapse of a civilization, detecting thematic changes, monitoring business activities in recessions, and identifying intellectual turning points. The second part of the chapter introduces the CiteSpace system and its application to the visualization of superstring revolutions.

We have emphasized the significant role of knowledge discovery and data mining techniques in the second generation of information visualization. The success of the first generation of information visualization is largely related to the structure-centric focus. We argue that the second generation of information visualization needs to go beyond the structure-centric mindset. One of the crucial components of the second generation is a dynamics-centric focus, which is an emphasis of increasing challenges to visualize the profound dynamics that govern rapid as well as gradual changes in so many practical issues. In this context, we also call for more substantial integration between knowledge discovery and data mining and the mainstream of information visualization. As information visualization extends to a wider range of practical domains, it is inevitable to incorporate technologies that can efficiently detect changes and emerging patterns.

Bibliography

Adams J, and Foote R (2003). Sudden climate change through human history. Retrieved Oct. 25, 2003, from the World Wide Web: http://dieoff.org/page127.htm

Ahlberg C, and Shneiderman B (1994). Visual information-seeking – Tight coupling of dynamic query filters with starfield displays. Proceedings of CHI '94, 24–28 April 1994, Boston, MA, pp. 313–317.

Ahlgren P, Jarneving B, and Rousseau R (2003). Requirements for a cocitation similarity measure, with special reference to Pearson's correlation coefficient. *Journal of the American Society for Information Science and Technology*, **54**(6), 550–560.

Albert R, and Barabási A (2002). Statistical mechanics of complex networks. *Reviews of Modern Physics*, **74**(1), 47–97.

Allan J (1997). Building hypertext using information retrieval. *Information Processing & Management*, **33**(2), 145–159.

Allan J, Lavrenko V, and Jin H (2000). First story detection in TDT is hard. Proceedings of the 9th International Conference on Information and Knowledge Management, pp. 374–381.

Allan J, Papka R, and Lavrenko V (1998). *Online new event detection and tracking.* Proceedings of ACM SIGIR. pp. 37–45.

Alley RB, Marotzke J, Nordhaus WD, Overpeck JT, Peteet DM, Pielke RA, Pierrehumbert RT, Rhines PB, Stocker TF, Talley LD, and Wallace JM (2003). Abrupt climate change. *Science*, **5615**, 2005–2010.

Alvarez-Gaumé L, and Witten E (1983). Gravitational anomalies. *Nuclear Physics B*, **234**, 269–330.

An Y, Janssen J, and Milios E (2001). Characterizing and mining the citation graph of the computer science literature. Halifax, Nova Scotia, Canada: Dalhousie University (CS-2001-02).

Anas J, and Ferrara L (2002). A comparative assessment of parametric and non parametric turning points detection methods: the case of the Euro-zone economy. Proceedings of Colloquium on Modern Tools for Business Cycle Analysis (Session: Turning Points Detection), November 28–29, 2002. Luxembourg.

Anderson J (1980). Cognitive Psychology and Its Implications. San Francisco, CA: WH Freeman.

Argyle M (1976). Personality and social behaviour. In R Harre (Ed.), *Personality*. Oxford: Blackwell.

Attneave F (1954). Some informational aspects of visual perception. *Psychological Review*, **61**, 183–193.

Baird JC (1970). *Psychophysical Analysis of Visual Space*. New York: Pergamon Press.

Bak P, and Chen K (1991). Self-organized criticality. *Scientific American*, **264**(1), 46–53.

Bak P, and Sneppen K (1993). Punctuated equilibrium and criticality in a simple-model of evolution. *Physical Review Letters*, **71**(24), 4083–4086.

Baker MP, and Bushell C (1995). After the storm: Considerations for Information Visualization. *IEEE Computer Graphics and Applications*, **15**(3), 12–15.

Baker P (1995). Thunderstorm visualization revisited, a collaboration with Edward Tufte. Retrieved November 21, 2003, from the World Wide Web: http://www.ncsa.uiuc.edu/~baker/Projects/storm.html

Barabási A-L (2002). *Linked: The New Science of Networks*. Cambridge, MA: Perseus Publishing.

Barabási A-L, Albert R, and Jeong H (2000). Scale-free characteristics of random networks: The topology of the world-wide web. *Physica A*, **281**, 69–77.

Barabási AL, Jeong H, Néda Z, Ravasz E, Schubert A, and Vicsek T (2002). Evolution of the social network of scientific collaborations. *Physica A*, **311**, 590–614.

Barrett E (Ed.) (1989). *The Society of Text: Hypertext, Hypermedia, and the Social Construction of Information*. Cambridge, MA: MIT Press.

Basseville M, and Nikiforov IV (1993). *Detection of Abrupt Changes: Theory and Application*. Englewood Cliffs, NJ: Prentice-Hall, Inc. http://www.irisa.fr/sigma2/kniga/

Batagelj V, and Mrvar A (1998). Pajek – Program for large network analysis. *Connections*, **21**(2), 47–57.

Batagelj V, and Mrvar A (2001). Layouts for GD01 graph-drawing competition. Retrieved, from the World Wide Web: http://vlado.fmf.uni-lj.si/pub/gd/01/report.pdf

Beckwith R, Fellbaum C, Gross D, and Miller GA (1991). WordNet: A lexical database organized on psycholinguistic principles. In U Zernik (Ed.), *Lexical Acquisition: Exploiting On-Line Resources to Build a Lexicon*, pp. 211–231. Hillsdale, NJ: Lawrence Erlbaum.

Bederson B, and Meyer J (1998). Implementing a zooming user interface: Experience building Pad++. *Software: Practice and Experience*, **28**(10), 1101–1135.

Bederson BB, and Shneiderman B (2003). *The Craft of Information Visualization: Readings and Reflections*. San Francisco, CA: Morgan Kaufman.

Bederson BB, Hollan JD, Perlin K, Meyer J, Bacon D, and Furnas G (1996). Pad++: a zoomable graphical sketchpad for exploring alternate interface physics. *Journal of Visual Languages and Computing*, **7**(1), 3–31.

Bederson BB, Shneiderman B, and Wattenberg M (2001). Ordered and quantum treemaps: Making effective use of 2D space to display hierarchies. *ACM Transactions on Graphics*, **21**(4), 833–854.

Benford S, Snowdon D, Greenhalgh C, Ingram R, Knox I, and Brown C (1995). VR-VIBE: A virtual environment for co-operative information retrieval. *Computer Graphics Forum*, **14**(3), C.349–C.360.

Benford S, Snowdon D, Colebourne A, O'Brien J, and Rodden T (1997). Informing the design of collaborative virtual environments. Proceedings of the international ACM SIGGROUP conference on Supporting group work: the integration challenge (GROUP '97), pp. 71–80.

Benyon DR (1993). Accommodating individual differences through an adaptive user interface. In M Schneider-Hufschmidt, T Kühmeand and U Malinowski (Eds), *Adaptive User Interfaces – Results and Prospects*. Amsterdam: Elsevier.

Benyon D, and Höök K (1997). Navigation in information spaces: Supporting the individual. Proceedings of Human-Computer Interaction: INTERACT '97, pp. 39–46.

Benyon DR, and Murray DM (1993). Adaptive systems: From intelligent tutoring to autonomous agents. *Knowledge-based Systems*, **6**(3), 197–219.

Bertin J (1983). *Semiology of Graphics: Diagrams, Networks, Maps*. Wisconsin: University of Wisconsin Press.

Bharat K and Broder A (1998). A technique for measuring the relative size and overlap of public web search engines. Proceedings of the 7th International WWW Conference. Australia.

Bly SA, Harrison SR, and Irwin S (1993). Media spaces: bringing people together in a video, audio, and computing environment. *Communications of the ACM*, **36**(1), 28–46.

Bookstein FL (1989). Principal Warps: Thin-plate splines and the decomposition of deformations. *IEEE Transactions on Pattern Analysis and Machine Intelligence*, **11**(6), 567–585.

Börner K, and Penumarthy S (2003). Social diffusion patterns in three-dimensional virtual worlds. *Information Visualization*, **2**(3), 182–198.

Borzo J (2004). Get the picture: In the age of information overload, visualization software promises to cut through the clutter. *The Wall Street Journal Online*, http://webreprints.djreprints.com/907210769198.html

Bosco P (1984). *Roanoke*. Connecticut, US: The Millbrook Press.

Botafogo RA, Rivlin E, and Shneiderman B (1992). Structural analysis of hypertexts: Identifying hierarchies and useful metrics. *ACM Transactions on Office Information Systems*, **10**(2), 142–180.

Bowers J, Pycock J, and O'Brien J (1997). Talk and embodiment in collaborative virtual environments. Proceedings of CHI '97.

Boyack KW, and Börner K (2003). Indicator-assisted evaluation and funding of research: Visualizing the influence of grants on the number and citation counts of research papers. *Journal of the American Society for Information Science and Technology*, **54**(5), 447–461.

Boyack KW, Wylie BN, Davidson GS, and Johnson DK (2000). *Analysis of patent databases using Vxinsight* (SAND2000-2266C). Albuquerque, NM: Sandia National Laboratories.

Boyack KW, Wylie BN, and Davidson GS (2002). Domain visualization using VxInsight for science and technology management. *Journal of the American Society for Information Science and Technology*, **53**(9), 764–774.

Boyd C, and Darken R (1996). Psychological issues of virtual environment interfaces. Proceedings of CHI '96. pp. 426.

Braam RR, Moed HF, and Raan AFJv (1991a). Mapping of science by combined co-citation and word analysis. II: Dynamical aspects. *Journal of the American Society for Information Science*, **42**(4), 252–266.

Braam RR, Moed HF, and Vanraan AFJ (1991b). Mapping of science by combined cocitation and word analysis. 1. Structural Aspects. *Journal of the American Society for Information Science*, **42**(4), 233–251.

Brandes U, and Corman SR (2002). Visual unrolling of network evolution and the analysis of dynamic discourse. Proceedings of IEEE Symp. on Information Visualization (InfoVis '02), Boston, MA, pp. 145–151.

Brandes U, and Corman SR (2003). Visual unrolling of network evolution and the analysis of dynamic discourse. *Information Visualization*, 2(1), 40–50.

Brandes U, and Willhalm T (2002). Visualization of bibliographic networks with a reshaped landscape metaphor. Proceedings of the 4th Joint Eurographics – IEEE TVCG Symp. Visualization (VisSym '02), pp. 159–164.

Branigan S, and Cheswick B (1999). The effects of war on the Yugoslavian network. Lumeta. Retrieved January 1, 2003, from the World Wide Web: http://research.lumeta.com/ches/map/yu/index.html

Bray T (1996). Measuring the Web. Proceedings of the Fifth International World Wide Web Conference, May 6–10, 1996. Paris, France.

Brin S, and Page L (1998). The anatomy of a large-scale hypertextual web search engine. Proceedings of the 7th International World Wide Web Conference, April 14–18, 1998. Brisbane, Australia.

Brooks TA (1995). Topical subject expertise and the semantic distance model of relevance assessment. *Journal of Documentation*, 51(4), 370–387.

Brown JA, McGregor AJ, and Braun HW (2000). Network performance visualization: Insight through animation. Proceedings of PAM2000.

Bry G, and Boschan C (1971). Cyclical analysis of time series: Selected procedures and computer programs: Technical Paper, Number 20. New York, NY: National Bureau of Economic Research.

Burge P, and Shaw-Taylor J (1997). *Detecting cellular fraud using adaptive prototypes*. Proceedings of AAAI-97 Workshop on AI Approaches to Fraud Detection and Risk Management. Menlo Park, CA. pp. 9–13.

Burgen AS, Dickens F, and Zatman LJ (1949). The action of botulinum toxin on the neuromuscular junction. *Journal of Physiology*, 109, 10–24.

Burns AF, and Mitchell WC (1946). *Measuring Business Cycles*. New York: National Bureau of Economic Research.

Burt RS (1992). *Structural Holes: The Social Structure of Competition*. Cambridge, MA: Harvard University Press.

CAIDA (1998). Skitter. CAIDA. Retrieved November 22, 1998, from the World Wide Web: http://www.caida.org/Tools/Skitter/

Caldarelli G, Capocci A, Rios PDL, and Munoz MA (2002). Scale-free networks without growth or preferential attachment: Good get richer. *Physical Review Letters*, 89, 258702.

Callan CG, and Thorlacius L (1998). World-sheet dynamics of string junctions. *Nuclear Physics B*, 534(1–2), 121–136.

Callon M, Law J, and Rip A (Eds.). (1986). *Mapping the Dynamics of Science and Technology: Sociology of Science in the Real World*. London: Macmillan Press.

Campagnoni F, and Ehrlich K (1989). Information retrieval using a hypertext-based help system. *ACM Transactions on Information Systems*, 7, 271–291.

Can F (1993). Incremental clustering for dynamic information processing. *ACM Transactions on Information Systems*, 11(2), 143–164.

Canter D, West S, and Wools R (1974). Judgments of people and their rooms. *British Journal of Social and Clinical Psychology*, 13, 113–118.

Canter D, Rivers R, and Storrs G (1985). Characterizing user navigation through complex data structures. *Behaviour & Information Technology*, 4(2), 93–102.

Card S, Mackinlay J, and Shneiderman B (Eds.). (1999). *Readings in Information Visualization: Using Vision to Think*. San Francisco, CA: Morgan Kaufmann.

Card SK, Robertson GG, and York W (1996). The WebBook and the Web Forager: An Information workspace for the World-Wide Web. Proceedings of the ACM Conference on Human Factors in Computing Systems (CHI '96), April 13–18, 1996. Vancouver, British Columbia, Canada, pp. 111–117.

Carlsson C, and Hagsand O (1993). DIVE: A platform for multi-user virtual environments. *Computer Graphics*, 17(6), 663–669.

Carpendale MST, Cowperthwaite DJ, and Fracchia FD (1997). Making distortions comprehensible. Proceedings of IEEE Conference on Visual Languages (VL '97), Capri, Italy, pp. 36–45.

Carpendale MST, Cowperthwaite DJ, and Fracchia FD (July 1997). Extending distortion viewing from 2D to 3D. *IEEE Computer Graphics and Applications*, 17(4), 42–51. http://pages.cpsc.ucalgary.ca/~sheelagh/personal/pubs/cga97.pdf

Carpenter MP, Cooper M, and Narin F (1980). Linkage between basic research literature and patents. *Research Management*, 23(2), 30–35.

Carreras BA, Newman DE, Dobson I, and Poole AB (2000). Initial evidence for self-organized criticality in electric power system blackouts. Proceedings of Hawaii International Conference on System Sciences. Maui, Hawaii.

Carroll JB (1974). *Psychometric tests as cognitive tasks: A new structure of intellect* (74–16). Princeton, NJ: Educational Testing Service.

Carroll JB (1993). *Human Cognitive Abilities: A Survey of Factor Analytical Studies*. Cambridge: Cambridge University Press.

Carroll JD, and Chang J-J (1970). Analysis of Individual Differences in Multidimensional scaling via an N-way generalization of "Eckart-Young" Decomposition. *Psychometrika*, **35**, 283–319.

Carruthers JDA (1992). Treatment of glabellar frown lines with c-botulinum-a exotoxin. *Journal of Dermatologic Surgery and Oncology*, **18**, 17.

Chalmers AF (1982). *What is this thing called science? an assessment of the nature and status of science and its methods*. Milton Keynes: Open University Press.

Chalmers M (1992). Bead: Explorations in information visualisation. Proceedings of SIGIR '92, June 1992. Copenhagen, Denmark, pp. 330–337.

Chalmers M (1996). *A linear iteration time layout algorithm for visualising high-dimensional data*. Proceedings of IEEE Information Visualization '96, October 28–29. San Francisco, CA. IEEE Computer Society Press. pp. 127–132.

Chapman RL (Ed.) (1992). *Roget's International Thesaurus* (5th edition). New York, NY: Harper Collins.

Charles MF, and Mattheyses RM (1982). A linear-time heuristic for improving network partitions. Proceedings of the 19th IEEE Design Automation Conference.

Chen SE (1995). QuickTime VR: An image-based approach to virtual environment navigation. Proceedings of the 22nd Annual ACM Conference on Computer Graphics (SIGGRAPH '95), pp. 29–38.

Chen C (1997a). Structuring and visualising the WWW with Generalised Similarity Analysis. Proceedings of the 8th ACM Conference on Hypertext (Hypertext '97), April, Southampton, UK, pp. 177–186.

Chen C (1997b). Tracking latent domain structures: An integration of Pathfinder and Latent Semantic Analysis. *AI & Society*, **11**(1–2), 48–62.

Chen C (1998a). Bridging the gap: The use of Pathfinder networks in visual navigation. *Journal of Visual Languages and Computing*, **9**(3), 267–286.

Chen C (1998b). Generalised Similarity Analysis and Pathfinder Network Scaling. *Interacting with Computers*, **10**(2), 107–128.

Chen C (1999a). *Information Visualisation and Virtual Environments*. London: Springer.

Chen C (1999b). Visualising semantic spaces and author co-citation networks in digital libraries. *Information Processing and Management*, **35**(2), 401–420.

Chen C (2000). Individual differences in searching through a spatial-semantic virtual environment. *Journal of the American Society for Information Science,* **51**(6), 529–542.

Chen C (2003). *Mapping Scientific Frontiers: The Quest for Knowledge Visualization*. London: Springer.

Chen C (2004). Searching for intellectual turning points: Progressive Knowledge Domain Visualization. Proceedings of the National Academy of Sciences of the United States of America, **101** (suppl. 1), 5303–5316. http://www.pnas.org/cgi/reprint/0307513100vi.pdf

Chen C, and Börner K (Forthcoming). From spatial proximity to semantic coherence: A quantitative approach to the study of group dynamics in collaborative virtual environments. *Presence-Teleoperators and Virtual Environments,* **14**(1).

Chen C, and Carr L (1999a). A semantic-centric approach to information visualization. Proceedings of International Conference on Information Visualization (IV '99), July 14–16, 1999, London, England, pp. 18–23.

Chen C, and Carr L (1999b). Visualizing the evolution of a subject domain: A case study. Proceedings of IEEE Visualization '99, October 24–29, 1999, San Francisco, CA, pp. 449–452.

Chen C, and Czerwinski M (1997). Spatial ability and visual navigation: An empirical study. *New Review of Hypermedia and Multimedia*, **3**, 67–89.

Chen C, and Czerwinski M (1998). From latent semantics to spatial hypertext: An integrated approach. Proceedings of the 9th ACM Conference on Hypertext and Hypermedia (Hypertext '98), June 1998. Pittsburgh, PA, pp. 77–86.

Chen C, and Davies J (1999). Integrating spatial, semantic, and social structures for knowledge management. Proceedings of the 32nd Hawaii International Conference on System Sciences (HICSS '32). Hawaii.

Chen C, and Kuljis J (2003). The rising landscape: A visual exploration of superstring revolutions in physics. *Journal of the American Society for Information Science and Technology*, **54**(5), 435–446.

Chen C, and Lobo N (2003). *Semantically modified diffusion limited aggregation for visualizing large-scale networks*. Proceedings of the 7th International Conference on Information Visualization (IV '03), July 16–18, 2003. London. IEEE Computer Society Press. pp. 576–581.

Chen C, and Morris S (2003). Visualizing evolving networks: Minimum spanning trees versus Pathfinder networks. Proceedings of IEEE Symposium on Information Visualization, October 19–24, 2003, Seattle, Washington, pp. 67–74.

Chen C, and Paul RJ (2001). Visualizing a knowledge domain's intellectual structure. Computer, 34(3), 65–71.

Chen C, and Rada R (1996). Interacting with hypertext: A meta-analysis of experimental studies. Human-Computer Interaction, 11(2), 125–156.

Chen C, and Yu Y (2000). Empirical studies of information visualization: A meta-analysis. International Journal of Human-Computer Studies, 53(5), 851–866.

Chen H, Houston AL, Sewell RR, and Schatz BR (1998). Internet browsing and searching: User evaluations of category map and concept space techniques. Journal of the American Society for Information Science, 49(7), 582–608.

Chen C, Newman J, Newman R, and Rada R (1998a). How did university departments interweave the web: A study of connectivity and underlying factors. Interacting with Computers, 10(4), 353–373.

Chen C, Thomas L, Cole J, and Chennawasin C (1999). Representing the semantics of virtual spaces. IEEE Multimedia, 6(2), 54–63.

Chen C, Czerwinski M, and Macredie R (2000). Individual differences in virtual environments: introduction and overview. Journal of the American Society for Information Science, 51(6), 499–507.

Chen C, Kuljis J, and Paul RJ (2001a). Visualizing latent domain knowledge. IEEE Transactions on Systems, Man, and Cybernetics, 31(4), 518–529.

Chen C, Paul RJ, and O'Keefe B (2001b). Fitting the jigsaw of citation: Information visualization in domain analysis. Journal of the American Society for Information Science, 52(4), 315–330.

Chen C, Cribbin T, Macredie R, and Morar S (2002). Visualizing and tracking the growth of competing paradigms: Two case studies. Journal of the American Society for Information Science and Technology, 53(8), 678–689.

Chi EH, Pitkow J, Mackinlay J, Pirolli P, Gossweiler R, and Card SK (1998). Visualizing the evolution of web ecologies. Proceedings of CHI '98, Los Angeles. pp. 400–407.

Chimera R, and Shneiderman B (1994). An exploratory evaluation of three interfaces for browsing large hierarchical tables of contents. ACM Transactions on Information Systems, 12(4), 383–406.

Chuah MC, Roth SF, Kolojejchick J, Mattis J, and Juarez O (1995). SageBook: Searching data-graphics by content. Proceedings of CHI '95, May 1995, Denver, CO, pp. 338–345.

Cleveland, WS, and McGill, R (1984) Graphical perception: Theory, experimentation, and application to the development of graphical methods. Journal of the American Statistical Association, 79(387), 531–554.

Cockburn A, and McKenzie BJ (2000). An evaluation of cone trees. Proceedings of People and Computers XIV: British Computer Society Conference on Human Computer Interaction 2000. Berlin: Springer. pp. 425–436.

Cockburn A, and McKenzie BJ (2001). 3D or not 3D? evaluating the effect of the third dimension in a document management system. Proceedings of CHI 2001, Seattle, Washington, USA, pp. 434–441.

Cockburn A, and McKenzie BJ (2002). Evaluating the Effectiveness of Spatial Memory in 2D and 3D Physical and Virtual Environments. Proceedings of CHI 2002, April 20–25, 2002, Minneapolis, Minnesota, USA, pp. 203–210.

Cohen J (1977). Statistical Power Analysis for the Behavioral Sciences. New York, NY: Academic Press.

Coleman MK, and Parker DS (1996). Aesthetics-based graphy layout for human consumption. Software – Practice & Experience, 26(12), 1415–1438.

Conklin J (1987). Hypertext: An introduction and survey. Computer, 20(9), 17–41.

Craik FIM, and Lockhart RS (1972). Levels of processing: A framework for memory research. Journal of Verbal Learning and Verbal Behavior, 11, 671–684.

Crane D (1972). Invisible Colleges: Diffusion of Knowledge in Scientific Communities. Chicago, IL: University of Chicago Press.

Crossley M, Davies J, McGrath A, and Rejman-Greene M (1999). The knowledge garden. BT Technology Journal, 17(1), 76–84.

Curtis P, and Nichols DA (1993). MUDs grow up: Social virtual reality in the real world, Palo Alto, CA: Xerox PARC.

Czerwinski MP, and Larson K (1997). The new web browsers: They're cool but are they useful? Companion Proceedings of HCI '97: People and Computers XII, Bristol, UK.

Czerwinski MP, Tan DS, and Robertson GG (2002). Women take a wider view. Proceedings of CHI '02, April 2002. Minneapolis, MN. New York: ACM Press. pp. 195–202.

Dahlbäck N, Höök K, and Sjölinder M (1996). Spatial cognition in the mind and in the world: The case of hypermedia navigation. Proceedings of the 18th Annual Meeting of the Cognitive Science Society, July 1996. University of California, San Diego.

Damer B (1998). *Avatars! Exploring and Building Virtual Worlds on the Internet*. Berkeley, CA: Peachpit Press.

Darken RP, and Sibert JL (1996). Wayfinding strategies and behaviors in large virtual worlds. Proceedings of CHI '96, Vancouver, BC, pp. 142–149.

Davidson GS, Hendrickson B, Johnson DK, Meyers CE, and Wylie BN (1998). Knowledge mining with VxInsight: Discovery through interaction. *Journal of Intelligent Information Systems*, 11(3), 259–285.

Davidson R, and Harel D (1996). Drawing graphs nicely using simulated annealing. *ACM Transactions on Graphics*, 15(4), 301–331.

Davies NJ, Weeks R, and Revett MC (1995). An information agent for WWW. Proceedings of the 4th International Conference on World Wide Web, December, 1995. Boston, USA. http://www.w3.org/pub/Conferences/WWW4/Papers/180/

Deerwester S, Dumais ST, Landauer TK, Furnas GW, and Harshman RA (1990). Indexing by Latent Semantic Analysis. *Journal of the American Society for Information Science*, 41(6), 391–407.

Del Negro M (2001). Turn, turn, turn: predicting turning points in economic activity. *Economic Review*, 86(2), 1–12.

Dertouzos ML (2001). *The Unfinished Revolution: Human-Centered Computers and What They Can Do for Us*. New York, NY: HarperCollins.

Di Battista G (1998). *Graph Drawing: Algorithms for the Visualization of Graphs*. Upper Saddle River, NJ: Prentice Hall.

Di Battista G, Eades P, Tamassia R, and Tollis I (1994). Algorithms for drawing graphs: An annotated bibliography. *Computational Geometry Theory and Applications*, 4, 235–282.

Di Battista G, Eades P, Tamassia R, and Tollis IG (1999). *Graph Drawing: Algorithms for the Visualization of Graphs*. Upper Saddle River, NJ: Prentice Hall.

Dieberger A (1997). Supporting social navigation on the World Wide Web. *International Journal of Human–Computer Studies*, 46, 805–825.

Diebold FX, and Rudebusch GD (1989). Scoring the leading indicators. *Journal of Business*, 64, 369–391.

DiGirolamo G, and Hintzman D (1997). First impressions are lasting impressions: A primacy effect in memory for repetitions. *Psychonomic Bulletin and Review*, 4(1), 121–124.

Dillon A, and Watson C (1996). User analysis in HCI: The historical lessons from individual differences research. *International Journal of Human–Computer Studies*, 45(6), 619–637.

Dillon A, McKnight C, and Richardson J (1990). Navigating in hypertext: A critical review of the concept. In D. Diaper (Ed.), Human–Computer Interaction – INTERACT '90, pp. 587–592. Elsevier.

Dillon A, McKnight C, and Richardson J (1993). Space – The final chapter or why physical representations are not semantic intentions. In C McKnight A Dillon and J Richardson (Eds), *Hypertext: A Psychological Perspective*, pp. 169–191. New York, NY: Ellis Horwood.

Dodge M, and Kitchin R (2002). *Atlas of Cyberspace*. London: Addison-Wesley.

Dorogovtsev SN, and Mendes JFF (2002). Evolution of networks. *Advances in Physics.*, 51, 1079–1187.

Dorogovtsev SN, Mendes JFF, and Samukhin AN (2000). Structure of growing networks with preferential linking. *Physical Review Letters*, 85, 4633–4636.

Dourish P, and Chalmers M (1994). Running out of space: Models of information navigation. Proceedings of HCI '94.

Drew P, and Heritage J (Eds) (1992). *Talk at Work: Interaction in Institutional Settings*. Cambridge: Cambridge University Press.

Dumais ST (1995). Using LSI for information filtering: TREC-3 experiments. Proceedings of the 3rd Text REtrieval Conference (TREC3), April 1995, pp. 219–230.

Eades P (1984). A heuristic for graph drawing. *Congressus Numerantium*, 42, 149–160.

Eckstrom RB, French JW, Harman HH, and Derman D (1976). Kit of factor–referenced cognitive tests. Princeton, NJ: Educational Testing Service.

Edwards D, and Hardman L (1989). Lost in hyperspace: Cognitive mapping and navigation in a hypertext environment. In R McAleese (Ed.), *Hypertext: Theory into practice*. Oxford: Intellect Books.

Egan D (1988). Individual differences in Human–Computer Interaction. In M Helander (Ed.), *Handbook of Human–Computer Interaction* pp. 543–568. Amsterdam: Elsevier.

Eisenberg M, Nishioka A, and Schreiner ME (1997). Helping users think in three dimensions: steps toward incorporating spatial cognition in user modelling. Proceedings of the 1997 international conference on Intelligent user interfaces (IUI '97), pp. 113–120.

Erickson T (1993). From interface to interplace: The spatial environment as a medium for interaction. Proceedings of the European Conference on Spatial Information Theory, pp. 391–405.

Erickson T (1996). The World Web as social hypertext. *Communications of the ACM*, 39(1), 15–17.

Erickson T (1997). Social interaction on the net: Virtual community as participatory genre. Proceedings of the 30th Hawaii International Conference on Systems Science. Hawaii, HA, pp. 23–30.

Erickson T, and Salomon G (1991). Designing a desktop information system: Observations and issues. Proceedings of CHI '91.

Erten C, Harding PJ, Kobourov SG, Wampler K, and Yee G (2003). Exploring the computing literature using temporal graph visualization (Technical Report TR0304): University of Arizona.

Erten C, Harding PJ, Kobourov SG, Wampler K, and Yee G (2004). Exploring the computing literature using temporal graph visualization. Proceedings of Conference on Visualization and Data Analysis (VDA), January 2004.

Estrella A, and Mishkin FS (1998). Predicting U.S. recessions: Financial variables as leading indicators. *Review of Economics and Statistics*, **80**(1), 45–61.

Fairchild K, Poltrock S, and Furnas G (1988). SemNet: Three-dimensional graphic representations of large knowledge bases. In R Guidon (Ed.), *Cognitive Science and its Applications for Human–Computer Interaction* pp. 201–233. Lawrence Erlbaum.

Feiner S, and Beshers C (1990). Worlds within Worlds: Metaphors for Exploring n-Dimensional Virtual Worlds. Proceedings of ACM Symposium on User Interface Software and Technology, pp. 76–83.

Fekete JD, and Plaisant C (2002). Interactive information visualization of a million items. Proceedings of IEEE InfoVis 2002, Boston, MA, pp. 117–124.

Foley JD, van Dam A, Feiner SK, and Hughes JF (1990). *Computer Graphics: Principles and Practice*. Reading, MA: Addison-Wesley.

Forgas JP (1979). *Social Episodes: The Study of Interaction Routines* (Vol. 17). London: Academic Press.

Forgas JP, Bower GH, and Krantz SE (1984). The influence of mood on perceptions of social interactions. *Journal of Experimental Social Psychology*, **20**(6), 497–513.

Forster EM (1927). *Aspects of the Novel*. New York: Harcourt.

Foster JD, Hope J, and Fraser H (1993). Transmission of bovine spongiform encephalopathy to sheep and goats. *Veterinary Record*, **133**(14), 339–341.

Fox E, Hix D, Nowell L, Brueni D, Wake W, Heath L, and Rao D (1993). Users, user interfaces, and objects: Envision, a digital library. *Journal of the American Society for Information Science*, **44**(5), 480–491.

French R (1953). The discrimination of dot patterns as a function of the number and average separation of dots. *Journal of Experimental Psychology*, **46**, 1–9.

Fruchterman TMJ, and Reingold EM (1991). Graph drawing by force-directed placement. *Software – Practice and Experience*, **21**, 1129–1164.

Fry B (2003). Anemone. Benjamin Fry. Retrieved Sept 8, 2003, from the World Wide Web: http://acg.media.mit.edu/people/fry/anemone/index.html

Furnas GW (1986). Generalized fisheye views. Proceedings of CHI '86, pp. 16–23.

Furnas GW (1997). *Effective view navigation*. Proceedings of CHI '97. Atlanta, Georgia. New York: ACM Press. pp. 367–374.

Furnas GW, and Bederson BB (1995). Space-scale diagrams: Understanding multiscale interfaces. Proceedings of ACM CHI'95 Conference on Human Factors in Computing Systems, pp. 234–241.

Gale, N, and Halperin, WC (1982) A case for better graphics: The unclassed choropleth map. *The American Statistician*, **36**(4), 330–336.

Gansner ER, Koutsofios E, North SC, and Vo K-P (1993). A technique for drawing directed graphs. *IEEE Transactions on Software Engineering*, **19**(32), 214–230.

Gansner ER, and North SC (1998). Improved force-directed layouts. In S. Whitesides (Ed.), *Graph Drawing 1998*. Berlin, Germany: Springer. pp. 364–373.

Garfield E (1994). Scientography: Mapping the tracks of science. Current Contents. *Social & Behavioural Sciences*, **7**(45), 5–10.

Garfield E, and Small H (1989). Identifying the changing frontiers of science. The S. Neaman Press. Retrieved June 26, 2000, from the World Wide Web: http://www.garfield.library.upenn.edu/ papers/ 362/362.html

Gaver WW, Smets G, and Overbeeke K (1995). A Virtual Window on media space. Proceedings of CHI '95, pp. 257–264.

Gershon N, and Page W (2001). What storytelling can do for information visualization. *Communications of the ACM*, **44**(8), 31.

Giddens A (1984). *The Constitution of Society: Outline of the Theory of Structuration*. Chicago, IL: Polity Press.

Girvan M, and Newman MEJ (2001). Community structure in social and biological networks. Retrieved Dec 7, 2001, from the World Wide Web: arXiv:cond-mat/0112110

Goffman E (1974). *Frame Analysis*. New York: Harper & Row.

Goguen J (2000). Information visualization and semiotic morphisms. Retrieved August 8, 2001 from the World Wide Web: http://www-cse.ucsd.edu/users/goguen/papers/sm/vzln.html

Gottsdanker R (1978). *Experimenting in Psychology*. Englewood Cliffs, NJ: Prentice-Hall.

Gower JC (1975). Generalized Procrustes analysis. *Psychometrika*, **40**, 33–51.

Granovetter M (1973). Strength of weak ties. *American Journal of Sociology*, **8**, 1360–1380.

Green MB, and Schwarz JH (1984). Anomaly cancellations in supersymmetric D = 10 gauge theory and superstring theory. *Physics Letters B*, **149**, 117–122.

Green MB, and Schwarz JH (1985). Infinity cancellations in SO(32) superstring theory. *Physics Letters B*, 151, 21–25.

Green SJ (1998). Automated link generation: Can we do better than term repetition? Proceedings of the 7th International World Wide Web Conference, April 14–18, 1998. Brisbane, Australia.

Greenhalgh C (1997). Analysing movement and world transitions in virtual reality tele-conferencing. Proceedings of The 5th European Conference on Computer Supported Cooperative Work (ECSCW '97), Sept 7–11, 1997, Lancaster, UK.

Greenhalgh C, and Benford S (1995). MASSIVE: A virtual reality system for tele-conferencing. *ACM Transactions on Computer Human Interaction*, 2(3), 239–261.

Gumperz, J (1982). *Discourse Strategies*. Cambridge: Cambridge University Press.

Gutwenger C, and Mutzel P (1998). Planar polyline drawings with good angular resolution. In S. Whitesides (Ed.), *Graph Drawing 1998*. Berlin, Germany: Springer. pp. 167–182.

Haake J, and Wilson B (1992). Supporting collaborative writing of hyperdocuments in SEPIA. Proceedings of Hypertext '92, pp. 138–146.

Hafner K, and Lyon M (1996). Where wizards stay up late: The origins of the Internet: Simon & Schuster. http://www.fixe.com/wizards//

Hamilton JD (1989). A new approach to the economic analysis of nonstationary time series and the business cycle. *Econometrica*, 57(2), 357–384.

Hanson A, Wernert E, and Hughes S (1997). Constrained navigation environments. Proceedings of Scientific Visualization: Dagstuhl '97, pp. 95–104.

Harel D, and Koren Y (2000). A fast multi-scale method for drawing large graphs. Proceedings of the 8th International Symposium on Graph Drawing, pp. 183–196.

Harrison S, and Dourish P (1996). Re-place-ing space: The roles of place and space in collaborative systems. Proceedings of CSCW '96, pp. 67–76.

Havre S, Hetzler E, Whitney P, and Nowell L (2002). ThemeRiver: Visualizing thematic changes in large document collections. *IEEE Transactions on Visualization and Computer Graphics*, 8(1), 9–20.

Healey CG, Booth KS, and Enns JT (1996). High-speed visual estimation using preattentive processing. *ACM Transactions on Computer-Human Interaction*, 3(2), 107–135.

Hearst MA (1995). TileBars: Visualization of term distribution information in full text information access papers. Proceedings of ACM CHI '95 Conference on Human Factors in Computing Systems, pp. 59–66.

Hearst MA (1997). Interfaces for searching the Web. *Scientific American* (3). http://www.sims.berkeley.edu/hearst/papers/scion0397hearst.html

Hearst M, and Karadi C (1997). Cat-a-Cone: An interactive interface for specifying searches and viewing retrieval results using a large category hierarchy. Proceedings of the 20th Annual International ACM/SIGIR Conference, July 27–31, 1997. Philadelphia, PA. pp. 246–255.

Heath L, Hix D, Nowell L, Wake W, Averboch G, Labow E, Guyer S, Brueni D, France R, Dalal K, and Fox E (1995). Envision: A user-centered database of computer science literature. *Communications of the ACM*, **38**(4), 52–53.

Hemmje M, Kunkel, C, and Willett A (1994). LyberWorld – A visualization user interface supporting full text retrieval. Proceedings of the 17th Annual International ACM-SIGIR Conference on Research and Development in Information Retrieval, Dublin, Ireland, pp. 249–259.

Hendley RJ, Drew NS, Wood AM, and Beale R (1995). Narcissus: Visualizing information. Proceedings of Information Visualization '95 Symposium, October 30–31, 1995, Atlanta, GA, pp. 90–96.

Herman I, Melançon G, and Marshall MS (2000). Graph visualization and navigation in information visualization: A survey. *IEEE Transactions on Visualization and Computer Graphics*, 6(1), 24–44.

Herndon KP, Dam Av, and Gleicher M (1994). The challenges of 3D interaction: A CHI '94 Workshop. *SIGCHI Bulletin*, 26(4), 36–43.

Hetzler B, Whitney P, Martucci L, and Thomas J (1998). Multi-faceted insight through interoperable visual information analysis paradigms. Proceedings of IEEE Information Visualization '98, October 19–20, 1998, Los Alamitos, CA, pp. 137–144.

Hightower RR, Ring LT, Helfman JI, Bederson BB, and Hollan JD (1998). Graphical multiscale Web histories: A study of PadPrints. Proceedings of the 9th ACM Conference on Hypertext and Hypermedia (Hypertext '98), Pittsburgh, PA.

Hill WC, Hollan JD, Wroblewski D, and McCandless T (1992). Edit wear and read wear. Proceedings of CHI '92 Conference on Human Factors in Computing Systems, May 3–7, 1992, Monterey, CA, pp. 3–9.

Hill W, Stead L, Rosenstein M, and Furnas G (1995). Recommending and evaluating choices in a virtual community of use. Proceedings of CHI '95.

Hjorland B (1997). *Information Seeking and Subject Representation: An Activity–Theoretical Approach to Information Science*. Westport, CT: Greenwood Press.

Hollands JG, Carey TT, Matthews ML, and McCann CA (1989). Presenting a graphical network: A comparison of performance using fisheye and scrolling views. Proceedings of the 3rd Int'l Conf. on Human–Computer Interaction, September, 1989, pp. 313–320.

Höök K, Dahlbäck N, and Sjölinder M (1996). Individual differences and navigation in hypermedia. Proceedings of ECCE-8 (http://www.cs.vu.nl/~eace/).

Huberman BA (2001). *The Laws of the Web: Patterns in the Ecology of Information*. Cambridge, MA: MIT Press.

Huffaker B, Nemeth E, and Claffy K (1998). Otter: A general-purpose network visualization tool. Retrieved, from the World Wide Web: http://www.caida.org/Tools/Otter/Paper/

Hummon NP, and Doreian P (1989). Connectivity in a Citation Network – the Development of DNA Theory. *Social Networks*, 11(1), 39–63.

Ihde D (1998). *Expanding Hermeneutics: Visualism in Science*. Evanston, IL: Northwester University Press.

ISI (1981). *ISI atlas of science: biochemistry and molecular biology, 1978/80*. Philadelphia, PA: Institute for Scientific Information.

Jankovic J (1991). Therapeutic uses of botulinum toxin. *New England Journal of Medicine*, 324(1186), 1186–1194.

Jankovic J, and Brin MF (1997). Botulinum toxin: historical perspective and potential new indications. *Muscle Nerve Suppl*, 6(S), 129–145.

Jeffrey P, and Mark G (1998). Constructing social spaces in virtual environments: A study of navigation and interaction. Proceedings of Workshop on Personalised and Social Navigation in Information Space, 16–17 March, Stockholm, pp. 24–38.

Johnson B, and Shneiderman B (1991). Tree-maps: A space filling approach to the visualization of hierarchical information structures. Proceedings of IEEE Visualization 91, October 1991, pp. 284–291.

Jolliffe IT (1986). *Principal Component Analysis*. New York: Springer.

Jones WP, and Dumais ST (1986). The spatial metaphor for user Interfaces: experimental tests of reference by location versus name. *ACM Transactions on Office Information Systems*, 4(1), 42–63.

Juléz B, and Bergen JR (1983). Textons, the fundamental elements in preattentive vision and perception of textures. *The Bell System Technical Journal*, 62(6), 1619–1645.

Kamada T, and Kawai S (1989). An algorithm for drawing general undirected graphs. *Information Processing Letters*, 31(1), 7–15.

Kandogan E, and Shneiderman B (1996). Elastic windows: Improved spatial layout and rapid multiple window operations. Proceedings of Advanced Visual Interfaces Conference 96, May 1996.

Kandogan E, and Shneiderman B (1997). Elastic windows: Evaluation of multi-window operations. Proceedings of CHI '97.

Kaplan N, and Moulthrop S (1994). Where no mind has gone before: ontological design for virtual spaces. Proceedings of ECHT '94, pp. 206–216.

Katz JS (1999). Bibliometric indicators and the social sciences. *Proceedings of SPRU*, Brighton.

Kazuhiro S, and Mostafa J (2003). An approach to protein name extraction using heuristics and a dictionary: Laboratory of Applied Information Research Tech Report: Indiana University, Bloomington, USA.

Keogh E, and Smyth P (1997). A probabilistic approach to fast pattern matching in time series databases. Proceedings of the Third International Conference on Knowledge Discovery and Data Mining. Menlo Park, CA, pp. 24–30.

Kernighan BW, and Lin S (1970). An efficient heuristic procedure for partitioning graphs. The *Bell System Technical Journal*, 29(2), 291–307.

Kessler MM (1963). Bibliographic coupling between scientific papers. *American Documentation*, 14, 10–25.

Kirkpartrick S, Gelatt Jr., CD, and Vecchi MP (1983). Optimization by simulated annealing. *Science*, 220(4598), 671–680.

Kleiberg E, van de Wetering H, and van Wijk JJ (2001). Botanical visualization of huge hierarchies. Proceedings of IEEE Symposium on Information Visualization 2001 (InfoVis '01), October 22–23, 2001, San Diego, CA, pp. 87–94.

Kleinberg J (2002). Bursty and hierarchical structure in streams. Proceedings of the 8th ACM SIGKDD International Conference on Knowledge Discovery and Data Mining, July 23–26, 2002, Edmonton, Alberta, Canada, pp. 91–101.

Kline P (1994). Review of Carroll's human cognitive abilities. *Applied Cognitive Psychology*, 14, 387–399.

Kling R (1980). Social analyses of computing: Theoretical perspectives in recent empirical research. *ACM Computing Surveys*, **12**(1), 61–110.

Kobsa A (2001). An empirical comparison of three commercial information visualization systems. Proceedings of IEEE Symposium on Information Visualization (InfoVis '01), San Diego, CA, pp. 123–130.

Kobsa A (2003). User experiments with three visualization systems (ISR Technical Report: #UCI-ISR-03-11). Irvine, CA: University of California, Irvine.

Kohonen T (1997). *Self-Organizing Maps*. Secaucus, NJ: Springer.

Kohonen T (1998). Self-organization of very large document collections: state of the art. Proceedings of the 8th International Conference on Artificial Neural Networks, London, UK, pp. 65–74.

Kohonen T, Kaski S, Lagus K, Salojärvi J, Honkela J, Paatero V, and Saarela A (2000). Self-organization of a massive document collection. *IEEE Transactions on Neural Networks*, **11**, 574–585.

Kontostathis A, Galitsky L, Pottenger WM, Roy S, and Phelps, DJ (2003). A Survey of Emerging Trend Detection in Textual Data Mining. In M Berry (Ed.), *A Comprehensive Survey of Text Mining*: Heidelberg, Germany: Springer.

Kosak C, Marks J, and Shieber S (1994). Automating the layout of network diagrams with specified visual organization. *IEEE Transactions on Systems, Man, Cybernetics*, **24**(3), 440–454.

Kraut R, Egido C, and Galegher J (1988). Patterns of contact and communications in scientific research collaboration. Proceedings of CSCW '88, September 1–12, 1988, pp. 1–12.

Kraut R, Egido C, and Galegher J (1990). Patterns of contact and communication in scientific research collaboration. In J Galegher, R Krautand and C Egido (Eds), *Intellectual Teamwork*, pp. 149–173. Hillsdale, NJ: Lawrence Erlbaum.

Krebs VE (2002). Mapping networks of terrorist cells. *Connections*, **24**(3), 43–52.

Krink T, and Thomsen R (2001). Self-Organized Criticality and Mass Extinction in Evolutionary Algorithms. Proceedings of the 2001 Congress on Evolutionary Computation, CEC2001, pp. 1155–1161.

Krumhansl CL (1978). Concerning the applicability of geometric models to similar data: The interrelationship between similarity and spatial density. *Psychological Review*, **85**(5), 445–463.

Kruskal WH (1975). Visions of maps and graphs. *Proceedings of the International Symposium on Computer Assisted Cartography*. U.S. Bureau of the Census and American Congress on Survey and Mapping. pp. 27–36.

Kruskal JB (1977). Multidimensional scaling and other methods for discovering structure. In K Enslein, A Ralstonand and H Wilf (Eds), *Statistical Methods for Digital Computers*. New York: Wiley.

Kuhn TS (1962). *The Structure of Scientific Revolutions*. Chicago, IL: University of Chicago Press.

Kumar A, and Fowler RH (1995). A spring modeling algorithm to position nodes of an undirected graph in three dimensions (Technical Report). Edinburg, Texas 78539: Department of Computer Science, University of Texas – Pan American.

Kuutti K, and Arvonen T (1992). Identifying potential CSCW applications by means of Activity Theory concepts: A case example. Proceedings of CSCW '92, pp. 233–240.

Lam W, and Mostafa J (2001). Modeling user interest shift using a Bayesian approach. *Journal of the American Society for Information Science & Technology*, **52**(5), 416–429.

Lamm SE, Reed DA, and Scullin WH (1995). Real-time geographic visualization of World Wide Web traffic. Proceedings of the Fifth International World Wide Web Conference, May 6–10, 1996. Paris, France.

Lamping J, and Rao R (1996). The hyperbolic browser: A focus plus context technique for visualizing large hierarchies. *Journal of Visual Languages and Computing*, **7**(1), 33–55.

Lamping J, Rao R, and Pirolli P (1995). A focus + context technique based on hyperbolic geometry for visualizing large hierarchies. Proceedings of ACM CHI'95 Conference on Human Factors in Computing Systems, pp. 401–408.

Lebert L, Salem A, and Berry L (1998). *Exploring Textual Data*. Boston, MA: Kluwer.

Lempel R, and Moran S (2001). SALSA: The stochastic approach for link-structure analysis. *ACM Transactions on Information Systems*, **19**(2), 131–160.

Lin X (1997). Map displays for information retrieval. *Journal of the American Society for Information Science*, **48**(1), 40–54.

Lin X, Soergel D, and Marchionini G (1991). A self-organizing semantic map for information retrieval. Proceedings of SIGIR '91, October 13–16, 1991, Chicago, IL, pp. 262–269.

Lokuge I, and Ishizaki S (1995). GeoSpace: An interactive visualization system for exploring complex information spaces. Proceedings of ACM CHI'95 Conference on Human Factors in Computing Systems, pp. 409–414.

Lokuge I, Gilbert SA, and Richards W (1996). Structuring information with mental models: A tour of Boston. Proceedings of CHI '96. pp. 413–419.

MacEachren AM (1995). *How Maps Work: Representation, Visualization, and Design*. New York: Guilford Press.

Mackinlay JD, Rao R, and Card SK (1995). An organic user interface for searching citation links. Proceedings of ACM CHI '95 Conference on Human Factors in Computing Systems, pp. 67–73.

Mackinlay JD, Robertson GG, and Card SK (1991). *The perspective wall: Detail and context smoothly integrated*. Proceedings of ACM CHI '91. New Orleans, LA. New York: ACM Press. pp. 173–179.

Mantei MM, Baecker RM, Sellen AJ, Buxton WAS, Milligan T, and Wellman B (1991). Experiences in the use of a media space, Proceedings of CHI '91, pp. 203–208.

Marshall CC, and Shipman FM (1995). Spatial hypertext: Designing for change. *Communications of the ACM*, 38(8), 88–97.

Marshall CC, Shipman FM, and Coombs JH (1994). VIKI: Spatial hypertext supporting emergent structure. Proceedings of ECHT '94, September 1994, Edinburgh, Scotland, pp. 13–23.

Masterman, M (1970). The nature of the paradigm. In I Lakatos and A. Musgrave (Eds.), *Criticism and the Growth of Knowledge* (pp. 59–89). Cambridge, England: Cambridge University Press.

McCahill M, and Erickson T (1995). Design for a 3-D spatial user interface for internet gopher. Proceedings of the World Conference on Educational Multimedia and Hypermedia (ED-MEDIA '95). Graz, Austria.

McConkie GW, and Currie CB (1996). Visual stability across saccades while viewing complex pictures. *Journal of Experimental Psychology: Human Perception & Performance*, 22(3), 563–581.

Melian CJ, and Bascompte J (2002). Complex networks: two ways to be robust? *Ecology Letters*, 5, 705–708.

Metropolis N, Rosenbluth A, Rosenbluth M, Teller A, and Teller E (1953). Equation of state calculations by fast computing machines. *Journal of Chemical Physics*, 21, 1087–1091.

Misue K, Eades P, Lai W, and Sugiyama K (1995). Layout adjustment and the mental map. *Journal of Visual Languages and Computing*, 6(2), 183–210.

Mitchell WC, and Burns AF (1938). *Statistical Indicators of Cyclical Revivals*. Cambridge, MA: National Bureau of Economic Research.

Mitton S (1997). Strings maintain tight wrap on physics top 10. *ScienceWatch*, 8(6), 7.

Mitton S (1999). Fifty orders of magnitude stretch physics to the limits. *ScienceWatch*, 10(2), 6.

Moore G (1991). *Crossing the Chasm*. New York, NY: Harper Business.

Morris SA, Yen G, Wu Z, and Asnake B (2003). Timeline visualization of research fronts. *Journal of the American Society for Information Science and Technology*, 55(5), 413–422.

Morrison A, Ross G, and Chalmers M (2002). *A hybrid layout algorithm for sub-quadratic multidimensional scaling*. Proceedings of IEEE Symposium on Information Visualization (InfoVis '02), October 28–29, 2002. Boston, MA. pp. 152–160.

Morrison A, Ross G, and Chalmers M (2003). Fast multidimensional scaling through sampling, springs, and interpolation. *Information Visualization*, 2(1), 68–77.

Mostafa J, Mukhopadhyay S, Lam W, and Palakal M (1997). A multilevel approach to intelligent information filtering: Model, system and evaluation. *ACM Transactions on Information Systems*, 15(4), 368–399.

Mostafa J, Mukhopadhyay S, and Palakal M (2003). Simulation studies of different dimensions of users' interests and their impact on user modeling and information filtering. Laboratory of Applied Informatics Research Tech Report 2003-1. Bloomington, IN, USA: Indiana University.

Mukherjea S (1998). Using VRML-based visualizations to facilitate information retrieval in the World Wide Web. *Virtual Reality: Research, Development, and Applications*, 3, 245–258.

Mukherjea S, and Hara Y (1997). Focus + context views of World-Wide Web nodes. Proceedings of Hypertext '97, Southampton, UK, pp. 187–196.

Mukherjea S, Foley JD, and Hudson S (1995). Visualizing complex hypermedia networks through multiple hierarchical views. Proceedings of ACM CHI'95 Conference on Human Factors in Computing Systems, pp. 331–337.

Munzner T (1997). H3: Laying out large directed graphs in 3D hyperbolic space. Proceedings of the 1997 IEEE Symposium on Information Visualization, Phoenix, AZ, pp. 2–10.

Munzner T (1998a). Drawing Large Graphs with H3 Viewer and Site Manager. Proceedings of Graph Drawing '98, Montreal, Canada.

Munzner T (1998b). Exploring large graphs in 3D hyperbolic space. *IEEE Computer Graphics and Applications*, 18(4), 18–23.

Munzner T, Hoffman E, Claffy K, and Fenner B (1996). Visualizing the global topology of the MBone. Proceedings of the 1996 IEEE Symposium on Information Visualization, October 28–29, 1996, San Francisco, CA, pp. 85–92.

Narayanasamy V, Mukhopadhyay S, Palakal M, and Mostafa J (2003). TransMiner: Mining transitive associations among breast cancer genes from PubMed (CSTR-2003). Indianapolis, IN: Computer & Information Science, Indiana University-Purdue University Indianapolis (IUPUI).

Nardi BA (1996). *Context and Consciousness: Activity Theory and Human–Computer Interaction.* Cambridge, Mass.: The MIT Press.

Narin F, Hamilton KS, and Olivastro D (1995). Linkage between agency supported research and patented industrial technology. *Research Evaluation,* 5(3), 183–187.

Narin F, Hamilton KS, and Olivastro D (1997). The increasing linkage between US technology and public science. *Research Policy,* 26(3), 317–330.

Newman M (2001a). Clustering and preferential attachment in growing networks. *Physical Reviews E,* 64(025102). http://aps.arxiv.org/abs/cond-mat/0104209/

Newman M (2001b). The structure of scientific collaboration networks. *Proceedings of Natl. Acad. Sci. USA,* 98, 404–409.

Nguyen QV, and Huang M (2003). Space-optimized tree: a connection + enclosure approach for the visualization of large hierarchies. *Information Visualization* 2(1), 3–15.

Noel S, Chu CH, and Raghavan V (2002). Visualization of document co-citation counts. Proceedings of the 6th International Conference on Information Visualisation. London, England, pp. 691–696.

North SC (1995). Incremental layout in dynadag. Proceedings of Graph Drawing (GD '95), pp. 409–418.

Nowell LT, France RK, Hix D, Heath LS, and Fox EA (1996). Visualizing search results: Some alternatives to query-document similarity. Proceedings of the 19th Annual ACM SIGIR Conference, August 18–22, 1996, Zurich, Switzerland, pp. 67–75.

Nowell L, Hetzler E, and Tanasse T (2001). Change blindness in information visualization: a case study. Proceedings of IEEE Symposium on Information Visualization 2001, pp. 15–22.

O'Regan JK (2001). Change Blindness. Retrieved, from the World Wide Web: http://nivea.psycho. univ-paris5.fr/ECS/ECS-CB/JK.html

O'Regan JK, Rensink RA, and Clark JJ (1999). Change blindness as a result of "mudsplashes". *Nature,* 398, 34.

Ocean Studies Board, Polar Research Board, and Board on Atmospheric Science and Climate (2002). *Abrupt Climate Change: Inevitable Surprises.* The National Academies Press. http://www.nap.edu/books/0309074347/html//

Okun AM (1960). On the appraisal of cyclical turning point predictors. *Journal of Business,* 33(2), 101–120.

Olsen KA, Korfhage RR, and Sochats KM (1993). Visualization of a document collection: The VIBE System. *Information Processing & Management,* 29(1), 69–81.

Olson J, Card S, Landauer T, and Olson G (1993). Computer-supported cooperative work: Research issues for the 90s. *Behaviour and Information Technology,* 12(2), 115–129.

Olssson F, Eriksson G, Franzen K, Asker L, and Liden P (2002). Notions of correctness when evaluating protein name taggers. Proceedings of the 19th International Conference on Computational Linguistics.

Ontrup J, and Ritter H (2001). Text categorization and semantic browsing with self-organizing maps on non-euclidean spaces. Proceedings of PKDD-01 the 5th European Conference on Principles and Practice of Knowledge Discovery in Databases, pp. 338–349.

O'Regan JK, Rensink RA, and Clark JJ (1996). "Mud splashes" render picture changes invisible. *Investigative Ophthalmology & Visual Science,* 37, 213.

Papakostas A, and Tollis IG (2000). Efficient orthogonal drawings of high degree graphs. *Algorithmica,* 26(1), 100–125.

Pastor-Satorras R, and Vespignani A (2001). Epidemic spreading in scale-free networks. *Physical Review Letters,* 86(14), 3200–3203.

Pedersen ER, and Sokoler T (1997). AROMA: Abstract representation of presence supporting mutual awareness. Proceedings of CHI '97, March 22–27, Atlanta, Georgia, pp. 51–58.

Pickover CA (1988). Pattern formation and chaos in networks. *Communications of the ACM,* 31(2), 136–151.

Pirolli P (1998). Exploring browser design trade-offs using a dynamical model of optimal information foraging. Proceedings of CHI '98, Los Angeles, pp. 33–40.

Pirolli P, and Card SK (1995). Information foraging in information access environments. Proceedings of CHI '95, Denver, CO, pp. 51–58.

Pirolli P, Pitkow J, and Rao R (1996a). Silk from a sow's ear: Extracting usable structures from the web. Proceedings of CHI '96, Vancouver, BC, pp. 118–125.

Pirolli P, Schank P, Hearst M, and Diehl C (1996b). Scatter/Gather browsing communicates the topic structure of a very large text collection. Proceedings of the Conference on Human Factors in Computing Systems, CHI '96, April 1996, Vancouver, BC, pp. 118–125.

Pirolli P, Card SK, and van Der Wege MM (2003). The effects of information scent on visual search in the hyperbolic tree browser. *ACM Transactions on Computer Human Interaction*, **10**(1), 20–53.

Plaisant C, Carr D, and Shneiderman B (1995). Image browsers: taxonomy and design guidelines. *IEEE Software*, **12**(2), 21–32.

Plaisant C, Grosjean J, and Bederson B (2002). SpaceTree: Supporting exploration in large node link tree, design evolution and empirical evaluation. IEEE Symposium on Information Visualization (InfoVis'02), October 2002, Boston, MA, pp. 57–64.

Polchinski J (1995). Dirichlet branes and Ramond-Ramond charges. *Physical Review Letters*, **75**(26), 4724–4727.

Powell WW, White DR, Koput KW, and Owen-Smith J (2002). The evolution of a science-based industry: Dynamic analyses and network visualization of biotechnology. Retrieved october 1, 2003 from the World Wide Web: http://www.fek.umu.se/dpcc/powell.pdf

Price DD (1963). *Little Science, Big Science*. New York: Columbia University Press.

Price DD (1965). Networks of scientific papers. *Science*, **149**, 510–515.

Purchase H (2000). Effective information visualization: a study of graph drawing aesthetics and algorithms. *Interacting with Computers*, **13**(2), 147–162.

Purchase H (2002). Metrics for graph drawing aesthetics. *Journal of Visual Languages and Computing*, **13**(5), 501–516.

Raje R, Mukhopadhyay S, Boyles M, Papiez A, Patel N, Palakal M, and Mostafa J (1998). A bidding mechanism for Web-based agents involved in information classification. *WWW Journal*, **1**(3), 155–165.

Ramond P (1971). Quark model of dual pions. *Physical Review D.*, **3**, 2415.

Rao R, Pedersen JO, Hearst MA, Mackinlay JD, Card SK, Masinter L, Halvorsen P-K, and Robertson GG (1995). Rich interaction in the digital library. *Communications of the ACM*, **38**(4), 29–39.

Redner S (1998). How popular is your paper? An empirical study of the citation distribution. *European Physical Journal B*, **4**(2), 131–134.

Reingold E, and Tilford J (1981). Tidier drawing of trees. *IEEE Transactions on Software Engineering*, **7**(2), 223–228.

Rensink RA, O'Regan JK, and Clark J (1997). To see or not to see: the need for attention to perceive changes in scenes. *Psychological Science*, **8**(5), 368–373.

Risden K, Czerwinski MP, Munzner T, and Cook DB (2000). An initial examination of ease of use for 2D and 3D information visualizations of Web content. *International Journal of Human-Computer Studies*, **53**(5), 695–714.

Rivadeneira W, and Bederson B (2003). A study of search result clustering interfaces: Comparing textual and zoomable user interfaces. Technical Report (HCIL-2003-36), University of Maryland. http://www.cs.umd.edu/local-cgi-bin/hcil/sr.pl?number=walky

Robertson GG, Mackinlay JD, and Card SK (1991). Cone trees: Animated 3D visualizations of hierarchical information. Proceedings of CHI '91, April 28–May 2, New Orleans, LA, pp. 189–194.

Robertson G, Card S, and Mackinlay J (1993). Information visualization using 3D interactive animation. *Communications of the ACM*, **36**(4), 57–71.

Robertson G, Czerwinski M, Larson K, Robbins D, Thiel D, and van Dantzich M (1998). Data mountain: using spatial memory for document management. Proceedings of the 11th Annual Symposium on User Interface Software and Technology (UIST '98), pp. 153–162.

Robertson GG, Cameron K, Czerwinski M, and Robbins D (2002). Polyarchy visualization: Visualizing multiple intersecting hierarchies. *Information Visualization*, **1**(1), 50–65.

Rooney SM, and Schmelkin LP (1996). Social episode cognition. *Basic and Applied Social Psychology*, **18**(1), 97–110.

Rosch E, Mervis CB, Gray W, Johnson D, and Boyes-Braem P (1976). Basic objects in natural categories. *Cognitive Psychology*, **8**, 336–356.

Rosenthal R (1987). *Judgment Studies: Design, Analysis, and Meta-Analysis*. Cambridge, England: Cambridge University Press.

Roth SF, Chuah MC, Kerpedjiev S, Kolojejchick J, and Lucas P (1997). Towards an information visualization workspace: Combining multiple means of expression. *Human–Computer Interaction*, **12**(1/2), 131–185.

Roy S, Gevry D, and Pottenger WM (2002). Methodologies for trend detection in textual data mining. Proceedings of the Textmine '02 Workshop at the Second SIAM International Conference on Data Mining, April, Washington, DC.

Salton G (1989). *Automatic Text Processing: The Transformation, Analysis, and Retrieval of Information by Computer*. Reading, MA: Addison-Wesley.

Salton G, Allan J, and Buckley C (1994). Automatic structuring and retrieval of large text files. *Communications of the ACM*, 37(2), 97–108.

Salton G, Singhal A, Buckley C, and Mitra M (1996). Automatic text decomposition using text segments and text themes. Proceedings of Hypertext '96, pp. 53–65.

Sarkar M, and Brown MH (1994). Graphical fisheye views. *Communications of the ACM*, 37(12), 73–84.

Schaffer D, Zuo Z, Bartram L, Dill J, Dubs S, Greenberg S, and Roseman M (1997). Comparing fisheye and full-zoom techniques for navigation of hierarchically clustered networks. Proceedings of Graphics Interface (GI '97), pp. 87–96.

Scherk J, and Schwarz J (1974). Interpretation of string theory as a theory of gravity *Nuclear Physics B*, 81, 118.

Schvaneveldt RW (Ed.) (1990). *Pathfinder Associative Networks: Studies in Knowledge Organization*. Norwood, NJ: Ablex

Schvaneveldt RW, Durso FT, and Dearholt DW (1989). Network structures in proximity data. In G Bower (Ed.), *The Psychology of Learning and Motivation*, 24, pp. 249–284. New York, NY: Academic Press.

Schwarz JH (1996). The second superstring revolution Retrieved October 1, 2002 from the world wide web http://arXiv.org/PS-caclhep-th/pdf/9607/9607067.pdf.

Scott AB, Rosenbaum A, and Collins CC (1973). Pharmacologic weakening of extraocluar muscles. *Invest Ophthalmology*, 12, 924.

Shneiderman B (1992). Tree visualization with tree-maps: A 2-d space filling approach. *ACM Transactions on Graphics*, 11(1), 92–99.

Shneiderman B (1996). The eyes have it: A task by data type taxonomy for information visualization. Proceedings of IEEE Workshop on Visual Language, September 3–6, 1996, Boulder, CO, pp. 336–343.

Shneiderman B (2003). Why not make interfaces better than 3D reality? *IEEE Computer Graphics and Applications*, Nov/Dec, 12–15.

Simons DJ, and Levin DT (1997). Change blindness. *Trends in Cognitive Sciences*, 1(7), 261–267.

Simons DJ, and Levin DT (1998). Failure to detect changes to people in a real-world interaction. *Psychonomic Bulletin and Review*, 5(4), 644–649.

Simons D (2000). Current approaches to change blindness. *Visual Cognition*, 7(1–3), 1–15.

Skupin A (2002). A Cartographic approach to visualizing conference abstracts. IEEE Computer Graphics and Applications, 22(1), 50–58.

Small H (1986). The synthesis of specialty narratives from co-citation clusters. *Journal of the American Society for Information Science*, 37(3), 97–110.

Small H (1994). A SCI-MAP case study: Building a map of AIDS research. *Scientometrics*, 30(1), 229–241.

Small HG (1977). A co-citation model of a scientific specialty: A longitudinal study of collagen research. *Social Studies of Science*, 7, 139–166.

Small H (1997). Update on science mapping: Creating large document spaces. *Scientometrics*, 38(2), 275–293.

Small H (1999a). A passage through science: Crossing disciplinary boundaries. *Library Trends*, 48(1), 72–108.

Small H (1999b). Visualizing science by citation mapping. *Journal of the American Society for Information Science*, 50(9), 799–813.

Small H (2000). Charting pathways through science: Exploring Garfield's vision of a unified index to science. *Web of Knowledge – a Festschrift in Honor of Eugene Garfield*, New York, NY: Information Today. pp. 449–473.

Small H (2003). Paradigms, citations, and maps of science: A personal history. *Journal of the American Society for Information Science and Technology*, 54(5), 394–399.

Small H, and Greenlee E (1989). A co-citation study of AIDS research. *Communication Research*, 16(5), 642–666.

Small HG, and Griffith BC (1974). The structure of scientific literatures I: Identifying and graphing specialties. *Science Studies*, 4, 17–40.

Sparrow M (1991). The application of network analysis to criminal intelligence: An assessment of the prospects. *Social Networks*, 13, 251–274.

Spence R (2001). *Information Visualization*. London: Addison-Wesley.

Spence R, and Apperley MD (1982). Data base navigation: An office environment for the professional. *Behaviour and Information Technology*, 1(1), 43–54.

Stahle DW, Cleaveland MK, Blanton DB, Therrell MD, and Gay DA (1998). The lost colony and Jamestown droughts. *Science*, 280, 564–567.

Stanney KM, and Salvendy G (1995). Information visualization: Assisting low spatial individuals with information access tasks through the use of visual mediators. *Ergonomics*, 38(6), 1184–1198.

Stasko J, Catrambone R, Guzdial M, and McDonald K (2000). An evaluation of space-filling information visualizations for depicting hierarchical structures. *International Journal of Human-Computer Studies*, **53**(5), 663–694.

Stevens SS (1975). *Psychophysics*. New York, NY: John Wiley.

Steyvers M, and Tenenbaum J (2001). Small worlds in semantic networks. Retrieved December 2001, from the World Wide Web: http://www.psych.stanford.edu/~msteyver/small_worlds.htm

Stick D (1983). Roanoke Island. Chapel Hill, NC: North Carolina University Press.

Stolfo SJ, Fan W, Lee W, Prodromidis AL, and Chan PK (1997). Credit card fraud detection using meta-learning: Issues and initial results. Proceedings of AAAI Workshop: AI Approaches to Fraud Detection and Risk Management, July, pp. 83–90.

Streeter LDV, and Wonsiewicz S (1985). How to tell people where to go: Comparing navigational aids. *International Journal of Man–Machine Studies*, **22**, 549–562.

Strominger A, and Vafa C (1996). Microscopic origin of the Bekenstein–Hawking entropy. *Physics Letters B*, **379**(1–4), 99–104.

Sugiyama K, Tagawa S, and Toda M (1981). Methods for visual understanding of hierarchical system structures. *IEEE Transactions on Systems, Man, and Cybernetics*, **11**(2), 109–125.

Sutcliffe A, and Patel U (1996). 3D or not 3D: Is it nobler in the mind? In MA Sasse, RJ Cunningham and RL Winder (Eds), *People and Computers XI*, pp. 79–94. London: Springer.

Swan R, and Allan J (1999). Extracting significant time varying features from text. Proceedings of Eighth International Conference on Information Knowledge Management (CIKM '99), November, Kansas City, Missouri, pp. 38–45.

Szirmay-Kalos L (1994). Dynamic layout algorithm to display general graphs. *Graphics Gem IV*. New York, NY: Academic Press.

Tamassia R (1987). On embedding a graph in the grid with the minimum number of bends. *SIAM Journal of Computing*, **16**(3), 421–444.

Tamassia R, Battista GD, and Batini C (1988). Automatic graph drawing and readability of diagrams. *IEEE Transactions on Systens, Man and Cybernetics*, **18**(1), 61–79.

Tang JC, Isaacs EA, and Rua M (1994). Supporting distributed groups with a Montage of lightweight interactions. Proceedings of CSCW '94, pp. 23–34.

Thagard P (1992). *Conceptual Revolutions*. Princeton, NJ: Princeton University Press.

Thomas JJ (1995). Information visualization: Beyond traditional engineering. Proceedings of the Workshop on Human–Computer Interaction and Virtual Environments, April 26–27, Hampton, Virginia, USA.

Thorndyke P, and Hayes-Roth B (1982). Differences in spatial knowledge acquired from maps and navigation. *Cognitive Psychology*, **14**, 560–589.

Thurstone LL (1931). Multiple factor analysis. *Psychological Review*, **38**, 406–427.

Tolman EC (1948). Cognitive maps in rats and men. *Psychological Review*, **55**, 189–208.

Tolva J (1996). Ut pictura hyperpoesis: Spatial form, visuality, and the digital word. Proceedings of Hypertext '96, Washington, DC, pp. 66–73.

Toomey L, Adams L, and Churchill E (1998). Meetings in a virtual space: Creating a digitial document. Proceedings of the 31st Annual Hawaii International Conference on System Sciences, Hawaii, pp. 236–244.

Triesman A (1985). Preattentive processing in vision. *Computer Vision, Graphics, and Image Processing*, **31**(1), 56–177.

Tromp J, Steed A, Frecon E, Bullock A, Sadagic A, and Slater M (1998). Small group behavior experiments in the Coven project. *IEEE Computer Graphics and Applications*, **18**(6), 53–63.

Tromp JG, Steed A, and Wilson JR (2003). Systematic usability evaluation and design issues for collaborative virtual environments. *Presence: Teleoperators and Virtual Environments*, **12**(3), 241–267.

Tufte ER (1983). *The Visual Display of Quantitative Information*. Cheshire, CT: Graphics Press.

Tufte ER (1990). *Envisioning Information*. Cheshire, CT: Graphics Press.

Tufte ER (1997). *Visual Explanations*. Cheshire, CT: Graphics Press.

Tukey JW (1962). The future of data analysis. *Annals of Mathematical Statistics*, **33**(1), 1–67.

Tukey JW (1977). *Exploratory Data Analysis*. Reading, MA: Addison-Wesley.

Tversky B (1993). Cognitive maps, cognitive collages, and spatial mental models. Proceedings of COSIT '93, Springer, Elba, pp. 14–24.

van Laarhoven PJM, and Aarts EHL (1987). *Simulated Annealing: Theory and Applications*. Dordrecht: D. Reidel.

van Raan A (2000). On growth, ageing, and fractal differentiation of science. *Scientometrics*, **47**(2), 347–362.

van Rijsbergen CJ (1979). *Information Retrieval* (2nd ed.). London: Butterworths.

van West CR (1991). Reconstructing prehistoric climatic variability and agricultural production in southwestern Colorado, A.D. 901–1300: A GIS approach. Proceedings of the Anasazi Symposium 1991, Mesa Verde, CO, pp. 25–34.

van Wijk JJ, and van de Wetering H (1999). Cushion treemaps: Visualization of hierarchical information. Proceedings of IEEE Symposium on Information Visualization (InfoVis '99), Oct. 25–26, San Francisco, CA, pp. 73–78.

Veerasamy A, and Belkin NJ (1996). Evaluation of a tool for visualization of information retrieval results. Proceedings of SIGIR '96. Zurich, Switzerland, pp. 85–92.

Vicente KJ, and Williges RC (1988). Accommodating individual differences in searching a hierarchical file system. *International Journal of Man–Machine Studies*, 29, 647–668.

Vygotsky LS (1962). *Thought and language*. Cambridge, MA: MIT Press.

Wainer H, and Thissen D (1981). Graphical data analysis. *American Review of Psychology*, 32, 199–202.

Ware C (2000). *Information Visualization: Perception for Design*. San Francisco: Morgan Kaufmann Publishers.

Ware C, and Franck G (1996). Evaluating stereo and motion cues for visualizing information nets in three Dimensions. *ACM Transactions on Graphics*, 15(2), 121–140.

Ware C, Purchase H, Colpoys L, and McGill M (2002). Cognitive measurements of graph aesthetics. *Information Visualization*, 1(2), 103–110.

Watts DJ, and Strogatz SJ (1998). Collective dynamics of 'small-world' networks. *Nature*, 393, 440.

Weiss R, Velez B, Sheldon M, Nemprempre C, Szilagyi P, Duda A, and Gifford L (1996). HyPursuit: A hierarchical network search engine that exploits content link hypertext clustering. Proceedings of Hypertext '96, Washington, DC, pp. 180–193.

Westerman SJ, and Cribbin T (2000). Mapping semantic information in virtual space: Dimensions, variance and individual differences. *International Journal of Human-Computer Studies*, 53(5), 765–787.

Wexelblat A (1999). History-based tools for navigation. Proceedings of the 32nd Annual Hawaii International Conference on Systems Sciences, Hawaii.

Wexelblat A, and Maes P (1997). Visualizing histories for Web browsing. Proceedings of RIAO'97: Computer-Assisted Information Retrieval on the Internet, Montreal.

White HD (2003a). Author cocitation analysis and Pearson's *r*. *Journal of the American Society for Information Science and Technology*, 54(13), 1250–1259.

White HD (2003b). Pathfinder networks and author cocitation analysis: A remapping of paradigmatic information scientists. *Journal of the American Society for Information Science and Technology*, 54(5), 423–434.

White D, and Houseman M (2002). The Navigability of strong ties: Small worlds, tie strength and network topology. Retrieved, from the World Wide Web: http://eclectic.ss.uci.edu/~drwhite/Complexity/SpecialIssue.htm

White HD, and McCain KW (1997). Visualization of literatures. *Annual Review of Information Science and Technology*, 32, 99–168.

White HD, and McCain KW (1998). Visualizing a discipline: An author co-citation analysis of information science, 1972–1995. *Journal of the American Society for Information Science*, 49(4), 327–356.

Whittaker S, Frohlich D, and Daly-Jones O (1994). Informal workplace communication: what is it like and how might we support it? Proceedings of CHI '94, April 24–28, pp. 131–137.

Wilhelmson RB, Jewett BF, Wicker LJ, Arrott M, Bushell CB, Bajuk M, Thingvold J, and Yost JB (1990). A study of the evolution of a numerically modeled severe storm. *International Journal of Supercomputing Applications*, 4, 20–36.

Wills GJ (1999). NicheWorks: Interactive visualization of very large graphs. *Journal of Computational and Graphical Statistics*, 8(2), 190–212.

Wise JA, Thomas JJ, Pennock K, Lantrip D, Pottier M, Schur A, and Crow V (1995). Visualizing the non-visual: Spatial analysis and interaction with information from text documents. Proceedings of IEEE Symposium on Information Visualization '95, October 30–31, Atlanta, Georgia, USA, pp. 51–58.

Yang Y, Pierce T, and Carbonell J (1998). A study on retrospective and online event detection. Proceedings of the 21st ACM International Conference on Research and Development in Information Retrieval, SIGIR '98.

Young P (1996). Three dimensional information visualization. Computer Science Technical Report No.12/96. Durham University.

Zhang J, Mostafa J, and Tripathy H (2002). Information retrieval by semantic analysis and visualization of the concept space of D-Lib magazine. *D-Lib*, 8(10), 3.

Zizi M, and Beaudouin-Lafon M (1994). Accessing hyperdocuments through interactive dynamic maps. Proceedings of ECHT '94, September 1994, Edinburgh, Scotland, pp. 126–135.

Index